Eighth Edition

CAMP COUNSELING

Eighth Edition

CAMP COUNSELING

Leadership and Programming
for the Organized Camp

Joel F. Meier
Professor Emeritus, Indiana University

Karla A. Henderson
North Carolina State University

WAVELAND

PRESS, INC.

Long Grove, Illinois

For information about this book, contact:
Waveland Press, Inc.
4180 IL Route 83, Suite 101
Long Grove, IL 60047-9580
(847) 634-0081
info@waveland.com
www.waveland.com

Chapter-Opener Photo Credits

Pages 11, 35, 69, 113, 153, and 181, courtesy of Bradford Woods Learning and Outdoor Center; pages 45, 159, 193, 201, 213, and 289 courtesy of American Camp Association; page 141, courtesy of Joel Meier.

10-digit ISBN 1-57766-713-1
13-digit ISBN 978-1-57766-713-1

Printed in the United States of America

7 6 5 4 3 2 1

To A. Viola Mitchell (1904–1984),
who provided inspiration, ideas, and sage advice
to legions of aspiring camps counselors
since she wrote the first edition of Camp Counseling in 1950.

Contents

PART IV
Outdoor Living, Camping, and Trail Skills 221

Preface

The Eighth Edition of *Camp Counseling* continues to do what the previous seven editions of this book have done—to emphasize leadership skills and programming ideas for the organized camp. This edition represents a 21st-century view of the trends, philosophies, and practices of the organized camp movement. It continues the original intent of *Camp Counseling*—to serve as a useful tool for people who are or will be engaged in positions of camp leadership in a variety of camp settings. Topics covered in these pages serve as an introduction and overview, with many online resources to supplement the ideas.

The text will be used primarily by students enrolled in college or university courses dealing with the subject of organized camps and leadership. However, the book may also be valuable to agencies or organizations that sponsor camp programs and related outdoor activities. This resource can be used in training courses or as recommended reading for prospective counselors and other camp personnel. *Camp Counseling* will also be useful to camp directors who conduct pre-camp or in-camp training courses, and to camp counselors and program staff who work independently to prepare to carry out their responsibilities.

Working in an organized camp offers many opportunities to make a contribution to society. Adequate training and skill are required of staff members who fill important leadership roles. A staff member must, first of all, develop a professional philosophy of organized camping that includes an understanding of its purposes, objectives, background, present status, and future trends. Part I addresses these issues.

Further, counselors and program leaders must work closely with people. They must have the knowledge and personal ability to lead campers successfully. These all-important people skills are a crucial component of successful camp experiences. Part II addresses these skills.

Campers want action and excitement and expect plenty of it in a variety of forms. Part III describes activities and programming techniques especially suited for use in the informal, experiential atmosphere of camps.

Part IV provides an overview of some of the skills needed for working in camps that focus on the outdoors. These skills represent the traditional core of the camp experience, although the nature of outdoor opportunities in camps varies greatly.

This new edition offers many useful ideas for providing positive camping experiences. Sources for additional information on many of these topics are included at the end of each chapter. Today's technology, particularly the Internet, facilitates access to the most up-to-date information about many of the strategies and activities discussed. Moreover, we've provided references for the excellent articles that have appeared in *Camping Magazine* over the past 10 years. These articles are available online at the American Camp Association website (http://www.acacamps.org/camping-magazine/archives).

New chapters discuss trends in organized camping, efforts to expand opportunities for camp participation, and ways to encourage increased physical activity among children and youth. Moreover, new photographs and illustrations have been added, and references at the end of each chapter have been updated to include the most relevant materials available today. This new edition highlights some of the more successful education techniques used today at camps. Also, we emphasize the importance of understanding and appreciating the natural environment and minimizing human impact on the land. *Camp Counseling* recognizes the interdependency of people and the natural environment and suggests ways to enjoy the outdoors without spoiling it for future generations.

We sincerely hope you will find the Eighth Edition of *Camp Counseling* to be a valuable, practical resource for promoting positive camp experiences for all.

Joel Meier and Karla Henderson

Acknowledgments

The first edition of *Camp Counseling* was published in 1950. As you can imagine, thanking all the organizations and people who contributed to previous editions is impossible. Nonetheless, many of the ideas and a few of their illustrations can still be found among the many new ones in this book.

Sincere appreciation goes to James Farmer for his early contributions to the project, and to Liana Dern, who assisted us in locating many of the resources that are offered in this new edition. Joel acknowledges his wife, Patricia, who has shown love and tolerance throughout the many hours spent on this book. Patricia has continued to be the real backbone for Joel's staying power, and he cannot adequately express his gratitude for her continuing encouragement. He also acknowledges Karla Henderson for her outstanding contribution as coauthor of this new edition of *Camp Counseling*. She has greatly refined and updated the book and brings a fresh new perspective to the subject of organized camping.

Karla would like to thank the many people with whom she has associated in the American Camp Association (ACA) over the years, particularly Dr. Deb Bialeschki. Deb has been invaluable with her recent work in developing a research agenda for ACA. We also wish to thank Laurie Prossnitz for her editorial assistance and diligence in moving the project forward, and the members of Waveland's production staff for their input and assistance.

Last, but not least, we appreciate and acknowledge the late Viola Mitchell, the leading coauthor of the first six editions of *Camp Counseling*. Almost everyone who has been involved in the camping profession at any time during the past six decades has become acquainted with one or more editions of this book. Consequently, Viola Mitchell's wisdom was imparted either directly or indirectly to the thousands who participated in organized camping over the years. The knowledge and skills she shared continue to have a lasting impact on attitudes about the value of camp experiences. This book is Viola Mitchell's ongoing legacy to the organized camping movement.

I

Growth, Structure, and Values of Organized Camps

*We do not see nature with our eyes, but with
our understandings and our hearts.*

— *William Hazlitt*

1

Organized Camps— What Are They?

Millions of people have participated in outdoor camping experiences of one type or another, ranging from short overnight excursions in nearby rural areas to extended outings of several weeks or more with friends or family. The term *camping* creates different images in people's minds depending upon the extent and nature of previous experiences. To some people camping means pulling a mobile shelter behind a car to a forest, park, or private campground and sleeping in it. Others associate camping with agency- or organization-sponsored outings at established group sites where nature-oriented programs are offered on a scheduled basis. Some people believe camping means carrying essential belongings in a backpack and hiking long distances into wilderness or backcountry areas far away from civilization.

The term *camp* also has different meanings. Soldiers go to boot camp. People pull their RVs into campgrounds. Some people "camp out" in line for concert tickets or for sales at stores. When you hear the word *camping* or *camp*, many images come to mind. For this book, we use the word *camp* to refer to experiences where people live, work, or play together generally in the outdoors within the structures of an organized program using trained leaders. Although other views about what constitutes camping may have some of those characteristics, we refer to camps as specific places where these elements of groups, outdoor activities, and supervision/leadership come together.

Why Go Camping?

The allure of camping usually is associated with a chance to get away from normal routines and an opportunity to refresh or relax—usually, but not always, in the natural world of the outdoors. Until the late 20th century, interest in the outdoors grew rapidly. More recently, however, such authors as Richard Louv (*Last Child in the Woods*, 2005) have expressed concern that people—especially children—have become disconnected from nature. This disconnect, or *nature deficit disorder* as Louv describes it, is a concern for many reasons.

As societies have evolved, people have grown less reliant on nature and therefore less familiar with it. The need to connect with the outdoor world is particularly critical since far more people today live in suburbs and cities than in rural areas. Camping and camps allow adults and children an opportunity to escape the routines of everyday existence and to experience our cultural and natural heritage firsthand. For some people, camping provides a chance to break away from the softness and ease of today's technology-reliant lifestyle. Camping is appealing because it provides an opportunity to challenge the self, to improvise and make do, to explore a relationship with nature, and to exercise personal initiative.

Camp experiences also have the potential to develop desirable physical, mental, social, and spiritual qualities. For instance, studies indicate that the effects of camp on an individual often include a positive, measurable outcome in terms of self-concept (including self-reliance and self-confidence), development of environmental awareness, aesthetic appreciation, cooperation, physical fitness, ability to deal with stress, and tenacity (American Camp Association, 2010). Thus, camp experiences enable people to acquire valuable skills and attitudes that they would not necessarily gain in school or from their usual daily activities.

Camping can be a prime way to develop and maintain close family and friendship ties. Camping offers opportunities for developing companionship with others, sharing joys and hardships, learning the meaning of humility, and for understanding the importance of communication. Since campers live and play together in groups, each individual has the opportunity to share the experience, cooperatively give and take, participate in group decision making, and build lifelong friendships. These outcomes can occur in campers as well as in those who assume a leadership role, such as camp counselors.

Structured Camp Experiences

A variety of camping experiences are available. In informal camping, people come and go as they please. This book, however, is primarily concerned with *organized* or *supervised* camping, so understanding more about the nature, design, function, and types of organized camps is important.

What Is Organized Camping?

As noted, several key characteristics differentiate an organized camp from other forms of outdoor recreation. For this book, we define **camp** as being comprised of a community of people living together as an organized group, usually in the outdoors, under the direction of designated leaders. Organized camps have traditionally occurred in the outdoors, but some camp programs today are run mainly in indoor facilities. The related educational programs and recreational activities are supervised by trained staff to meet the needs, interests, and safety of the participants. Camps are usually associated with children but adults can also go to camp, and organized family camping is a growing trend.

The camp program consists of the *total* of all experiences or events in the camp, whether or not they are structured and/or associated with the outdoors. Many camp programs focus on the natural environment and take advantage of experiences that are inherent to living in the outdoors. Nevertheless, in today's technology-driven society, camps can be quite varied in their approach to using the outdoors. The outdoors, however, is what distinguishes camps from other youth-serving organizations such as clubs, after-school programs, or churches. In this book, the focus is on camps that occur in outdoor environments, although that environment can range from a multi-day wilderness experience to a trip to the zoo for day-camp participants.

Four components or principles generally encapsulate the basic philosophy of organized camps.

1. The program consists of the total of all experiences that take place while at camp.

The organized camp offers a broad and varied range of activities, and the program consists of every experience each camper has throughout the duration of the camp, whether it is a day camp or an 8-week resident camp experience. The camp program consists of unstruc-

tured or informal aspects of camp life as well as the more structured and formal recreation activities. Thus, campers are participating in camp life whether they are hiking as a group in the woods or washing dishes after the evening meal. Living fully in a camp community can involve participants in many relationships, experiences, and activities that are part of social and educational growth.

2. The organized camp revolves around group living experiences in an organized community.

The basic unit of camp life consists of campers (e.g., children, youth, or families) and staff members who work, play, and often live together in small groups. Cooperation and teamwork are necessary to successfully meet the requirements of camp life. The camp structure often represents a microcosm of a democratic society. Through this group process campers develop skills in cooperating, sharing, decision making, and assuming leadership and citizenship responsibilities.

3. The organized camp relies on trained and well-qualified staff.

The staff consists of the camp director and camp counselors as well as other personnel who are involved in the operation of the camp, including program specialists, maintenance personnel, health supervisors, and cooks. People who work at an organized camp must be mature and interested in working with people. They usually have a range of interests and skills, including an understanding of the campers, and a commitment to the goals of the camp and positive human development. Because campers and staff associate with one another over an extended period of time, it is essential that camp personnel be capable of providing guidance and support to campers to aid in their physical, emotional, social, and spiritual growth.

4. Organized camps usually focus efforts on the natural environment in an outdoor setting.

The camp program may concentrate on activities that are natural to the outdoor environment like camping, hiking, nature appreciation, and other skills associated with living outdoors. Similarly, the camp facility usually focuses on the beauty of a natural setting in addition to offering some of the amenities of urban living.

Types of Camps

Organized camps commonly are established for young people from 7 to 16 years old, although many camps offer programs for adults, older adults, and families. Regardless of age group, all camps provide opportunities for participants to work, recreate, and live together under the guidance of a staff of counselors and camp personnel. Organized camps include several types and are conducted for many purposes.

Camps may be classified into six major types (although various combinations can occur):

- Resident camps
- Day camps
- Trip or travel camps
- Specialized camps
- School camps
- Conference and retreat centers

The majority (62%) of the estimated 12,000 camps in the United States are resident camps (American Camp Association, 2010). These resident camps may also offer trip, specialized, or school camps within their programs. Day camps are the fastest growing type of camp, with about one-third of camps falling into that category.

Resident Camps

A resident or residential camp is one in which campers live for a period of time, usually from a few days to eight weeks or more. These camps are sometimes called *overnight* or *sleepover* or *sleepaway* camps. They typically have permanent buildings surrounded by a broad expanse of woods and meadows that are left as much as possible in their natural state. The camps are located away from the main roads to provide privacy and freedom from intrusion by the public and/or people without legitimate camp connections.

Resident camps have many similarities; yet each camp has a distinct personality based on its mission, location, and traditions. Some camps are purposely kept primitive and rustic and feature a rugged and simple way of life that is quite different from the average camper's home environment. Other camps go to the opposite extreme and provide many of the refinements and conveniences of urban life such as air conditioning. Most camps fall somewhere in the middle on this continuum. All successful camps, no matter how rustic or urbanized, maintain the qualities essential for safe and healthful living as well as positive human development.

In resident camps, campers and staff may live in rustic cabins, tents on wooden platforms, or in sleeping lodges, which usually are grouped into separate units of from 8 to 20 campers with their counselors. Each unit is somewhat segregated from the others to promote a feeling of group identity and privacy. In some camps each living unit is entirely self-sufficient. However most camps feature centrally located buildings, including a common dining room and kitchen, a large lodge or recreation room, an arts and crafts shop, washrooms, showers, toilets, laundry facilities, a camp office, tool houses and sheds for camp storage and the caretaker's equipment, a health center, trading post, counselors' lounge or retreat, camp library, and a facility to house equipment and supplies for cookouts or trips away from camp.

Some resident camps have fields and courts for such sports as tennis, archery, softball, badminton, horseshoes, riflery, and golf; an amphitheater; an outdoor chapel; and a council ring. Some camps specialize in activities like tennis, horseback riding, or water sports. Other camps offer a variety of activities ranging from woodworking and ballet dancing to technical subjects such as electronics and nuclear physics. Most camp programs, however, lie somewhere in between specialties and a broad program.

Located at the ends of certain trails and at some distance from the main camp will sometimes be outposts or remote campsites where campers with sufficient outdoor skills can live comfortably and simply under more primitive conditions. Some camps may have a stable, tack room, riding ring, and riding trails. A popular spot might be the waterfront on a lake, river, or seashore with an array of rowboats, canoes, sailboats, and possibly even jet skis and power boats. Many camps also have a swimming pool, although some camp locations feature natural bodies of water that are clean and safe for swimming. A resident camp represents a big investment and may be populated by as many as a hundred or even several hundred campers and an appropriate number of counselors and other personnel.

Each resident camp has a personality of its own.

Canvas tents on platforms offer more basic accommodations.

Day Camps

A day camp is set up to accommodate campers who commute from home each day. The camps ordinarily operate from one to five days, although sometimes campers attend more than one week-long session. Children arrive by bus or private car soon after breakfast and return home in the late afternoon. Some camps may lengthen the hours to accommodate the children of working parents. The children spend the day participating in various recreation activities and may cook part or all of their lunch, have a catered lunch, or bring food from home.

Day camping is most common in or near metropolitan areas, and often the camp uses parks or other recreational facilities. A public parks and recreation agency or service organization such as the Boy Scouts, Girl Scouts, Camp Fire Inc., Boys' or Girls' Clubs, YMCA or YWCA, may sponsor the camp. Many privately owned day camps are operated for profit from fees paid by those attending. Some day camps are based in a recreation center or other such indoor facility, where much of the day is spent inside with occasional field trips or outdoor nature programs.

Nearly all the activities of a resident camp are possible in a day camp, except for those conducted in the early morning or nighttime and, of course, sleeping at the camp. However, some day camps do sponsor overnight sleepouts and occasional trips for campers interested in participating. Programming in a day camp is especially challenging since campers may choose to return each day or skip a day, depending upon how appealing the previous day's activities were. Day camps make an important contribution to camping by extending their benefits to those who are too young or financially unable to attend resident camps. They also prepare beginning campers for later participation in a resident or travel camp.

Trip and Travel Camps

Campers participating in *trip* camping start from a common base then travel by foot, canoe, bicycle, horseback, sailboat, a horse-drawn covered wagon, or almost any other self-propelled means of transportation. In contrast, groups that are *travel* camping are transported by car or bus, and they usually make camp each night at a new location. Some travel groups consist of older campers from a resident camp who earn this privilege by demonstrating their knowledge and skills in camping techniques. Other groups are made up of individuals who come together for the express purpose of making the trip.

Specialized Camps

Most organized camps offer a well-rounded program that includes a mix of activities like outdoor skills, aquatics, nature study, and arts and crafts. Some camps, however, concentrate on only one or a few activities to serve those with special interests or needs.

Specialized camps can be classified as either special interest camps or special purpose camps. Examples of *special interest* camps include aquatic camps, ranch camps, farm camps, mountain-climbing camps, and trip and pioneering camps. These camps develop programs around their particular environments and interest. For example, *wilderness, pioneer,* or *survival camping* is a specialized form of primitive camping undertaken by older campers specially trained for it. Participants are usually transported to a takeoff spot where they set out with only rudimentary equipment and supplies. They may obtain some of their food and other necessities from what nature provides along the way. Two or more skilled counselors or guides are in charge, and the trip may last from a week to an entire summer. Other special interest camps may stress specific activities like field hockey, tennis, aquatics, basketball, horseback riding, nature or science study, dramatics, music, dance, religious education, tutoring, or language study. The term "camp" is sometimes used to refer to any grouping of people pursuing the same activities, though such groupings may not meet the principles of organized camps described earlier. Nevertheless, many of these special interest camps exist.

Special purpose camps typically serve special clientele such as campers with diabetes, epilepsy, hearing impairments, mental disabilities, or physical challenges. Some camps are coed, and others accommodate specific groups such as families, adults, or older adults. Although the trend in working with people with disabilities is to provide inclusive services so that participation is possible at any camp, many campers with disabilities and their parents prefer a specialized camp. The important thing is that such campers are able to choose the camp experience they wish to have.

Outdoor Education and School Camping

Although people sometimes use the terms *outdoor education* and *school camping* interchangeably, they are not the same. *Outdoor education* is a learning process that takes place in the outdoors. It broadly includes environmental education, conservation education, adventure education, school camping, wilderness therapy, and some aspects of outdoor recreation. Among the curricular areas often associated with outdoor education are language arts, social studies, mathematics, science, nature study, and music. Outdoor education includes all types of experiences that improve people's knowledge, attitudes, or skills in the outdoors and help facilitate an appreciation and enjoyment of the outdoors. Outdoor education may involve anyone, of any age, at any time, and in various situations. In schools, a child's first experience with outdoor education may occur when a teacher takes a class out on the playground to observe cloud formations, soil erosion, or the activities of the surprisingly large number of plants and animals living there. Outdoor education may consist of a trip to a farm, zoo, museum, dam, wildlife refuge, fish hatchery, or municipal/state park. It may include viewing films and slides about nature and ecology, or growing plants or caring for pet animals in the classroom. Instruction in fishing, hunting, hiking, or camping techniques may also be included.

School camping is one aspect of outdoor education. It consists of a camping trip to a regular camp by one or more school classes and their teachers and other personnel. The trip may last from a few days to several weeks. Neither school camping nor outdoor education is new. The objectives of school camping are somewhat similar to those of general organized camping except that an intentional effort is made to closely connect the camp experience with what is occurring in the classroom. Thus, when properly carried out, it supplements and makes more meaningful certain phases of the regular school curriculum. This type of camping can make an important contribution in the educational process.

School camping, however, has lost popularity over the years, in part due to movements like "No Child Left Behind," which focus on academic subjects in the classroom. Nevertheless, where school camping occurs, all children have the opportunity to have an outdoor experience. Thus, school camping fills a need by offering this opportunity for all children—including those who may not otherwise have camp opportunities.

Camp, Conference, and Retreat Centers

Many facilities that offer residential camp programs may also serve as conference centers during the summer and especially during other times of the year. A number of residential camps report offering services other than summer youth camp programs (ACA, 2010). More than 40% of respondents indicated that they offered a retreat center, family camp programs, or outdoor/environmental education programs. Furthermore, over 30% of all residential camps offer weekend or daily rentals, site rental by other camps, day-use programs, or trip and/or travel camp. Some conference and retreat facilities are located in outdoor settings but may have similar amenities as resorts. These types of camp provide opportunities for a wide range of campers, including adults and families. The programs often include educational opportunities as well as recreational pursuits. Some of these camps and conference centers are incorporated as part of religious (e.g., Episcopal Conference Centers) or agency centers (e.g., YMCA of the Rockies).

Camp Affiliations

Camps are administered and organized in many ways. The most commonly used categories to describe particular affiliations or sponsorships of camps are:

- organization or agency not-for-profit camps
- independent for-profit or private camps
- religiously affiliated camps
- government-sponsored camps

The American Camp Association (2010) indicates that 54% of camps are agency affiliated or independent not-for-profit, 22% are private independent camps, 23% are religiously affiliated, and less than 2% are public/municipal sponsored. These percentages, however, are debatable since less than one-fourth of the US camps are associated directly with ACA. Getting a clear picture of the exact number of camps and their sponsorship is difficult.

Organization, Agency Camps, or Independent Not-for-Profit Camps

Youth organizations or independent not-for-profit organizations provide camp opportunities to serve youth, adults, and families as a means for furthering their mission and objectives. These camps may be tailored to meet specific purposes. Many of these organizations are supported by the public through the United Way or some other combined campaign, government funds, fund-raising projects, and memberships and donations. Campers usually pay only nominal fees, which makes camping opportunities available for low-income groups. Grants or scholarships are often made available for deserving children to attend camp.

Youth organizations provide camp opportunities as a way of fulfilling their mission and objectives. (Photo courtesy of Bradford Woods Learning and Outdoor Center)

Since the facilities are limited and such camps must accommodate large numbers, a child's stay is often limited to a week or two. With Girl Scout or Boy Scout camps, the camp experience is often an extension of what the child has been doing in the organization's regular program. An organization camp is usually located near the campers it serves, which reduces transportation costs. These camps have high standards and follow recommended camping practices. Since organization or agency camps handle so many children from different social strata, they play an important role in making camp experiences available to all.

Many organizations promote camping as a part of their programs—providing a complete listing is impossible. Noteworthy examples are included in exhibit 1.1.

Independent or Private Camps

Independent or private camps are owned by an individual or individuals and are usually run for profit. They are often incorporated as businesses. Since they receive no public funds, they must usually charge a large fee. A camper in a private camp ordinarily remains four to eight weeks, which allows enough time to thoroughly acclimate the child and make progress toward achieving camp objectives. Children from wealthier families often attend these camps, although many grants and scholarships are available to selected children from lower income families. Private camps often draw their clientele from widespread geographic areas as well as other countries. Campers therefore get opportunities to live with a variety of people whose customs and ways of life may be different.

The greater financial resources of private camps sometimes enable them to provide more options in the summer camp program. However, they do not necessarily offer better programs than other camps. Most directors of private camps, nevertheless, are public spirited and sincerely dedicated to conducting their camps in the best interests of children, youth, and adults. Throughout their history, private camps have generally been quite progressive and have made valuable contributions to the camp field.

Religiously Affiliated Camps

The mission of religiously affiliated camps is to nurture spiritual growth through the camp and retreat experience. Many camps exist along a spectrum of religiosity from highly religious to nonreligious. The differentiation along this spectrum usually depends on the specific religious group with which the camp is affiliated. If this connection is with an orthodox, conservative, or evangelical organization, camp life probably focuses more heavily on religious activities.

The staff and campers usually identify themselves with a particular faith. Religion typically fits into the daily program of activities. Other types of camps also have important spiritual components to their program such as daily vespers or mealtime prayers, but these are not the focus of the camp. Religious camps usually emphasize that a major part of each camp day includes worship and Bible, Torah, or Koran study. These camps may integrate religious themes into everyday games, songs, stories, and sports. Most religious camps are designed to serve children whose families are members of a particular religious group, or who are members of a specific church, synagogue, or mosque. However, many camps do not discriminate relative to who can attend their camps.

Government-Sponsored Camps

Government agencies acting on behalf of the public may use tax funds to support camp programs. Government sponsorship means that camp services usually are either free or entail a minimal fee to help defray expenses. Public parks and recreation agencies provide numerous day camps in towns and cities across the country. Other government sponsors might be school systems, social service departments, and state-owned hospitals or rehabilitation centers.

Camp and Camper Characteristics

Residential and day camps traditionally operate during the summer months, which are often called the *camp season*. In some camps, the season may be divided into several shorter periods known as *camp sessions*. In *long-term camps*, campers may stay for half or the entire camp season of four to eight weeks. In others, their stay may be limited to one session that lasts a week, ten days, or two weeks. These are known as *short-term camps*. Because they must serve a large number of campers, most camps sponsored by agencies, organizations, or religious groups are short-term camps.

Many camps extend their seasons by offering camp opportunities on weekends throughout the year. In addition, with growing adoption of the year-round school concept, some agencies now offer programs during breaks between school sessions.

The wide array of camp types mirrors the diversity in camp populations, though ascertaining the composition of camp populations is difficult because many camps are not accredited by the ACA. For example, the racial and ethnic breakdown of campers has not been adequately documented. Resident camps have typically had more white campers than campers of color. However, many day camps—especially in urban areas—serve a high population of racial and ethnic minorities. The majority of camps accredited by ACA are coed. However, many camps offer programs for only boys or only girls.

Organized camps have changed greatly in the past 20 years, expanding their focus to serve a wide array of populations. Although camp has traditionally been associated with outdoor experiences, the intensity of these experiences varies substantially depending on the location, philosophy, and activities offered at the camp. Although traditionalists argue that the outdoors is what differentiates camp from other recreation opportunities, some camps focused on youth development using highly skilled leaders do not emphasize outdoor activities and may, in some cases, be based primarily indoors.

A 2007 survey of ACA camp directors inquired about the role of camp in fostering nature-based experiences for campers (James, Henderson, & Garst, 2008). The majority of camp directors believed that (1) fostering children's connection to nature requires purposeful programming, (2) opportunities to connect with the natural environment at camp are important for children, and (3) camp plays a more important role today in fostering children's connection to nature than in the past. No differences were found in agreement with these statements based on camp affiliation, day/resident camp, programming focus (traditional outdoor or not), camp location, or camper attributes of income level, gender, age, or abilities. Regardless of programming focus (i.e., traditional outdoor or not), almost all camp directors (94%) reported that their campers spend more than four hours outdoors every day, and 83% stated that their programs were conducted primarily outdoors. Thus, although some successful camps make little use of the outdoors, the majority of camps remain highly focused on providing outdoor opportunities.

REFERENCES

American Camp Association (2010). Various articles retrieved from http://www.acacamps.org.

James, P. A., Henderson, K. A., & Garst, B. (2008). Camp directors' beliefs regarding nature-deficit disorder and camp. *Camping Magazine, 81*(4), 34–39.

Louv, R. (2005). *Last child in the woods.* Chapel Hill, NC: Algonquin Press.

WEB RESOURCES

The American Camp Association (ACA) (http://www.acacamps.org) has numerous materials describing many aspects of camp.

International Camping Fellowship (www.campingfellowship.org) provides news from camps around the world.

Summer Camp Handbook (www.summercamphandbook.com) is an invaluable resource, providing an overview of such topics as camp terminology, camp goals, camp types, checklists, homesickness, health and safety, and care packages, just to name a few.

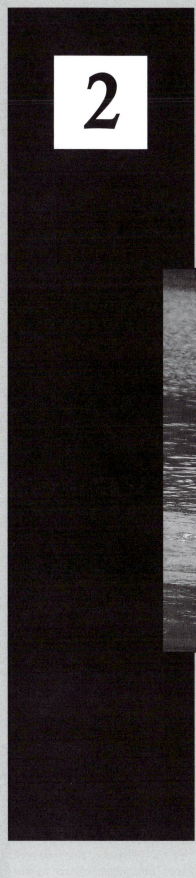

2

History of Organized Camps

Camps have a rich past. In 2010, organized camps celebrated their 150th anniversary and the American Camp Association (ACA) celebrated its 100th anniversary. The strength of camp experiences today is based in part on the rich traditions and successes of camps over the years. To understand the breadth and depth of today's camp movement as well as its future direction, it is necessary to explore its past.

Early Campers

Camping is as old as human existence. Early people were often nomadic, moving with the changing seasons in search of food or better climate, or in pursuit of or flight from their enemies. Some ancestors lived in caves, while others constructed temporary and sometimes portable shelters. Although they may not have had any alternatives "to camp," they nevertheless were involved in an intimate relationship with nature and the outdoors.

The American Indians might also be considered campers prior to the European invasion and settlement. Their ability to survive was based on a respect for and compatibility with nature. The first settlers who came to the New World became campers as well since they immediately needed to construct shelter and find nourishment from the land.

Almost everything growing in the wild was of interest to early settlers. Many plants were valuable as sources of food, tools, medicine, clothing, or shelter. Other native materials were a hindrance to be gotten rid of to make room for crops, buildings, or cattle. These people *had* to know nature intimately. There was no time for mistakes when selecting the proper wood for a box or axe handle or finding food to eat or herbs to relieve illness and pain.

Hunting and trapping animals for fur, food, leather, and clothing required cunning and an understanding of animal life. The history of America is rich in the lore of early explorers and settlers who matched wits with nature in a constant struggle for survival.

Early Rural Life

When the US Constitution was signed, 98% of the population lived in rural areas. With the coming of the industrial revolution, manufacturing enterprises were established in the larger towns and cities. As lucrative employment opportunities appeared in the more populated areas, people left the farms and turned the settlements into towns and the towns into cities. Now more than 200 years later, only about 2% of the US population lives on farms. This exodus from the farm to the city, with its mechanization and gadgetry, greatly affected people's lifestyles.

In the farm environment of several generations ago, boys and girls grew up with knowledge of nature. Children learned a wide variety of useful skills since most things were grown or made at home and repaired by the user. Thus, woodworking, arts and crafts, and homemaking were learned and practiced from an early age under the close supervision of parents or grandparents. Formal school training in "readin', writin,' and 'rithmetic" was confined to a few winter months when the children could be spared from their farm duties.

Farm chores furnished vigorous exercise. Large, close-knit families provided the companionship of brothers, sisters, and cousins as they worked and played together. Guests provided welcome diversion and were urged to make an extended stay. Distances were too great and traveling too hazardous and uncomfortable to warrant brief overnight or casual evening visits. Local communities organized social affairs like corn huskings, house and barn warmings, taffy pulls, and spelling bees. Attendance at church services was regular, and religious "camp" meetings drew people from great distances.

This way of life changed as people moved to cities and began to specialize in one trade or occupation, and to earn wages that they used to buy services or commodities from other specialists. People began to lose the daily contact with nature they had experienced while tilling the soil or rambling over woods and fields.

Urban Life

Today, children spend nine or ten months attending schools that may be overcrowded. That school year is further extended if they attend summer school. Children are regulated by daily schedules and subjected to the formality of teaching methods that are necessary when large numbers of students must meet course and credit requirements.

Too many children today get insufficient exercise. Adolescent obesity and overweight are critical public health problems. The 2005–2008 National Health and Nutrition Examination Survey (NHANES) reported that from 1980–2008, obesity rates doubled for adults and tripled for children in the United States (Centers for Disease Control and Prevention [CDC], 2010a). In 2007–2008, almost 17% of children and adolescents aged 2–19 years were obese. The Youth Risk Behavior Surveillance for 2009 (CDC, 2010b) found that 12% of high school students were obese, and another 16% were overweight. Unfortunately, except for a few perfunctory physical education periods each week, little more than lip service is paid to this aspect of health and physical development.

In contrast to earlier rural households, many families today see both parents employed outside the home. When working parents spend their free time in pursuits that continue to segregate them from their offspring, this further reduces the family's time together. Instead of providing their children with companionship, understanding, and sympathy, some parents try to substitute with liberal allowances for movies, television, videos, computer games, and other material "things" that are supposed to supply happiness.

Another distinction between today's urbanized children and the rural children of the past is that children now have a great deal of leisure time. Unfortunately, too many quickly fall into the pattern set by their parents and become afflicted with "spectatoritis," an overreliance on commercial organizations and technical equipment to supply them with ready-made entertainment. Given such circumstances, it is easy to understand why children derive so much enjoyment from participating in camp activities that provide exciting, meaningful, and often novel opportunities.

The Beginnings of Organized Camping

As early as the latter half of the 19th century, some people who had rushed to the city for its advantages found that the city life was not as idyllic as anticipated. Problems immediately arose, as they do when many people live in close proximity to one another. Of great concern to some was the manner in which their children were growing up. Although children from poorer families were kept busy with household chores and apprenticeships at trades or other outside jobs, those young people from well-to-do families had servants to satisfy their needs, which left them with time on their hands.

For those children, camping seemed to offer an acceptable solution to the disconnect with nature as well as with other children. Organized camping began in the United States as devoted men and women organized groups of young people for outings in the woods. Organized camping was originally a "Yankee notion" conceived and fostered in New England. It spread quickly across the country and exists today throughout many parts of the world.

First School Camp (1861)

The distinction as to which camp was the "first" camp is debatable, however as historian Eleanor Eells (1986) notes, deciding who was "first" is of far less importance than the impact made by this new approach to experiential learning. The Round Hill School was founded in Northampton, Massachusetts, in 1823 as a preparatory school with a strong emphasis on outdoor life. However, this school did not focus on overnight excursions so many do not consider it the first camp.

Frederick William Gunn generally is regarded as the father of organized camping. He was the founder and head of the Gunnery School for Boys in Washington, Connecticut. With the coming of the Civil War, his students, like typical boys, wanted to "play soldier," and sometimes were permitted to march, roll up in their blankets, and sleep outdoors. Since the school operated through part of the warmer summer months, in 1861, yielding to the wishes of the boys, Mr. and Mrs. Gunn packed them up for a gypsy trip to Milford on the Sound, four miles away. They spent two weeks boating, sailing, hiking, and fishing. The experiment proved so successful that it was repeated in 1863 and 1865, with some former students returning to join in the excursion.

Later, the Gunns selected a new site for these excursions—Point Beautiful on Lake Waramauge, seven miles from the school, and the name was changed from Camp Comfort to Gunnery Camp. The camp continued to exist until 1879. Although Mr. Gunn's camp might be considered the forerunner of school camping (he simply moved his school program outdoors for a brief session), the objectives and procedures of today's school camping are quite different from those of the first Gunn camp. However, his camp is recognized as the first organized camp in the world and established the United States as the birthplace of organized camping.

First Private Camp (1876)

Dr. Joseph Trimble Rothrock was a practicing physician in Wilkes-Barre, Pennsylvania, who combined his hobbies of forestry and conservation with his desire to do something for frail boys by establishing the North Mountain School of Physical Culture. He felt that the children's health would improve by living outdoors in tents while continuing their education. The school was located on North Mountain in Luzerne County, Pennsylvania, and operated from June 15 to October 15 with 20 pupils and five teachers. Each student paid $200 tuition, but this income failed to cover expenses, and after one year, Dr. Rothrock abandoned the idea in favor of spending the following year on an Alaskan expedition. Various attempts to revive the school under different leadership proved similarly unprofitable and it was permanently closed within a few years.

First Religiously Affiliated Camp (1880)

The Reverend George W. Hinckley of West Hartford, Connecticut, established a camp because he saw in its informal atmosphere an opportunity to get to know the boys of his congregation better and, perhaps, to influence them more permanently. In 1880 he took seven members of his church on a camping trip to Gardner's Island, Wakefield, Rhode Island. The results must have been gratifying, because he later founded The Good Will Farm for Boys at Hinckley, Maine. Hinckley's schedule called for a "sane and sensible" religious and educational morning program; afternoons spent in activities such as swimming, baseball, and tennis; and evenings devoted to singing, talks, and other forms of entertainment.

First Private Camp Organized to Meet Specific Educational Needs (1881)

In 1880, while Ernest Berkley Balch was traveling on Asquam Lake near Holderness, New Hampshire, he chanced upon Burnt Island, which appeared to be unowned. It was an ideal spot to realize his aspiration to give boys from well-to-do families a summer of adventure instead of letting them idle away in resort hotels. Consequently, in 1881 he returned with five boys and erected a small frame shanty that they christened "Old '81." The campers were surprised by the unexpected appearance of a man who claimed to own the island, but their offer of $40 as complete payment for the entire island was accepted, and so they bought it. They called their retreat Camp Chocorua because of its superb view of Chocorua

Mountain 30 miles away. The camp continued for eight more summers, until 1889.

The boys wore camp uniforms of gray flannel shorts and shirts with scarlet belts, caps, and shirt lacings. The boys were divided into four work crews, each with a leader called the "stroke." One crew was off duty each day while the other three spent about five hours as kitchen, dish, or police crews. Spiritual life was planned carefully, and the services must have been quite impressive as the boys came singing through the woods, dressed in cotta and cassock (a short, outer garment worn over a long garment reaching to the feet) to the altar of their chapel, which was set deep in a grove of silver maples.

The camp's five staff members oversaw 25 boys who competed in tennis, sailing, swimming, diving, and baseball. Winners were awarded ribbons bearing their names, the event, and the date. Balch was the first to formulate specific objectives for his camp, which included instilling in each boy a sense of responsibility both for himself and others, and an appreciation of the value of work. The Camp Chocorua silver pin was given annually to the two or three campers who best demonstrated the qualities of manliness, justice, truth, and conscientiousness.

First Agency Camp (1885)

Sumner F. Dudley, a young resident of Brooklyn, was employed with his father and brother in the manufacture of surgical instruments. His first venture into camping was to take seven members of the Newburgh, New York, YMCA on an eight-day fishing, swimming, and boating trip to Pine Point on Orange Lake. Since the boys shaved their heads in what they deemed proper preparation for the trip, their camp was appropriately dubbed Camp Bald Head.

Dudley spent the next several years conducting other camping trips for boys and joined the YMCA staff as a full-time worker in 1887. He died in 1897 at the age of 43. His last camp on Lake Champlain near Westport, New York, was renamed Camp Dudley in his honor and is the oldest organized camp still in existence.

Camping for Girls (1890, 1892, and 1902)

The first camping experiences for girls occurred a bit later than for boys. In 1890, Luther Halsey Gulick opened a private camp for his daughter and her friends. He later founded the Camp Fire Girls, which was more recently changed to Camp Fire, Inc. In 1891, Professor Arey of Rochester, New York, established Camp Arey as a natural science camp and a year later he lent it for a month's use by girls. Andre C. Fontaine and his wife took over the camp in 1912 and thereafter conducted it exclusively as a camp for girls. Laura Mattoon founded what generally is regarded as the first camp exclusively for girls in 1902 at Wolfeboro, New Hampshire, calling it Camp Kehonka for Girls.

Developmental Periods of Camping

Early organized camping has been classified by Dimock (1950) into three stages of development according to the main emphasis at the time. These include (1) the *recreational stage*, (2) the *educational stage*, and (3) the stage of *social orientation and responsibility*. Ramsing (2007) suggested that the period after 1970 might be considered the *new directions* stage. Based on the trends since 2000, the current developmental period of organized camps might be considered the *outcomes-based* stage of camping. As with any movement, precise dates cannot be demarcated for these stages because they evolved gradually and overlapped. Moreover, there was never perfect unanimity among leaders or uniformity as to the programs and practices of the various camps.

Recreational Stage (1861–1920)

Early camps were sponsored mainly by conscientious, public-spirited men who saw in camps a chance to get boys into natural, outdoor environments and away from potentially harmful pursuits in the city. They believed that the rugged outdoor life would strengthen the boys physically and keep them engaged in wholesome, enjoyable activities. Bible study often played a prominent part in the program, and high moral and spiritual values were held in esteem. These early leaders believed that values, like mumps or measles, could be contracted merely by association with the right people. Financial gain was not important; however, the lack of adequate monetary backing caused the early demise of many camps.

Commonly one or two adults led an excursion with as many as 40 or 50 boys and a meager supply of equipment. The expeditions were, almost without exception, built around the strong personality of the leader, who earned the respect and admiration of the boys through unselfish motives, sympathetic understanding, tactful leadership, and sound principles concerning the roles of work and play. Ralph Waldo Emerson's statement that "every institution is but the lengthened shadow of a man" certainly applied to these early camps.

The camping movement was slow to gain adherents. No more than 25 to 60 camps were in existence in 1900.

Educational Stage (1920–1930)

Significant changes often follow wars. The years after World War I were no exception. The number of organized camps increased rapidly, with marked changes in methods and programs. *Progressive education*, with its foundations in psychology and mental hygiene, fostered an emphasis on satisfying the needs of each child instead of trying to fit all children into a preconceived mold. In response to this progressive trend, camps added such activities as dramatics, arts and crafts, dancing, and music that were designed to supplement the expanding school curriculum.

Almost every hour of a camper's day was regimented strictly and campers were enrolled in scheduled classes much as when they were in school. Competition, often with an elaborate system of awards, was stressed. One reason for this change in philosophy was the development of new testing methods that demonstrated that personality, character, and spiritual growth were not inevitably acquired through association with the right people but rather must be taught through well-planned programs to obtain optimum results. This idea was the precursor of intentional or purposeful programming, a common feature of 21st century camps.

Social Orientation and Responsibility Stage (1930–1970)

Camping enthusiasts who had assumed that an active outdoor life was invariably invigorating and healthful were shocked when a 1930 study of more than 100

The developmental emphasis of organized camping has changed over the years, but fun and adventure remain primary components.

camps showed that camping was sometimes detrimental to health and that the longer children stayed in camp the more likely their health was to suffer. To remedy the situation, camp directors added physicians, nurses, and trained dietitians to their staffs and instituted more healthful practices in their programs. Campers were allowed more freedom to choose activities, which emphasized principles of citizenship and democracy, and the hectic tempo of camp life was reduced.

Some in the camp movement were also concerned about the effect of the Great Depression on children. A significant outcome of this concern was the declaration that play should be the right of every child (Chudacoff, 2007). This philosophy recognized the emerging importance of play and recreation experiences in contributing to quality of life. In addition, New Deal programs built campgrounds that were used for organized camping (Van Slyck, 2006), making outdoor experiences accessible to more people.

The strength of a society is only as great as that of its individual citizens. People in the United States as well as citizens of other parts of the free world are aware that the best way to strengthen and preserve democratic government is to give each citizen a solid foundation in the principles of democracy. Early in the camp movement, camping leaders realized that they had not only the opportunity but also the responsibility to foster democracy, especially since they were dealing with young people in their formative years. Consequently, progressive camps tried to offer young people a chance to experience democratic living in a community atmosphere. Camping was considered an experience in group living at its best in that campers were encouraged to develop independence, self-control, and self-reliance as they planned and accepted responsibility for their own daily camp life. Camp personnel encouraged positive outcomes by adapting programs to meet the needs of individuals. In addition, a camp accreditation program that addressed many health and safety issues in camps was launched and gained momentum during this period.

New Directions (1971–1999)

The tumultuous times leading into the 1970s witnessed major societal changes, including the civil rights movement, the women's movement, the environmental movement, and the introduction of the technological age. Camps had to address issues such as integration, environmental degradation, and sedentary children. Camps also began to try to meet the demands of a *youth culture* that rejected some of the values held by their parents. More emphasis was put on environmental education and stewardship as well as on diversity and specialization. Adventure/challenge courses including ropes courses fostered skills and self-confidence. Games focused on inclusion rather than competition. More awareness existed regarding interactions among various groups of people, and changes were made in the conduct and organization of camps. Advances in technology provided new means for marketing camps as well as new policies regarding the use of this technology at camp by campers.

Outcomes-Based Camp Programs (2000–present)

From their beginning, camps were associated with positive outcomes, particularly with regard to character development. In the first decade of the 21st century, the value of camps relative to positive youth development as well as human development has become a prominent focus. An emphasis on purposeful or intentional programming to attain desired outcomes in campers is widely accepted. More about this approach will be discussed in the chapter on program planning.

Camps in the 21st century are often challenged to maintain the traditional aspects and activities of camping while integrating the forces of culture, society, and technology in the development of new programs. Many camps now offer educational programming of more breadth as well as leadership training, and many have incorporated technological advancements at the expense of the rustic approach to camping. As time constraints on children's summer schedules have become more demanding, the opportunity for a lengthy stay at camp has decreased, while parental desire for greater educational gain has heightened.

The modern camp movement has struggled to maintain its identity due to overgeneralization of what constitutes a "camp" and the diminishing interest of youth in the outdoors. Nevertheless, the contributions to youth development through group interaction, planned programs, trained leadership, and potential outdoor experiences remain the mainstay of camp experiences.

The Organization of the Camp Movement

Early camps were highly individualized projects conducted largely according to the beliefs, past experiences, and particular ideals and aspirations of the person or organization sponsoring them. Over time, the more progressive camp directors and other interested individuals recognized the value of meeting informally for fellowship and to discuss common successes, problems, and failures. These gatherings proved so helpful and inspirational that a formal meeting was held in Boston in 1903 with about 100 people in attendance.

In 1910 the *Camp Directors' Association of America* was established with 11 charter members. Charles R. Scott served as its first president. The *National Association of Directors of Girls' Camps* was formed in 1916, with Mrs. Luther Halsey (Charlotte) Gulick as president. The *Mid-West*

Camp Directors' Association followed in 1921. These three organizations joined forces as the *Camp Directors' Association of America* in 1924, with George L. Meylan serving as president. In 1926 the Association began publication of a magazine called *The Camp Directors' Bulletin,* later changed to *Camping Magazine.* The following paragraphs highlight two early leaders and provide further context for understanding the beginnings of the camp movement.

Dr. William Gould Vinal

In the 1910s, Dr. William Gould Vinal, known as Cap'n Bill, began his tenure in the field of camping education. Cap'n Bill played a significant role in setting the foundation and outline for school camps, guidelines that would resonate until the 1950s. Cap'n Bill spent time teaching and directing the Nature Lore School, participated in the Boy Scouts of America, and was a nature guide at Yosemite National Park. He was elected president of the Camp Directors' Association in 1925. Cap'n Bill was a prolific writer and speaker and initiated and directed summer programs for graduate students, nature guides, members of the National Camp Directors' Association, and many other organizations. Following his tenure at Columbia University, Cap'n Bill went to the University of Massachusetts in Amherst, where he maintained his fieldwork and worked closely with Life Camps and with Dr. Lloyd Burgess Sharp.

Cap'n Bill promoted the idea of a decentralized camp in which small groups of people would split apart from the established camp to create their own self-sufficient community. Guiding students in exploration and reflection were principles that Cap'n Bill embraced. He allowed others the freedom to explore and answer their own questions, and in the process made a significant impact on the experiential education field.

Dr. Lloyd Burgess Sharp

Lloyd Burgess Sharp, often referred to as the "Chief," was an educator first and an academic second. Sharp has been described as the originator, promoter, and chief authority in the methodology of outdoor education. Sharp grew up in a rural Kansas farm community, which had a great impact on his life, philosophies, and methods. Upon graduating from college, enlisting in the U.S. Navy and completing his tour of duty, and teaching in a secondary classroom, he enrolled at Columbia University and received his PhD in 1929 as the first person to earn a doctorate in camping education. While attending Columbia, Sharp's influential faculty members consisted of educators such as John Dewey.

In 1925 Sharp began his tenure at Life Camps. Life Camps began in 1887 when John Ames Mitchell, the original editor of *Life Magazine,* founded the Life Fresh Air Fund to take underprivileged children from the summer heat of city slums to the clean air and sunshine of a country farm. The camps offered "free vacations for children at two places known as Fresh Air Farms" (Rillo, 1964). These camps were established to offer underprivileged children the opportunity to leave New York City for a brief period and experience life away from the city. However, by the mid-1920s the program was in disarray and the facilities were falling into disrepair.

Sharp was hired by Edith Shatto King to assist in evaluating and reconstructing Life Camps. Sharp agreed to do so with the stipulation that the name would be changed from Life Fresh Air Farms (1887–1925) to Life Camps (post–1925). Sharp discovered that the programming at Life Camps was unlike what he and his colleagues had spent time researching, implementing, and promoting. The program at Life Camps consisted of a highly structured, militaristic/dictatorial style of leadership. The ratio of staff to campers surpassed 50 to 1. The staff and campers were treated differently, eating in different locations and from different menus. Sharp recognized that a new style of leadership was necessary. He focused his reorganization on the idea that camping was "loving to live in the woods and open spaces."

Sharp's PhD dissertation had promoted what he called "camping education." He believed that camping programs provided opportunities for real-life learning moments. The residential summer camp was a miniature community and in such a setting, campers could exercise self-reliance and their own judgment to maintain success and safety in their activities.

Dr. Sharp also influenced the camping industry through his research dealing with the effects of camping programs on and in educational settings. Promoting the idea that school grounds and camping facilities should be used year round, Sharp supported the notion that camping was as beneficial in the winter as in the summer and that public school camp should be open all year. Sharp further realized the need for professional standards and training in the field of camping education and thus implemented leadership training through New York University. During these training seminars, students learned about and became part of the public school camping movement. In response, other colleges and universities began to develop their own camping facilities, programs, and training. Sharp's emphasis on professional organization resulted in the formation of many new camping programs across the nation.

The American Camp Association (ACA)

The Camp Directors' Association was renamed the American Camping Association in 1935, with another name change in 2004 to the American Camp Association. Leaders in 2004 observed that organized camping

Figure 2.1   The American Camp Association logo.

Used with permission. The American Camp Association logo is a registered trademark of the American Camping Association, Inc.

was often associated with public and private campgrounds and wanted to further distinguish the nature of camps for children.

ACA is a nationwide nonprofit professional organization dedicated to the promotion and improvement of camp experiences for children. ACA is a community of camp professionals who, for 100 years, have shared knowledge and experience to ensure high-quality camp programs that give children and adults the opportunity to learn lessons in community, character-building, skill development, and healthy living.

The association is committed to helping members and all camps provide:

- camp communities committed to a safe, nurturing environment
- caring, competent adult role models
- healthy, developmentally appropriate experiences
- service to the community and the natural world
- opportunities for leadership and personal growth
- discovery, experiential education, and learning opportunities
- excellence and continuous self-improvement (ACA, 2010)

ACA has more than 7,000 members in 50 states and 10 foreign countries. Among its members are camp owners, camp directors and staff, educators, clergy, commercial firms that supply camp materials, family camping leaders, and others with diverse training and experience who are interested in camps and human (primarily youth) development. Categories of membership include:

- individual
- individual with an international address
- ACA Standards Visitor
- volunteer
- educator
- expanded learning staff

- retiree
- student

Through 2010 the American Camp Association was composed of five geographic regions further divided into sections. Organizational changes are occurring due to the 20/20 Vision Plan and the ACA is therefore becoming more centralized due to the pervasiveness of technology and the need to maximize resources. National conferences are held annually, while each section also holds meetings. Much of the work of the organization is carried out by volunteers; however, a team of full-time staff members that includes a Chief Executive Officer (CEO) works directly with a National Board of Directors. The national office is at Bradford Woods, an outdoor education and camping center 25 miles south of Indianapolis, Indiana.

Since 1926, the ACA's official publication has been *Camping Magazine,* which is published six times a year (semi-monthly). The publication covers topics on education, guidance, programming, business management, and other important subjects. The *CampLine* newsletter, published three times per year, provides camp-specific knowledge on legal, legislative, and risk-management issues. In addition, *ACA Now* is an online newsletter published weekly that highlights activities occurring within ACA. Numerous book titles are available through the ACA bookstore, which is managed by Healthy Learning.

In 2010, ACA embarked on a Professional Development Center, which will be built upon a framework of knowledge, skills, and abilities identified with and related to work in the camp and youth development profession. The center will provide information about core competencies needed to be a camp professional or to work in a camp. Resources that will be coordinated include opportunities from educational partners, job services, online learning communities (e.g., message boards, discussion groups, Facebook, Linked In), a registry of camp mentors, and professional development courses offered through events, the e-Institute, webinars, and other endorsed courses.

The Outdoor Living Skills (OLS) program has been a component of ACA for many years. In 2005 ACA began to phase out the OLS program as it was then known and transitioned to a program called Leave No Trace. The Leave No Trace Center for Outdoor Ethics and ACA are formal partners in promoting environmental ethics. The Leave No Trace Center is a national nonprofit organization dedicated to promoting and inspiring responsible outdoor recreation through education, research, and partnerships. The Leave No Trace program builds awareness, appreciation, and respect for wildlands and has a variety of program offerings and curricula to teach and share the seven Leave No Trace principles (www.lnt.org). Camps are encouraged to work with the Center in developing environmental stewardship programs associated with outdoor living.

One of the newest initiatives of ACA is its research program. Since 2000, ACA has conducted and coordinated a variety of studies to examine such issues as camper outcomes, healthy camps, enrollment trends, business operations data, emerging trends, and programming in different settings. Research is promoted through an annual Research Symposium at the national conference, a column devoted to research in *Camping Magazine*, involvement in the national Collaboration for Youth, and the awarding of the annual Marge Scanlin Outstanding Student Research Award in honor of Marge Scanlin, an ACA staff member who was instrumental in establishing its research agenda. The ACA website contains many of its sponsored research reports.

ACA also offers a crisis hotline for camps to use in the event of emergency situations at camp. The ACA staff who respond to calls provide the most up-to-date legal and ethical recommendations for camp staff to consider if a problem emerges, such as child abuse or death of a camper.

The ACA lobbies state and national legislators regarding laws and public policy that impact camp management and employment. ACA teams with numerous partners, sponsors, and educational alliances for promoting its work. The official ACA website (www.acacamps.org) includes a plethora of resources regarding accreditation, education, research, and current news. Moreover, potential job seekers can visit ACA's jobs site.

Accreditation

One of the notable accomplishments of the ACA has been its contribution to the general upgrading of camp operation and performance. Since 1935, standards of performance have been developed and approved by the members of the association. Since 1948, the process of visiting camps to verify compliance with those standards has been in practice. The ACA standards are regarded as the industry standards by government entities, the courts, and the public in general. ACA is the only body with national standards that are applicable to all kinds of camps: day and resident, independent, not-for-profit, religious, or government sponsored.

The accreditation program is based on the following premises:

- Camp professionals care about the successful development of children.
- Camp is for everyone—all interests, ages, abilities, budgets, and personal schedules.
- Camp offers a supervised, positive environment in the outdoors where kids can laugh and grow within a set of controlled boundaries.
- Camp is more than a place; it is an experience that does kids a world of good.

- Camp experiences provide opportunities to develop key life skills: responsibility, cooperation, courage, and self-esteem (ACA, 2010).

To be accredited by ACA, a camp must be visited by trained ACA Standards Visitors who verify compliance with standards in eight areas (see exhibit 2.1).

Exhibit 2.1	
ACA Standards Categories	
Site and facilities	Human resources
Health and wellness	Program design and activities
Transportation	Aquatics
Operational management	Trip/travel

The standards establish guidelines for needed policies, procedures, and practices. The camp, then, is responsible for ongoing implementation of these policies. The accreditation program is educational and allows administrators to evaluate their own program against nationally established criteria and develop plans for improvement. Verification of the completion of this educational process by the ACA Standards Visitors occurs at least once every three years.

Accreditation is also useful as a guide to prospective camp staff members and parents seeking a camp for their children. However, while accreditation can assist the public in choosing a camp that has voluntarily submitted itself to this external verification process, it is not a guarantee that the camp will meet the campers' expectations.

Nevertheless, during an average year, approximately 5 million children and adults attend the 2,400 camps that have been accredited or approved by ACA. Accredited camps are permitted to display the Accredited Camp logo shown in figure 2.2.

Figure 2.2 Only camps accredited by the ACA may display this emblem.

Used with permission of the American Camp Association.

The American Camp Foundation

The American Camp Foundation (ACF) is the administrator for various gifts given to the American Camp Association. ACF's purpose is to raise funds to support needed and worthwhile projects that cannot be included in the regular ACA budget. Its general management is the responsibility of an elected board of trustees, and it depends entirely upon voluntary contributions from individuals, sections of the ACA, foundations, and other sources.

Other Professional Organizations

The following is a brief summary of several other professional or public organizations involved in one or more aspects of camping and outdoor adventure programming, which includes provision of technical assistance, leadership training, and publications.

International Camp Fellowship (ICF)

ICF is a worldwide assembly of camping professionals interested in sharing their enthusiasm, knowledge, and commitment to the camping experience. It was founded in 1987 by an energetic group of individuals intent on creating "a better world through camping" and who believe that people can make a difference by "bringing together the world of outdoor experience." The ICF is committed to coordinating the exchange of news and information between individuals, camps, and organizations in different countries. Bilateral and multilateral exchanges are encouraged to achieve international understanding and global living, leadership, and ecological action through organized camping and outdoor experiences.

Association of Experiential Education (AEE)

AEE is committed to the development and promotion of adventure-based experiential learning while supporting professional development, research, and the evaluation of experiential education programming and methods. It represents the efforts of diverse groups to create a formal, international network that provides both support and impetus to the development of experience-based teaching and learning techniques and to their application to the traditional aims of education and human development. The organization was founded in the early 1970s. AEE grew from the need for communication among those who conduct programs that use camping, adventure education, outdoor pursuits, and other experiential approaches. The AEE's major undertakings are sponsorship of the Annual Conference on Experiential Education and publication of *The Journal of Experiential Education*.

The National Camp Association (NCA)

The NCA was established in 1983 to help parents find the right camp for their children. NCA's free summer camp referral services provide summer camp program information for parents looking for camp experiences for their child. All NCA camps are accredited programs (i.e., by NCA, not ACA) that have met health, safety, and programming standards and have been evaluated by NCA staff.

The Council for Adventure & Outdoor Education/Recreation (CAOER)

The council supports and promotes innovative and challenging educational/recreational adventure and other outdoor activities. It is a council within the American Association for Physical Activity and Recreation, which is a unit within American Alliance for Health, Physical Education, Recreation and Dance (AAHPERD). CAOER recognizes that holistic programming with a focus on personal growth in the outdoors, developing the self, understanding group dynamics on challenge courses, and greater awareness of environmental issues is now a critical part of K–12 school and university curricula, camp programs, and the leisure pursuits of physically active people worldwide. CAOER is a professional resource for cutting-edge training, high-quality programs, and established standards for all people across the life span. Membership in the council is open to all members of AAHPERD who by experience or training have demonstrated a professional interest in outdoor education.

The Association of Outdoor Recreation and Education (AORE)

A national organization, AORE was developed to link outdoor recreation and education professionals and students. AORE's mission is to provide members with opportunities to exchange information, promote the preservation and conservation of the natural environment, and address issues common to college, university, community, military, and other not-for-profit outdoor recreation and education programs. Founded as a grassroots movement in 1993, AORE promotes networking and communication throughout the outdoor recreation field.

Coalition for Education in the Outdoors (CEO)

CEO is a nonprofit network of outdoor and environmental education centers, nature centers, conservation and recreation organizations, outdoor education and experiential education associations, institutions of higher learning, public and private schools, fish and wildlife agencies, and businesses that share a mission—the support and furtherance of outdoor education and its goals. Goals include personal growth and moral development, team building and cooperation, outdoor knowledge and skill development, environmental awareness, education, and enrichment. The coalition was established in 1987 at the State University of New York at Cortland by a group of outdoor educators from around the country. CEO fills a need in the outdoor education community for an organization that "unites outdoor associations, institutions, businesses, and agencies to better serve both professionals and consumers in the outdoors." CEO sponsors a semi-annual Research Symposium and publication, *Research in Outdoor Education*. In addition, *Taproot* is published twice a year to share news and resources about outdoor education.

REFERENCES

ACA (2010). Celebrating 100 years. *Camping Magazine, 83*(1), entire issue.

Centers for Disease Control and Prevention (2010a). Prevalence of obesity among children and adolescents: United States, Trends 1963–1965 through 2007–2008. Retrieved from http://www.cdc.gov/nchs/data/hestats/obesity_child_07_08

Centers for Disease Control and Prevention (2010b). Youth Risk Behavior Surveillance—United States, 2009. Surveillance Summaries, June 4, 2010. *Morbidity and Mortality Weekly Report 2010*, 59 (No. SS-5).

Chudacoff, H. P. (2007). *Children at play: An American history.* New York: New York University Press.

Dimock, H. S. (1950). *Administration of the modern camp.* New York: Association Press.

Eells, E. P. (1986). *History of organized camping: The first 100 years.* Bradford Woods, IN: American Camping Association.

Ramsing, R. (2007). Organized camping: A historical perspective. *Child and Adolescent Psychiatric Clinics of North America, 16*(4), 751–754.

Rillo, T. (1964). *Historical background and development of camping and outdoor education.* Eric Reports 067-171.

Van Slyck, A. A. (2006). *A manufactured wilderness: Summer camps and the shaping of American youth.* Minneapolis: University of Minnesota Press.

WEB RESOURCES

AAPAR's Council for Adventure & Outdoor Education/Recreation (http://www.aahperd.org/aapar)

ACA Timeline (www.acacamps.org/anniversary/timeline)

Association for Experiential Education (http://www.aee.org/)

Association for Outdoor Recreation and Education (http://www.aore.org/)

Coalition for Education in the Outdoors (http://www.outdooredcoalition.org/)

Cyclic trends in the history of camping: Reflections on the past/implications for the future (http://www.acacamps.org/handouts/James%20Penny%20-%20Cyclic%20Trends%20in%20the%20History%20of%20Camping.pdf)

Development of organized camping (http://www.infed.org/association/sum-camp.htm)

History of organized camping (http://www.acacamps.org/media_center/about_aca/history.php)

International Camping Fellowship (http://www.campingfellowship.org)

Leave No Trace Center for Outdoor Ethics (http://www.lnt.org/)

National Camp Association (http://www.summercamp.org/)

PRINT RESOURCES

Bond, H. E. (2003, July/Aug). Children's camps in the Adirondacks. *Camping Magazine, 76*(4). Describes camps in the Adirondacks, some of the earliest organized camps.

Cohen, H. (2003, July/Aug). A camp director remembers World War II. *Camping Magazine, 76*(4). Interesting description of what camp was like during this time.

Dunn, B., & Frebershauser, D. (2002, Sept/Oct). Native Americans—the first campers. *Camping Magazine, 75*(5). Discusses how to honor Native American traditions properly in camp.

Nicodemus, T. (2003, July/Aug). Camp through the decades. *Camping Magazine, 76*(4). Brief overview of the history of camps.

3

Values in Organized Camping

Organized camping provides an environment to address many learning objectives. The aim of all education is to help people develop into happy, healthy, and well-adjusted contributing members of society. Unfortunately, for too many people education is only what takes place within the confines of a classroom. However, every experience people have during their waking and sleeping hours plays a part in human development. Every person encountered has the potential to leave an impression. People are influenced also by the organizations to which they belong, as well as the books read, websites visited, television programs watched, and the movies attended. Many of these influences are positive; some are not.

Camping Is Education

Learning is a lifelong process. It is neither age-specific nor place-specific. However, learning has been traditionally associated with children and youth in school settings. Although schools are important, learning occurs in venues across the life span—including resident and day camps. As you discovered in chapter 2, camps have provided young people with outdoor experiences for 150 years. The early camps were founded to complement didactic school work and to give youth opportunities to participate in nature, physical exercise, play, and adventure experiences. Although people need to be "book smart" and "numbers smart," learning also involves acquiring behaviors, skills, values, and understandings that are not traditionally academic. Children as well as adults should have multiple intelligences that include being body smart, music and culture smart, people smart, self smart, and nature smart (Louv, 2005).

A well-conducted camp opportunity can be educational and beneficial when learning becomes fun. A good camp will take advantage of its unique environment to strengthen the values already instilled in campers by others and to teach new values that are particularly meaningful in both the camp setting and daily lives of the campers. Howard and Howard (2005) described how camps must use their unique environments to promote creativity and diversity. They suggested that for camps to realize their full educational potential, four steps must be addressed:

1. Embracing the truth that camps are a unique educational institution,

2. understanding why a focus on youth development is desperately needed,

3. accepting the challenge that each camp must decide what it fundamentally believes, and

4. facing the real challenge of challenge education, which means translating beliefs into action.

Characteristics and Benefits of the Camp Environment

Many characteristics of organized camps set them apart from other learning environments. The following sections discuss these characteristics and the many potential benefits.

Camp As a High-Dosage Experience

Camp can possess campers completely when they eat, sleep, work, and play intensely for 8–24 hours a day every day of the week with few outside influences or distractions. Campers get a high dose of opportunities in a compact period of time. Campers live in their own world, associate closely with counselors and others in their cabin or program group, and often do activities with their unit or the camp as a whole. Parents usually do not spend as much time with a child each day as do counselors and fellow campers. In terms of total hours, eight weeks spent in camp are the equivalent of a whole year in school. Camp becomes home, school, friends, place of worship, and playground all in one setting (i.e., usually outdoors) that contrasts strongly with the urban or school environment.

The Outdoor Setting

Most resident camps are located on varied terrain that is relatively primitive and undeveloped. Campers spend much of their waking moments, as well as an appreciable amount of their sleeping hours, in the open air. In a 2007 study (James, Henderson, & Garst, 2008), camp directors indicated their campers spent *at least* four hours each day in the outdoors, with an average of almost eight hours. Campers' senses undergo constant stimulation by the smells, sights, sounds, textures, and even tastes of nature.

Some potential benefits of these outdoor settings for campers are:

1. An **appreciation of and knowledge about nature and ecology** as well as a lasting love of the outdoors that can lead to a lifelong interest in outdoor activities and related hobbies.

2. Insight into nature's blueprint for **keeping balance** and an appreciation of the interdependence of all living things and of humans' proper place in the natural world.

3. A meaningful **spiritual experience** as campers develop appreciation and concern for others as well as knowledge about the universe itself. A sense of awe and inspiration can occur when campers see the majesty of a high mountain, the peace of a quiet valley, the beauty of a colorful sunset, the glint of sunlight on a lake, or dewdrops glistening on a spider web.

4. An understanding of the need to **conserve natural resources** for future generations to enjoy. Observant campers will notice a camp's practices of recycling, conservation, and ecology and can be influenced to continue these practices at home.

5. The development of **aesthetic tastes** as campers live with nature's panorama of beauty. Campers can come to gain an appreciation of nature's peace and serenity.

Living with Others of Varied Backgrounds

Many young people spend their nonschool time with children who have similar social backgrounds. In camp, children often live and play with individuals with different personalities and backgrounds.

Some potential benefits of this social diversity for campers are:

1. Learning to **accept diversity** in others, appreciating their good qualities and hoping they will reciprocate.

2. Learning that **flexibility, sharing, and consideration for others** are essential for harmonious group living.

3. Reinforcing **good manners**, or helping to develop manners when youth are lacking in such areas as politeness, flexibility, and satisfactory eating and health habits.

4. Developing **lasting friendships** with peers, older youths, and adults through the shared experiences of camp living.

5. Gaining **maturity** by learning self-confidence and self-reliance.

Living in a Democratic Community

The usual camp method of handling problems and topics of general interest in a group is through group discussion with a counselor, or sometimes with a camper serving as leader. Matters concerning the whole camp similarly may be handled through the Camp Council, which is usually composed of representatives and staff from each of the smaller groups. Campers thus have an opportunity to share in forming procedures and rules that are within their province. Some camps have used the ideas of *negotiable* and *nonnegotiable* rules. Campers are told what elements are negotiable and have a say in establishing the behavior expectations at camp. In other cases because of safety or other reasons described below, some rules are simply nonnegotiable.

Regardless, the benefits of democratic group living for campers might include the following:

1. Learning how the **democratic process** works, how to serve effectively as a leader or follower, and how to express oneself clearly without being obnoxious or monopolizing time or attention.

2. **Understanding and accepting camp rules**, since there is a necessity for some nonnegotiable regulations to protect the rights of each individual and to keep the program running smoothly. Small group discussions teach campers to become cooperative camp citizens since people are less likely to break rules when they understand the reasons for them, especially if they have shared in discussing and negotiating them.

3. Gaining the courage to **take an active part** in a meeting and to express opinions, even when they may not coincide with what is popular. Democratic living can help campers not only recognize the right of others to differ but also teach them to listen and think about what others are saying.

4. Learning to **abide by the will of the majority** while still having concern for the rights and wishes of the minority. Willingness to compromise instead of insisting on having one's own way is essential to democratic living.

5. Learning to **get the facts before making a decision**, consulting knowledgeable people or references if necessary, and then analyzing and evaluating all the pros and cons as well as costs and benefits before making up one's mind.

6. Learning to **bring problems and disputes into the open** instead of sulking, grumbling, becoming bitter, or discussing them only with those who are no better informed or in no better position to do anything about the situation.

7. Gaining experience in **problem solving**, since camp living frequently involves questions about what to do and how to do it.

The Program of Activities

Most camps offer a variety of activities, with special emphasis traditionally placed on outdoor adventure activities. These activities are unlikely to be available at home, or at least not in the same form, since many depend on an outdoor environment and the general atmosphere of a typical camp.

Some potential benefits of a varied program are:

1. Developing **lifetime recreational pursuits or hobbies**, and perhaps even a vocation. Participation in new experiences at camp often uncovers unsuspected interests and aptitudes, broadens perspectives, and enables campers to appreciate the interests and accomplishments of others. The average camp tries to develop general, all-around abilities rather than specialized ones, as is so often done in school sports and other activities in which only a few participate and the majority are left to cheer on the sidelines.

2. Encouraging campers to **try their best** as they attempt to improve their own performance. Although competition can challenge campers with superior ability, most camps emphasize self-improvement.

3. Becoming **gracious losers** by accepting defeat without bitterness or excuses.

4. Having *fun* **and enjoying the excitement of new and challenging experiences**, but doing so in a safe way. Young people who learn to satisfy their desire for adventure and fun in wholesome ways will likely not resort to socially unacceptable ways (e.g., drugs or reckless driving) to obtain excitement.

5. Satisfying **curiosity** and the desire to investigate and learn. The guided discovery approach of camp is "let's go together and find out."

6. Learning how to properly **balance work, play, and rest**. Campers can alternate vigorous activities with quieter ones, while observing regular times for rest.

The wide variety of activities offered by camps allows children to broaden their perspectives and discover new abilities.

7. Learning the wise **use of leisure time**. Campers should be able to choose activities that offer enjoyment and satisfaction rather than merely kill time. By participating in varied camp activities such as canoeing, swimming, hiking, rock climbing, kayaking, backpacking, sailing, fishing, camping out, nature study, photography, tennis, and horseback riding, participants develop lifelong skills and interests. In contrast, few individuals will continue as adults to participate in the team sports they played in school.

8. Enjoying **simple pastimes** that cost little or nothing, and learning to be self-sufficient instead of depending on others or commercial entertainment. Campers can learn much about the world around them by watching baby birds fledge or appreciating a beautiful sunset.

9. Increasing feelings of **patriotism** and appreciation of heritage through participation in such activities as flag-raising ceremonies, Fourth of July celebrations, studying local history, and living somewhat like pioneers and early explorers.

10. Learning to appreciate **seriousness and thoughtfulness** through participation in services and campfire programs developed around thought-provoking themes and rituals.

Free Time for Dreaming

Society often seems intent upon converting children into adults as rapidly as possible. Youth clothing, games, and social activities often are patterned closely after those of adults. Many children's after-school hours are crammed with structured activity, with an emphasis on *being productive*. Sometimes setting aside time for rest and simple relaxation is rejected. Although many children today spend unstructured hours behind computer screens, they often do not take time or even know how to meditate or exercise their own imaginations. Summer vacations often no longer provide lazy carefree days to spend fishing, wading in a brook, browsing in a book, or just relaxing.

Camps long ago recognized the folly of cramming each day with a frenzy of activities. The pace and scheduling of today's camp should provide opportunity for rest and relaxation. Having time to think and reflect often gives young people an avenue to better understand who and what they are as well as the meaning of the world around them. Acquiring a sense of calmness and well-being is essential to being human. At camp, children can participate in physical activities that create a healthy fatigue as well as relax at something they enjoy—whether it is just chatting with friends or sitting and dreaming.

(Photos on this page and on opposite page, left, courtesy of Bradford Woods Learning and Outdoor Center.)

Ratio of Trained Staff to Campers

The typical camp consists of a community of young people and selected leaders playing and living together in small groups. The American Camp Association requires the following ratio of counselors to campers according to age group (Standard HR-9).

Table 3.1   Number of Campers Served per Individual Counselor (Staff to Camper Ratios)

Camper Age	Number Staff	Overnight Campers	Day Campers
4–5	1	5	6
6–8	1	6	8
9–14	1	8	10
15–18	1	10	12

*Camps may have smaller ratios depending upon the ability level of campers and the specific activities.

A camp staff usually includes a nucleus of older experienced adults supplemented by college students, younger counselors (e.g., counselors-in-training or leaders-in-training), teachers, and specialists trained and interested in working with people. Children and youth need and usually want advice and crave a sympathetic adult or older person to whom they can express their hopes, frustrations, accomplishments, and problems.

Some potential benefits of a high ratio of staff to campers are:

1. Learning to **regard adults** in a new light. A cabin counselor or group counselor acts as a sort of big buddy and establishes a friendly atmosphere by planning, working, sharing, laughing, and having fun with the children. Other staff specialists (e.g., sports instructors, swimming instructors) play a similar role and can present a picture of adults as interesting, helpful people whom campers can trust and enjoy.

2. Learning **desirable traits and characteristics** by example. Both desirable and undesirable traits are more likely to be acquired by association or example rather than by teaching, although teaching is also important. Informal camp life creates an atmosphere of closeness and camaraderie that is favorable for learning by associating with others. Most young campers are in the stage of "hero worship" and a counselor or other staff member may well be chosen as an influential model. The familiar saying that "your actions speak louder than words" is certainly evident in staff/camper relationships.

Simple Living

Not all camps focus their programs around the outdoor environment. While some have retained simple living and rustic facilities, others offer cabins and program areas with electricity, air conditioning, bathrooms, and even computer networks for campers to keep in touch with friends and family who are not at camp. Nevertheless, the classic appeal of a simple setting has benefits for today's campers, whether in day or resident camps.

Many camps maintain a rugged, outdoorsy appearance. Even buildings that are fully equipped to serve a distinct purpose often do so without decoration or unnecessary gadgetry. Such facilities as the health center and food services must adhere to strict standards of cleanliness and sanitation, but can retain an outdoor feel with large, screened windows and, ideally, a beautiful lake view!

"Do it yourself" is an often-used motto used to teach campers to care for their cabins and possessions and share in the upkeep of buildings and common areas. Campers also share in such chores as setting tables, sweeping the lodge, and preparing and cooking outdoor meals. They learn to dress for the weather and pack and carry their own gear as well as a share of the group equipment.

Some potential benefits to campers of simple camp living are:

1. Acquiring new self-respect and self-confidence as campers learn to **take care of themselves** and do things others may previously have done for them.

2. Gaining a new and more realistic **sense of values** as campers note the relative unimportance of such things as money, computers, video games, and fancy clothes in assessing the true worth of an individual. In camp they find that the happiest, best liked, and most respected counselors and campers have earned their status because of their character and personality rather than their outward appearance and material possessions.

3. Gaining a feeling of **community and camp pride** from serving others as they share in maintaining the camp or assist in projects to improve the camp for the present and future campers.

4. Taking pride in their **ability to improvise** and make do with what they have, since they can't run to the store to replace something they have damaged or run out of.

5. Acquiring a feeling of being at **home in the outdoors** as they learn the unique role each element plays in the makeup of the total environment.

6. Learning **respect** for the dignity of work and the satisfaction that comes from the sustained effort needed to complete individual or group projects.

7. Taking pride in the **good health and physical fitness** that camp activities bring as they stimulate the lungs and heart, exercise the large muscles, and produce a healthy appetite for the meals cooked outdoors or served indoors by the food service staff.

8. Acquiring skill in resident camp **household tasks** like making beds, sweeping, washing dishes, planning

and cooking well-balanced meals, setting tables, and constructing, repairing, and maintaining equipment and clothing.

9. Learning to **appreciate history and culture** through appropriate programs that include dramatics, storytelling, reading, and trips to nearby points of historical interest.

Camps and Positive Youth Development

We've just listed the characteristics of camps that uniquely position them to have a positive influence on participants. Camp may offer these benefits for any participant, but the major focus of camps has been on young people. Although general concern for the development of youth is not a new idea, the notion of positive youth development has been extensively applied over the past two decades by people working with children and adolescents. The focus of positive youth development is not on the problems of youth but on how to move youth toward successful adulthood. Therefore, the emphasis is on determining what youth need to function well now and into the future.

Youth development specialists have indicated that in addition to academic excellence, youth need opportunities to grow toward physical, social, emotional, civic, and social competencies. They need a variety of supports to reach these competencies and camp is one place that can offer opportunities in addition to the home, school, and other community organizations. Evidence is mounting that well-designed and well-implemented youth programs that consciously focus on positive youth (or human) development have positive outcomes (National Collaboration for Youth, 2006). Many camp professionals have adopted these ideas in this era of outcomes-based camp programs. A number of positive youth development models exist, but they all point to what Lerner and her colleagues (2005) described as the 5 C's: competence, confidence, character, connection, and caring.

A great deal has been written about positive youth development and how it can be applied to camps (e.g., Bialeschki, Henderson, & James, 2007). However, most studies about the outcomes of camp have been conducted in a single camp. Further, many people believe that camp is inherently good and research is not needed to document that fact. However, with the new focus on outcomes, research is needed to quantify what camps have to offer.

The ACA has renewed its commitment to the foundational aspects of the camp experience through its positive youth development focus. In addition, the ACA has identified research as a central component necessary to understand camp's value and to improve the quality of camping. Camp provides an opportunity for community living away from home in an outdoor recreational setting that appears to accelerate youth development beyond what would be expected by maturation alone.

Two national studies directed by ACA staff and volunteers to measure developmental outcomes resulting from camp experiences (Bialeschki et al., 2007) showed that the areas influenced most strongly were social skills, physical and thinking skills, positive identity, and spirituality (i.e., mostly for those camps that had this outcome as a goal). Camps were particularly good at providing supportive relationships but had the most room to improve when providing physically and emotionally safe spaces and opportunities for youth involvement (e.g., leadership and decision making).

Youth Development Outcomes of the Camp Experience (ACA, 2005) provided a starting point for describing developmental outcomes at camp. For this research effort, questionnaires for campers, parents, and staff were constructed and pilot tested. Data were collected from a national representative sample to ascertain: (1) whether developmental change occurred in key developmental domains and (2) whether some camp attributes (e.g., supervision ratios, program elements, staff training) were associated with change in outcomes.

Children's self-reports indicated statistically significant growth from pre-camp to post-camp on most of the ten constructs. *Adventure and exploration* showed the largest change. Other areas where significant change occurred were *self-esteem, independence, leadership, friendship skills, environmental awareness,* and *spirituality.* Children's self-reports at the six-month follow-up indicated that gains realized at camp were mostly maintained. In the case of *independence, leadership, social comfort,* and *peer relationships,* additional statistically significant gains occurred over post-camp levels.

Parents' reports on their children indicated statistically significant growth from pre-camp to post-camp in all ten constructs measured. Parents' reports on their children at the six-month follow-up also indicated that gains realized at camp were mostly maintained. For *leadership* an additional statistically significant gain was seen by the parents beyond post-camp levels.

Camp counselors' reports on their campers indicated statistically significant growth from the second day of camp until the penultimate day in all four of the developmental domains measured: *positive identity, social skills, physical and thinking skills,* and *positive values and spirituality.* Growth was modest, with *physical and thinking skills* showing the largest effect.

As predicted, children whose self-report scores were lowest at pre-camp showed the greatest gains from pre-camp to post-camp. In other words, campers who started out with the lowest scores gained the most. Those children who started out with high self-reports may have encountered a ceiling effect because of the nature of the measurements used.

Children's and parents' responses to additional items on the post-camp versions of the questionnaires illuminated some of the positive outcomes of the experience. For example, three-fourths of children and over two-thirds of parents agreed "a lot" with the statement: "Camp helped [me/my child] make new friends." Over two-thirds of children and three-fourths of parents agreed "a lot" with the statement: "The people at camp helped [me/my child] feel good about [myself/him/herself]." More than three-fourths of children indicated that they had learned something new at camp, with almost as many indicating they had improved their skill in some area while at camp.

In summary, *Youth Development Outcomes of the Camp Experience* provided confirmation of the conventional wisdom concerning the value of camp as a developmental growth experience. The convergence of opinion among children, parents, and staff provided scientific validity that camp is not only fun, but also enriching and educational. This first national study of outcomes demonstrated that important developmental changes occurred in youth at camp and pointed the way to the next step—further defining the developmental processes through a focus on intentional programming and reaching the goals of camp.

Reaching Goals

Camps can accomplish many outcomes, but not by being a camp in name only—coasting along on the good reputation of organized camps. Worthwhile achievements are attained only when those who are in charge of a camp have made intentional and purposeful plans that are based on the belief that positive youth (human) development is central to camps. Organized camps, therefore, should outline their specific purposes and design a program of activities to attain them. The task of administrators is to lay the groundwork and unite the staff into a team that pulls together to achieve these common goals. This process will be discussed in greater detail in the chapter on planning programs.

The words *purpose*, *goal*, *end*, or *aim* are synonymous and connote an ultimate objective. For instance, one common goal of camping is for campers to experience individual growth and development, while another is for campers to learn to live outdoors and become acquainted with the natural environment. Although these aims are admirable and worthy, such broad statements do not provide any specific guidelines on how to achieve them through the program offerings and services of the camp. Thus, definite directions are needed for a camp program to meet such stated goals. These directions are developed through the formulation of objectives that serve as stepping stones toward the goal. (Objectives will be discussed more fully later in this book.)

In actuality, camp sponsors and administrators place varying emphasis upon particular goals and objectives, depending on the individual camp's purposes and philosophy. For instance, a church camp probably will stress spiritual values, while a private camp might emphasize certain recreational skills. Although the goals and objectives may vary, all camps are established for the purpose of creating positive personal opportunities for participants. Since camps offer unique learning experiences that draw upon a group living situation, they reinforce the importance of transferring experiences learned in the outdoor environment to normal daily living. Some of the common goals established by camps for their participants are illustrated in figure 3.1.

The second national ACA study about supports and opportunities in camp programs, *Developmental Supports and Opportunities of Youths' Experiences at Camp* (ACA, 2006a) was undertaken to specifically examine how intentional youth development might occur when using a community action framework (Gambone, Klem, & Connell, 2002) applied to camp settings. In this study, ACA researchers sought to understand how youth participants viewed the provision of developmental supports and opportunities in the camp setting. The first step in this two-part effort provided benchmark data on four domains of developmental supports and opportunities at camp: *supportive relationships, safety, youth involvement*, and *skill building*. These four areas were dimensions uncovered in the first national study. Researchers also wanted to discover how the developmental quality of camp experiences and the goals set could be used for program improvement.

The overall results showed that optimal levels of support and opportunity were highest for the domain of *supportive relationships* followed by *skill building* and *safety*. The optimal levels of *supportive relationships* and *skill building* at these 80 representative camps appeared to exceed the averages of other community-based organizations and schools. Levels for *youth involvement* and especially decision making and youth leadership fell below camp directors' expectations, with 39% of the campers reporting insufficient levels of involvement.

The second phase of this study focused on a program improvement process that assessed significant changes in the level of supports and opportunities of the participating camps (ACA, 2006b). Camps designed and implemented strategies to intentionally target particular areas of supports and opportunities. The findings from this second phase showed significant positive changes in 83% of the participating camps. Improvement was most evident when camps implemented program-improvement strategies in a holistic and integrated fashion. In other words, the greatest change occurred when camps set specific goals to address these developmental outcomes.

ACA standards require camps to establish a written statement of overall goals, identify in writing specific observable behavioral outcomes, provide materials and

Figure 3.1   Common goals of organized camps.

training strategies to help staff achieve the established outcomes, and inform parents and campers of the goals of the camp experience (ACA Standards, Program Design 6A-D). This approach provides a framework for determining what outcomes are possible. Camp administrators, staff, parents, and campers can then work together to determine how to best meet these goals.

Camp is not only a valuable experience, for some it can be life changing. However, as a staff member you should have realistic expectations about what can be accomplished in the time available. There will be some disappointments and setbacks, since habits are hard to break and personality changes come slowly. A clear understanding of objectives will help you assess progress and, perhaps, alter your goals as experience and a better understanding of your group dictate. Try to help each person to achieve at least one new competency during the camp session.

One of the best ways to change attitudes and instill new ideas is to present yourself as an example. Another is to recognize and take advantage of the "teachable moments" that arise during the activities of the day. These moments occur when campers are truly interested in what they are doing and recognize the need for guidance or information. During these moments they are alert and ready to look, listen, and learn. At such times, a brief anecdote (even if you have to make it up) is often an effective way to make your point.

Each day, think about and evaluate what has been accomplished with each individual and with the group. Informal chats with individuals and the group will help you develop your initial objectives and keep tabs on how each camper feels about the progress being made. Think about strategies that can be used to emphasize the positive outcomes of camps.

REFERENCES

American Camp Association (2005). *Youth development outcomes of the camp experience: Directions.* Retrieved from http://www.acacamps.org/research/ydo.pdf

American Camp Association (2006a). *Inspirations: Developmental supports and opportunities for youths' experiences at camp.* Retrieved from http://www.acacamps.org/research/Inspirations.pdf

American Camp Association (2006b). *Innovations: Improving youth experiences in summer camp programs.* Retrieved from http://acacamps.org/research/Innovations.pdf

Bialeschki, M. D., Henderson, K. A., & James, P. A. (2007). Camp experiences and developmental outcomes for youth. *Child and Adolescent Psychiatric Clinics, 16,* 769–788.

Gambone, M. A., Klem, A. M., & Connell, J. P. (2002). *Finding out what matters for youth: Testing key links in a community action framework for youth development.* Philadelphia: Youth Development Strategies, Inc. and Institute for Research and Reform in Education. Retrieved from http://www.ydsi.org/YDSI/pdf/Whatmatters.pdf

Howard, A. H., & Howard, T. H. (2005, Sept/Oct). Notes from the margins. *Camping Magazine, 78*(5), 40–45.

James, P. A., Henderson, K. A., & Garst, B. (2008). Camp directors' beliefs regarding nature-deficit disorder and camp. *Camping Magazine, 81*(4), 34–39.

Lerner, R. M., Lerner, J. V., Almerigi, J., & Theokas, C. (2005). Positive youth development: A view of the issues. *Journal of Early Adolescence, 25*(1), 10–16.

Louv, R. (2005). *Last child in the woods.* Chapel Hill, NC: Algonquin Press.

National Collaboration for Youth (2006). *Making a difference in the lives of youth.* Washington, DC: National Human Services Assembly.

WEB RESOURCES

Afterschool.gov (www.afterschool.gov)

America's Promise Alliance (www.americaspromise.org) provides an overview of children's needs and resources addressing those needs.

American Youth Policy Forum (www.aypf.org) is a series of articles covering a variety of youth development topics.

Benson, P. L., & Saito, R. N. (2006). *The scientific foundations of youth development.* Minneapolis: Search Institute. Retrieved from http://www.ppv.org/ppv/publication/assets/74_sup/ydv_4.pdf

Bibliographies of camp-related research can be found at: (http://www.acacamps.org/content/bibliographies-camp-related-research-24). As a service to members, educators, students and the general public, ACA has compiled and annotated a comprehensive listing of camping-related research.

Center for Youth Development Policy and Research. (2003). What is youth development? Retrieved January 15, 2007, from http://cyd.aed.org/whatis.html

Character education book lists, available from Michigan State University Extension (http://4h.msue.msu.edu/4h/resources/character_dev_educ_biblio), lists books for children and adults that focus on character development and education.

Character Education Partnership (www.character.org) includes principles of character education, standards, lesson plans and activities, and assessment tools.

Character Education (www.goodcharacter.com) offers teaching guides, character education in sports, discussion starters, and discussion techniques.

Child Trends (www.childtrends.org) has information on child poverty, childhood development, positive development, indicators of child well-being, and youth development.

Community Network for Youth Development (www.cnyd.org) provides links and a framework for community networks.

CYFERnet (www.cyfernet.org) includes educational materials, learning environments, youth development, and program development.

Explaining the value of camp (http://findarticles.com/p/articles/mi_m1249/is_n5_v66/ai_15262703/).

Finding out what matters for youth (http://www.ydsi.org/ydsi/pdf/WhatMatters.pdf) is a research report on youth development.

Henderson, K. A. (2001). Camping gives kids an endless world of good—research (http://findarticles.com/p/articles/mi_m1145/is_11_36/ai_80448467/).

Josephson Institute of Ethics (http://josephsoninstitute.org) offers lesson plans, resources, and guides.

Search Institute (www.search-institute.org) provides an overview of developmental assets, spiritual development, downloads, and links.

The Whole Child (www.pbs.org/wholechild/index.html) includes information on developmental milestones, thinking skills, communication skills, physical development, activity ideas, tips, and articles.

Virginia Commonwealth University Life Skills Center (www.lifeskills.vcu.edu/lifeskills.html) provides an overview of life skills.

PRINT RESOURCES

Bialeschki, M. D., & Scanlin, M. (2005 Sept/Oct). The camp experience: Being all that you can be. *Camping Magazine, 78*(5).

Bialeschki, M. D., Younger, T., Henderson, K., Ewing, D., & Casey II, M. (2002). Happy but sad. *Camping Magazine, 75*(1), 38–41.

Boffey, D. B., & Overtree, C. E. (2002, Sept/Oct). Life changers. *Camping Magazine, 75*(5). Discusses life changers like love, humor, humility.

Brannan, S., Arick, J., & Fullerton, A. (1997). Inclusionary practices: A nationwide survey of mainstream camps serving all youth. *Camping Magazine, 70*(1), 32–34.

Cameron, S. (1999, May/June). The growing camper. *Camping Magazine, 72*(3). Discusses developmental traits, typical behavior for age groups.

Carnegie Council on Adolescent Development (1992). *Task force on youth development and community programs: A matter of time.* Washington, DC: Author.

Catalano, R. F., Berglund, J. A. M., Ryan, H. C., Lonczak, H. C., & Hawkins, J. D. (1998). *Positive youth development in the United States: Research findings on evaluations of positive youth development programs.* Paper submitted to US Department of Health and Human Services, Office of the Assistant Secretary for Planning and Evaluation and National Institute for Child Health and Human Development.

Dworkin, J. G., Larson, R., & Hansen. D. (2003). Adolescents' accounts of growth experiences in youth activities. *Journal of Youth and Adolescence, 32,* 17–26.

Eccles, J., & Gootman, J. A. (Eds.) (2002). *Community programs to promote youth development.* Washington, DC: National Academy Press.

Gambone, M. A., & Arbreton, A. J. A. (1997). *Safe havens: The contributions of youth organizations to healthy adolescent development.* Philadelphia: Public/Private Ventures.

Gilmour, B., & McDermott, W. (2008, May/June). Avoiding the "pinball machine approach" to promoting social competence. *Camping Magazine, 81*(3). Discusses the social skills campers need and how they can acquire them.

Gucker, P. L. (2001, Sept/Oct). Camp teaches life lessons. *Camping Magazine, 74*(5). Discusses the elements that promote self-assurance, self-esteem, and self-confidence.

Jacobs, J. (2002, Sept/Oct). Starfish values program. *Camping Magazine, 75*(5). Describes a character education program and how to implement it.

Kinnamon, R. (2003, Jan/Feb). The importance of character development. *Camping Magazine, 76*(1). Covers character building, core values.

Kohn, A. (2003, Sept/Oct). Rethinking character education. *Camping Magazine, 76*(5). Information on promoting social and moral growth, key elements of character education.

Kurtines, W. M., Ferrer-Wreder, L., Berman, S. L., Lorente, C. C., Silverman, W. K., & Montgomery, M. J. (2008). Promoting positive youth development: New directions in developmental theory, methods, and research. *Journal of Adolescent Research, 23*: 233–244.

Larson, R. W. (2000). Toward a psychology of positive youth development. *American Psychologist, 55*(1), 170–183.

Leffert, N., Benson, P. L., Scales, P. C., Sharma, A. R., Drake, D. R., & Blyth, D. A. (1998). Developmental assets: Measurement and prediction of risk behaviors among adolescents. *Applied Developmental Science, 2*(4), 209–230.

Marsh, P. (1999). Does camp enhance self-esteem? *Camping Magazine, 72*(6), 36–40.

McKinlay, B. (1999, May/June). Tips for camp counselors. *Camping Magazine, 72*(3). How to nurture development, guide positive behavior.

National Academy of Sciences. (2001). *Community programs to promote youth development.* Washington, DC: National Research Council, National Academy of Sciences.

Peterson, C. (2004). Positive development: Realizing the potential of youth. *The Annals of the American Academy of Political and Social Science, 591,* 202–220.

Pittman, K., Irby, M., & Ferber, T. (2000.) Unfinished business: Further reflections on a decade of promoting youth investment. Takoma, MD: The Forum for Youth Development.

Roth, J. L., & Brooks-Gunn, J. (2003). What exactly is a youth development program? Answers from research and practice. *Applied Developmental Science, 7,* 94–111.

Scanlin, M. (2001, Jan/Feb). "What is camp about?" *Camping Magazine, 74*(1). Discusses outcomes and objectives of youth development.

Schweinhart, T. (2002, March/April). The camp community and the world community. *Camping Magazine, 75*(2). Information on building community, service learning at the Institute for IDEAS.

Wallace, S. (2005, May/June). The myth of risk. *Camping Magazine, 78*(3). Discusses positive risk taking.

Wallace, S. (2006, May/June). Rites of passage. *Camping Magazine, 79*(3). Discusses teen transitions.

Wallace, S., & Seifer, B. (2009, May/June). The boy in the boat. *Camping Magazine, 82*(3). Covers the five metrics of success—self-reliance, self-confidence, exploration, respect, responsibility.

Waltemire, M. E. (1999, Jan/Feb). A kaleidoscope of opportunity. *Camping Magazine, 72*(1). Includes descriptions of the seven life skills identified by 4-H.

4

Trends in Camping

As in other phases of American life, rapid changes are occurring in the camp movement. Such changes are necessary and desirable. Improving that which is good regarding camp experiences and incorporating promising innovations is essential to the future of organized camping. This chapter discusses ongoing trends as well as emerging issues that will be reinforced throughout this book.

Camp Growth

The American Camp Association (ACA) accredits about 2400 camps in the United States. However, the exact number of camps is much higher than this figure. Some sources estimate there are over 12,000 camps in the country, depending, of course, on one's definition of "camp." For example, many university athletic departments have summer sports camps. Public parks and recreation departments appear to offer an increasing number of day-camp opportunities in local parks rather than in a typical outdoor camp site. Youth organizations such as the YMCA and Boys and Girls Clubs offer day-camp programs that are conducted indoors. Therefore, tracking the changes in the number and types of camps is difficult. Although some states have inspection and licensing procedures for any organization serving children in particular, no national requirements exist. Therefore, quantifying trends in the number of camps is a highly speculative venture.

Although some decrease in the number of traditional resident camps is apparent—especially among the smaller camps and among organizations like the Girl Scouts of the USA that went through a major reorganization at the turn of the century—other camps have ex-

panded to accommodate even more campers. Day camps, in particular, seem to be growing at a fast rate across the country. Specialized camps such as trip and family camps also appear to be growing in number. Likewise, trends indicate an increase in the number of therapeutic and/or rehabilitative programs focusing on the abilities and needs of specific populations such as individuals with developmental disabilities and physical disabilities, as well as for people who experience difficult or unusual situations (e.g., bereavement camps, obesity).

In addition to the number of camps, the enrollment in camps is of key interest, particularly given ACA's goal to have more than 20 million children attending camps by 2020. Although the estimates vary, the current number of campers attending camp each year is likely between 5–10 million. Therefore, making sure that available camps are at their capacity and helping to initiate more camp opportunities is essential.

ACA has been conducting periodic enrollment surveys in the past several years. Although not enough data exist yet to make trend projections, several observations were made in 2007 that indicate positive trends in enrollment statistics (ACA, 2010a):

- More than half the camps identified the 2007 summer as one of their best in the past five years. Of these camps, one-third said the 2007 summer was the highest enrollment ever.

- Half the directors said they reached 90–100% total capacity for the 2007 summer. Over 71% of directors said they had reached their targeted capacity.

- When asked about enrollment based on specific camper characteristics, most camps again said that 2007 was a summer of increases. For example, more than 40% of camp directors said that compared to

2006, they had increased numbers for boys and girls and for all age groups.

- More than half said they had between 50–74% camper return rates, which were about the same as 2006.
- About a fourth of directors said their minority camper numbers had increased in 2007. Most other directors indicated that the number of minority campers had stayed about the same.
- Over half the camps had about the same number of financially supported campers as in 2006, but 26% had more than a year ago.

These data represent only one year, but suggest that camp numbers are growing. However, the economic downturn of 2008–2009 has made continuation of such trends uncertain. Preliminary data for 2010 indicated that about two-thirds of the camps anticipated higher or about the same number of enrollments, that the number of returning campers was the same or higher than 2009, and resident camps were up more than day camps (but both were higher). Almost half the camp directors said they had more requests for financial aid. In addition, they indicated that they were trying to keep their numbers up by keeping costs down so camp fees did not need to be increased, offering sibling discounts, and offering discounts for enrollment in multiple sessions.

The potential for future enrollment increases may be most evident among new populations that were not as visible in traditional camp programs. The trends regarding these new camper populations are discussed in more detail in the next chapter.

Camp As a Learning Environment

Although camp has always been an environment for learning, an emerging trend is to position camps specifically as a learning opportunity. This positioning is based on a broad definition of learning. Learning happens in the classroom. It can also occur through venues such as family outings, community organizations, and camps. Unfortunately, many children do not have access to these types of educational activities nor to healthy, safe, and supervised environments, especially during the summer. Research has shown that young people experience learning losses over the summer when they do not participate in some type of learning opportunity. Moreover, many children are at risk for weight gain over the summer because of the absence of structured school activities.

Camps can provide holistic learning in a safe, healthy, and fun environment. They facilitate opportunities to be physically active through adventure activities, to bond with others through songs and skits, to learn social skills in a group situation, to gain confidence in one's abilities,

and to appreciate nature. In addition to these life skills, camps also provide a place where "kids can be kids."

Play is a learning tool for children. Many schools have decreased the amount of physical education and recess time while increasing homework, which is counterproductive in the overall development of children. A 2005 conference at Yale University entitled "Play = Learning" documented the importance of play for children's intellectual, emotional, social, and physical development. Play is at the heart of camp programs and play opportunities must be a focus of any child's learning.

Camp professionals are focusing on the fact that for 150 years, camps have provided unique settings that offer young people opportunities for community living away from home with a recreational premise, typically in natural environments. No other positive youth development experience combines these factors, and few can offer the same well-documented outcomes. Camp is not optional learning; rather, it is an essential, powerful, and important complement to school-based and lifelong learning. This message is a key trend being reinforced through ACA and related allies and is applicable to all types of camps.

Camps provide holistic learning in a safe, healthy, and fun environment.

Camp Physical Structures

Early camps were laid out in the manner of military camps, with living quarters arranged in straight lines on either side of a central street or in the form of a hollow circle or square with common-use buildings such as the mess hall and camp lodge in the center. Multiple-occupant sleeping units, like army barracks, contained cots arranged in long rows. The emphasis was on all-camp activities or on various activities from which campers could choose, so that campers usually associated with either the entire camp group or with a constantly changing group of individuals who had chosen similar activities. This type of organization was usually called **centralized camping**.

As camps grew larger, with some enrolling as many as a hundred or more campers, the participants sometimes found themselves in an impersonal atmosphere that lacked the warmth, camaraderie, and personal attention essential to a positive camp experience. Some camps responded to this problem by dividing their enrollment into smaller living units that functioned more or less independently. Nearly all camps, even those of modest size, have now adopted what is known as a **decentralization** plan, which was pioneered by the Girl Scouts many years ago.

In this decentralized model, the entire camp is divided into groups of 12 to 24 campers, with each group functioning like an independent camp. Each group, usually called a unit, section, division, or village, is fairly homogeneous with its members selected on some common basis such as age, camping experience, or interests. This model of decentralized camping—with many variations—is found in almost all types of camps today. Many day camps also incorporate this model of young people being a part of a small group for most of the day.

Along with the move toward decentralization, many older camp facilities have been renovated and new camp buildings designed with features such as heating and air conditioning systems so that campers can be comfortable year around. Computer technology has been installed in most camps, allowing staff and campers alike to stay in contact with the non-camp world during their time at camp. All new camp buildings today also must be able to accommodate people with physical disabilities.

In an attempt to meet constantly spiraling costs and still maintain a reasonable return on a considerable investment, many camps are now promoting multiple and year-round use of their facilities. Among the positive results of this trend have been innovative programs and greater possibilities for year-round employment for professionals with camp program and administrative skills. Off-season use may include such activities as winter sports, school camping and outdoor education, college camping and administration workshops, environmental education programming, orientation programs, senior citizen camping, family camping, and family reunions.

Camps also are used as retreats for conferences and vacations during the off-season.

Appealing to Camper Interests and Needs

Camps encounter competition in their quest for campers. Only about 10% of the youth of typical camp age (i.e., 6–17 years) participate in camp experiences each year. Thus, the potential for new campers is great, and is being actively pursued through ACA's 20/20 Vision Plan. However, for some children camp is but one of many options in the summer. Camps face great competition from alternative activities such as Little League, year-round basketball programs, traveling sport teams, extensive park and recreation programs, tutoring in special subjects or summer school, summer travel, and year-round schools. Nonetheless, not all children have these enrichment opportunities in the summer and these are the campers who would probably gain the most from a camp experience. Many young people never get the opportunity to go to camp either because they are unaware of camp opportunities or do not have the financial means to attend camp.

Another issue, however, is the apparent disconnect that many children feel for nature and the outdoors (Louv, 2005). Because today's youth are more worldly and technology-dependent, they may be disenchanted with camps that offer traditional programs. Such programs might be considered dull by today's youth who live in a fast-paced, immediate gratification culture. In response, many camps are successfully promoting exciting new programs that have appeal for young people. Such activities might include mountain biking, photography, movie making, zip lines, self-defense, and a number of other contemporary activities in addition to traditional camp activities. Some of these new activities will be discussed in more detail later in this book.

Program changes to capture campers' interest have been matched with schedule changes to accommodate campers' availability. Camps, particularly private independent camps that once offered longer sessions (i.e., 4–8 weeks) during the summer, now offer several short sessions so that young people can attend camp and still have time for other summer activities. Moreover, in communities with year-round schools, organizations like the YMCA now offer day-camp programs during the fall, winter, and spring to accommodate children during the intersessions.

Camps also are trying to attract more children through *camperships*—a means to provide financial aid for youth who cannot afford camp. Expanding the number of community and organization scholarships is essential in expanding the camper base and in addressing the needs of low-income children who would benefit greatly

Many camps promote exciting programs that appeal to young people. (Photo courtesy of American Camp Association)

from the camp experience. The majority of camps now make a conscious effort to bring together campers and staff from various social, religious, and economic backgrounds. Instead of remaining largely a middle-class institution, camps are becoming melting pots, attracting more minority and inner-city kids with targeted efforts.

Professionalization of Camp Staff

Many years ago camp counselors were often college students selected because of their athletic ability, their primary appeal derived from their prowess on field or court. These staff often knew little about the needs, desires, and personalities of children. With changes in camp philosophy and programs have come a demand for counselors and other staff who not only enjoy children but also know how to work with them in an atmosphere of mutual trust and friendly rapport. Although program specialists still are needed in such areas as trip camping, aquatics, health, and arts and crafts, the current tendency for campers and counselors to do most activities together

as a cabin or unit has produced a need for counselors with broad interests, versatility, and training and skills in group leadership.

Camp staff must have certain characteristics as required by ACA standards. For example, HR-10A states that at least 80% of the staff must be 18 years of age or older. For camps that serve people with special needs, the standard requires that 100% are 18 or older. HR-10B states that all staff must be at least 16 years old and must be at least two years older than the campers they are leading. In addition, the standards require specific credentials for all specialists, such as individuals who supervise aquatics (PA-1), adventure/challenge (PC-1), horsemanship (PH-2), and trip leadership (PT-4). Furthermore, the ACA standards also require particular procedures for staff hiring (HR-3) as well as mandatory staff screening (HR-4). All staff who work at camp must have first-aid certification and CPR certification (HW-23).

Camp staff have a great deal of information available to them prior to beginning their camp positions. For example, a wide array of camp literature is available online to make potential staff aware of the opportunities available that best fit their interests and abilities. Each camp staff member must be provided with a job description (HR-6) as well as specific training for the job (HR-7). The pre-camp staff training period conducted by camps is now considerably longer and better planned. The ACA standards recommend a minimum of at least three days of training for day-camp staff and five to six days for resident camps (HR-11). This standard also stipulates that training should address outcomes, developmental needs of campers, safety considerations and emergency procedures, expectations of staff performance, behavior management techniques, and issues related to child abuse. The pre-camp session must be used to *train* counselors, in contrast to the earlier custom of using the pre-camp period to get free help from incoming counselors in doing the physical work of getting the camp ready to open.

Many camps are now "growing" their own counselors by conducting excellent Counselor-in-Training (CIT) or Leader-in-Training (LIT) opportunities for older campers. These opportunities provide older campers with skills that may be useful if they decide to become camp counselors.

Flexible Camp Programming

Early centralized camps rigidly scheduled their programs. Activities were planned like school classes and each camper was required to participate in most of the offerings. The program was planned by the camp or program director, sometimes with the assistance of a few chosen counselors. The program often was intended to fill every waking moment of the day.

The narrow view that the program is merely the schedule of activities offered each day or each week is no

longer adequate. Rather, the camp program is the sum total of every experience campers have from the time they enter camp until their final good-bye. Most camps today offer more flexibility, giving campers some freedom to choose where they will go and what they will do. Ideally campers, counselors, and general staff all share in planning the camp program. Camps have become person-centered with an emphasis on positive youth development, as attuned to developing the campers as people as they are to developing skills.

The focus on outcomes as well as the changing interests and needs of campers have influenced camp programs. The traditional outdoor living skills remain important for many camps. Some have adopted creative approaches to keep campers motivated. For example, some maintain an elaborate system of achievement charts and awards given as participation incentives. Other camps do not use such systems. Although prizes and awards may be useful, keep in mind some of the negative ramifications of an overemphasis on winning awards:

1. Campers become so intent on working for awards that they miss the real values inherent in the activities themselves.

2. Regardless of the care taken in planning any system of awards, for every winner there must be one or several losers. Since some campers or groups seldom win, they may acquire a "what's the use of trying" attitude.

3. The desire to win sometimes becomes so keen that it leads to regrettable incidents. An overemphasis on competition can result in petty bickering and jealousies that are in direct conflict with the atmosphere camps are trying to create.

Though competition in some manner may exist, the majority of camps give awards while minimizing the importance of winning and losing. Campers are encouraged to do their best rather than attain top marks in a specific event. Many camps have adopted a philosophy of cooperation rather than competition. The focus is on the success of the group rather than on individual success. High camp morale, tradition, a word of commendation from sincere and enthusiastic counselors, the self-satisfaction individuals feel at having done their best, and the impetus of group approval usually furnish the best types of rewards in camp programs.

Health Practices and Healthy Camps

Health always has been an important objective of camping, but early camp staff deluded themselves into believing that good, nourishing food plus an active life in the outdoors inevitably would produce good health. This formula was not entirely successful. Therefore, camps must now adhere to a number of health standards. For example, ACA Standard HW-2 requires that every day camper, resident camper, and seasonal staff member must have a signed health history before they can attend camp. HW-6 states that each camper and staff must have had a health examination within 24 months of attending camp. In addition, all camps must have appropriate information available about each camper or staff member in case of an emergency (HW-5). All resident camps must have a process for health screening when campers arrive at camp (HW-8).

Camp staff, especially at resident camps, realize that scheduling campers in a nonstop round of strenuous activities from reveille to taps is counterproductive. Many camp programs now plan for quiet time, and campers, with counselor guidance, are more often permitted to pursue their own interests, even though these may occasionally involve nothing more strenuous than sitting under a tree daydreaming or watching a colony of ants at work. Often a rest hour is scheduled after lunch, and campers are encouraged to balance active and inactive pursuits.

Researchers in ACA (2010c) have recognized the need to provide surveillance of the illnesses and accidents in camp. A five-year study is currently underway to track camp illnesses and injuries, monitor trends in camp health, identify risk and protection factors, and track/analyze appropriate intervention strategies. Although the study remains ongoing, it has produced several broad preliminary recommendations:

1. Control the spread of infectious/communicable diseases. Promote hand-washing and good hygiene.

2. Reduce slips, trips, and falls by requiring all campers and staff to wear closed-toed shoes at all times.

3. Improve health monitoring by tracking injuries and illnesses to determine when, where, and how camper and staff health is being impacted. Make changes in appropriate areas as suggested in ACA Standard OM-4.

In addition to the above, other specific strategies include increasing the use of protective equipment, taking knife-safety seriously, reducing the impact of fatigue since accidents are more likely to happen when staff and campers are tired, assessing what happens during the campers' free time, and discussing these concerns at staff training (Garst & Erceg, 2009; Garst, Erceg, Baird, & Thompson, 2010).

Due to increasing occurrences in the US of extreme weather conditions, school violence, and terrorist activities, camp staff must also consider, evaluate, and plan for unforeseen crises and emergencies since no program is immune to such events. Risk-management plans have been adapted to include the possibility of intruders to the camp, violence from within the camp, and events which may arise in surrounding communities. The ACA Standards require that risk-management planning is conducted (OM-3), written procedures address intruders in

camp (OM-6), search and rescue procedures exist for a missing person (OM-14), and that the camp has written, site-specific emergency procedures established that address the possibilities of storm, earthquake, or fire (OM-7). Along with these specific requirements, communication procedures must be established (OM-15). Many of these standards have evolved over the years as social and environmental conditions have changed.

Camp staff must understand the complexities of the possible events and be prepared to act accordingly to minimize the risk to campers in their charge. First aid and safety precautions must be taken, evacuation plans need to be developed, and communication systems must equip camp personnel to respond to a multitude of situations. Moreover, these plans must be practiced during pre-camp training so that all staff are aware of the policies and procedures for their specific camp.

Camp Standards and Government Involvement

The American Camp Association has spent years developing, refining, and evaluating camp standards, which are based on prevailing practices in working with youth. Adoption of the ACA Standards is voluntary; however, they represent the best research available that can be put into practice.

The ACA Standards provide a valuable resource since no national, governmental standards exist that directly relate to all camps. A number of states now have regulations concerning such practices as food handling, sewage and garbage disposal, fire prevention, milk supply, and licensing of the camp store as well as boating, fishing, and minimum wage laws. Recently, camps have been affected by regulations concerning the use of pesticides, solid waste disposal, air pollution produced by refuse burning and other types of fires, child welfare and day care, and legislation such as the Occupational Health and Safety Act.

No degree of accreditation or government control can make camps 100% free of accidents or illness. Camps experience the same problems that exist in the general population. For example, the outbreak of H1N1 flu in the summer of 2009 occurred in camps as well as other places. ACA, however, responded quickly to the concerns and offered a number of suggestions for how camps could deal with this epidemic while continuing to offer camp programs. The procedures developed became standard practices for all youth organizations.

Research and Evaluation

As noted in previous chapters, more interest has emerged relative to camping research. Many camps now conduct evaluation studies to address the outcomes at their camps. ACA has a battery of instruments available and more are being developed. These tools focus on ten outcomes common to many camp programs. They include questions that ask if the camp experience has helped campers develop:

- friendship skills (i.e., make friends and maintain relationships)
- independence (i.e., rely less on adults and other people for solving problems and for their day-to-day activities)
- teamwork (i.e., become more effective when working in groups of their peers)
- family citizenship (i.e., encourage attributes important to being a member of a family)
- perceived competence (i.e., believe that they can be successful in the things they do)
- interest in exploration (i.e., be more curious, inquisitive, eager to learn new things)
- responsibility (i.e., learn to be accountable for their own actions and mistakes)
- affinity for nature (i.e., develop feelings of emotional attraction toward nature)
- problem-solving confidence (i.e., believe they have abilities to resolve problems)
- camp connectedness (i.e., feeling welcomed and supported at camp)

These tools are camp-specific, easy to administer, age-appropriate, statistically tested for reliability and validity, and can be used individually depending on the construct a camp wishes to measure. One version was developed for 6–9-year-olds called *Camper Learning*. Two versions were constructed for 10–17-year-olds: *Basic Camp Outcomes Questionnaires* and *Detailed Camp Outcomes Questionnaires* (ACA, 2010d).

Ecology and Conservation

As land for camping becomes scarcer and more expensive, those responsible for operating camps have become more invested with caring for what they have. For example, primitive camping programs no longer depend largely upon natural resources but rely mainly upon manufactured products (stoves for cooking and warmth, lanterns for light). The use of wood for lashing elaborate camp facilities or for campfires often is discouraged, and is prohibited by law in some states and in certain federally owned areas. The new philosophy embraces the concept that campers take everything they need to the campsite, and then bring it all back again so they disturb the environment as little as possible. "Leave no trace" is the motto.

Camp programs today teach young people about the importance of preserving the natural environment.

Camp personnel are interested in preserving their natural heritage and voluntarily support these conservation practices. ACA Standard PD-3 recommends that all camps evaluate their environmental impact and implement procedures to minimize any detrimental effects. Owners and users of land now feel a greater sense of stewardship or responsibility for its wise use and care, including planting trees to replace those lost to disease, accident, fire, or old age.

The ACA, like other organizations, has placed major emphasis on going "green." Benton, Guzik, and Nozik (2005), for example, described how green design and sustainability are at the forefront of new camp construction. They noted that the green philosophy about how structures are designed, built, and operated will have a dramatic impact today and for future generations. The idea is to make development sustainable and to design and construct structures that fit with the environment, conserve energy, and safeguard people's health. Camp staff may have little control over building design, but many other aspects of the camp can be green. Additional suggestions to stay green at camp offered by ACA (2010b) include:

1. Form a "green committee" of staff, volunteers, and campers and get everyone's input on ways to stay green.

2. Start a Captain Planet (or some other type of environmental) program for campers.

3. Switch to compact fluorescent light bulbs in camp facilities.

4. Keep camp beautiful! Pick up litter and clutter; make your green space enticing. Eliminate as much paper, plastic, and Styrofoam as you can from program, food service, and maintenance areas.

5. Get campers involved in conserving electricity and water. Put up friendly signs by faucets and light switches as reminders.

6. Research recycling methods for your area and put a recycling plan into action at your camp.

7. Compost plant material and install composting toilets.

8. Review what you buy. Buy recycled supplies from local sources and buy in bulk, which uses less packaging. Avoid purchasing products that have been shipped around the world in containers.

Emerging Issues

The ACA has conducted an emerging issues questionnaire for the past five years. The focus of this questionnaire is to determine what directors consider to be new issues that can be addressed through educational programs. The results from the 2009 study indicated some interesting findings regarding camp concerns (ACA, 2009).

• Almost all directors indicated that communicating with parents, staff screening and hiring, and camp training were ongoing concerns.

• Generating relevant programs, dealing with problem behaviors, crisis management, and financial stability were acknowledged by more than 90% of camp directors.

• Concerning staffing issues, about a third of the directors indicated they were doing one or more of the following to address financial concerns: making staff to camper ratios slightly higher, lowering salaries and bonuses, reducing training costs, and using more volunteers in formerly paid positions.

- Directors indicated that issues concerning romantic relationships between staff and the use of alcohol by staff during free time had decreased somewhat in the past five years.
- Directors reported that registrations for camp occurred later than in the past.
- About half of directors said they were using an online system for registration.
- More than half of directors said the marketing of their camps had increased in the past year. The most important messages communicated through marketing were the value of camp, camp is a safe place to send children, lifelong skills can be developed at camp, and camp is a place for positive youth development.

Some of these issues relate to ideas previously discussed. New concerns arise each year and successful camp staff will be able to recognize them and seek ways to resolve issues, whether new or ongoing. Camp is a microcosm of the larger society in many ways and is influenced by an external world. Nevertheless, a camp staff with the mind-set of continual improvement will be well prepared to meet head-on any emerging issues and to maintain the safe, nurturing environment of their camp.

REFERENCES

ACA. (2009). Emerging Issues. Retrieved from http://www.acacamps.org/sites/default/files/images/research/improve/2009_emerging_issues_summary.pdf

ACA. (2010a). Enrollment Trends. Retrieved from http://www.acacamps.org/sites/default/files/Spring2010enrollmentpulse.pdf

ACA. (2010b). Green Techniques. Retrieved from http://www.acacamps.org/campmag/0711topten

ACA. (2010c). Healthy Camps Study. Retrieved from http://www.acacamps.org/research/enhance/reduce-injury-illness

ACA. (2010d). Outcome Tools. Retrieved from http://www.acacamps.org/research/youth-camp-outcomes-battery

Benton, M. E., Guzik, J. D., & Nozik, N. K. (2005, March/April). Green and sustainable design for camp facilities: Why should you implement it at your camp? *Camping Magazine, 78*(2).

Garst, B., & Erceg, L. E. (2009, March/April). Ten ways to reduce injuries and illnesses in camp. *Camping Magazine, 82*(2), 47–52.

Garst, B., Erceg, L. E., Baird, S., & Thompson, S. (2010, March/April). Healthy camp study update. *Camping Magazine, 83*(2), 48–50.

Louv, R. (2005). *Last child in the woods*. Chapel Hill, NC: Algonquin Press.

5

Expanding Opportunities for Camp Participation

A key trend in promoting camp as a positive developmental experience for all is to focus on populations of people who have not necessarily been associated with camp in the past. Although organized camping has existed in a variety of forms, it traditionally has been associated with white, middle- to high-income, able-bodied, heterosexual children and staff. Further, camps have been associated with rugged, outdoor experiences that are not necessarily desired by or possible for some groups of people.

The reality is that all people can benefit from camp experiences. More emphasis should be placed on reaching unserved as well as underserved populations. This focus does not mean that the traditional audience should be left out; however, it does suggest that our pluralistic society should be reflected in the pluralism of camps. This chapter will briefly examine characteristics of groups of children and adults who may benefit from the camp experience. If the ACA motto of "better camping for all" is to be embodied, camp counselors must recognize the diversity of campers.

Diversity, Special Needs, and Cultural Competence

Before embarking on a discussion of specific groups, establishing a context for the issues that exist in today's world may be helpful. **Diversity** is a term commonly used to simply describe differing from one another—whether referring to ecosystems or people. Diversity exists at many levels, whether related to age, gender, weight, race, geographic origin, sexual identity, occupation, and so on. In US society the notion of diversity usu-

ally refers to racial and ethnic diversity. However, the concept is far broader. The bottom line, nevertheless, is that along with diversity must come acceptance and respect for the differences. Promoting diversity in camps requires the development of cultural competence in all camp staff.

Cultural competence refers to an ability to interact effectively with people of different cultures, with culture defined broadly. **Culture** refers to a learned and shared system of values, beliefs, and attitudes that shapes and influences behavior. Culture can refer to ethnic background, age cohorts, sexual identity, identification with a sports team, or any number of shared values that influence one's perceptions, including identification with a particular camp. Cultural competence comprises having an awareness of one's own cultural worldviews, knowledge of different cultural practices, and cross-cultural skills. Camp counselors who develop cultural competence have the ability to understand, communicate with, and effectively interact with people across cultures.

Each staff member and camper is a product of a particular culture with a variety of characteristics. Some cultural characteristics are dominant in a society, such as middle income socioeconomic status and male gender. The usefulness of cultural competence lies in understanding the situation of individuals who are not in dominant groups in society.

Vaughn (2007) describes how the ideal camp staff should encompass people with diverse backgrounds and communication styles who work together to provide the best experience for every staff member as well as every camper. Cultural competence is a continuum, from complete ignorance to advanced competence where culture is held in high esteem. Believing that culture makes no difference is cultural blindness. Camp staff should strive for

advanced competency, but the reality is that most people are at a level of pre-competence—they accept and respect differences and are continually in a process of self-assessment. Learning to recognize and celebrate some of the differences among people is a way to move toward cultural competence.

Sometimes individuals who are different in some way are thought to have special needs. The reality is that everyone—including every camper—has special needs. Some needs seem *normative* while others seem more unusual or extreme. Camp counselors should strive to meet the needs of all campers. Some needs are visible, such as physical disabilities, while others are invisible, as with emotional issues like dealing with grief. While addressing everyone's special needs may seem a daunting task, counselors who work from the basic premise that each camper is an individual will contribute to promoting positive human development through camps.

As camps become more diverse, an understanding of camper characteristics and backgrounds becomes more critical to the development of successful programs. For example, some campers may arrive at camp with no previous camp experience and minimal contact with the outdoors. Their approach to camp experiences will be different than someone whose family has been camping for generations. Other groups whose approach to camp might differ include millennials, people with disabilities, at-risk youth, Latino populations, LGBQT campers and staff, older adults, and nuclear as well as multi-generational families.

Millennials

Millennials are the generation born in 1982 and after. Most campers and many staff members will fit this category. People who grow up during particular periods of time are heavily influenced by the history and social movements of that time. For the Baby Boomers that influence included social consciousness, while for Generation X it was market-driven economies (Howe, 2007).

Much has been written about the differences among generations, but several distinguishing characteristics have implications for camp. Millennials see themselves as special. Many have been sheltered by parents and these children accept and rely upon that security. These individuals are confident about the future. They develop strong team instincts and tight peer bonds. Millennials tend to be somewhat conventional in their thinking and do not typically push the boundaries. Many feel a great pressure to excel in whatever they do. They want to be successful. These young people, however, are diverse and more willing to accept diversity than their parents (Howe, 2007).

These characteristics are obviously overgeneralized, but they suggest that many of these children expect to have structure in their activities. They also suggest that when you work with these children, you are also working with their parents. Further, opportunities to achieve in a variety of ways should be considered. These suggestions apply to campers as well as young staff who may be within this generation.

Campers with Disabilities

Camps for people with disabilities have existed for some time. Many of these have served particular groups, such as individuals who are wheelchair users, those who have autism, or those who are visually impaired. Since passage of the Americans with Disabilities Act in 1990, camps have been expected to make reasonable accommodations for any individual regardless of ability or disability. Many camps have redesigned buildings to make them wheelchair accessible. However, much more must be done if campers with disabilities are to feel welcome at camp.

When discussing people with disabilities in camps, two models exist. One is the **integrated** camp where children with and without disabilities camp together. The other option is a **disability specific** camp that may focus one or more weeks to a specific group—for example, children with diabetes, children with severe burns (i.e., burn

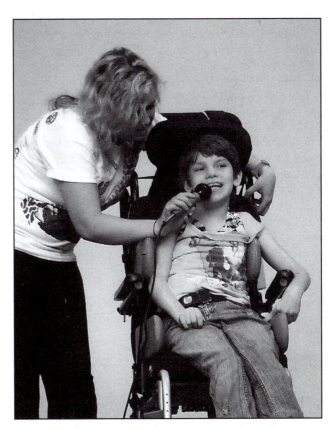

Camp counselors should strive to meet the needs of all campers. (Photo courtesy of Bradford Woods Learning and Outdoor Center)

camps), and children living with cancer. Some camps offer programs for siblings of individuals with disabilities. Regardless of the model, camp counselors are likely to encounter individuals with various disabilities in camps and should be familiar with the concept of inclusion.

The practice of welcoming, valuing, empowering, and supporting people of all abilities is called **inclusion**. Inclusion is a process by which all campers, including those with disabilities, attend camp together and enjoy the same program. This philosophy of inclusion is based on the belief in every person's inherent right to fully participate in society, whether as students, employees, or recreationists. Inclusion implies acceptance of differences and makes room for individuals who might otherwise be excluded. Thus, inclusion is more than just providing an opportunity. It also means making that opportunity of high quality for all individuals involved.

One of the issues that individuals with disabilities sometimes face in society is a lack of understanding regarding their abilities. This lack of understanding may also be found in camp. Those who have experienced being teased, laughed at, and left out of activities may fear the same will happen at camp. Camp should be a safe environment in which children and adults can learn about themselves and experience the world around them. For campers with and without disabilities, camp should be a place where they are exposed to differences and learn how to respond to these differences. For campers with disabilities, camp should provide a place where all are accepted and allowed to be as *normal* as possible. Camp staff and campers need to learn how to interact with people with disabilities to assure this normalcy.

Camp staff and administrators who have not been exposed to or educated about disabling conditions are likely to be uncomfortable in an integrated situation. Attitudes and perceptions that may have developed early in one's life need to be adjusted. Camp can be a place to dispel some negative attitudes about people with disabilities. For example, our society's emphasis on body image suggests everyone should look thin, fit, and physically attractive. In reality, only a small percentage of society meets this false standard of appearance. People in wheelchairs, overweight individuals, people with disfiguring scars, or anyone else who does not meet this ideal can be perceived negatively. Further, for individuals who have to move or think slower than most people, competition is particularly stressful in a society where being fast, strong, and first is valued.

Sometimes people without disabilities feel uncomfortable that they can walk, see, or hear when the person next to them cannot. Therefore, they choose to interact in environments where they will not encounter people with disabilities. Moreover, people unaccustomed to interacting with those with disabilities are sometimes guilty of *spread*. Spread occurs when people identify one specific characteristic (e.g., inability to hear) and apply it to the entire person (e.g., intellectually disabled). One type of disability does not mean that an individual has multiple disabilities, although some people may have more than one disability.

Several strategies can be employed to alleviate misconceptions of people with disabilities and to promote positive interaction among all campers and staff members. Depending on the type of camp and the history of attendance of children with disabilities, pre-camp training can teach campers and staff to be comfortable with people who are different from them. Although camp counselors need to know about various disabilities and feel comfortable working with such campers, they also should know how to work with campers without disabilities to encourage and facilitate friendships and networks between the two groups.

Camp staff members have endless opportunities to influence interactions with people with disabilities. This process requires planning, however. Camp staff must establish systematic programming and planning, and evaluate and modify as needed. Staff should be aware of a camper with disabilities coming to camp before he or she arrives at camp. In addition to staff preparation, counselors should be mindful of the need to always ask the camper what he or she needs, and let the individual make decisions about personal care and activity comfort level that is desired. The camp's responsibility is to send a consistent message of inclusion to campers and the community (Evans & Pemberton, 2007).

Educating about disabilities also requires an understanding of the appropriate terminology. **People-first language** recognizes that a camper (or staff, parent, guardian, volunteer) is much more than just a condition. Evans and Pemberton (2007) posed a riddle: "What do you call a person with a disability? Answer: Call the person by his or her name" (p. 58). Each camper has a name, and brings gifts, talents, and challenges with them. With practice and a conscious effort, you can change the way you speak about individuals. Here are two other examples of people first language:

Old language: "Bobbie Camper is autistic."
People-first language: "Bobbie Camper loves soccer, spicy food, and has autism."

Old language: "My group has a diabetic camper."
People-first language: "We have a camper with diabetes this week."

Common Disabilities at Camp

A full discussion of all the disabilities you might encounter at camp is impossible within the parameters of this text. Numerous resources on the Internet can provide detail about specific illnesses and conditions. Many of these resources also offer strategies to use in all types of social interactions that might be encountered at camp. The following are some of the more commonly encountered conditions.

Autism

Autism is a spectrum disorder. It is defined by a certain set of behaviors, but children and adults with autism can exhibit any combination of these behaviors in any degree of severity. Two children, both with the same diagnosis, can act completely different from one another and have varying capabilities. Different terms are used to describe children within this spectrum. More important than the term used to describe autism, however, is understanding that whatever the diagnosis, children with autism can learn and show functional improvement with appropriate treatment and education.

Every person with autism is an individual, and like all individuals, has a unique personality and combination of characteristics. Some individuals who are mildly affected may exhibit only slight delays in language and greater challenges with social interactions. They may have difficulty initiating and/or maintaining a conversation. People with autism also process and respond to information in unique ways. Persons with autism may exhibit some of the traits listed in exhibit 5.1. Note that these characteristics MAY exist but should not be stereotyped to all individuals with autism. Contrary to popular belief, many children with autism do make eye contact. Many children with autism develop good functional language skills and others develop alternative communication skills such as sign language or use of pictures. Children do not "outgrow" autism, but symptoms may lessen as the child develops and receives treatment.

Exhibit 5.1

Behavior That May Be Present in Individuals with Autism

- Insistence on sameness and resistance to change
- Difficulty in expressing needs; using gestures or pointing instead of words
- Repeating words or phrases in place of normal, responsive language
- Laughing (and/or crying) for no apparent reason
- Preference for being alone and difficulty mixing with others
- Not wanting to cuddle or be cuddled
- Little or no eye contact
- Unresponsive to normal teaching methods
- Sustained odd play
- Obsessive attachment to objects
- No real fears of danger
- Noticeable physical overactivity or extreme underactivity
- Uneven gross/fine motor skills
- Nonresponsive to verbal cues (Autism Society of America, 2010)

Asperger's Disorder

Though long considered one aspect of the autism spectrum, Asperger's now is distinguished from autism. What distinguishes Asperger's from autism is the severity of the symptoms and the absence of language delays. Children with Asperger's disorder frequently have good language and cognitive skills. To the untrained observer, a child with Asperger's may seem just like any child, albeit behaving differently. Individuals with Asperger's disorder usually want to fit in and have interaction with others. They simply do not know how to do it. They may be socially awkward, not understanding conventional social rules, or show a lack of empathy. Their interests in a particular subject may border on the obsessive. Children with Asperger's disorder frequently have good language skills but use language in different ways. Speech patterns may be unusual, lack inflection, have a rhythmic nature, or be too loud or high pitched. Children with Asperger's may not understand the subtleties of language such as irony and humor, or they may not understand the give-and-take nature of a conversation (What Is Asperger's, 2010).

Tourette Syndrome (TS)

Tourette syndrome is a neurological disorder that becomes evident in early childhood or adolescence, typically before the age of 18 years (Tourette Syndrome Association, 2010). TS is defined by multiple motor and vocal tics. The first symptoms usually are involuntary movements (tics) of the face, arms, limbs, or trunk. These tics are usually frequent, repetitive, and rapid. Verbal tics (vocalizations) may occur with the movements. These vocalizations include grunting, throat clearing, shouting, and barking. The verbal tics may also be expressed as the involuntary use of obscene words or socially inappropriate words and phrases or obscene gestures. The symptoms of TS vary from person to person and range from very mild to severe. Most cases fall into the mild category and these individuals can lead productive lives and have positive experiences at camp.

Down Syndrome

Down syndrome is a prenatal, chromosomal disorder that results when an individual has three, rather than two, copies of the 21st chromosome (National Down Syndrome Society, 2010). This additional genetic material alters the course of development and causes the characteristics associated with Down syndrome. The common physical traits of Down syndrome are low muscle tone, small stature, an upward slant to the eyes, and a single deep crease across the center of the palm. Every person with Down syndrome is a unique individual and may possess these characteristics to different degrees or not at all. In addition, people with Down syndrome have an increased risk for certain medical conditions such as congenital heart defects, respiratory and hearing problems, Alzheimer's disease, childhood leukemia, and thy-

The philosophy of inclusion emphasizes providing high-quality experiences for all campers. (Photo courtesy of American Camp Association)

roid conditions. Many of these conditions are now treatable, so most people with Down syndrome lead healthy lives. All people with Down syndrome experience cognitive delays, but the effect is usually mild to moderate and is not indicative of the many strengths and talents that each individual possesses.

Attention Deficit Hyperactivity Disorder (ADHD)

One of the most common childhood disorders, ADHD can continue through adolescence and adulthood (National Institute of Mental Health, 2010). Symptoms include difficulty staying focused and paying attention, difficulty controlling behavior, and hyperactivity (overactivity). All children can be inattentive, hyperactive, or impulsive sometimes. However, for children with ADHD these behaviors are more severe and occur more often.

ADHD can be mistaken for other problems. Adults may think that these children just have emotional or disciplinary problems. Sometimes children with symptoms of inattention do not seem to have the disorder because they are quiet and less likely to act out. They may sit quietly, seeming to work, but they are often not paying attention to what they are doing. They may get along well with other children.

Staff may consider some of the following suggestions for working with ADHD children:

- Frequent, immediate feedback
- Frequent changes in reinforcements or rewards
- Motivating incentives

- Praise and more positive feedback
- Better eye contact
- Tasks presented one at a time
- Repeating back instructions
- Light physical touch for focusing
- Positive commands (what you want as opposed to what you want stopped)
- Simple, clearly stated, posted rules
- Tasks broken down into smaller pieces

Juvenile Diabetes

This disease is characterized by an insufficient supply of insulin available to act on carbohydrates; therefore, sugar accumulates in the blood (Juvenile Diabetes Research Foundation, 2010). A person who has juvenile diabetes has to use a needle to inject insulin two or three times a day (or use an insulin pump). He or she must also monitor blood sugar levels and follow a careful schedule of eating and exercise. Diabetes will probably mean lots of changes to the day-to-day life of the camper. For example, the child may not be able to eat snacks with everyone else. He or she may need to inject insulin in the middle of an activity, or stop playing to eat. Having to adjust their schedule, and sometimes missing out on things, may make children with diabetes feel angry or upset, or just plain different from everybody else. Camp counselors who understand these issues and take them in stride will help a camper with diabetes accept any modifications.

Physical Disabilities

Physical impairments cover a wide range of abilities. Physical impairment refers to disabilities that may include orthopedic, neuromuscular, cardiovascular, and pulmonary disorders. People with these disabilities often must rely upon assertive devices such as wheelchairs, crutches, canes, and artificial limbs to obtain mobility. The physical disability may either be congenital or a result of injury, muscular dystrophy, multiple sclerosis, cerebral palsy, amputation, heart disease, pulmonary disease, or other condition. Some people may have hidden (i.e., not visible) disabilities which include pulmonary disease, respiratory disorders, epilepsy, and sensory impairments (Physical Disabilities, 2010).

Although strategies for working with people with disabilities are numerous, here are some key ideas to consider in working with these campers:

- If a person uses a wheelchair, conversations at different eye levels are difficult. If possible, sit down, kneel, or squat and share eye level.

- A wheelchair is part of the person's body space. Do not automatically hang or lean on the chair since it is similar to hanging or leaning on the person.

- Using words like "walking" or "running" are appropriate. Sensitivity to these words is not necessary. People who use wheelchairs use the same words.

- When it appears that a person needs assistance, ask if you can help. Most people will ask for assistance if they need it. Accept a "no thank you" graciously.

- Accept that a disability exists. Not acknowledging the disability is the same as not acknowledging the person.

- People with physical disabilities are not "confined" to wheelchairs, they are wheelchair users.

- If a person's speech is difficult to understand, do not hesitate to ask him/her to repeat.

Mental Health Issues

One in five youth has been diagnosed with a mental health problem that can cause at least mild impairment (Carlson, 2009). Children with mental illness—whether undiagnosed or diagnosed and under treatment—are likely to come to camp. Camp personnel can enhance their capacity to accommodate such individuals by understanding child development, recognizing significant signs of distress, gaining prior knowledge, and learning how to use behavior management plans (discussed later in this book). Severe mental health problems are not likely to be found in most camps, but camp staff should recognize that all children with mental or behavioral problems can benefit from the camp experience.

Campers from At-Risk Communities

Campers from at-risk communities, sometimes called at-risk youth, are gaining more opportunities to come to camp. Sometimes special camps are designed for these children and other times they are integrated into a regular camp group, especially if scholarships are available to send them to camp. Camps are increasingly taking on the challenge to incorporate youth from these so-called at-risk communities.

The term "at-risk youth" covers a broad category. Some youth development specialists suggest that all youth are at risk. However, certain characteristics are more likely to be associated with youth who are at risk (Grayson, 2001):

- Live in chronic poverty
- Attend an underperforming school
- Have poor school performance
- Are in a negative peer group
- Have poor social skills
- Use drugs themselves or have a caretaker who does
- Are a racial or ethnic minority
- Have a family situation characterized by stress
- Live in a bad neighborhood

None of these characteristics alone defines an at-risk youth, but they cumulatively increase the possibility. A child with one or two of these characteristics might be at minimal risk, but the more these circumstances describe a young person's environment, the more likely he or she is to be at risk.

Children who come from at-risk communities can rise above these circumstances and become successful. The term used to describe this potential is **resiliency**. These children have resources that might include family support, personal characteristics, mentors, good schools, or responsive communities that help them overcome risk factors. Camp is one resource that can help foster this resiliency (Grayson, 2001).

If means can be found to get these at-risk children to camp, they have the opportunity to participate in programs that focus on positive youth development. Camps can influence the personal characteristics of young people, particularly self-confidence, self-esteem, and social skills. Camps are educational organizations, but offer creative ways to learn. Therefore, campers who may not be successful at school with standard pedagogical techniques may thrive in the experiential world of camps. Camps also offer the potential for highly trained staff who can provide interpersonal support to campers, in addition to serving as role models and mentors.

While camps cannot necessarily produce miracles during one camp session, they can set the stage for new behaviors. If at-risk children have the opportunity to return to camp for more than one summer, the potential for behavior change is greatest. Even if camps do not result in monumental change, Grayson (2001) suggests that they can be beneficial in several other important ways:

- Children receive a respite from a negative environment
- Children see that there are alternatives to their daily routine
- Children are exposed to a healthy community
- Children learn new ways of using their free time
- When children are at camp, they are not getting into trouble at home

Children from at-risk communities can benefit greatly from camp. Though an increasing number of camps are beginning to focus on these children, many more opportunities are needed.

Latino/Latina Populations

Census data and other statistics note the growing number of Hispanic and Latino/Latina populations in the United States. Going to camp, however, has not been a part of the cultural traditions of many Latino people. Camp directors are aware of the lack of Latino youth represented in camps and are seeking ways to increase participation in both resident and day camps. Research has uncovered several interesting findings influencing the attendance of Latino/Latina youth in camps.

Magana, Hosty, and Hobbs (2006) describe how personalism and familism are important in Latino cultures. This means that individual decisions consider the needs of the family. In addition, personal face-to-face contact is important. Some families are overly protective of daughters. Further, overnight experiences are not common in the Latino culture, so some parents are troubled by the thought of overnight camps. Some Latino parents fear their children may experience discrimination while at camp. Parents need to understand that the camp staff will assume the role of parent while the child is at camp. Since camp experiences have not been a part of the Latino culture, parents have not gone to camp and do not understand the value and context of camp. Finally, some Latino families have limited resources, so financial concerns, lack of transportation, and lack of technology for registration may be a problem.

Lukanina (2008) conducted research directly with parents and uncovered many similar findings to those of Magana et al. (2006). She recommended that since Latino parents do not understand camp, staff must make an extra effort to gain the trust of parents and help them feel comfortable with being away from their children for a camp session. Safety and security are natural concerns, and Latino parents may need more reassurance on these issues. The availability of bilingual marketing tools may be useful. Lukanina also suggested allowing parents to have contact with their children at camp. Many camps do not allow phone calls, but Latino parents indicated that they wanted this connection.

The parents in Lukanina's (2008) study indicated that if they sent their children to camp, they hoped their children would enjoy interacting and communicating, would become more disciplined and mature, and would become more independent and responsible. The potential for positive youth development for Latino/Latina children is high, but overcoming parental misgivings is a necessary first step toward getting these children to camp so they can enjoy the experience.

Lesbian, Gay, Bisexual, Queer, and Transgendered Campers and Staff

Not all children and certainly not all staff who attend camp are heterosexual. With society's increased discussion of lesbian, gay, bisexual, queer, and transgendered people (LGBQT) comes the need for camp staff to be aware of the issues involved. The presence of LGBQT staff and campers has been a controversial issue in the camping field; however, their existence cannot be ignored. Since issues of sexual identity and preference are highly visible in most young people's lives, they become issues that camps must consider.

The following terminology is associated with those who are LGBQT. *Lesbian*, *gay*, or *homosexual* refers to a person who is emotionally and physically attracted to people of the same biological sex. *Bisexual* is a person who may be attracted to either sex. *Queer* is a term used by some young people to show a breadth of possible sexual choices. *Transgendered* refers to individuals who have the body of one sex but an emotional identification with the other sex. Some of these individuals may undergo a sex change operation.

People today are more likely to disclose their sexual preference since it is such an important part of their identity. Alexander and Kriesel (2003) advocate that camp staff should not assume all campers (or all fellow staff members) are straight. If camps are to be inclusive, they must consider how to make camp a safe environment for LGBQT participants. Some camps may choose not to hire LGBQT staff, but that decision must be clear at the time of hiring. Regardless, camps cannot prevent LGBQT campers from attending camp.

Although society in general has become more accepting of nontraditional sexual identities, LGBQT young people still face discrimination. Camp directors must consider a number of issues, including hiring policies, campers with LGBQT parents, the prohibition of discriminatory or derogatory language, and whether pol-

icies regarding opposite sex and same sex couples are equitable. All staff benefit by understanding what *coming out* means in terms of a staff member or camper acknowledging that he or she might be LGBQT. Although discussions about LGBQT do not need to be initiated in camp, they should never be ignored if they arise. Campers who are LGBQT or have LGBQT relatives and friends should feel that they are as respected as anyone else in camp.

Older Adults

Although older adults are not typically associated with camps, these individuals may be involved in organized camping as campers, staff, or volunteers. If camp is a positive and beneficial experience for all, then the senior community should not be overlooked as a potential emerging group of campers (Fornaciari & Martin-Fornaciari, 2009). Statistics indicate that the senior population will continue to grow rapidly in coming years.

Camp programs for older adults differ from those of children in varying degrees, depending on the characteristics of the campers. Some older people attended camp as children, but others may not be experienced with it. They need to know what to expect. In planning a program or working with older adults, staff should recognize that variety is needed, and that each individual should be able to choose what he or she wishes to do, or is capable of doing. Camp facilities need to be able to accommodate older adults, especially those who may have medical issues.

For younger and older people alike, one of the most important elements of a successful camp program is creating emotional connections (Fornaciari & Martin-Fornaciari, 2009). Most of the activities and rituals of camp that appeal to youth also appeal to senior citizens. They want camp to feel like a community or family. Camps for older adults will never supplant camps for younger people, but this group constitutes an important population that may benefit greatly from camping in the future.

Family and Multi-Generational Camping

A final group that is emerging with more opportunities for camp experiences is families and family units.

Many camps provide opportunities for entire families to come to camp together for a week or a weekend. To reach children today, it is often necessary to reach the family—especially among families that have not had a history with camp (Hoefner, 2006). The philosophy of most of these camps is that the camp does not serve as a pseudo-resort. Rather, an intentionally planned program is designed to involve the entire family in aspects of the camp such as meals, campfires, and special programs.

Many family camps are organized around specific themes. For example, religiously affiliated camps often have programs and retreats designed for the entire family. Families with particular characteristics may come together at camp, such as families that have a child with autism (Kabot, 2009) or families that have adopted children from a particular country like China or Vietnam.

Several camps have organized what is called "Grand Camps." In this case, a grandparent and grandchild come to camp together and experience various programs (Nicodemus, 2006). This unique opportunity gives different generations an opportunity to get to know one another in ways that would not occur outside the camp environment.

Family camps can be designed in a variety of ways. They offer great potential for organized camp experiences in the future.

An Inclusion Audit

Camp is clearly a special environment that can benefit children and adults of all types, abilities, ages, and backgrounds. Kelly and Maurer (1999) suggest that each camp may want to conduct an inclusion audit. This audit is a means to evaluate the messages that the camp sends and the publicity used to invite children and families to be a part of camp. The audit can include various aspects, but certainly promotional materials and the images portrayed are important components of such an audit. For example, does the mission statement indicate that all campers are welcome regardless of background and ability? Does the camp have a diversity policy? Are positive role models hired? These are just a few of the aspects that can be evaluated. The goal is to make every effort to ensure that all campers are welcomed.

REFERENCES

Alexander, R., & Kriesel, C. (2003, Nov/Dec). Don't assume I'm straight. *Camping Magazine, 76*(6), 24–27.

Autism Society of America. (2010). Retrieved from http://www.autism-society.org/site.

Carlson, K. P. (2009, Jan/Feb). What now? Understanding and supporting campers with mental health issues. *Camping Magazine, 82*(1), 50–54.

Evans, F., & Pemberton, J. (2007, Nov/Dec). Change yourself, change the world: How to play with campers with disabilities. *Camping Magazine, 80*(6), 54–58.

Fornaciari, G. M., & Martin-Fornaciari, A. S. (2009, Nov/Dec). Senior citizens in day and resident camping. *Camping Magazine, 82*(6), 52–58.

Grayson, R. (2001, Jan/Feb). Serving at-risk youth at camp. *Camping Magazine, 74*(1).

Hoefner, L. J. (2006, Jul/Aug). Camp gives families a world of good. *Camping Magazine, 79*(4), 20–22.

Howe, N. (2007, Jan/Feb). Millennials: Shaping the future. *Camping Magazine, 80*(1), 26–31.

Juvenile Diabetes Research Foundation. (2010). Retrieved from http://www.jdrf.org/.

Kabot, S. (2009, July/Aug). Camp Yofi: A family camp for children with autism. *Camping Magazine, 82*(4), 12–15.

Kelly, M., & Maurer, L. (1999, March/Apr). The inclusion audit: Evaluating your camp's efforts to include diverse populations. *Camping Magazine, 72*(2).

Lukanina, M. (2008, March/Apr). Guidelines for attracting the Latino population to a summer overnight camp. *Camping Magazine, 81*(2), 54–59.

Magana, M., Hosty, M., & Hobbs, B. B. (2006, Nov/Dec). Recruiting Latino youth to participate in resident camps. *Camping Magazine, 79*(6), 34–38.

National Down Syndrome Society (2010). General information retrieved from http://www.ndss.org/

National Institute of Mental Health. (2010). Retrieved from http://www.nimh.nih.gov/health/publications/attention-deficit-hyperactivity-disorder/complete-index.shtml.

Nicodemus, T. (2006, July/Aug). Camp for all: Expanding the tradition. *Camping Magazine, 79*(4), 14–18.

Physical disabilities. (2010). Retrieved from http://www.csun.edu/~sp20558/dis/physical.html.

Tourette Syndrome Association (2010). Retrieved from http://www.tsa-usa.org/Medical/whatists.html.

Vaughn, G. (2007, Sept/Oct). Cultural competency: The key to hiring diverse staff. *Camping Magazine, 80*(5), 42–47.

What Is Asperger's Disorder? (2010). Retrieved from http://www.aspergers.com/aspclin.htm.

WEB RESOURCES

American Academy of Child and Adolescent Psychiatry (www.aacap.org) offers links, publications, and facts related to mental health issues in children.

Autism Research Institute (www.autism.com) provides information on understanding autism, treatment, and research.

Camp For All (www.campforall.org) is an example of a camp for groups with special needs.

Children and Adults with Attention Deficit/Hyperactivity Disorder (www.chadd.org) offers tips for understanding ADHD and provides links to related resources.

Epilepsy Foundation (www.epilepsyfoundation.org) offers information on understanding epilepsy, treatment, first aid, and research.

National Association for Gifted Children (www.nagc.org) offers general information and resources.

National Association of Therapeutic Wilderness Camping (http://natwc.org) provides summaries of therapeutic wilderness camping organizations, resources, newsletters, and conferences.

National Center for Learning Disabilities (www.ncld.org) helps laypeople better understand learning disabilities, and lists publications and resources.

National Dissemination Center for Children with Disabilities (www.nichcy.org) describes disabilities, laws, resources, and research.

National Mental Health Information Center: Children's Mental Health Facts (www.mentalhealth.samhsa.gov/publications/allpubs/CA-0006/default.asp) provides information on disorders including anxiety, depression, bipolar, ADHD, learning, conduct, eating, autism, and schizophrenia.

Program Development Associates: The Professional's Choice for Disability and Diversity Resources (www.disabilitytraining.com) offers a bookstore, and newsletter with resources and articles.

University of Illinois: Resources for Working with Youth with Special Needs (http://urbanext.illinois.edu/specialneeds/) includes information on specific special needs: cerebral palsy, deaf/hearing impaired, epilepsy, learning disability, mental retardation, speech/language disorders, spina bifida, visual impairments, and other health impairments.

PRINT RESOURCES

Brannan, S., Arick, J., Fullerton, A., & Harris, J. (2000, July/Aug). Inclusive outdoor programs benefit youth. *Camping Magazine, 73*(4). Describes a study that looks at inclusionary sites (mainstream) and their program's benefits.

Ditter, B. (2009, May/June). 20/20 toolbox: Everybody's in, nobody's out. *Camping Magazine, 82*(3). Discusses embracing diversity and differences among campers.

Durall, J. (1999, Jan/Feb). Toward an understanding of ADHD. *Camping Magazine, 72*(1). Describes common characteristics of ADHD.

Leiken, J. (2009, May/June). Heightened awareness camp counseling. *Camping Magazine, 82*(3). Describes how to be a great counselor by sharing passion, telling stories, reaching out to all.

McDonald, J. (2002, May/June). Helping your counselors welcome all campers. *Camping Magazine, 75*(3). Training counselors to overcome fears of working with campers with disabilities.

Peniston, L. C. (1999, Jan/Feb). Learning disabilities in campers. *Camping Magazine, 72*(1). Discusses accommodations and modifications to implement for a broad variety of learning disabilities.

Raps, M. A. (2003, May/June). Working with children with special needs. *Camping Magazine, 76*(3). Discusses the personal benefits of working with campers with special needs.

Simpson, C., & Armstrong, S. A. (2007, July/Aug). Camp El Tesoro de la Vida: A camp experience for bereaved children. *Camping Magazine, 80*(4), 32–35.

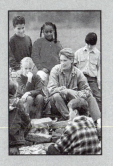

II

The Role of Camp Staff

It is good to realize that if love and peace can prevail on earth, and if we can teach our children to honor nature's gifts, the joys and beauties of the outdoors will be here forever.

—Jimmy Carter

6

The Camp Counselor

Camp employment is a seasonal opportunity for thousands of people each year. Some individuals also have the privilege and responsibility of being involved professionally with camping on a full-time basis. Few positions are more demanding, require a greater level of responsibility, and provide more satisfaction than working in camps.

A seasonal staff member needs to be versatile and multifaceted, able to improvise, a team player, willing to work long hours, and above all, love working with people, especially children. Over the course of a traditional camp season an individual is typically asked to care for a group of young people between the ages of 7–17 years, sometimes younger and sometimes older. Duties may include leading campers into outdoor settings with unknown variables, being on duty almost 24/7 as in the case of a resident camp, promoting an atmosphere of belonging and acceptance, instructing on a variety of topics, and perpetuating self-reliance, personal growth, and a positive developmental experience for all campers. Throughout these efforts, the counselor always is responsible for first aid, reacting to emotions, and assuring the health and safety of campers.

In this chapter the term *camp counselor* refers broadly to the roles of all seasonal staff whether they are cabin or group counselors or activity specialists (e.g., arts and crafts directors, lifeguards, or wranglers). Although living and working with the same campers all day is different than seeing a range of campers for activity periods, most of the same principles apply. Thus, the use of *camp counselor* here refers to all camp staff involved in any way working directly with children. We realize that many other staff are employed at camp, such as kitchen or maintenance workers, who may or may not have much direct contact with campers. All positions are important

and each facilitates a way to promote positive developmental experiences.

Regardless of the position at camp, employees must be able to provide guidance to ensure the best camp experience possible. Skills and attributes such as patience, caring, empathy, honesty, enthusiasm, love of the outdoors, responsibility, and dependability produce the greatest bond between the camper, the counselor, and the camp experience. Knowing how to teach a canoeing class fulfills a specific role, but knowing how to interact positively with campers fulfills a broader purpose throughout the camp. What makes a camp job attractive, the expectations or requirements for a camp position, and how one goes about getting a camp position are discussed in this chapter.

Characteristics of a Good Counselor

Appreciation of and Liking for People

To be a fully functional member of the camp staff, a camp counselor MUST enjoy working with all sorts of people. After all, camp life involves associating with an assortment of personalities—often for almost 24 hours a day depending on the type of camp. Someone contemplating the possibility of working at camp also should be able to fit in with a diverse group of colleagues. Furthermore, all associates on the job will have different personalities, interests, and experiences as well as specific camp duties or responsibilities. Thus, a camp counselor must be versatile and multifaceted enough to work with such varied staff members as the camp nurse, the head cook, the waterfront director, the camp caretaker, the camp director, and others. High camp morale and good working relationships do not always develop automatically. Rather, they result when each staff member shows an enthusiastic willingness to combine with all others into a harmonious camp family regardless of the differences that may exist.

A camp counselor must be able to tolerate frequent and prolonged contact with children and adults while maintaining patience and good humor. A counselor is many things to campers—a substitute parent, teacher, friend, confidante, motivator, and role model. Consequently, a good camp counselor must understand other people, be able to find good traits or qualities to appreciate in each of them, and have the ability to ungrudgingly accept others' quirks and peculiarities, whatever they may be. These traits are all part of a broad base of cultural competency. A successful camp counselor is able to seek out and acknowledge each camper's intrinsic worth and extrinsic abilities.

A camp counselor must enjoy adults and children, even when they are noisy, uncooperative, impulsive, or demanding. A counselor needs to pay attention to all campers, not just those who are likeable. For example, shy, socially awkward children need affection and appreciation more than those with outgoing personalities who effortlessly attract others to them. All individuals have hidden potential. Your concern for each child as an individual will often win their trust and friendship, and ideally help them gain acceptance by the entire group of campers.

Serving as a camp counselor means being many things to many people. In addition to liking children, you must be prepared to intervene or discipline campers when their actions endanger their welfare or conflict with camp program objectives. Maintaining their friendship and respect can be challenging as you skillfully weld them into a harmonious camp community.

Empathy

The ability to put oneself in the place of others and actually sense how they feel is called **empathy**. This rare and valuable quality is more likely to be acquired if a person has had many experiences and felt a variety of emotions—joy, sadness, love, hate, anger, fear, depression, and loneliness. Such a broad background provides the basis for recognizing and correctly interpreting these emotions in others. In this way, the problems and emotional needs of others can be sensed and the counselor can determine how best to offer help.

Being a Good Role Model

A leader must exemplify personal habits and behavior that honors the ideals and objectives of organized camping. An ability to interact comfortably and positively with children is a valuable asset, but a counselor must first set a good example.

The ability to interact comfortably and positively with children is a valuable asset, but a counselor must first set a good example. (Photo courtesy of American Camp Association)

Pretense and phoniness are spotted easily in the intimacy of camp life. Everything a counselor says and does will be carefully observed by young people who will be quick to detect and point out hypocritical behaviors. Youth is the period of hero worship and children are seeking adults that they can admire, trust, and love. Consequently, nothing is more painful or demoralizing to children than to discover that a beloved counselor is phony or fake. All prospective counselors must ask themselves if they are prepared to inspire their campers.

Counselors must try to be worthy of emulation, since they are the leaders who set the pattern, especially for younger, impressionable campers who may be away from parental authority for the first time. Counselors must capitalize on opportunities to help campers of any age recognize and develop their own potential.

Enthusiasm

Enthusiasm is key to providing a fun and memorable experience. Counselors should be mindful of this even when (especially when) they aren't feeling particularly peppy. An enthusiastic counselor, for example, can recruit 15 kids to help clean horse manure from the pasture, while an uninspired counselor may find zero participants interested in joining him or her on a canoe trip down the Blue River.

A counselor's enthusiasm will make or break the experience in a group. Not all people exhibit the same energy as others, but internal excitement can establish the external enthusiastic connection to the moment and the child. If the counselor demonstrates a genuine commitment to the task or activity, the campers will follow suit. Whether leading storytelling around a small campfire, setting up for kitchen duties, or initiating an all-camp game of capture the flag, enthusiasm for the task at hand will be perceived and acted upon by campers. Enthusiasm breeds fun even in routine tasks.

Being Dynamic

Camp counseling is about being dynamic—having the energy and flexibility to adjust to changing situations. For example, suppose Michelle is on her day off and forgot to get someone to cover her dish duties. John left on a canoeing trip and another lifeguard is needed for the dive tower. Sienna could use an extra hand down at the climbing wall. You fulfilled your dish duties that morning, would prefer to have a relaxing day playing on the raft, and are not interested in rock climbing at all. Working at camp, however, means that a counselor's time is not always his or her own. Counselors are often expected to pitch in wherever help is needed.

The demands of camp counseling are nothing short of a quasi parental role. Consider what many parents go through in a typical day: shuffling kids around, work, meetings, and household chores. A camp counselor may have to do the same for 8–10 children at once. The success of the camping season depends upon the energy and flexibility of the staff. Counselors have to bend and push their comfort levels for the good of the camp and the sake of the kids. In addition, a willingness to accept these challenges also results in personal growth for individual counselors.

Youthful Spirit, Mature Judgment

The camp environment demands that counselors exercise mature judgment. In fact, as one of its requirements for accreditation, the American Camp Association has stated that at least 80% of a camp's counselors and program staff must be at least 18 years old (HR-10). However, mature judgment is not always a matter of age or experience. Some people attain it early, whereas others live a lifetime without ever having demonstrated maturity. Campers cannot be entrusted to staff whose actions are determined by impulse and whim. Ideally, counselors balance good judgment with a youthful spirit and sense of curiosity that keeps them open to new experiences.

Love of the Outdoors

Many resident camps have rustic surroundings and facilities since these settings are necessary for accomplishing some of the traditional camp objectives. Counselors and campers may spend many hours in the open air participating in a variety of activities in all types of weather. Therefore, a counselor must enjoy the outdoors and have the ability to adapt to such environments. Some young adults choose camp employment because they want to be connected to the outdoors every day. Inexperienced counselors may find themselves captivated with outdoor living before the season is over.

Initiative

At camp you will have plenty of opportunities to show initiative, whether leading an all-camp activity, organizing the supply room, sweeping the outhouses, developing a new program area or game, or helping out on an overnight trip. The key is to embrace these opportunities and do your best. Although the camp environment is structured, numerous opportunities exist to try new ideas. Counselors capable of recognizing opportunities and taking action when the situation requires added effort or creative thinking will not go unnoticed, and their commitment will improve the camp program for both staff and campers.

Patience

Patience can be a counselor's greatest asset. For example, on the first day of a 14-day wilderness backpacking trip, a camper named Max turned to his counselor and said, "You know, it was my parents' idea that I go on this trip. I know I'm going to have a terrible time." Later that week, this same city boy had some of the greatest accomplishments of his life. Max learned how to use a compass, camp in the wilderness, climb a mountain, and was not ready to leave the woods when the trip finished. The counselor's patient encouragement helped this camper learn to enjoy the outdoors.

Many of the children who come to camp are not only first-time campers, but also are experiencing their first time away from home for an extended period. Campers need counselors' ultimate patience as they try, and sometimes falter, but eventually succeed at camp. Camp is a setting where every participant should experience success. Without the patience and encouragement of counselors, many kids would not experience the joys and satisfaction that camp has to offer.

Humor and Happiness

Noted comedian Joel Goodman once said that humor is a universal language. At camp, humor is often the primary language. Practical jokes are played, minor mishaps occur, and sleepless nights are often spent under the cover of a plastic tarp during a thunderstorm. Nevertheless, staff and campers can walk away from those experiences with smiles and laughter. Many occasions that provoke anger can also provoke laughter. Though camps are serious places with dangers both known and unknown, camps are also filled with happiness. To have humor in camp is to have joy in camp.

Camping Skills

Counselors, depending on the nature and location of camp, should have some outdoor knowledge and skills that contribute to the camp program. A camp counselor may excel in general and/or specialized areas such as archery, outdoor cooking, swimming, or canoeing. Al-

Counselors should have outdoor knowledge and skills that contribute to the camp program.

though some staff members are hired specifically because of their skill in a particular camp program area, counselors often need to know something about a variety of activities. These skills might relate to nature and ecology, telling stories, singing, playing an instrument, or performing reasonably well in some phase of arts and crafts.

If you do not possess these skills, it is essential that you be willing to acquire them during pre-camp training and over the course of the camping sessions. Numerous opportunities are available to learn from others. Many of the best counselors acquire their knowledge and "know-how" on the job.

Persistence

A camp counselor must find self-satisfaction in doing a job well and in serving others without concern for ego or personal gain. In other words, the counselor must intrinsically value the benefits of being a camp counselor. A counselor in any type of camp must be willing to do hard work. Counselors in resident and trip camps have only brief periods of free time since they are on duty 24/7. The saying that genius is but "1% inspiration mixed with 99% perspiration" is true at camp. Spending a summer at camp is a great challenge and opportunity. Unlike an hourly job at McDonald's, the demands go way beyond a fixed number of hours.

Although the job is demanding, time away is necessary to allow staff members to rejuvenate. The ACA Standards state that for resident camps, all staff should have at least two hours off each day when they are not on call, and 24 hours or more every two weeks in blocks of not less than 12 hours (e.g., a night off each week: HR-21). Persistence is important, but having adequate time

off from camp duties is necessary and helps staff members avoid burnout.

Self-Appraisal

A camp counselor is expected to zealously fulfill all responsibilities and be a contributing camp citizen. Therefore, when contemplating camp employment, young adults should consider their talents, capabilities, and limitations. Assessing strengths and weaknesses is necessary in examining special skills, talents, and competencies.

To better assess one's potential for success and enjoyment as a counselor, consider the criteria in exhibit 6.1 and exhibit 6.2. This assessment may help you evaluate strengths and weaknesses as they apply to camp employment.

Exhibit 6.1

Self-Appraisal: Physical Health

Do you . . .

- Have stamina enough to last through a strenuous day
- Eat well-balanced meals regularly
- Get regular sleep in sufficient quantity
- Have the endurance to do moderate exercise each day
- Smoke (Note: ACA Standards state that a camp must prohibit smoking or allow it only in designated areas away from children and nonsmokers)
- Use alcohol or other non-prescriptive drugs (Note: ACA Standards state that a camp must have a written policy regarding alcohol and drug use, personal sports equipment, vehicles, animals, and weapons)

Exhibit 6.2

Self-Appraisal: General Qualities

Are you . . .

- Curious (i.e., want to know about many things just for the sake of knowing)
- Well-mannered
- Tactful (i.e., speak truthfully, but without offending or hurting others)
- Cooperative, even when carrying out the plans of others
- Cheerful (i.e., no sulking or moodiness)
- Warm (i.e., a friendly personality that attracts others to you)
- Poised, even in emergencies or embarrassing situations
- Flexible (i.e., can happily change plans to fit in with others or the weather)
- Prompt at all appointments and in performing all tasks
- Dependable (i.e., do *what* you say you will *when* you say you will)
- Persistent (i.e., finish what you start)

Do you . . .

- Have a sense of humor, even when the joke is on you
- Communicate well verbally
- Appreciate beauty in actions, nature, music, and literature
- Sincerely like people, and especially children (i.e., even unattractive and obnoxious ones)
- Work well with others
- Work hard even though it means getting dirty
- Have skills and knowledge for outdoor living
- Follow as well as lead
- Love having fun and see the possibilities for enjoyment in almost any situation
- Have an interest in many things
- Have skill in at least one camp activity that children like to do
- Possess initiative (i.e., ability to start without outside prodding or suggestion)
- Exhibit good personal hygiene

Other Ideas about Maturity and Camp Employment

Emotional Maturity

Camp directors consider emotional maturity to be one of the surest indicators of a counselor's probable success. A counselor cannot help campers to mature unless he or she can set an example for them. People who are emotionally immature are often unhappy since their behavior keeps them constantly at odds with themselves and with their peers, and they often feel mistreated and deprived.

Physical and intellectual maturity are not necessarily related to emotional maturity, as evidenced by adults who have not yet learned to face life squarely and to solve their own problems in an adult way. A college student may be a straight "A" scholar but may be unable to apply emotional intelligence to solving problems or to interacting with other people.

How often have we heard someone say in exasperation, "Why don't you grow up?" What actions and attitudes determine why one person is considered mature while another is not? Mature people realize that every person has wants and needs similar to their own and that everyone cannot always have his or her own way. Mature people try to persuade others to agree with their way of thinking by reasoning with them, not by pouting, flattering, or being so obnoxious that others give in rather than suffer the consequences.

Mature individuals also realize that learning to accept criticism is a necessary part of growing up. They have pride and faith in themselves, yet are modest. They do not make excuses for their shortcomings or blame others. On the other hand, a mature person is not a doormat who lets people walk over him or her. Expressing anger or opinions about things that really matter is important on occasion.

Understanding Yourself

Many psychologists believe that feelings of security are engendered by successful experiences, from childhood onward. Gradually such people develop an increasing sense of competence and self-confidence sufficient to meet new circumstances. Emotionally mature people are able to realistically analyze their own behavior patterns and personality components to better understand actions, reactions, and personal motives. A better understanding of self helps you develop keener insights into others in recognizing their same desires and needs as well as how they attempt to satisfy them.

Other Signs of Maturity

An emotionally mature individual takes pride in influencing others and leading them in the right direction. Great satisfaction should come from watching young campers become increasingly independent. A mature counselor readily and easily adapts to the routines of camp living and cheerfully accepts camp rules and realizes they are important regarding the rights and privileges of everyone at camp. A mature person is thoughtful of others and considerate of their needs and wishes, even

though they sometimes conflict with one's own. Perhaps the surest indication of emotional maturity is that people's actions are governed by reason, not by emotions.

The Counselor's Rewards

The characteristics and demands of a camp counselor are tremendous. However, the experience also offers numerous benefits to the counselor. The satisfactions and rewards of camp counseling, as with any other occupation, will vary with the individual and the situation. Being a seasonal camp counselor not only provides economic benefits, but social, emotional, and intellectual growth and development. The degree of effort put into the job will largely determine what you will receive from the experience.

A counselor's rewards! (Photo courtesy of American Camp Association)

Counselors have almost unlimited opportunities to achieve the objectives of organized camping for themselves. Living and working in an outdoor environment, forming close and lasting friendships, developing successful group living techniques, and improving leadership skills are just some of the benefits. The opportunity to learn and practice valuable "life skills" such as organizing, scheduling, supervising, communicating, and mastering human relations is also valuable. Camp counselors often get to enjoy helping young people grow and mature. They can experience the deep and rewarding satisfaction that comes with making a contribution toward developing good citizens who will become the leaders of the future.

Camp Gives Staff a World of Good

Great emphasis is placed on positive development for campers, but camp is an experience that also benefits counselors. Many staff members are emerging adults and as such can be greatly influenced by camp experiences.

Bialeschki, Henderson, and Dahowski (1998) conducted a number of focus group and personal interviews with staff as they looked back on their camp experience several years after their employment. Analysis of the group interviews revealed a number of positive personal and professional outcomes.

These positive outcomes focused on relationships with other staff and campers (e.g. long-lasting friendships, finding a balance between being a friend and a responsible adult when working with campers, being able to make a difference in a camper's life), appreciation of diversity (e.g., different backgrounds of campers and staff), interpersonal skills (e.g., communication, problem-solving), group cohesion (e.g., establishing bonds, feeling a sense of community at camp), leadership and responsibilities, role modeling/mentoring, technical skill development (e.g., recreation skills), personal growth (e.g., character development, confidence, spiritual growth), administrative skills (e.g., risk management, safety considerations), and teamwork.

Staff also indicated some negative aspects of the camp counseling experience. These issues related to dealing with diversity (e.g., not being able to work with everyone), low wages, lack of time for self, negative perceptions from influential others such as their own parents, frustration with campers (e.g., not being able to successfully address problem behaviors), and cliques (e.g., among staff). Staff indicated that their experience was more positive if their philosophy was compatible with the camp, they had good staff training, and the staff was supportive of one another.

If camp is indeed a microcosm of the real world, then the skills learned will carry over to that world. Many individuals interested in careers with children (e.g., teaching) find their experience at camp invaluable in understanding the developmental stages of children. Yet, the broader skills that are learned such as scheduling, decision-making, communication, and team building have application in almost any future job. Sometimes the benefits of being a camp staff member are not realized until later in life when the experiences can be applied to employment and one's personal life.

Economic Rewards

Staff salaries for seasonal summer employees vary depending on type of position, responsibilities assigned, experience, and tenure at the camp. Recent statistics from a 2009 study completed by the ACA (2010) are presented in table 6.1. Due to variable length of summer camp staff employment, a breakdown of the salaries can best be presented on a weekly rather than monthly basis.

Although not always the case, camp staff salaries are sometimes relatively low, especially for those with no experience or special training. The staff members in the Bialeschki et al. study (1998) indicated that salary was a negative drawback of their camp experience. On the other

Table 6.1   Weekly Salaries of Seasonal Camp Staff in 2009

Position	Day Camp Median Weekly*	Resident Camp Median Weekly*
Summer Camp Director	$833	$600
Assistant Camp Director	$588	$500
Program Director	$750	$440
Activity Director	$488	$318
Head/lead counselor	$440	$350
Counselor	$306	$235
Waterfront Director	$560	$350
Pool Director	$545	$350
Nurse	$600	$650
Doctor/MD	—	$1000
Food Service Dir/Supv	$750	$600
Food Service Staff	$375	$300
Housekeeping Dir/Supv	—	$425
Housekeeping Staff	—	$300
Maintenance Dir/Supv	$750	$500
Maintenance Staff	$375	$300
Videographer/Photographer	$425	$275
Office Clerk/Admin	$450	$300
Room/Board weekly cash value	**	$150

*Gross weekly wage; **more than 50% do not offer room and board
Source: ACA Compensation and Benefits Report, 2010.

hand, lodging and food normally are provided in resident camps. These benefits should not be dismissed. In addition, camps sometimes pay for part or all of the staffs' transportation expenses and some provide free laundry service. Another advantage of working as a counselor is that there are few needs and little temptation to spend money in camp. It is easier to save whatever salary you receive.

Getting a Job Offer

Camps are a major employer of young people, especially college students between the ages of 18 to 23 years. Nonetheless, job hunting for camp positions is not always easy, and many people wonder where and how to start. An early start (e.g., 5–6 months before employment will start) is usually essential. Winter is the time when most camps start to advertise their jobs, and most positions are filled by late spring.

As noted earlier in the list of salaries, a variety of positions exist. Being part of the kitchen staff as a dishwasher is a much different experience than being a cabin counselor who is with children 24/7. Likewise, many camps have "activity specialists" who may be responsible for a specific activity such as aquatics, arts and crafts, or sports. Although these specialists deal with campers all day, they frequently do not live with campers in the same cabins. Therefore, in considering work at a camp, a potential staff member must consider the self-appraisal questions earlier in this chapter and also determine what types of positions might be of most interest as well as what skills an individual might be able to offer, or be willing to learn. Not everyone wants to be with children all day, but may enjoy teaching them a specific sport or outdoor skill.

Once potential counselors have some idea of the job they would like to have, they can then seek opportunities. Possible sources for learning about and applying for positions may include the following:

1. The Internet
   a. individual camp websites
   b. outdoor recreation websites
   c. job banks
   d. ACA employment website (http://www.acacamps.org/jobs)
2. University career and placement bureaus
3. University departments of physical education, recreation, park administration, social work, teacher education, child development
4. Local camping associations
5. Municipal social, welfare, and youth-service agencies such as Boy Scouts, Girl Scouts, Camp Fire, YWCA, and YMCA
6. Private employment agencies as well as state and federal employment services
7. Advertisements in newspapers and magazines that feature camp listings and job opportunities
8. Personal contacts (i.e., word of mouth)

Many colleges and universities hold summer employment or camp job fairs in the winter, which provide opportunities to meet and interview with directors personally while also learning specifics about the various camps and available positions. You can contact several of your nearest institutions of higher education to learn about upcoming events.

Learning as much as possible about specific camps that are of interest is essential. A potential counselor can check out camp websites, read brochures, and, if possible, talk with current or former counselors and campers. Also, such aspects as location, length and dates of the camp season, general policies, programs, objectives, and types and ages of campers served should also be considered.

Putting Together a Résumé

All employers are interested in learning as much as possible about their prospective employees. Therefore, providing such information in a neat and logical order is important. A one- or two-page summary can be developed along the lines of the sample résumé presented in exhibit 6.3, or other alternatives are possible. Résumés may be hard copy or in pdf format for electronic mailing.

Exhibit 6.3

Sample Résumé

James Wannabecounselor

1210 Canterbury Ct.
Raleigh, NC 27707
Mobile- 777-524-3136
jwannabe@gmail.com

Objective: To obtain a camp counseling position at Camp Big Lake

Education: *Bachelor of Arts, Secondary Education, Social Studies*
North Carolina State University (2004)
Masters of Parks, Recreation, and Tourism Management
North Carolina State University (2012)

Professional *Co-Director, Camp Palawopec, Nashville, Indiana*
Experience: June 2000–August 2005
- Co-director during the summers of 2002, 2004, and 2005.
- Increased camper enrollment by 176% by developing a new marketing campaign.
- Designed and coordinated the first staff training week in 2002, which has continued each year since.
- Managed the hiring, evaluation and dismissal of staff for three seasons.
- Participated as a campsite counselor, ages 12–15.
- Horseback program specialist, 2001.
- Facilitated backpacking, mountain biking, and spelunking programs for kids ages 7–15.
- Coordinated 2002 two-week scuba diving adventure in the Florida Keys.
- Coordinated 2001 two-week mountaineering expedition in the Gunnison National Forest, CO.

Adventure Trip Coordinator, Indiana University Outdoor Adventures, Bloomington, Indiana
August 2000–May 2005 and January 2009 to Present
- Planned, organized, and facilitated wilderness trips for university students, staff, faculty, and local community citizens.
- Instructed R110 outdoor recreation courses through IUOA and Indiana University, School of HPER.
- Concentration in backpacking, flat water canoeing, and hiking programs, along with leave no trace camping techniques.

High School Adventure Club, Columbus North High School, Columbus, Indiana
September 1997–May 2000
- CNAC is an extracurricular club that centers on teaching students about outdoor recreation, concentrating in low-impact camping principles. Coordinated and facilitated weekend and weeklong outdoor recreation adventure trips for high school students.

Professional *Fundamentals of Search and Rescue*, NASAR, October 2003
Development: *Geography Educators Network*, Conference, March 2012
Middle School Boot Camp, Peace College, July 2010
Team Building Facilitator Training, Experiential Resources, April 2008
Tremont Outdoor Education Consortium, Great Smoky Mountain National Park, Tremont Institute, March 2009

References: References are available upon request.

Considerations for analyzing your experience and ability might include asking:

1. What have I successfully accomplished and for what achievements have I been commended?

2. What jobs have I held?

3. What specific skills do I have that are appropriate for a camp leadership position?

4. What are the things I really like to do as well as those things I don't like to do?

Cover Letter or Letter of Application

Since often a camp requires an application form and a résumé, a cover letter to the camp where employment is desired does not need to be lengthy. However, the personal letter should briefly explain why you are attracted to a particular camp and also describe those qualities that will enable you to make a contribution to it.

A well-written cover letter is important and worth the time and effort since it may lead to a personal interview; it may also be influential in opening the door to future contacts. An applicant should be honest and not overstate abilities or experience. Statements should be specific and targeted to the kind of job for which you are applying. Keep the cover letter brief, clear, concise, interesting, courteous, and convincing. Address it to the proper person and be sure to provide ways that a director might contact you (e-mail address, phone, mailing address).

Interview and Follow-Up

Camp employers are as concerned about an applicant's personality as they are about the factual information included in the résumé. When two applicants have approximately equal qualifications, the interview usually determines who will get the job. If invited for an interview, the goal is to present yourself as a valuable product.

Ideally you will have a chance for a face-to-face interview, although that opportunity is not always possible. You may be invited for a telephone, video, or Skype interview. Regardless, as with any merchandise, a product always sells better when it is attractively packaged. Thus, having a neat appearance as well as a clear and alert mind is important. Think before answering a question, and give polite, accurate, and honest responses without appearing to brag. Be confident and enthusiastic, but do not bluff. Not knowing exactly how to answer a question is not necessarily a problem as long as the applicant is honest. Conduct yourself in a businesslike manner, and be polite, tactful, and show proper respect.

The purpose of an interview, whether in-person or via telephone, is to exchange pertinent information in a relatively short period of time. The camp director wants to know what you are like, what you have done in the past, and what you have to offer the camp. Be prepared to talk about yourself in terms of the needs or require-

ments of the camp. What do you have to offer that would make you an asset to the camp? Why do you want to be there, and why will the director be glad to have you?

Consider the following questions as preparation for describing what you have to offer. They are likely the types of questions that will be asked:

1. Why do you want to work for a camp? At this particular camp?

2. Tell me about yourself.

3. What experience do you have?

4. How would you describe yourself?

5. What is it about this particular job that you think you will enjoy?

6. What special training do you have for this job?

7. What activities have you been involved in while going to school?

8. Why should we hire you at this camp?

9. What are your major weaknesses/strengths?

10. What do you know about our camp?

11. What are some of your outside activities and interests?

12. How would your friends and former employers describe you?

13. What questions do you have about the camp and/or the job?

In responding to some of these questions, keep in mind that the camp director will want to know if you have had any prior experience in working with people in a leadership capacity. For example, have you supervised or taught others, organized programs or projects, or accepted other major responsibilities? Prior to the interview, take the time to think through your previous job and school experiences. You may be surprised at how much prior involvement or experience you actually have in some of these areas.

The interview, however, is not a one-way exchange. A potential camp counselor should also be assessing the camp and the camp director to see if this employment is really what he or she wants. You are interviewing the camp director as well, so it is important to learn as much as possible from the director about the camp, the job, and the expectations. If you are a qualified individual, you may have more than one personal interview and will want to choose the job that is best for you.

A camp director will often ask, "Do you have any questions you would like to ask me?" The interview should provide an opportunity to ask questions about the camp, the program, the living conditions, and other important details. Therefore, prior to the interview, do some research on the camp's website and carefully read any available materials about the camp. Give some thought to pertinent areas in which you want to obtain further information. Do not ask these questions if the information has been provided to you. However, if you need any clarification, you might ask questions about:

1. The philosophy and program structure of the camp
2. The camp setting itself and its location
3. The exact dates on which your job would begin and end
4. General camp policies
5. Whether the camp specializes in particular activities such as aquatics, riding, or arts and crafts, or does it instead provide a balanced general program
6. Living quarters and conditions provided for staff (will you share a cabin with other staff members or be expected to live in the cabin with your campers?)
7. The age group with which you will be working
8. The regulations regarding time off, smoking in camp, the use of alcohol in and out of camp, having your own car, bringing pets, etc.
9. The compensation, including possible transportation to and from camp, use of camp equipment, and extras such as riding and boating privileges
10. Your definite responsibilities and duties on the job. Accredited camps should be able to furnish you with such information through a definite and detailed written job description (ACA Standard HR-6). Ask about it. (For a more detailed discussion of the job description, see the next chapter.)

Although you are also interviewing the camp director, recognize that some of these questions are more important than others in your ultimate decision regarding whether or not you are interested in the camp. Prioritize your questions. A good camp director will gladly supply you with answers so take your cues from that director during the interview. Some reminders for successful interviewing are listed in exhibit 6.4.

Throughout the interview the camp director will be evaluating your maturity, cooperativeness, physical and mental alertness, motivation, enthusiasm, and any other qualities that will help in assessing your willingness to work and your ability to get along with others.

Following the interview, send a brief follow-up note or e-mail thanking the interviewer for the meeting and expressing appreciation for the courtesy and consideration extended to you. This gesture allows you to reaffirm your interest in the camp position. Such action is not only polite, but also shows special interest and enthusiasm for the job.

Additional Aspects of Securing a Camp Job

Most camps will want to learn more about you from other people who know you. The ACA Standards (HR-4C) require that at least two reference checks are done on all new staff. The camp application will likely ask you for a list of references who can be contacted regarding your suitability for the camp position. These sources of information should be people who know your work well. College professors, employers, or volunteer supervisors might serve as possible references. Keep in mind that the person who is giving you a recommendation should be someone

---

Exhibit 6.4
Successful Interviewing DOs and DON'Ts

DOs

1. Be prompt, neat, polite, and appropriately dressed.
2. Act naturally. Be poised and friendly and remember to smile.
3. Try to overcome nervousness or shortness of breath. (It may help to take a deep breath and sit back comfortably in your chair as you talk, whether face-to-face or over the telephone.)
4. Answer questions honestly and in a straightforward manner. Look the interviewer in the eye in a personal interview.
5. An interview is a two-way street, so feel free to ask for information about the camp and its policies.
6. Recognize your limitations.
7. Indicate your flexibility and readiness to learn.
8. Make sure the interviewer understands what you mean. Enunciate clearly and use good grammar and sentence structure.
9. Modestly point out the specific contributions you can make to the camp.
10. Give the employer an opportunity to express himself or herself and listen closely to what is said.

DON'Ts

1. Don't be late for the interview.
2. Don't be extreme in mannerisms, grooming, or dress.
3. Don't display a passive or indifferent attitude.
4. Don't be inflexible.
5. Don't become impatient or emotional.
6. Don't make claims if you can't deliver on the job.
7. Don't be a "know-it-all" or a person who can't take instructions or suggestions.
8. Don't speak indistinctly or in a muffled voice. Keep your head up and look directly at the employer as you talk.
9. Don't overemphasize salary.
10. Don't unnecessarily prolong the interview. Watch for signals that indicate that the interviewer is ready to conclude the interview and follow his or her lead.

who knows you fairly well and can speak to your work ethic as much as your character and personality. The references are usually contacted by phone or e-mail, so make sure that the potential camp employer has accurate information. Also, be sure to ask your references whether you can use their names before you give the information to the potential employer. If the reference knows something about the job or jobs for which you are applying, he or she will be in a better position to discuss your abilities.

The ACA Standards (HR-4A and 4B) require that all camps have a process for screening staff that will have contact with campers. You will be asked to sign a voluntary disclosure form and your name will be checked with the National Sex Offender Public Website and/or the state's registry. New camp staff will undergo a criminal background check as well.

Accepting a Position

If you receive an offer of a position, do not accept the job unless you can give it your utmost loyalty and commitment. In other words, prior to accepting be reasonably sure that the camp's philosophy is sufficiently compatible with your own. Clear up all questions and doubts. If you accept a job offer either verbally or through a writ-ten contract, you have assumed responsibilities that you are obligated to fulfill. Do not accept a job unless you are absolutely sure the position is the one for you.

If you have applied to several camps and receive an offer from one before hearing from others in which you are interested, it is entirely appropriate to call those other camps to determine the status of your application. Do not feel shy about inquiring. Your honesty and initiative usually will be appreciated. Answer all correspondence promptly, since the director may lose other desirable applicants while you are trying to make up your mind. A signed contract is your word of honor that you will arrive on schedule prepared to carry out your assignments to the best of your ability.

After returning the signed contract, you will receive various literature and correspondence from the camp. Read it carefully to better orient yourself and fix pertinent details in your mind. Begin to prepare to assume your duties. If possible, enroll in, or at least audit, helpful school courses and get any necessary training that will be useful or that may be required. Start a camp journal or notebook in which to jot down useful information and helpful ideas that come your way. Also, as a final suggestion, take advantage of all opportunities to gain further experience in working with groups of people. Good luck!

REFERENCES

American Camp Association Compensation and Benefits Report (2010). Retrieved from www.acacamps.org/research/camp-compensation-and-benefits-report-2010

Bialeschki, M. D., Henderson, K. A., & Dahowski, K. (1998, July/Aug). Camp gives staff a world of good. *Camping Magazine, 71*(4), 27–31.

WEB RESOURCES

ACA Employment Center: (www.acacamps.org/jobs/) allows you to view jobs, post résumés, subscribe to a listing of year-round camp jobs, and get a list of job fairs and tips.

Camp Channel (www.campchannel.com/) features a job board and the option to post a résumé.

Camp Jobs (www.campjobs.com) allows you to search for camp jobs by type, position, state, job length, type, and religious preference; able to post/edit résumé on site.

Camp Page (www.camppage.com) provides a search engine for summer camps and wilderness programs in the U.S. and Canada, with an option to search for camp jobs by state, type, or activity.

Camp Staff (www.campstaff.com) is an online application process; matches summer camps with prospective employees.

Great Camp Jobs (www.greatcampjobs.com) offers tips, résumé tips, description of various camp jobs, and an online application feature.

InterExchange (www.interexchange.org) matches young adults from around the world with camp jobs in the U.S.

Summer Camp (www.mysummercamps.com) provides a job database with search options.

YMCA Careers (www.ymca.net/camp_vacancies) allows you to search for YMCA residential or day-camp jobs.

PRINT RESOURCES

Ball, A., & Ball, B. (2004). *Basic camp management: An introduction to camp administration* (6th ed.). Martinsville, IN: ACA.

Ditter, B. (2007, Sept/Oct). Determining competency. *Camping Magazine, 80*(5). Contains sample interview questions, qualities directors look for, and interview steps.

Garst, B., & Jacobs, J. (2006). Get a real job. *Camping Magazine, 79*(6), 3–5.

Lowe, H. (ed.). (2007). *Child and youth development: By the expert.* Martinsville, IN: ACA.

Starkman, N. (2002). *Walking your talk: Building assets in organizations that serve youth.* Martinsville, IN: ACA.

Yerkes, R. (2009, Sept/Oct). A career in organized camping: Stand up and be counted! *Camping Magazine, 82*(5), 26–31.

7

Counselors on the Job

amps vary greatly, as discussed throughout this book. Individual camps also provide camp experiences in different ways. Therefore, a camp counselor's duties will reflect the type of camp and the facilities and activities that are emphasized as part of its mission. This chapter surveys some of the general aspects of a counselor's duties. Before accepting a job at a camp, prospective staff should read and understand the job description. Staff members should be aware of both specific job duties and general duties that all camp staff undertake to enhance positive experiences for campers.

Figure 7.1 shows the lines of responsibility that might exist in the staff organization of a typical resident camp. Variations exist as each camp tailors its plan to its mission and size, staff capabilities, program and facilities, and the objectives and personal preferences of the director or sponsoring agency. The chart, however, does give an overall view of staff organization and indicates lines of authority and the particular staff member to whom each person is directly responsible. Note that one individual is in charge of each of the five main areas of health, food, program, maintenance, and business, and that each is directly accountable to the director for the conduct of his or her particular area.

Camp Staff

Camp Director

The camp director is at the top of the chart. He or she is the highest authority in camp and is ultimately responsible for everything that occurs there. All staff members are accountable to the director, even though they may be under the immediate supervision of someone to whom the director has delegated responsibility. General camp policies and rules cover routine procedures. Staff in charge of a certain area may be authorized to make important decisions in that area. However, decisions of major importance must be referred to the camp director for final approval and consent.

The director is responsible for the welfare of each camper and staff member and carries out these responsibilities through the abilities and training of the staff as well as through the camp rules, philosophy and objectives, and the strategies used to carry them out. The director must possess diverse abilities since he or she serves simultaneously as an administrator, financial wizard, child welfare expert, educator, recreation director, and advisor to counselors and other staff members.

Since the director realizes that a camp is only as strong as its staff, he or she tries to recruit the best personnel available. To obtain the optimum in total team performance, the director must recognize the inherent potential of each team member and help each to develop and use his or her abilities to the best advantage in combination with whatever physical and natural resources the camp offers. At the same time, the director must realize that each staff member also has needs and desires that must be fulfilled. The director, then, is the hub of the wheel and staff members are the spokes.

Assistant Director

The person second in command is called by various titles such as assistant director or program director, and generally serves as the liaison or coordinator of the whole camp program. This person is accountable to the camp director and works directly with program specialists and unit directors. The morale of both campers and staff is

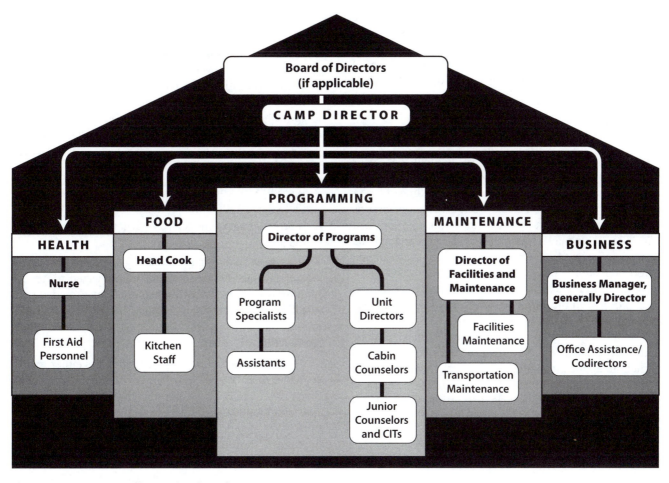

Figure 7.1   Camp staff organization chart.

largely dependent upon this person. The specific duties of the assistant director will vary according to the size, philosophy, and general setup of the camp.

Program Specialists or Department Heads

Program specialists or department heads usually are employed in resident camps or those tending toward a more centralized system, although nearly every camp has some specialists, like a riding instructor or a waterfront director. They head such specialized areas as sports, horseback riding, arts and crafts, ecology and nature programs, aquatics, trip camping, music, adventure activities, and dramatics. Each specialist or department head may also have an assistant to help carry out the program.

Program specialists perform their duties in many ways. In some camps, the specialist keeps the work area open at definite hours for any campers who wish to come. In other cases, each camper group is scheduled for the program at a certain time. In camps operating under the decentralized program philosophy, each group has more leeway in planning and carrying out its own activities. Consequently, small groups may ask for the services of the program specialist when required.

A program specialist may or may not be assigned regular cabin duties, depending on the philosophy of the camp and the demands of the specialty. In addition to instructing and advising, the program specialist's duties usually include requisitioning the supplies needed and seeing that the work quarters and equipment are kept in good condition. She or he usually will be held responsible for taking inventory, packing away supplies at the end of the season, and listing supplies needed for the following year.

Unit Directors and Counselors

A unit director, sometimes called a village or section head, presides over a unit of four to six groups, cabins, or tents. Usually this person has assistant unit heads or counselors in direct charge of campers who comprise a day-camp group or a resident-camp cabin or tent.

Prior to camp opening, the unit director works closely with the counselors in planning a skeleton unit program for the summer that is suited to the needs and interests of their particular campers. The details of the plan are then worked out and altered, if necessary, with the help of the campers after they arrive. The unit director generally works with counselors to decide such matters as the division of unit duties and time off, and serves as their liaison with the assistant director. He or she must see that the unit program coordinates with the overall program of the camp and with its general objectives and philosophy.

The Job Description

A job description is a written statement that spells out the exact terms of employment for a particular staff member and includes not only a detailed outline of a person's responsibilities to the camp, but also the obligations of the camp to the employee. The job description in a particular camp may develop in various ways and may be revised in succeeding years as experience or changing camp philosophy and customs dictate. At the end of a season, the camp administration usually reviews the job description with the employee to receive any suggestions he or she may have for ways to improve it.

When applying for a job, the applicant should be shown the job description during the interview. As noted earlier, an applicant should certainly ask for it in specific and written form before making a final decision to accept so that the expectations are clear regarding what the job involves. According to ACA Standards (HR-6), all staff should be given a written job description.

What a Job Description Includes

Job descriptions may be written in different ways, but all should include the following information:

1. Title of the position
2. To whom the employee is accountable
3. General responsibilities: degree of responsibility and performance expected
4. Specific duties
5. Qualifications: prior training and experience, skills and interests needed
6. The relationship of the position to other positions in the camp as well as to the camp's total program

Advantages of a Job Description

A job description aids the camp by: (1) helping to recruit staff specifically suited for a particular position, (2) serving to remind an immediate supervisor of exactly what each of the subordinate's duties are to avoid having duties overlap or leaving important areas unassigned, (3) serving as an objective basis for evaluating an employee's performance during and at the end of the season, and (4) producing more satisfied and more confident staff members since each knows what he or she can expect and what is expected of that person before accepting the job. The job description also serves as a guide for the counselor to follow on the job.

The job description is important to staff members because:

1. It prevents the misunderstandings and confusion that often result from verbal discussions. It informs the person of what his or her particular job entails, where to turn for help and guidance, to whom he or she is responsible, with whom he or she works, their positions in relation to his or hers and how they interrelate.
2. It lends status to a position and helps the staff member take pride in the job.
3. It assures that the camp is efficiently administered and that concern for its personnel is a high priority.
4. It provides a specific reference when questions arise on the job.
5. It helps in planning by supplying definite information about what and when things are expected to get accomplished (e.g., what reports are to be provided periodically and at the close of camp).

Staff Manual

Most camps have a staff manual that is either sent to staff members before camp opens or given upon arrival. Some camps may post their staff manuals on their websites. The manual should be a comprehensive reference book with specific information and material that should be studied thoroughly and kept for future reference. It probably will contain information concerning the camp's mission, philosophy and objectives, brief history of the camp, the camp staff organization chart, personnel policies and privileges, camp customs, sample record forms, a description of the camp layout with a map of the units and facilities, emergency procedures, policies regarding staff time off and staff use of equipment and facilities, staff meetings, in-camp training procedures, and a risk management plan.

Pre-Camp Training

Counselors and other staff personnel customarily are required to report to the camp site for pre-camp training several days to a week or more ahead of the campers. ACA Accreditation Standards (HR-11) require five to six days of pre-camp training at resident camps and three days at day camps. This pre-camp training session provides an important orientation period for new counselors as well as a review for returning staff. The training should give everyone a chance to get acquainted with one another and to become familiar with the camp site, routines, program, and customs and traditions. Ball and Ball (2004) cite the following common objectives of pre-camp staff training:

1. Infusing staff with the basic philosophy and objectives of the camp and defining their implications for procedures and operations.

2. Fostering a sense of pride in the camp job and a harmonious working relationship among staff.

3. Teaching and/or practicing necessary program skills.

4. Developing an understanding of the characteristics of age groups and providing an insight into working with these ages.

5. Providing an opportunity for staff to understand working policies and procedures as they relate to individual staff responsibilities.

6. Preparing, inspiring, and motivating staff towards a successful summer.

7. Developing esprit de corps and team building among staff.

The pre-camp training program allows staff to plan for the summer both individually and with others. During this time counselors probably will have an opportunity to learn or review skills as well as go through some of the routines and activities their campers will be doing. Counselors may be assigned specific readings and may be asked to participate in discussions conducted by members of the staff. Also, unit staff meetings likely will be held to plan for specific unit programs. The pre-camp training program is also an ideal time to certify staff in CPR, first aid, and other emergency techniques so that staff members are prepared if and when such skills are needed. Exhibit 7.1 on the following page delineates topics that might be covered in pre-camp training as they relate to ACA Standards.

Previewing Campers

Pre-camp training may include learning about incoming campers. ACA Standards (HW-6, HW-9) require that each camper submit a health history prior to coming to camp. This record contains information about the camper which may be of a highly personal nature and is viewed only by the health supervisor—who will give the counselor any information that is needed. Other information might also be available from registration forms. Use the information solely to gain a better understanding of the campers before you meet them face to face. It may be your responsibility to note any limitations regarding strenuous activities and any allergies or food idiosyncrasies to assure that recommendations regarding them are carried out. The information may help staff anticipate and prevent behavior problems. General registration information may reveal the possible interests and abilities of the camper as well as provide an overall impression of all campers coming to the camp.

If a camper previously attended the camp, records of earlier accomplishments and staff evaluations of his or her personality, social adaptability, adjustment to adult and peer groups, and general behavior may be available. Wise handling of pre-camp assessments will require maturity and good judgment. Because these records contain only factual information, a person examining them could jump to conclusions and form inaccurate judgments based upon single or isolated bits of information. It is also unwise and unfair to assume that episodes that may have occurred during one period of a camper's life necessarily forecast what he or she will do at a later period.

Counselor Relationships with Other Staff

Camps offer an intense experience, albeit during a relatively short period of time, for staff as well as campers. Considering relationships with the camp director and other staff is instrumental in assuring a successful camp counseling experience.

With the Camp Director

A camp director usually spends months preparing for the approaching season. Though the director may have delegated duties and responsibilities to others, she or he still retains the primary responsibility for the administration of the camp, and is held accountable for any serious errors in judgment made by the staff. Obviously, the director has a comprehensive view of the whole camp situation and the multitude of details and problems demanding attention.

The counselors' actions should be directed toward helping to bear the load instead of unnecessarily adding to the director's burdens by making thoughtless, selfish requests or by failing to fully and efficiently carry out all assigned tasks. Counselors should neither ask for nor expect special favors since no administrator should show partiality. Counselors are expected to obey the spirit as well as the letter of camp rules and regulations. All required reports should be turned in on time and be complete.

Counselors must keep the aims and objectives of the camp foremost in mind and direct all efforts toward their accomplishment. Be conscious always that *camp is for the campers* and that their moral, spiritual, and physical welfare must take precedence over the self-centered desires of any individual or group.

Though it will often be difficult, a counselor must be able to distinguish between problems and decisions that can be directly handled and those that should be referred to superiors for their action or advice. On the one hand, a staff member has been hired because of mature judgment and should be able to make minor decisions within one's jurisdiction instead of passing responsibility along to someone else. On the other hand, counselors must be quick to recognize major problems that should be referred to the unit head, the camp nurse, or the head counselor. If the problem is of great urgency or importance, a counselor should go directly to the camp director.

With Fellow Staff Members

Camp offers a fun and satisfying way to spend time; it also is a way of life. It is a valuable experience in living harmoniously in close association with others—often 24 hours a day. The *esprit de corps* of the staff largely determines the spirit of the entire camp. No person can be happy and do a good job when working in a tense environment, with vague feelings of insecurity and frustration. Thus, good staff morale almost invariably is the vi-

tal component found in every successful camp. Each person should make a conscientious effort to promote cooperative relationships. This cooperation is essential not only for a counselor's state of mind but also for the well-being of the campers and for the attainment of camp objectives. Campers are quick to perceive any lack of staff unity and, like their elders, will discuss it among themselves and may even pick sides in an open feud. Petty gossip or a careless comment can cause the first break in

---

Exhibit 7.1

Pre-Camp Training Topics with Reference to ACA Accreditation Standards

Site and Food Service
- Proper handling and use of power tools—SF-11
- Proper handling of hazardous materials, e.g., kerosene, cleaning agents—SF-2
- Required general maintenance routines, e.g., cleaning, reporting maintenance problems—SF-7 written
- Food preparation, storage, and handling procedures (as applicable)—SF-19 through SF-28, some written

Transportation
- Bus/van safety procedures and group management—TR-8 and TR-9 written
- Orientation of safety regulations and procedures in vehicles provided for passengers—TR-10
- Procedures in case of accident during transportation—TR-7 written
- Safety procedures for orderly arrival and departure and for loading and unloading of vehicles—TR-3
- Training for vehicle drivers—TR-17 and TR-18 written
- Transportation of persons in nonpassenger vehicles—TR-4
- Transportation policies that specify supervision ratios of staff to campers, availability and location of health information, and permission-to-treat forms—TR-6 written

Health and Wellness
- Procedures for informing staff of special needs of campers—HW-10
- Responsibilities of staff for camper health care—HW-13 written
- Providing health care and emergency treatment when out of camp—HW-14
- How prescription and nonprescription drugs are stored at camp—HW-20
- Records kept in health log and incident reports filed—HW-21, A and B

Operational Management
- Camper security procedures—OM-17 written
- Emergency communications plan—OM-15 written
- General camp safety regulations and rules—OM-9 written, OM-8, and OM-12
- Procedures for camper supervision in public areas—OM-16 written

- Completing incident and accident reports—OM-13
- Missing persons procedures—OM-14 written
- Policy and procedures covering personal property—OM-10 written
- Smoking policy—OM-11
- Procedures for dealing with possible intruders—OM-6 written

Human Resources
- Behavior management—HR-16 written
- Camper/staff ratios—HR-9 written
- Personnel policies—HR-8 written
- Pre-camp staff training (specific topics to be covered)—HR-11
- Sensitive issue policy—HR-17
- Staff/camper interaction—HR-15
- Staff training in diversity—HR-5
- Camp staff responsibility for general camp activities—HR-14 written
- Supervision of staff—HR-18 written
- Supervisor training—HR-19 written
- Training for their particular job—HR-7

Program Design and Activities
- Details for designated person left in camp—PD-14
- Emergency information—PD-13
- Environmental practices and activities—PD-3, PD-12
- Supervision of specialized activity areas—PD-18
- Operating procedures for each specialized activity—PD-19 written
- Skill verification and activity supervision—PD-16, PD-17 written
- Procedures for controlled access of activity areas—PD-18
- Procedures for overnights and trips—PD-1 written
- Participant competency demonstration—PD-21
- Program goals and outcomes—PD-6 written
- Safety orientation for participants—PD-20
- Use of program equipment—PD-4

(Adapted from ACA Accreditation and Standards, 2010).

staff morale. Therefore, counselors must avoid being critical of other staff members.

Camp consists of a blending of different activities and experiences. Most of the positive outcomes of camp result from this blending into a whole, rather than from the parts individually. At times this blending is difficult for conscientious counselors to remember since they can become absorbed in trying to conduct their own particular part of the program and, consequently, lose sight of the bigger picture. Immature counselors often can be spotted by their attempts to vie with each other in attracting the campers' attention, which is short-sighted and selfish and may jeopardize the welfare of both the camp and the campers.

Forming cliques should be avoided since exclusive friendships among counselors can damage camp morale. Returning counselors, who are reuniting after a winter's separation, must be especially careful. Their joy at being together again may unconsciously exclude new staff members, making them feel lonely and estranged from the rest of the camp family. Nevertheless, long-term friendships are fostered at camp. One of the major reasons that many staff return from year to year is because of their relationships with other staff. Acknowledging this point allows a counselor to realize the importance of the previous bonds, while also highlighting the importance of welcoming and integrating new staff members into the staff community.

Counselors should take their jobs seriously, but not themselves. Worthwhile personal relationships, *esprit de corps,* and good camp morale are the end products when staff members work together and acknowledge what each person has to contribute to achieving the camp mission.

The First Day of Camp

Planning for Camper Arrival

Day, resident, trip, and school camps will all have different procedures. Most of the following suggestions are directed toward resident camp staff, although the principles apply across all types and sponsorships of camps.

If you are a cabin counselor at a resident camp, you will be living closely with a small group of campers and will come to know them well. A defining quality of the camp experience is living and playing in a small group in which each member has an important role and enjoys the feeling of being an integral part of the group by sharing in its work, play, joys, and sorrows just as in a closely knit family. This living arrangement should give each camper a feeling of security and belonging.

Many activities will involve only the small group. Yet like any family, the group will frequently engage in community activities with other groups and the camp as a whole. The counselor's job is to teach campers to function effectively in their own and in larger groups. The

proceedings during the first few camp days will be instrumental in setting the stage for this undertaking.

First contacts and first impressions will largely determine the attitude of the campers toward one another and you. Therefore, planning what you will do and how you will do it during these first crucial hours and days is important. A large share of this time should be spent in the small group so that the counselor can weld them together and build a climate of "oneness" and loyalty that will instill in each the courage to go out and take his or her place with larger groups.

Some long-term resident camps ask the counselors to send brief notes or e-mails to campers and their parents a few days before they head for camp. This strategy helps campers face the new experience more confidently, knowing someone is looking forward to his or her arrival. You will not want to do this, however, unless someone in authority has approved it in advance.

The Journey to Camp

Campers likely will have been anticipating their arrival at camp for several weeks (if not months) prior to arriving at camp. Many times parents find bags packed and gear stowed well in advance of their child's departure for camp. However prepared the camper might be, those first-day jitters still exist. The following narrative offers one insight into a camper's mind from the standpoint of an adult looking back:

> I remember the feeling I would get each year as my parents drove me down from the city to my camp 200 miles away. The weeks or month preceding camp were filled with anticipation, yet the butterflies in my stomach would still appear. As we bounced on the gravel roads making our way to the remote region where camp was, the butterflies would move about a bit quicker as we got closer. Finally, we would pull into the camp drive and up the long stand of pine trees that lined the drive. As we rounded the bend into the parking lot I would be looking for familiar faces: my counselor from last year, the director and his wife, or just someone to connect to. Once I found someone, the butterflies were gone.

This story is not unlike what many kids may experience en route to camp. Counselors and camp staff members must constantly remind themselves of the nuances associated with leaving home, family, and comfortable surroundings. The first moments and day at camp are paramount in establishing vital camper-staff relationships that persist throughout the camper's stay at camp.

When Campers Arrive

The process of getting campers settled at camp will differ depending on whether they arrive simultaneously on a bus, come singly, or arrive in small groups. If all the campers arrive at one time, all staff members should be present together. All staff will be needed to take care of a multitude

A "get to know you" activity helps break down barriers when campers first arrive at camp. (Photo courtesy of Bradford Woods Learning and Outdoor Center)

of details. If campers dribble in a few at a time, one unit staff member may remain in the quarters as a host to greet the campers, show them their bunks, and help them get settled. Program specialists and other staff may act as guides, receiving the newcomers, assigning them to quarters, and keeping an accurate record of who has checked in. Spare staff or returning campers may act as "runners" to help the new arrivals with their baggage and show them to their living units. A staff member may be assigned to meet those coming by train, bus, or plane at some central gathering place and to transport them to camp.

As a guide to your conduct at this time, imagine yourself as a small child leaving your parents, friends, and familiar surroundings for the first time. You probably would be overwhelmed by feelings of excitement and anticipation; tempered somewhat by uncertainty and anxiety. At a time like this, being greeted by a friendly counselor who tells you his or her name and makes a genuine attempt to help you get settled is greatly appreciated. Calling someone by his or her first name is a boost to anyone's ego. This practice of calling someone by name is known and practiced by anyone who wants to quickly make friends and establish rapport.

Campers should also be introduced to each other and provided with a name tag that can be read easily from a distance. Getting everyone started on a first-name basis breaks down barriers and launches the camp session with a spirit of friendliness. A "get to know you" activity or some sort of "name game" might also be used. For example, have each child choose an animal whose

name starts with the first letter of her or his name. You can continue this in a circle, having each child recite the name and animal of the person or persons going before, and then adding her or his own to the list. Finally the game can end with the counselor culminating all names and animals together, reciting each correctly. Icebreakers like this are helpful and can be found by searching for initiatives or icebreakers in the camp library or the Internet.

Encourage the camper to unpack, put his or her belongings in a personal storage place, make up a bed, and get into comfortable camp clothes. These tasks help the camper feel at home and settled for a long stay. This approach also helps to dispel the instinct to turn away from the unknown and unfamiliar and run back home. As long as the bags are packed, the new camper may yield to her or his fears and latch onto any excuse to return to familiar surroundings.

The camp director probably will have provided each camper with a list of gear to bring to camp. As the campers unpack their baggage, make a practice of checking off each item when it is unpacked and, if there is a discrepancy, report it to the camp office. At some camps, the inventories should be filed in the camp office to use later when it is time to pack to return home. Campers are usually requested to put their name on all items that they bring to camp. Another common procedure is to collect return trip tickets, money, and other valuables for safekeeping in the camp office or other designated place.

HCA Standards (HW-8, HW-20) require a health screening upon arrival at a resident camp and require that prescription medicines be collected and turned over to the health supervisor for administration. Anyone needing medical attention, no matter how minor, must be referred to the health care professional in charge. Unless specifically directed otherwise, a counselor should not give any kind of medical treatment except first aid in an emergency.

Veteran campers placed in a cabin unit with new campers can become a problem. Veterans may become bossy or dictatorial and may attempt to run the cabin for you, or they may try to play practical jokes on the newcomers. Such showing off might be an attempt to gain what they consider to be their rightful recognition and to cover up underlying feelings of insecurity. In contrast, such needs often can be satisfied constructively by having these veteran campers assume various responsibilities such as helping newcomers unpack and get settled, showing them around the camp, preparing and passing out name tags, or running errands. Tactfully but firmly remain in charge and in full control of the situation, welcoming all campers and using the services of the returning campers as much as is reasonable.

When the parents do not bring the child to camp, having the child write a card to go out in the first mail or sending a quick e-mail or text message to tell parents of the safe arrival may be a good idea. A worthwhile gesture on your part may be to send the parents a short note within a day or two to establish rapport and to assure them that their child is in good hands, but only if that practice is sanctioned by your supervisor.

As the occasion presents itself, talk about some of the main points of camp life such as mail call and basic camp rules, and discuss with your campers their contributions to the general welfare of the camp family. Campers do not resent reasonable rules if they understand the reasons for them and especially if they have some say in the negotiable rules concerning camp living. Most campers want to know the rules and boundaries that exist in camp. When possible—in both day and resident camps—let campers formulate some of the rules that will affect them, since this helps give them a sense of responsibility in the camp community. Since the word *rules* often carries a negative connotation and may arouse antagonism and resentment in some, you may want to give them a more innocuous name such as *guidelines* or *camp customs*.

Developing Group Unity and Feelings of Acceptance

As soon as campers settle in and seem ready, proceed with some activities to break the ice further and get them on easy terms with one another. Play some familiar fun group games or take them on a tour of the camp. Pairing campers off in a "buddy" system for a designated period may help establish bonds with at least one other person at the beginning.

When it seems appropriate, launch into an informal group discussion suggesting exciting adventures your campers may want to plan for the near future or long-term projects to think about now and decide on later. Notice the emphasis on *group* discussion, which means encouraging each and every one to contribute. Try to generate enthusiasm, keep their minds occupied, and crowd out any feelings of insecurity and loneliness that are particularly likely to appear the first night.

Dining room procedures should be discussed before the first meal to give campers an idea of what to expect. Later on, as the need arises, dining room conduct and table manners can be delved into more deeply. Stress the importance of personal cleanliness when in the dining room. Ask returning campers to volunteer to wait on tables and carry out other duties until newcomers have had a chance to observe operations and become familiar with procedures.

The First Night at Resident Camp

Camps often have an all-camp council ring or other all-camp meeting on the first night to give everyone a chance to see the whole group and have the entire staff introduced. At this time, the staff may put on a skit or other entertainment to introduce themselves in a more informal way. Some camps prefer to arrange for unit or cabin programs, believing that a camper should become well acquainted with the small group before tackling the large one.

The time just before dark is a critical period. New campers may need a little extra attention from you. It may be desirable to have your campers wash and perform other bedtime rituals before dark, and you should personally check to see that these chores are performed adequately. Leave some time for a short evening discussion or a bedtime story before lights out. Explain the wake-up procedure and breakfast routine, some of the activities going on the next day; ask what campers are interested in doing; and stress that a time is set after the evening program for silence with everyone in bed and ready for sleep. This first night, take a little extra time to show personal interest in each camper. Many of these children may never have camped before, so unfamiliar sounds such as a tree creaking in the wind might be alarming in the unaccustomed stillness of an outdoor environment. Settling in on the first night may take a while because of the campers' excitement. Be patient. Each night will get easier and you will actually get some sleep.

Those Important First Days

Set an example from the start by maintaining a positive outlook and trying to see the funny side of things. Joking and good-natured banter can help start the day on a cheerful note. Perform the morning routines of washing, brushing teeth, and combing hair as efficiently as possible.

Encourage campers who awaken early to read or write letters so they will not disturb others. Be sure to accompany your campers to breakfast each morning. Promoting a healthy lifestyle and group unity by attending camp events together is important. This time might also be used for attending to morning medications, sorting out the day's events with fellow counselors, and developing a game plan for the day with your cabin.

Homesickness is likely to occur during the first few days of camp. One of the best ways to cope with it is to get individuals deeply involved in things that absorb them. Continually plan exciting adventures for the future so there is always something to look forward to. If you spend extra time with campers during the first two days and work hard to achieve a spirit of camaraderie and cooperation, this cohesiveness can be maintained throughout the camp session regardless of its length.

Seize every available opportunity for informal chats to get to know the campers. Find out why they came to camp, what their hobbies and interests are, and what they look forward to experiencing at camp. Listen attentively to campers' chatter. It provides insight into their current hopes, plans, interests, capacities, and ambitions. By initiating conversations with your campers, individually and in groups, you will quickly become at ease with one another. Be sure to make a special effort to include loners and introverts. These conversations also will provide an opportunity for you to spot any campers who show a tendency to stir up trouble or dissension within the group.

Gradually introduce your campers to such things as camp *kapers* (camper duties), and work out a rotation system for keeping cabins and unit quarters neat and clean. Present information as the need for it arises. Ears are keener and minds more receptive when an individual sees that what is being presented can be put to use right away. Appropriate occasions will arise to inform your group about such matters as camp traditions, programs, special events, camp government and how it works, waterfront procedures, fire drills, safety and health practices, and sick call.

One of the first things campers may want to do depending on the length of their stay is to make their living area comfortable and attractive. Let them help decide what to do. This worthwhile project might be intentionally planned by having the cabins stripped of decoration to allow newcomers to create their own cabin decor. Energy can also be devoted to sprucing up the unit grounds. Many other improvements will suggest themselves once the campers get started.

Resident Camp Housekeeping

Good housekeeping skills are important for peaceful group living. Many camps have tent or cabin inspection at least once a day, usually unannounced and at varying times, to encourage habitual orderliness rather than a periodic tidying up for an inspection. Cabins or units that have met high standards sometimes are recognized or given an award. Immediately following breakfast is an ideal time for the whole group to straighten up the cabin and adjacent unit area. Campers may also be expected to help out in cleaning up the entire camp. Making a checklist for each job is advisable so campers will know how to proceed. The counselor's attitude toward camp duties is important, and you should pitch in enthusiastically as a role model so campers will follow suit.

Campers may be expected to help with various chores such as keeping unit showers, latrines/outhouses, cabins, unit houses, and the main lodge in order and/or collecting and disposing of trash. Counselors should pitch in when their group is on duty and see that the work is done properly. Cooperate in devising ways to complete the job more quickly and efficiently and discourage tendencies to procrastinate.

Let campers help you work out some equitable way to share camp duties. For instance, you might wish to develop a rotating kapers (duties) chart such as the one shown in figure 7.2, or place slips with the names of duties or symbols for them (such as a fork for dish washing or a broom for cleaning the cabin) in a hat and let each camper draw one out, or conceal them under the campers' plates at the table.

After meals, some groups may be assigned certain duties such as cleaning up the dining room. Some camps may have campers wash the dishes but most camps today

	Aarti	Latoya	Mia	Chloe	Lindsay	Megan	Maria
Clean-up squad—sweep cabin floor	Su	M	Tu	W	Th	F	S
Woodperson—clean out ashes in fireplace, bring in wood	M	Tu	W	Th	F	S	Su
Table setters—set tables and help prepare vegetables	Tu	W	Th	F	S	Su	M
Hoppers—wait on and clear tables	W	Th	F	S	Su	M	Tu
Groundskeepers—clean up campsite	Th	F	S	Su	M	Tu	W
Kitchen police—help do dishes	F	S	Su	M	Tu	W	Th
Unit duty—help at the Unit house	S	Su	M	Tu	W	Th	F

Figure 7.2   A typical kapers chart.

use dish-washing machines to assure that all dishes are properly sanitized. These cleaning or dish-washing responsibilities usually are rotated among groups, or each table is held responsible for taking care of its own things. Dish washing and cleanup need not be dreaded chores. They often become enjoyable group experiences, with campers joking, singing, and telling stories while they work.

Other Camp Responsibilities

Although all counselors want to keep their individuality intact, they need to set an example for the campers. If you wear dirty clothes, skip your shower, or fail to stow your stuff away neatly, what can be expected from your campers? Like you, they should wear clothing appropriate for the weather and the activity. For health and accident prevention reasons, campers and staff should wear shoes in conjunction with camp policies, and these should be appropriate for the activities in which campers are participating.

Being at camp is no excuse for disregarding personal hygiene. A swim is no substitute for a daily shower. Even on backcountry trips, a wash pan can be used if no other facilities are available. Hair should be washed frequently and the counselor should help if necessary. Many campers will be reluctant to use open showers with multiple stalls. Remind them that it is ok to shower with swimsuits on, as long as all parts of the body are getting cleaned and rinsed free from soap and dirt. See that campers use fresh towels and washcloths as needed and, of course, they should never use anyone else's. Toiletries and towels should never be borrowed, and other borrowing should be discouraged and is permissible only with the express permission of the owner. Casually inspect campers daily for cleanliness, and inconspicuously call any deficiencies to their attention if necessary.

Impress upon your campers the importance of washing hands before eating and after going to the bathroom and make sure they brush their teeth each morning and again before bed. The best way to prevent the spread of illness is to wash hands frequently. See that campers put on fresh clothing each day and put their dirty clothes in the proper place. Make sure your campers rotate wearing the clothing they have brought. Young people often have a few favorite garments they put on day after day and never completely unpack all the items they have brought with them. Also, some children may be inclined to stuff wet clothing or swimsuits in a corner, under the bed, or in a suitcase or laundry bag in their rush to get on to something else.

Be wary of bed-wetting that sometimes takes place with younger age groups. If this happens, many campers will stuff the soiled clothing in their baggage to hide it from the rest of the cabin. This situation is very delicate; when addressed improperly it can cause serious embarrassment for the child and the cabin mates. A simple way

to check is to do a bed check each day for grit, feeling at the same time for dampness within the bed linens.

In addition to ensuring personal cleanliness, you must also work closely with the health care staff to protect and maintain the health of your campers. During pre-camp training, you probably will become familiar with the health facilities. Most camps have one or more nurses or health specialists on duty and a physician is usually on call. These health staff are required by ACA Standards (HW-16) to have their headquarters in a health-care center that has ample space for campers who are ill or in need of special food, rest, or care. These specialists will provide the camp staff with special instructions or guidelines to assist them in identifying health problems. Each morning while campers are dressing, eating breakfast, or doing cabin cleanup, you should observe them for signs of illness or injury and note any symptoms or sicknesses such as headache, sore throat, indigestion, sneezing, cough, fever, skin rashes, paleness, swelling, cuts or other irritations, and signs of fatigue such as listlessness, irritability, or excitability.

If you suspect a child is injured or ill, send him or her to the health supervisor immediately. Better yet, escort the person there yourself. A camper sometimes avoids the infirmary from fear that he or she will be prevented from pursuing a favorite activity such as swimming. Show the camper the wisdom of taking a few moments now to prevent the development of an illness that could curtail future activities.

When signs of fatigue are widespread in a group, it indicates an overly strenuous program. Prevent fatigue by alternating quiet and active pursuits, and see that competition is not carried to the point of overstimulation. Be firm about rest times and bed times.

A few common ailments have grave consequences if the infection spreads to others in the camp. Easily transferable illnesses/epidemics can truly disrupt the camping experience for the masses. Contagious illnesses/parasites/bacteria such as pink eye, lice, and staph infections are among the most contagious and easily transferable among children in a camp environment. The setting is conducive to a fast spread of all these ailments. Furthermore, other potential outbreaks exist, so observe your campers for signs of illness each day.

Most camps send a camper home or to the hospital if an illness is likely to last several days or is of a serious nature. However, even minor illnesses may detain the camper at the infirmary for what may seem like many long hours. If those in charge approve, the time will pass faster if a camper's friends make a get-well card, write an original poem, make a small arts and crafts gift, or serenade the ill camper from outside. A visit is welcome if permitted. If not, just waving to him or her through the window helps. The specific gesture is not as important as simply letting the camper know that your group is thinking of him or her.

Safety

Your camp should have an established risk-management plan as well as rules and guidelines regarding safety that you will need to interpret for your campers. ACA Standards require the posting of rules of behavior in all activity areas. More importantly, you will need to develop in campers a proper attitude toward safety and safe procedures. Camp safety standards are based upon long years of experience, as reflected in state and federal law and in the recommendations of authoritative bodies such as the American Red Cross. As a leader, you should respect and observe good practices yourself, which will help elicit a similar response from campers.

Safety does not begin and end with merely obeying established rules. Safety also involves developing an awareness of potential hazards (e.g., keeping a careful eye on children using knives or other possibly dangerous equipment). When you are about to lead your group in potentially dangerous experiences (e.g., going boating or canoeing), try to anticipate any possible hazards and then brief your campers regarding necessary precautions to take. Follow through by preventing needless risk-taking and correcting faulty techniques. If the welfare or safety of anyone is compromised, you must be authoritative, firm, and insist on an immediate response to your directions. Adventurous and challenging experiences are desirable components of the camp experience, but always err on the side of caution. As with many other camp issues, be proactive. A group discussion may enable your campers to devise safe procedures that they willingly follow.

The advice in exhibit 7.2 will help reduce the elements of danger and risk in camp activities and in the camp environment.

Dining Room Procedures for Resident Camps

Entering the Dining Hall

Counselors and campers should arrive on time for meals with their hands and faces washed. Those arriving early often enjoy singing or playing a quick game while waiting to enter the dining room. Some camps have developed a tradition of assembling early to sing or carry on some other activity such as a flag ceremony or inter-cabin competition.

Many different plans exist for seating in the dining area. In some cases, campers and counselors walk in and sit in previously assigned places, or a counselor will lead an assigned group to a table. The group may be the counselor's regular living unit, or a rotating system may be used to enable each individual to widen his or her circle of acquaintances. A less formal procedure consists of having campers enter the dining room first and fill in camper places at tables as they choose. The counselors then follow and seat themselves at tables, making a point to choose a different table at each meal. All these methods avoid the melee that can occur when counselors enter first followed by the campers who often engage in a mad scramble to find seats with the most popular counselors.

Meal Time Procedures

Counselors customarily occupy the places at the foot and head of a table where they can act as hosts, serving the food, seeing that refills are provided as needed, giving second servings as requested, and signaling for the tables to be cleared. In some camps, campers stand quietly behind their benches or chairs until the counselors are seated, then the meal opens with a grace, song, or thought for the day. With younger campers it is better to serve plates family style, since heavy or hot platters often cause accidents when passed around.

Camps usually serve tasty, well-balanced meals that often have been carefully planned by a dietician. These efforts will be wasted, however, if campers are allowed to pick and choose what they eat. Although you must make allowances for food allergies or stipulated special diets, do not accept a camper's word about these since he or she may be using them as an excuse to avoid eating certain foods. Consult the health staff about problems in this respect, and report a child who is absent from a meal to the proper person. You can allow an individual to ask for only a small portion if he or she really dislikes the item, but insist that something of it be eaten. Campers often learn to like something they have never tasted before. Serve small portions, especially to younger campers, encouraging them to clean their plates before asking for seconds. You are doing campers a favor when you encourage them to broaden their tastes and learn to eat a variety of foods. Seconds and even thirds usually are available for those who want them but only after others, particularly slow eaters, have had their fair share. This procedure encourages good table manners.

Promote healthy eating habits among your campers. The best way is to lead by example. Attempt to promote the consumption of a balanced diet rather than one that consists of only French fries or peanut butter and jelly. Many camps today offer healthy options like fresh fruit and a salad bar at lunch and dinner so that campers always have this option. In planning cookouts, explain the necessity of maintaining a varied and well-balanced diet. When children understand the importance of each item, they usually become more cooperative about their eating.

Dining Room Atmosphere

The dining room atmosphere should be one of leisurely relaxation and conversation. A counselor can set the pace by keeping his or her voice well modulated and

---

Exhibit 7.2

Proactive Safety Issues to Consider

1. Do not encourage programs or activities that are too dangerous to be practical. Be objective when evaluating such programs and seek advice when necessary to ensure safety for all participants. Counselors and other camp staff must constantly measure the goals and values they expect to derive from the experience against whether they are worth the risk and the cost.

2. Inspect all equipment for defects before any activity. If a defective piece of equipment could cause injury, do not use it. Likewise, use only quality equipment, use it appropriately and, if it is to be worn as a protective device, be sure it fits properly.

3. Confine your programs to known areas or locations. You should have previous firsthand experience in these areas before the activity begins. If you are embarking into the unknown, the proper pre-trip planning should have presupposed the experience, notifying the program director of your whereabouts, time of departure, arrival back to camp, with the consideration of how to minimize the risks in the situation.

4. Know the camp's emergency plans and practice them to ensure readiness. For example, if your camp has a severe weather plan, make sure you know it long before the severe weather strikes.

5. Recognize that you are not necessarily an ensurer of safety. On the other hand, you are expected to protect your campers against foreseeable harm by performing as a reasonable and prudent camp professional or a prudent parent. Therefore, *reasonable* preparation is needed for activities involving potential risk. The greater the danger or risk, the higher the preparation and care. Your preparation as a camp counselor should be much greater than what is required or expected from campers.

6. Stay current in first aid and emergency procedures specific to the activities that you conduct. Likewise, when conducting activities away from the main camp site, always carry an adequate medical kit (with your campers' medications if the situation necessitates). Keep in mind that activity leaders should know causes and prevention of environmental injuries (e.g., heat exhaustion, dehydration, altitude sickness, snake bites, poison ivy) as well as more common types of injuries. Medical training for an outdoor leader includes advanced first aid and CPR training, as well as possibly a wilderness first aid course.

7. Develop safety rules, policies, and procedures for each activity under your responsibility. A written copy should be kept in the form of a field manual or handbook.

8. The ability to avoid accidents is related to one's physical and/or emotional health. Therefore, to be reasonably assured that your campers are able to withstand the rigors of a particular activity or program, you should know about their general level of fitness, overall health status, and previous experience or performance in similar types of activities. Medical exams, experience records, and a conditioning routine can be helpful and possibly should be required from participants. With this type of information, experi-

enced camp counselors often can accurately assess those campers most likely to avoid accidents and those who are more susceptible to accidents. For instance, a person who is fatigued, stressed, or depressed might be more prone to an accident. Campers who are fearful or timid need special encouragement and attention.

9. Follow or exceed the industry safety standards and instructional practices. To achieve this objective, however, you must know the standard safety practices and adjust them to the camp activity.

10. Participation should be in accordance to abilities and readiness for the activity. Do not encourage campers to seek out activities that are too far above their abilities. Consider screening and ability grouping and, for activities with potentially high risk, establish qualifying programs or prerequisites. To gage a camper's state of readiness for an activity and to match skill and challenge difficulty, the counselor must attempt to analyze the camper's performance to learn as much as possible about his or her baseline experience, physical condition, and awareness of risks.

11. Skills should always be taught by proper progression of difficulty (e.g., in a rock-climbing program, first teach knots, then belaying skills, then climbing techniques).

12. Always use proper safety procedures. Instruct participants regarding the activity's proper safety procedures and know and perform the "duties" that are inherent in the activity. For example, correct belaying is a duty inherent in the activity of rappelling. Requiring the use of life vests is an inherent duty in boating activities. Be sure campers appreciate the risks involved in violating safety rules and practices. Enforce the rules and always lead by example.

13. Your ego should not get in the way of good leadership. Attempts to impress other staff members or campers, or to live up to some real or perceived expectations can lead to problems. Do not give false qualifications or profess competence, expertise, and knowledge you do not possess. Likewise, do not guess. When the safety of others depends on the accuracy of information you provide, make sure it is correct. If you do not know, say so.

14. Develop safety consciousness within your group of campers and encourage self-reliance. Encourage participants to be fundamentally responsible for their own safety and to rely on their own abilities. Do not create a false sense of security by inviting them always to rely on you, even though you are always responsible.

15. Prevent reckless action by keeping campers under control. Do not let anyone act or use equipment in a way that may create an unreasonable danger to others. Enforce discipline. Horseplay has no place when serious injury or life may be at stake.

16. Remember that all the risks of camping and the outdoors cannot be completely eliminated, even with proper care and supervision. Nevertheless, do your best always. Do any action or activity you undertake to the best of your ability.

by trying to introduce topics of general interest instead of letting a few monopolize the conversation. These conversations can provide good social training, as each camper learns to respect the right of the person speaking to finish what is being said before adding his or her own comments. Keep your voice low as an example. When a few individuals or a whole table becomes boisterous, others must raise their voices to be heard and soon the whole dining room is an uproar that is anything but relaxing. You may want to inconspicuously seat a shy or unpopular child next to you during the first few meals to draw that person out and give him or her self-confidence.

Camps have different ways of calling for silence when an announcement is to be made. Some have a pleasant chime, which is certainly better than banging loudly on glasses or the table. Another method that proves quite successful is for the person wanting attention to merely raise a hand and then each person nearby raises his or her own hand and stops talking as soon as the signal is seen. This presumes the idea of "hand up, mouth shut." When all hands are up, everyone is ready to listen.

Good Table Manners

Observe all the basics of good table manners. Everyone at a table should, for example, wait to eat until all are served. No one but *hoppers* (i.e., the individuals responsible for bringing food to the table) should leave the table until all are ready to go. Remind campers about such common table manners as not playing with utensils while waiting to be served, not to talk when the mouth is full, to cut meat a piece at a time as it is eaten, to handle knife and fork properly, and to chew food with the mouth closed. Complaints about the food and bickering at the table make it hard for everyone to enjoy the meal, so nip this in the bud. Do not publically draw attention to a camper who has violated good etiquette. It is usually better to discuss it with him or her privately. Such lapses are more likely to result from a lack of training, being ill at ease, or a desire for attention rather than intentional misbehavior. In addition, consideration must be given to differences in children's eating habits and cultural backgrounds.

After Eating

Each camp usually has a system for clearing tables. Commonly, serving dishes are removed first. When all have finished eating, campers pass their dishes to the counselor at the head of the table who scrapes them, stacks them neatly, and signals the hopper to clear them from the table. Most camps forbid taking anything edible from the dining hall except on certain occasions when specific permission is given.

Singing songs, especially those requiring movements, distracts slow eaters and interferes with clearing tables, washing dishes, and putting food away. It is probably better to wait until tables are cleared and then engage in a songfest led by a designated song leader. Obviously, no activity should be scheduled too soon after the meal to prevent campers from racing through the meal to get on to something else.

Each camp usually has a system for clearing tables. The schedule for hoppers indicates which group is responsible for clearing dishes on a particular day. (Keystone Science School, Keystone, Colorado; Photo by Joel Meier)

Eating Between Meals

Camp meals should be substantial enough to satisfy normal needs, and campers are consequently not encouraged to supplement them with between-meal soft drinks, candy, and other goodies that may offset the good effects of the carefully planned diet. When snacks are permitted, a limit is usually set on the daily amount and when the snack shop is open. If campers are truly hungry, usually the cook staff can provide a piece of fruit or some healthy snack to tide them over until the next meal.

No matter what steps the camp takes, it seems that many parents must demonstrate their love by sending their children treats from home. Some camps warn parents before camp that such food will be confiscated. Encourage parents to substitute fruit or small items such as a piece of camping equipment if they feel they must send something to show their affection.

Campers readily understand the reason for not keeping or eating food around living quarters when you point out to them that ants, flies, mice, raccoons, possum, and other unwelcome "guests" will be attracted by the crumbs.

Rest and Sleep at Resident Camps

Rest Hour

Busy camp life makes campers and counselors thankful for the rest hour, which usually comes after lunch to rejuvenate them for the remainder of the day. Campers can sleep or engage in some quiet activity such as reading, writing letters, telling stories, playing quiet games, or working on a craft project. It may be desirable to stay with your campers to see that they observe this period, and set an example by observing it properly yourself. Your camp may choose an individual name for the rest hour, such as Siesta or FOB (Feet on Bed and Flat on Back).

Sleep

Camp life is strenuous. Campers (and staff) who get plenty of sleep can keep up and enjoy it to the fullest. As a general guideline, the following amounts of sleep (in addition to the one-hour rest period) are recommended:

Ages	Hours of Sleep
6–8	11
9–11	10½
12–14	10
15–17	9
Staff	8

Children, like adults, differ in their reactions to the excitement and activity of camp life. Some campers may need to rest over and above this amount. Others can do with less.

As previously mentioned, a common mistake has been to try to crowd too many activities into the camp day. The smart camp programmer tries to adopt the saner practice of spreading special events over the session so that campers can leave camp rested and healthy instead of completely frazzled.

Bedtime

The period just before bedtime usually provides one of the best opportunities for developing group rapport. After routine hygiene tasks, plan to leave a few minutes for group activities, such as a discussion period, planning future activities, inactive games, a quiet bedtime story, stargazing, singing, or listening to soft music before lights out. Creating the right atmosphere just before your campers go to sleep is important. Do your best to answer campers' questions, to get to know them, and encourage them to get some rest. Avoid roughhousing, exciting games, or scary stories; otherwise you will have difficulty getting them to quiet down and go to sleep. Take time to participate with them wholeheartedly instead of hurrying them into bed to squeeze out more time for yourself. Taps, however, should be an enforced signal for lights out and absolute quiet beginning the first night at camp.

A designated rest hour provides an opportunity to either sleep or engage in some quiet activity.

Other Considerations

Visitors' and Parents' Days

Each resident camp has its own policies regarding visitors' and parents' days based upon its own philosophy, the length of the session, the nature of the camp, camp activities, and the ages of the campers. Visitors are always a disturbance to the smooth-running routines of a camp and, for this reason, some short-term camps discourage or prohibit visitors, or plan to carry on their regular activities so that interference is minimized and visitors get a better picture of regular camp operation.

Long-term camps of six to eight weeks sometimes set aside specified hours and days for visitation and encourage family and friends to come in the belief that it boosts camper morale and satisfies natural parental concerns. Many camps plan special events for these occasions such as horse shows, aquatic activities, campfire programs, and sightseeing tours around the camp grounds. If parents must travel a great distance, the camp sometimes sends them advance information about places nearby where they can stay overnight. Inviting parents to eat in the camp dining room or at an outdoor cookout helps avoid the problem of parents who want to take their child out of camp to eat, which is a practice most camps discourage.

Having visiting days or having parents in camp is fun for the children, but it can create problems for young people who do not have visitors. They need your special attention so they will not feel left out. One way to do this is to keep these campers busy by using them as guides to escort parents to their child's living unit or to help prepare for the coming program. You can also encourage campers to include friends without visitors in some of their activities, although they should reserve some time to be alone with their parents.

Successful visiting days require careful planning and preparation. Meeting campers' families lays the groundwork for better understanding on everyone's part. Since you have been serving as substitute parent, friend, and guide to each camper of your group, you will have at least one very important thing in common with parents—the welfare of their child. Parents have a deepened sense of security when favorably impressed by their child's counselors. Be diplomatic in talking with them, remembering that the center of their attention is their child. Comment positively about any good points, achievements, or signs of improvement you have noticed, but be sincere in what you say, since most parents are fully aware that their children fall short of being perfect. Since many camps wisely prohibit monetary and expensive gifts to camp personnel, you should closely adhere to the camp's policy on accepting tips from parents.

As guests leave at the end of the day, you may be faced with emotional reactions by campers, some of whom may even want to return home with their families.

Planning exciting activities to follow parental departures to regain campers' attention and reestablish the normal tempo and atmosphere of camp life is important.

Communicating with Home

Several common methods are used for communicating with parents at home. Whether it be through the use of the Internet, text messaging, or traditional mail, parents, friends, and campers alike appreciate correspondence with one another.

Each camp probably will have its communication policy, which may require that campers write home regularly or send an e-mail. Some camps leave communication up to the discretion of the camper. No matter what guidelines are established, you will find it advantageous to encourage your group to set aside time for this activity. You may be called on for guidance, especially to help your younger campers spell difficult words and master the essentials of good letter writing. Suggest topics to write about such as the activities they have been engaging in, the new skills acquired, new friends, the food, and the weather. Encouraging them to write about the positive side of camp life keeps them from recounting minor grievances and incidents that often are only products of the moment and will be forgotten soon.

Records and Reports

You may be asked to keep various records concerning your campers. Although these chores may seem tedious and a waste of time, they actually are important and take only a few moments if you keep up with them. They serve to give the camp director and head counselor a composite picture of what is really happening throughout the camp, and this information sometimes proves to be quite important later on.

Written reports mean different things to different people and you should never regard them as just busy work. Unfortunately, counselors are sometimes not told the ultimate purpose of these records and the exact information they should include. Ask for more information if you feel you need it. Here are a few simple basic rules to follow in writing reports:

1. Try to be *completely objective* and *impartial* in every statement made. Report the facts, not your interpretation of the facts.

2. Record all observations *accurately* and *correctly*. It is better to omit something than to risk being incorrect in important details.

3. If an incident with a camper has produced a strong emotional reaction in you, delay recounting it until you have had time to calm down and look at it objectively.

4. It often helps to include a brief description of the background or social setting in which certain actions took place.

The reports that the sponsoring agency, camp director, or head counselor send to parents or headquarters are based partially upon your evaluations. Therefore, completing reports in an honest, objective, and thorough manner is important.

Staff members are commonly asked to make a written report of any accident or injury to a camper, no matter how trivial. Counselors are usually furnished with a form on which to do this, which should be filled out as soon as possible following an injury and before you have forgotten exactly what happened. Be accurate in your report, and provide detail about what happened and what actions you took—this will become extremely important if later complications or questions arise. Be sure these reports are filed in the appropriate place. The paperwork may be necessary to sort out an issue at a later date when you are back at school or unable to be contacted.

You may also be asked to submit certain reports at the end of the season, such as inventory of the equipment and supplies in your unit or cabin, or an activity with which you have worked, together with recommendations for additions or changes for next year. Again, devote time and thought to the procedure. It will be instrumental in helping you or your successor do a better job next season.

Time Off

All camps give counselors some time off—usually several hours each day and/or a longer period each week or every two weeks. The ACA Standards require at least two hours a day in resident camps and a 24-hour period every two weeks. This interlude can and should be of great benefit to both the counselor and the camp. Dealing with many personalities can deplete physical and emotional energy and cause patience to grow short. Counselors sometimes are unaware of a gradual accumulation of emotional and nervous fatigue and become so attached to their jobs that they are reluctant to leave them, even when given time off. Such overdevotion to duty can be a mistake, and sooner or later it will reduce job effectiveness.

Camp staff should get away from their job responsibilities and their campers for an adequate time. The purpose of time off is for you to return rested and with renewed enthusiasm. You must plan so that this purpose is accomplished. During daily breaks you may be allowed to use camp equipment and facilities for your own leisure time enjoyment. At other times you may plan to be away from the camp for a visit to a nearby community. When out in public, remember that you represent your camp and should dress and conduct yourself accordingly.

Personal Habits

All ACA accredited camps require that counselors who smoke or use smokeless tobacco do so in designated places, but never in front of campers. Such requests are not based on moral issues, but reflect the example that a sincere counselor would want to present in view of the well-known medical findings concerning the health dangers of smoking as well as in recognition of the fire hazard created by indiscriminate smoking. The use of alcoholic beverages is generally prohibited on the camp site, even when all campers are away, and sometimes prohibited on time off. If you drink during your time off, it is not wise for you to come back to camp with a hangover. You have an enormous responsibility when on duty so you need to be as alert as possible. It should go without saying that the use of recreational drugs is inappropriate as well as illegal.

Loyalty

You owe loyalty first, last, and always to your camp and camp director. Most likely you initially chose a camp because it seemed compatible with your objectives and ideals. However, as in any situation, you may find things that are not to your liking. Keep your opinions to yourself and think them over for a few days—you will likely see the situation in a different perspective as camp life unfolds and you get a better picture of the whole scene. If your problem still seems important, do not complain or talk to others who are as unable as you to interpret things from a different perspective or to do anything about them. Instead, go to someone who can provide the right context, such as the camp director. If you still cannot accept or adjust to the situation, consider asking for a release from fulfilling the rest of your contract. You and the camp may be better off parting company. Never, under any circumstances, criticize the camp to outsiders or other counselors, and, of course, never do so in front of campers. Even when started as good-natured small talk, griping will sooner or later hurt morale and also will reflect negatively on you.

Counselor-In-Training Programs

Many camps conduct counselor-in-training (CIT) or Leader-in-Training (LIT) programs designed to prepare older campers for possible future positions as full-fledged counselors. Candidates are usually 16–18 years old and have had several seasons of successful camping experience. Although they sometimes admit outsiders, many camps use the training program as a means of "growing" some of their own future staff members by choosing outstanding campers with definite leadership qualities and abilities. Being chosen as a CIT is an honor since stringent requirements usually are formulated and only those former campers who are deemed worthy of consideration as future staff members are admitted. Each camp has its own standards, rules, regulations, fees, and course content, but most have similar objectives in mind.

The CIT course is carried out on the camp site during the regular camp session and may last over two seasons to do justice to all the material to be covered. It is conducted by one or more trained leaders who are familiar with the purposes of the program, their responsibilities as instructors, and proper course content and teaching methods. A sample four-week CIT schedule appears in figure 7.3.

A well-conducted CIT program provides an opportunity for the discussion of such topics as camp philosophy, history and development, objectives, program and activities, and the growth and behavior patterns of children at different ages, as well as their varying individual needs and how to understand and meet them.

The program also permits participants to enjoy satisfying experiences with peers while observing the workings of group dynamics. Further, it gives older campers the opportunity to perfect or learn new skills and to increase their appreciation of and sense of security in the outdoors. A good CIT program allows participants to work with campers so that they can apply and practice directly the techniques and skills they have been studying. As their skills develop, they are allowed to assume increasing responsibility by assisting in planning and carrying out such camp activities as evening programs, cookouts, song leading, initiating games, planning activities for rainy days, assisting in special areas such as aquatics or arts and crafts, and sometimes living with and working closely with counselors and their cabin group under close supervision and with the guidance of an older, more experienced person.

Although CIT training involves hard work, the trainees usually find it enjoyable. They usually receive special privileges such as living in their own cabin without a counselor, developing and enforcing their own codes of behavior, and planning their own social programs. CITs often set the tone of the whole camp and inspire others by their youthful enthusiasm and upbeat personalities. Their special status in younger campers' eyes constantly challenges them to set a good example by adhering closely to all camp rules and regulations. Because of their proximity in age, their young protégés often adopt them as models and try to emulate their behavior and attitudes. The CIT program is an important professional undertaking and can be fun and rewarding to the individuals involved. See appendix C for more information on CIT programs.

Top Counselor Responsibilities

A number of duties and procedures have been suggested in this chapter. Future chapters will talk more specifically about working with campers, but Friedman (2010) presented the Top 10 Cabin Responsibilities that counselors should consider. These responsibilities also apply to day-camp counselors even though they may not be in a cabin:

1. Explain your reasons for accepting responsibility for campers' care and safety.
2. Define your expectations of acceptable group behaviors and consequences for noncompliance.
3. Establish the adult (parent substitute) relationship.
4. Learn the individual needs of each camper.
5. Establish an individual relationship with each camper.
6. Know in advance of any physical and emotional issues of campers.
7. Observe and report any inappropriate behaviors.
8. Put the needs of your campers before those of yourself.
9. Serve as an appropriate role model 100% of the time.
10. Request immediate assistance when you are unclear about how to react to a situation.

	MONDAY	**TUESDAY**	**WEDNESDAY**	**THURSDAY**	**FRIDAY**
Week 1	• Icebreaker or game • Review CIT/JC Manual expectations • Introduce learning-to-teach activities	• Crushes and personal issues • Sexual abuse and contact	• Teambuilding activities • Technology cautions	• Emergency procedures • Health care with camp nurse	• Trip requests • Evening event planning • Choose theme night • Begin planning
Week 2	• Lesson planning • Intentionality • Risk management	Theme night planning	Behavior management	Creating cohesive cabins	Changeover procedures
Week 3	Prep for theme night	Process theme night	Child development	• Trip requests • Evaluations	Perfect counselor activity
Week 4	CIT/JC trip expectations	All-day trip visiting other camps	• Process trip • "Camp in 10 years"	Teambuilding	Closing activity

Figure 7.3   Four-week counselor-in-training schedule.

REFERENCES

ACA Accreditation and Standards. (2010). Retrieved from http://www.acacamps.org/accreditation

Ball, A., & Ball, B. (2004). *Basic camp management: An introduction to camp administration* (6th ed.). Martinsville, IN: ACA.

Friedman, N. (2010, May/June). Top 10 cabin counselor responsibilities. *Camping Magazine, 83*(3), 16.

PRINT RESOURCES

ACA. (1996). Selected summer staff resources. *Camping Magazine, 68*(6), 34–35.

Aycock, K. (2009, May/June). Chance vs. choice. *Camping Magazine, 83*(3). Discusses making deliberate choices about everyday activities, thus ultimately requiring less effort for routines.

Aycock, K. (2010, May/June). Big deal or no big deal: A framework for co-counselors. *Camping Magazine, 83*(3), 70–75.

Brandwein, M. (2003). *Learning leadership: How to develop outstanding teen leadership training programs at camp.* Martinsville, IN: ACA.

Coleman, J. (2009, May/June). The power of camp. *Camping Magazine, 83*(3). Offers tips for being an effective counselor.

Fleischner, D. (2003, May/June). Opening day blues. *Camping Magazine, 76*(3). Describes a walk-through of the first day of camp and how to handle situations.

Grayson, R. (2001). Successful counseling. *Camping Magazine, 74*(3), 24–26.

Leiken, J. (2007). Seven absolutes of camp counseling. *Camping Magazine, 79*(3), 3.

Leiken, J. (2007, May/June). Bringing professionalism to camp counseling. *Camping Magazine, 80*(3), 30–32.

Schafer, E. (2009, May/June). Do it your way. *Camping Magazine, 82*(3). Suggests that understanding your own personality can maximize your talents as a counselor.

Wallace, S. (2006). Rites of passage: Camp pays off in youth development, happiness, health, and safety. *Camping Magazine, 79*(3), 1–5.

Wallace, S. (2007, May/June). Under the influence: Respect, responsibility, and the conduct of camp counselors. *Camping Magazine, 80*(3), 20–22.

8

Understanding Human Development

To be happy in this world, people must be able to get along with others. People who say they do not care what other people think of them are almost always covering up deep disappointment and frustration by pretending to reject what they really desire—the respect and affection of others. Getting along well with others is most important to camp counselors. Counselors will not be happy or successful in influencing campers unless they gain respect, admiration, and cooperation.

The three main components of camp life that have a major effect on the camper's growth and improvement are (1) the camp environment or facilities, (2) the camp program; that is, what is done in camp, and (3) the camp leadership and personnel. The last component is by far the most important of the three. Not only do camp staff influence campers by their actions, words, and example, but also by their skills within the camp environment and with the program. To function most effectively in this role, counselors must understand the needs of campers and how to satisfy them. Counselors who try to promote positive camper behavior and attitudes must consider the ways they can influence others.

How to Influence Others

Assume you have a mental picture of what you want to accomplish and are trying to find a way to induce campers to comply with your objectives. One way is to order the campers to do what *you* want, and perhaps threaten to withhold something *they* want (such as a regular swimming period) if they disobey. This approach may bring about the desired action, but it is not likely to encourage lasting improvement in the campers' behavior. As soon as the threat is removed, the campers proba-

bly will revert to their earlier behavior and may even resent the experience so much that they behave worse than before. The experience may also teach them to dislike and resist authority and anyone who symbolizes it. Campers may rebel inwardly, but from fear will keep their feelings bottled, gradually building resentment. Some individuals eventually may come to hate whatever activity you had ordered them to do, despite their initial feelings toward it, because of the coercive nature of the whole experience.

A better method to accomplish your goals is to persuade people to act in a certain way because *they* want to. Almost everything people do is a response to a need or want. For instance, a person goes to bed because he or she needs to rest, eats because of the taste of food or to satisfy hunger, or works to buy things with the money earned. People practice long hours on sports skills because they want to be good athletes or because they seek the social prestige that comes from playing on a team. Trying to persuade others to do something because *we* want them to is futile, especially if they have no interest in it. People, including campers, are primarily motivated by their own needs and desires.

A camp counselor must be able to recognize the genuine needs and interests of a camper rather than simply impose his or her values on that individual. Instead of manipulating campers to get them to do what you want, consider how you can work with the campers to achieve goals and aspirations. The relationship between camper and counselor requires feedback, including a two-way flow of information and ideas. This process allows the leader to recognize the wants and needs of the followers and then plan activities and programs that help to meet these needs. This quality in a leader comes about with an understanding and knowledge of people.

Almost all people are selfish to some degree and often more interested in themselves than in anyone else. Therefore, lasting changes in other people's behavior can be made more successfully when they realize that changes will satisfy their wants or needs. For instance, suppose a camper wants to pass an endurance test in swimming to qualify for a canoe trip. He or she probably will follow recommended guidelines for eating and rest if it is understood that these are essential for swimming endurance. The outcome and the attitudes of campers will be much better if generated by this process than if the counselor tries to force adherence to the requirements. Although this example is somewhat simplistic, it does illustrate the positive rather than the negative approach to a problem, and how to use self-motivation to accomplish objectives or achieve desired actions. This approach works, but counselors must practice the technique and use it skillfully. The important point is to *help people to do those things that will satisfy their needs or desires.* Different needs and desires are evident in all people.

The Fundamental Desires

People are different, but they are also alike in many ways. Five desires (sometimes called needs or wishes) are common to nearly every person. Though these desires vary in intensity, they are usually so strong and compelling that almost anything a person does is an attempt to satisfy one of these needs. Well-adjusted people find ways to fulfill their desires in a socially acceptable manner. When they cannot do so they may resort to unacceptable ways. Compelling inner demands require fulfillment, no matter how accomplished. When attempts to satisfy needs are carried to antisocial extremes, socially unacceptable or criminal behavior may result.

The Need for Affection

One powerful wish is to be accepted and regarded affectionately by friends and associates. Fulfillment of this basic desire can come about when campers feel their peers have accepted them in a friendly way. The longing to be loved, appreciated, needed, and missed is universal. When satisfied, people experience a feeling of well-being and contentment. When unsatisfied, people are lonely and unhappy. Therefore, counselors must be alert for the camper who shows dislike for the group or who does not want to mix with other campers. The chances are that this person really is miserable and longs to be accepted. A counselor may need to exercise tact and persistence to penetrate the "wall" that this person may erect, but when successful, a happier, better adjusted camper will emerge.

From the first day, counselors' efforts to build group morale and a feeling of unity and camaraderie are aimed at helping each newcomer feel wanted and accepted. Spe-

The need for affection is a basic, universal desire. (Photo courtesy of Bradford Woods Learning and Outdoor Center)

cial attention may be given to shy campers who are more difficult to get to know by counselors as well as other campers. Some campers will fit into the group much easier than others, with greater acceptance from the group as a whole. The job of a leader and counselor is to work with those campers who do not easily "fit in" and search for good points to help that person assimilate into the group. Find out why a camper is disliked or ignored, then use your interpersonal skills to help remedy the situation.

The camp program should be broad and varied enough to provide for every camper's interests and abilities—whether as an athlete, a musician, a social planner, or crafter. A thoughtful counselor can find many ways to satisfy campers' desire for attention: giving a friendly "hello," a willingness to listen to their achievements, a pat on the back and a "well done," a bedtime story, or a moment spent asking about the activities of the day.

When you notice children who need help, spare their pride by using an indirect, tactful approach and unobtrusively devising ways to draw them into the group. Occasionally a counselor might approach the problem directly and have a frank talk with the isolated camper. Such conversations must be handled skillfully; the goal is to help the person realize that his or her own actions cause others to avoid his or her company. On some occasions, especially with more mature groups of children, it may be best to choose a time when the troubled camper is absent to discuss the situation with other campers. They often can help by making a special effort to include him or her in the group. Most children basically are sympathetic and good-hearted and will change their behavior when shown how their thoughtlessness is hurting someone else. Tolerating and forgiving the shortcomings of others are desirable traits to cultivate, and an alert counselor can do much to facilitate campers' awareness in this area.

A serious case of maladjustment or a continued failure to fit in may necessitate referral to the camp director or head counselor. Leaving the situation to staff with insufficient training and experience often only compounds the problem. Sometimes transferring the camper to another cabin is possible, but should be a last resort. Better results occur when a counselor can help the child confront and solve the problem rather than run away from it.

The Need for Achievement

Everybody wants to count for something in this world. The need to be successful and to have others believe in you is universal. Campers achieve satisfaction when they learn to master a physical skill or to discipline themselves to finish a challenging project. Learning to master the backstroke or catching and cooking one's own fish dinner are examples of such achievements. Opportunities to perform in a leadership role also provide campers with a constructive outlet for demonstrating control over a situation. Satisfaction may be realized when a camper serves as chairperson of a committee, steering it to successful conclusion of its duties or persuading others to see his or her way of thinking during a group discussion. On the other hand, a bully may exercise misdirected power and try to control others through intimidation, or may try to dominate or do the thinking for weaker followers.

The need to achieve can be satisfied in part by an individual's participation in activities that allow him or her a degree of success and personal enjoyment. A feeling of accomplishment gained from one task can be a powerful spur to further accomplishments. Consequently, broad and varied camp activities must be provided that are appropriate to the skill levels of different age groups. A camper can suffer frustration and disappointment when asked to compete with older campers who are more experienced, or who have more ability. Carrying competition to extremes is counterproductive. One alternative is to de-emphasize competition or to reasonably control it. Another possibility is to provide activities that are self-testing, which allow individuals to compete against themselves. For example, bettering a previous performance or passing standardized tests in activities such as swimming or canoeing are self-testing. The key is having a program that includes something in which *each* camper can experience a satisfactory degree of success.

The Need for Security

The need for security includes freedom from fear, apprehension, danger, insecurity, and pessimism. People want to feel safe and secure in their surroundings and with their associates. Campers, particularly those away from home for the first time, miss their familiar routines and ways of life. They may be inexperienced in playing and living with other children their own age and associating with unfamiliar adults. In situations like this, a camper's security seems threatened, especially if others make rude remarks, show outbursts of temper, or appear to be angry. Such responses from fellow campers or staff members can hurt a person's ego and reduce his or her confidence and optimism. A young camper may respond by running to someone else for sympathy, or may retreat into a shell and brood. The overall effect of a threat to a camper's security may be a bad case of homesickness or even more lasting problems. For instance, some children who are constantly worried and afraid may react by stuttering, wetting the bed, fighting back, criticizing others, or engaging in malicious gossip.

Several responses can add to the camper's sense of security. Be friendly and pleasant, but be firm when the need arises. Above all be consistent; a counselor who is full of fun one minute and angry or temperamental the next will certainly not give campers a sense of security.

Encourage your campers to talk freely with you and feel flattered when they disclose their emotions. Never betray their confidences or let them overhear you discussing their personality or problems with others. Establish yourself as a reliable friend to whom they can feel free to communicate their hopes and dreams as well as their worries and concerns.

The Need for New Experiences

The desire for new experiences is basic to all humans. All people need opportunities in their lives for thrill, excitement, and adventure. Although opposite to the need for security, the desire to do something different and to experiment in unconquered fields is a strong drive. When it is denied too long it can cause boredom, bad temper, and poor behavior. Varying camp routines and letting campers assist in planning their own programs—including suggesting new and exciting things that interest them—helps satisfy this need.

Keeping campers busy at activities that give them a feeling of accomplishment is one of the secrets of a successful camp. Being in an outdoor environment naturally provides plenty of new opportunities, but many other activities can give campers a chance to try something new, like camp plays, dancing, or art projects.

Another consideration is to avoid unnecessary rules and regulations that impede or prohibit opportunities for campers to fulfill their need for adventure. In some cases, camp programs are so formal or so structured that participants are not allowed adequate freedom to express spontaneous behavior.

The Need for Recognition and Approval

The need for recognition includes a desire to be accepted by adults and peers, to be noticed and gain attention, to receive praise, and to achieve status, prestige, and distinction. Every person wishes for and seeks ego support and social approval.

Like everyone else, a camper has a deep-seated desire to stand out as an individual and to do at least one

Camp is a great place to experience the excitement of trying new activities. (Photo courtesy of American Camp Association)

thing better than anyone else. Campers will work diligently to run faster, swim further, swear more fluently, make more noise, or do whatever it takes to get attention. From early childhood, this deep urge drives some people from one field of endeavor to another in search of activities in which they can excel.

Often a camper's reluctance to engage in an activity is based on a fear that he or she cannot do it well. For instance, a person's reluctance to go in the water during a swimming period may stem from self-consciousness about a lack of ability that is heightened by teasing from fellow campers or a counselor. The camper's attitude may change to one of tolerance or even enthusiasm if a counselor offers a compliment or suggestion that boosts the camper's confidence. To work successfully with young people—or with people of any age—you need to remember that praise produces better results than criticism. As we've all heard, "You can attract more bees with honey than with vinegar." Praise campers frequently, but avoid overdoing it or giving praise when none is deserved. Kids are quick to detect insincerity and consequently will lose respect for you.

Most young people desire to be accepted by their peers and receive recognition from them for their accomplishments. Sometimes the camp program can be rearranged to make use of a talent not called for by the regular routines. A quieter child who does not easily make friends could possess a special ability in art or music, and may really shine when given a chance to demonstrate those special skills or talents. For example, a camper named Jean had an outstanding trait in her ability to make more noise than anyone else. Her counselor, realizing that her frequently annoying behavior was in reality an unconscious attempt to get the personal attention she could get no other way, decided to stage a contest to see who could yell the loudest. Jean won as anticipated, and achieved her place in the limelight.

Campers would prefer to have *favorable* distinction if they can get it. However, their desire for recognition is so strong that they sometimes will go to almost any length to satisfy it, and will settle for unfavorable attention if necessary. The actions of the constant troublemaker or camp comic may be explained in this way. He or she can at least achieve some distinction and would rather be known unfavorably than be treated as a nonentity. Nevertheless, troublemakers often have a sense of inadequacy and unhappiness, and a counselor can help by showing them how to achieve distinction in a more satisfactory way. No quick cure can be expected, but you have to start somewhere.

Meeting Needs and Desires

All people exhibit both good and bad behavior. When children behave badly, it is usually because they have not found a satisfying and socially acceptable way to fulfill one or more of their basic needs. Therefore, when trouble arises, seek and eliminate the cause. Basic desires, needs, and wishes are strong motivators of behavior. Most people want to fulfill these needs in positive ways; others may need more guidance.

All people want a sense of well-being and of living at peace with themselves and the world. Well-adjusted individuals recognize their strengths and weaknesses. They have learned to expect and accept disappointment in life but have kept their sense of humor and can laugh at themselves. They like people and have learned that it is wiser to emphasize the good traits of others than to look for faults. They are friendly and outgoing, but not artificial. They are cheerful and optimistic, yet recognize and meet problems and take constructive steps to solve them instead of wasting time in ineffective worry and indecision. What is perhaps most characteristic of well-adjusted people is that they have gone beyond childish self-interest and have developed a concern for others and a desire to use their emotions, time, and talents in ways that make the world a better place in which to live.

Basic Emotions

To work with campers and to understand oneself as a counselor requires an understanding of basic needs as well as emotions such as love, fear, worry, inferiority, anger, and jealousy. *Love* can be of several types and is one of the universal aspects of normal development. It begins in the young child with self-love, and later grows to include affection for family, for friends, and then intimate love for another individual.

Fear is characterized by dread of impending harm to one's physical or emotional well-being and makes individuals want to either fight or flee from whatever threatens them. Fears generally are learned reactions since most babies have no fears. A swimming instructor may be faced with a camper who is afraid of water yet wants to learn to swim, or a counselor may have a camper who is afraid of the dark and loudly protests when lights go out at taps. A certain amount of fear is normal and important, since it causes people to temper actions with caution and to avoid taking reckless chances. However, children as well as adults sometimes have unreasonable or unduly magnified fears that may have developed from past traumatic experiences or from observing other people's fear. Fears may also result from exposure to too many violent or scary media images.

Worry is a form of anxiety about possible future events. Though sometimes related to dread of a specific thing or event, worry is often quite vague and is merely a general feeling that something bad may happen. Some children are constant worriers and may manifest such symptoms as insomnia, indigestion, nail-biting, or bed-wetting. Chronic worriers often have deep feelings of insecurity and inferiority. Counselors' efforts to help young people feel valued and wanted may result in cessation of these often seemingly unrelated worries.

Inferiority feelings probably are present occasionally in everyone. Even some of the most outwardly self-confident people confess to having butterflies in their stomachs from time to time regardless of the activity. Some campers, however, experience such feelings almost constantly and in nearly everything they do because they are convinced that they are inferior to their associates either physically, mentally, or socially. A counselor can help address these inferiority feelings by helping children and youth find activities that they can do well and then trying to instill confidence to do well in other activities.

Anger usually results when one's plans or desires are thwarted. A camper may respond to such frustration by throwing a temper tantrum or by screaming, biting, crying, or throwing things. The child may have found these tactics to be effective in getting his or her own way in the past and may have practiced them so often that they have become almost unconscious reaction patterns. A counselor can help the camper acknowledge his or her anger and find ways to address it through other behaviors such as talking it out, or attempting to modify the situation causing the anger.

Jealousy results from the actual or feared loss of the affection of someone close, such as a parent or friend, or

the failure to attain some goal that the individual prizes, such as winning a tennis match or being elected to an office. Jealousy is often directed at the person who did win the coveted goal and may cause the jealous person to intensely dislike and even belittle the winner. Feelings of fear and inferiority usually accompany jealousy. People with these jealousy feelings often respond in ways that promise the most satisfaction and pleasure. They may show some of the symptoms of a chronic worrier in an effort to gain the sympathy and attention they crave. Such behavior should not go untreated or without attention. Do not hesitate to solicit the help of other professionals at camp to address severe jealousy situations.

Developmental Characteristics

Each counselor and camper has emotions and a unique personality created from genetic background and the totality of experiences and knowledge absorbed from their environments. No person is average, but average or typical characteristics of people can be discussed. These typical characteristics represent basic patterns that can be related to individual personalities. Understanding the stages of maturation and patterns of growth and development of children and older campers can help counselors design meaningful programs for them. Keep in mind, however, that not all characteristics of these age groups apply to all campers.

Campers Age 6 to 8

This period might be termed the *individualistic period* since a child's thoughts are still largely self-centered with only a superficial and transitory interest in others. A friend may be completely spurned or disliked one minute and accepted again as a best friend a short time later. Children of this age often show more interest in pleasing adults than in pleasing their contemporaries. They can be easily motivated to demonstrate desirable behavior by praise or other signs of approval.

Children in this age group tend to be physically active and cannot be restrained for long. Their interests are keen but fleeting, and they may suddenly drop a project or game in which they have been absorbed and clamor for something entirely new and different. They are impulsive, highly unpredictable, and also like to be first and to win. Their imaginations know no bounds and much of their free play involves make believe or fantasy. They love, for example, to creep through the woods acting like a dinosaur and yet only moments later, transform themselves into astronauts piloting their space shuttle towards the moon.

Encouraging 6–8-year-olds to try their skills in many areas and to sample everything to discover where their true interests and abilities lie is important. Although they

Campers age 6 to 8 have wonderful imaginations and much of their free play involves make-believe or fantasy. (Photo courtesy of Bradford Woods Learning and Outdoor Center)

are greatly excited about trying anything new, their physical coordination is not fully developed and their endurance is poor. Control over the finer muscle activities is often poor, so concentrating on painstaking and exacting tasks can be tiring and unsatisfying. Simple large-muscle activities such as running and jumping are, therefore, best. These children also need to be protected against overexcitement and fatigue, which tend to interfere with their getting sufficient rest and sleep.

Campers Age 9 to 11

Campers from 9–11 years are beginning to prize the approval of their peers above that of parents and other adults. At the same time, they are entering the age of hero worship and may adopt some adult, perhaps a famous athlete or even their camp counselor, as a model for patterning their behavior. They seek a close relationship with one or two special buddies and share closely-guarded secrets. These children have abundant energy. A counselor needs to watch them closely for signs of fatigue or overexcitement and make sure they observe rest hour and get adequate sleep.

Children in this age group have a good sense of humor, although it may be of the slapstick variety. At times they can be quite talkative, sometimes imagining or exaggerating things. Their interests are many and varied and they often are intent on learning everything they can about the world and enjoying their surroundings. They are far less concerned with their personal hygiene or keeping their cabins tidy. They want to know the "why" of everything and will take something apart to figure it out. They like to read, but at the same time enjoy being outdoors.

The improved coordination and muscle control of 9–11-year-olds enable them to acquire new skills like tennis, swimming, crafts, or the use of simple tools for outdoor living. They enjoy working in a group on such activities as planning a skit, an outdoor cookout, or a project for their group or cabin. They have a tendency to throw themselves wholeheartedly into a new task and will work furiously, but after a day or two may lose interest and abandon the project even though not yet finished.

Campers of this age may be prone to bragging or exaggeration. However, a counselor should avoid responding with sarcasm. These tendencies may indicate an underlying lack of confidence and a desire for attention. This age group is striving to grow up and exercise more independence, and consequently will resent it if an adult is bossy or dictatorial. A friendly approach that attempts to elicit their cooperation by "let's" instead of by direct orders usually is more productive. Their imaginations are active and they usually find doing things much more fun when they can picture themselves as a character from a TV show or movie.

Campers Age 12 to 15

This 12–15 age group can be referred to as the *group age* because self-interests are now becoming subservient to a deeper loyalty to the group, squad, crew, inner circle, or gang (used loosely to refer to a team and not a bunch of criminals). Desire for the approval of the group is usually so strong that to be different or to stand out from the rest is a source of embarrassment. The majority of youth want to act and dress as nearly alike as possible, even to the extent of engaging in antisocial behavior or wearing

Campers age 12–15 have deep loyalty to the group and a keen desire for the group's approval.

spection. Predicting what any camper will do or say next is difficult. Whether this period with its rapid change of moods, interests, and physical development is harder on the camper or on those around him or her is hard to say. Girls often become self-conscious about their changing physical appearance, while boys may be embarrassed by their changing voices. Arms and legs lengthen and hands and feet rapidly increase in size, which may leave the young person feeling awkward. Puzzled by these rapid physical, emotional, and social changes, a young adolescent often covers up self-consciousness by loud talk and laughter and general boisterousness. These campers need self-assured role models and someone to confide in, and a counselor can be instrumental.

Campers or CIT Staff Members Age 16 to 18

Older adolescents are nearing both physical and mental adulthood and the rapid changes taking place may both embarrass and puzzle them. They are gregarious by nature, anxious to achieve a level of status and acceptance with their peers. They usually conform to whatever is currently popular in matters of dress, language, or behavior within the group with whom they identify (e.g., jocks, band nerds, geeks, goths). They sometimes may sacrifice their own personal standards if group approval demands it. The combination of peer pressure and the older teenager's desire for new experiences often provides the impetus for experimentation with tobacco, drugs, alcohol, or other forms of risky behavior.

Their maturing sexual development intensifies their quest for sex information, and they are much more interested in sex and in seeking social contact. Dating is common because it provides status and desired companionship. Some members of this age group have a surprisingly casual attitude toward sex.

Campers or CIT staff of this age want to be accepted as thinking, self-reliant adults by other adults. They often resist suggestions or advice from elders or those in positions of authority. They are in a transitional stage in which they are no longer children but not yet adults. Striving for identification as persons in their own right, these 16–18-year-olds struggle to resolve the conflict between what adults expect of them, what they expect of themselves, and especially what their peers expect. They want adults as well as their peers to take them seriously. They want to respect themselves as people who matter, and if they fail to achieve recognition in accepted ways they may be inclined to find less desirable means for their expression.

This stage often is a period of idealism and of wanting to participate in social causes to "save the world." These older adolescents are interested in a variety of topics, including those of national and international scope as well as topics of a religious and philosophical nature. Group discussions and informal discussion sessions are popular. Participation by older counselors who have had

outlandish clothing. A counselor should not forcibly try to stop this tendency—young adolescents usually resent authoritative methods and their antagonism can be easily aroused. The best approach may be to try to employ peer pressure in constructive ways to further camp objectives. A camper of this age is anxious for independence but must be encouraged to recognize that more independence always brings increased responsibilities.

This loyalty to and enthusiasm for working as a group, plus a growing ability to discuss and see several sides of a question, make this age an ideal time to give campers more responsibility for planning their own program and working out common problems. Encouraging camper leadership is essential whenever it can be done safely. Campers in this age group can accept responsibility as individuals and as team members, and should be encouraged to recognize their responsibility for and obligations to others.

These young adolescents are often at a stage of acute hero worship and *crushes*. The choice of the right role models can be a powerful force for good. Campers admire thoughtfulness, self-sacrifice, bravery, and honesty in their models, and they themselves (even though sometimes protesting) want to be held to high standards, with reasonable rules and regulations consistently and fairly enforced. Counselors must avoid the mistake of striving for personal popularity by being overly lenient or by trying to be one of the group. These young people will take advantage of this mistake and may lose respect for counselors in the process.

These 12–15-year-olds will vacillate between clowning around and showing off and moodiness and intro-

interesting experiences is welcome. A sense of values and standards is rapidly taking form and these young people can be a challenge to camp counselors.

Campers and young staff of this age crave adventure and activities that challenge their growing skills and ability to plan and solve problems. To retain this interest, a progressive program is necessary that is free from repetition of activities of previous years. Camp counselors need to acknowledge the power of self-direction among these older adolescents by letting them play a major role in program planning and camp policies. A minimum of guidance is still necessary, however, since these fledgling adults are inclined to fluctuate between their new-found maturity and their former immaturity. Their help can be enlisted in planning longer events and trips, more elaborate unit improvements and outpost activities, coed activities, and opportunities to explore and satisfy individual interests and developing skills. Many camps have found that a counselor-in-training (CIT) or junior counselor program is highly effective with campers of this age.

Campers Are Individuals

The summaries just provided are generalizations of typical characteristics of children according to age. Changes do not occur because of a birthday. Development proceeds at different rates in different individuals and even in the same individual. For example, a child may suddenly increase in height and weight while remaining relatively immature emotionally and socially. A 12-year-old might have the physique of a 14-year-old, a 10-year-old's mentality, the social skills of a 9-year-old, and the emotional development of only an 8-year-old.

Campers usually are placed in living groups according to such factors as chronological age, camping experience, and school grade in an attempt to obtain as homogeneous a grouping as possible. However, counselors will undoubtedly see great diversity within an age group due to variations in personal development.

Similarities exist among individuals, and yet no one in the whole world is exactly like anyone else. Each person's personality results from his or her particular heredity, environment, and associates. Even during a young camper's short lifetime, she or he has been in contact with hundreds or even thousands of people, situations, and experiences, all of which have influenced the individual. The importance of developing what can be called a *good personality* cannot be overestimated. It opens many doors to individuals and helps them fit happily into society by fulfilling basic needs and desires in socially acceptable ways. Everyone recognizes someone with a good personality, but actually defining a good personality in specific terms is challenging. Generally, **personality** refers to the general impression a person makes based upon such diverse qualities as general appearance, facial ex-

Campers achieve fulfillment when they can assert their own individuality while still being accepted by their peer group. (Photo courtesy of American Camp Association)

pressions, voice, choice of vocabulary and manner of speaking, manners, and, most importantly, how a person reacts to others. Personality development—for good or bad—is an ongoing process.

A counselor must be mature enough to understand and accept each camper and encourage them to be individuals rather than try to change them to fit into a common mold. Individual camper personalities can be shaped by others. However, individuals attain a feeling of fulfillment when they can assert their own individuality while still conforming and adapting enough to be accepted by the group.

Counselors often notice and perhaps give more attention to confident, outgoing children due to their capacity to successfully approach new situations, their sense of security, and their eagerness to accept responsibility. Counselors need to concentrate attention on the quiet campers who tend to shrink into the background and are often subservient to others to please them and gain reassurance. All children need understanding and encouragement to help them recognize and develop their unique qualities and contributions as they develop their personalities.

Counselors must recognize that children will respond differently to efforts to help them reach their potential. Some will respond well to suggestions and encouragement. For others, you must be careful about pushing them beyond their capacities. Thus, working with children requires determining the proper proportion of pushing and restraint with each camper.

How Learning Takes Place

A number of approaches and tools exist to assist in determining how to best work with campers of all ages. Behavior management and other psychological tools are available to counselors to use in specific situations. These principles can be referred to as **laws of learning**. Camp leaders who are aware of these principles are better prepared to understand camper behavior and to react to it appropriately to encourage camper learning. For the most part, application of these principles involves common sense, but the theoretical area of human behavior is complex. To master the techniques, they need to be understood and practiced. The strategies include laws of exercise, readiness, effect, and reinforcement.

1. *The law of exercise* states that people learn by practice. Repetition produces habits. Campers learn what they practice or repeat, including bad actions as well as good ones. Each time bad habits are exercised, they become more difficult to break. However, practicing good techniques also reinforces their value. This law also suggests that discussing virtues such as kindness or honesty will not necessarily alter conduct if they are not accompanied by practice. A counselor could explain how to build a campfire but until it is practiced successfully by campers, they will not really understand how to build a fire in the future.

2. *The law of readiness* maintains that when someone is ready to act, doing so is satisfying. In other words, when campers are not ready to learn an activity, forcing them to learn will likely cause resistance and a lack of interest. Individuals differ greatly in what interests them. Consequently, learning generally will not take place and certainly will not last unless a basic physiological or psychological need for the person to learn exists. Campers may only be enthusiastic about an activity if it seems enticing, desirable, or necessary to them. Effective leaders can take advantage of those times when a camper is in a proper frame of mind for learning and is motivated and ready to learn. This time is often referred to as a **teachable moment**.

3. *The law of effect* states that people repeat those things that they find satisfying and avoid those that are dissatisfying. Thus, if campers are going to form good habits, they should experience satisfaction or enjoyment in the things they do. Fortunately, most of what children do in an organized camp program is fun and, consequently, satisfying to the individual. Even so, counselors must do what they can to assure the internal satisfaction of each camper so they can use the skills they learn at home.

4. *The law of reinforcement* states that when satisfying conditions follow a response, then the bond between the stimulus and the response is strengthened, which increases the probability that the response will recur. Behaviors that are positively reinforced or rewarded are more likely to recur. If the behavior is not rewarded, it is not as likely to be repeated. Reinforcement is one of the most important principles for changing people's behavior, and often it is not practiced enough by those in leadership positions. Reinforcement can be used to maintain or increase appropriate behavior as well as to eliminate inappropriate behavior.

All these laws suggest that performance will not improve unless an individual understands that what he or she has done is right or wrong. Without feedback, improvement in learning may not occur. Knowledge of the effects of performance functions to reinforce whatever behavior or action resulted in the improvement. For example, if a person were blindfolded and then asked to shoot an arrow at a target, there would be no improvement in skill (no matter how many times it was attempted) because there would be no visual clue regarding where the arrow might land. The same idea applies to learning social behaviors. A child who wants to make friends might take actions or make comments that will gain attention and approval. If the action or comment elicits positive reactions such as smiles, friendly comments, and the like, such positive feedback or reinforcement will probably encourage the camper to repeat the same actions or behavior. On the other hand, if the other campers pay no attention or respond negatively (e.g., making derogatory comments or facial expressions that show disapproval), the original behavior might be altered until approval is received. If behavior is not rewarded with reinforcement acceptable to the individual, then the likelihood of the behavior being continued is reduced.

The Psychology of Learning

The laws of learning provide a basis for understanding how people learn—both formally as well as informally. Other strategies are worth consideration whether you are formally teaching an activity or informally talking to a camper.

Three major theories of learning (Schafer, 2004) are particularly applicable to teaching in camp:

1. Active learning is better than passive learning.
2. Spacing learning out is better than cramming it into one session.
3. Personal relevance must be created.

Most people do not enjoy being talked *at*. They would rather be talked *with*. Thus, *active learning* must be interactive. It also must include a logical sequence. Any teaching session should include three parts: (1) tell them what you are going to teach them, (2) teach them, (3) review what you taught. The teaching is obviously the major part of the experience, but people need to have a context for what they are going to learn and then also need to be reminded of what they have learned.

Tate (2006) described professional learning strategies that can engage the brain. Camp provides many active opportunities where these strategies can be employed in teaching:

- Brainstorming and discussion
- Drawing and artwork
- Field trips
- Games
- Visuals, charts, pictures
- Humor
- Hands on activities
- The use of metaphors (e.g., X is like . . .)
- Use of movement
- Music, rhythm, rhyme, or rap
- Project-based experiences
- Peer coaching and cooperative learning
- Role plays, drama, pantomime, charades
- Storytelling
- Journaling or writing

The second theory described by Schafer (2004) is spacing out learning. You cannot teach something effectively in one long sitting. Cramming is seldom a good way to learn and retain information. Therefore, short sessions with opportunities for campers to try out skills as well as think about what they are learning may be a far better way to teach. Teaching requires using a variety of techniques to introduce skills or concepts in small chunks, and then linking these segments over time.

For learning to be effective, it must have a context. People remember things better when they matter personally and when they can be applied to real life. We earlier referred to the idea of a teachable moment. When a camper asks a question, he or she is intent on the answer. Therefore, answering a question or exploring a topic as it is raised is an important way to make learning relevant. This idea of a teachable moment is applicable whether during a formal session of teaching or in an informal conversation. The more you incorporate specific examples and not just abstract ideas, the more likely campers are to learn not only about facts or skills but also about appropriate behavior that matters to them.

Muchnick and Bryan (2010) describe how camps can be a place to focus on *positive learning*. They recognize that learning is a social and personal experience. Learning occurs within the space of a triangle with the teacher (i.e., counselor), learner (i.e., camper), and the material to be learned. They also indicate, as do others, that learning encompasses more than academic subjects but also includes sound, space, movement, interpersonal relations, self-knowledge, and nature. Although some learning occurs naturally in camps, counselors should also consider what they can intentionally teach to help campers learn about themselves, others, and the world around them.

Behavior Management

Behavior, thus, is based on human needs and desires, emotions, typical characteristics, and learning. **Behavior** can be defined as any observable and measurable act, response, or movement by an individual. To maintain a positive environment, everyone attending a camp must behave together in a cooperative manner. Good behavior is desired in all campers. Unfortunately, not everyone is friendly and well-behaved. Dealing with the misbehaviors demands the best from camp counselors. Even the most experienced staff member can be challenged when dealing with a difficult child. Nevertheless, behavior management techniques exist that can be applied in camp situations. Some techniques depend on time and experience to be fully developed. However, an awareness of useful techniques should increase the confidence of any camp counselor.

Many different approaches can be effective in working with campers as well as staff. Several examples are provided in this book, but you will need to determine a style that works well for you. Ditter (2009) has written a great deal about counseling skills and problem-solving. He suggests that there are three basic tools and four procedures that are essential.

The basic tools are validation, listening, and inquiry. *Validation* is the most critical skill as it acknowledges the feelings, opinions, or stories of others and helps them to feel that they have been heard. Validation might include acknowledging their feelings (e.g., "I can see how angry you must be"), courage (e.g., "I respect your honesty in telling me"), their positive attempts to handle something (e.g., "I know that you really wanted to help"), and your contribution to the problem (e.g., "I apologize because I did not understand how upset this made you." You do not have to agree with the feelings, but you must establish a relationship first.

The second tool is *listening*. Listening is a skill that must be developed. Frequently people are so anxious to talk that they do not take the time to listen. People also tend to talk too much, which inhibits listening. Listening can often be done best in a private place. Be open and interested in what the camper has to say. Your body language is an important indicator of how well you are listening.

The third tool is *inquiry*. You need to get good information before you can help a camper. You must assume the role of a detective or scientist. However, you do not want to pressure an individual. Try to approach children as if they were the expert on their behavior. Use follow-up questions and make them as open-ended as possible. Ask, "What was it about the evening that was scary" rather than "was it scary" or "why was it scary?"

Ditter (2009) cautions that it is important to know how to use these tools—when to validate, when to ask a question. To manage camper behavior, he suggests four procedures: joining, setting the table, behavioral planning, and follow-up. *Joining* means that you are signaling to the camper that you are a friend. *Setting the table* refers to determining with the camper what the expectations for behavior are. *Behavioral planning* is the practical aspect of identifying specific strategies to shift behavior. Getting the child's input is important. The final procedure is *follow-up*, where you set a time to check back in and talk to the camper to assess the success of the plan.

Contain-Discuss-Plan

Another successful example of a positive behavior plan, presented by Cohen and Carlson (2007), is labeled contain-discuss-plan (CDP). This approach is based on a philosophy of assuring the emotional and physical safety of everyone at camp and believing that all campers want to do their best. The approach is aimed, as are all approaches, at helping the camper be successful. It focuses on setting up the environment for program success (i.e., proactive strategies) and intervening quickly.

CDP includes three aspects. When a negative behavior occurs, the camper is contained, which means the staff member increases physical proximity, notices behavior, and tries to slow the behavior. Discussion is used to seek the camper's view and understanding of the behavior and why it occurred. It requires reflecting and accepting feelings and providing an adult perception of what took place. The exact behavior is identified and named. The final component is to agree on a plan for avoiding future problems. The child has input, but the plan must also be realistic and age appropriate. As part of this third step, it may be useful to actually practice the planned behavior for the future.

Empowerment and Self-Regulation

Other behavior management strategies include empowerment and self-regulation, which are implied in the suggestions already presented. These facets promote the idea of an individual recognizing the appropriateness, or inappropriateness, of certain behaviors and adjusting to what is acceptable within the camp community.

The ideas of self-regulation and empowerment are closely connected. Campers must learn the relationship between stimulus and their actions. They are fully capable of deciding what to do in the most appropriate manner, and thus, carry out the most acceptable reaction/behavior for the situation. Being able to regulate one's own behavior and feeling empowered to make decisions can be a great benefit for both the individual and other campers. Promoting individual empowerment and self-regulation can be the catalyst for long-term behavior management by the individual.

Although no one changes behavior overnight, self-regulation can be promoted and encouraged throughout a camper's stay at camp. Camp counselors use several techniques for promoting self-regulation.

- Model self-control and self-regulation in words and actions when in a frustrating situation.

- Provide structure and predictability. Too much freedom and flexibility is more likely to lead to uncontrolled behaviors. A balance of freedom and structure would likely benefit campers learning their self-regulation abilities.

- Anticipate transitions and announce changes in the upcoming schedule so that campers can adjust to changes internally as well as externally.

- Reward children with good self-regulation capabilities the freedom and flexibility that offers opportunities for spontaneous fun. The concepts of behavior modification may work in conjunction with supporting self-regulation.

- Try to identify the most impulsive campers and attempt to match them with others that exhibit a high level of self-control who can be role models.

- Remember that campers who may be impulsive and aggressive can create an atmosphere of chaos and fear that inhibits the capacity of others to enjoy the experience. Do not be afraid to immediately redirect inappropriate words and actions. Your actions will make the rest of the campers feel safer.

- Seek help. Don't be afraid to ask other staff members and camp personnel for advice and assistance with specific campers.

- Be sure to communicate calmly and directly with the camper, noting examples of both the appropriate and inappropriate behaviors.

Behavior Modification

Another aspect of behavior management is external *behavior modification*, which involves the application of procedures designed to change behavior. Understanding introductory techniques of behavior modification can provide staff with helpful facilitation procedures when working with campers (Dattilo & Murphy, 1987). The appropriate application of these procedures can help camp staff more effectively encourage individuals to properly interact with other individuals and participate in enjoyable camp activities.

Behavior modification concepts originate from the belief that behaviors are learned, rather than inherent, and that behavior can be altered or modified by additional learning. **Target behavior** is a behavior that is the focus of programmed efforts aimed at alteration or modification. Behavior modification does not attempt to explain behavior by analyzing a person's impulses or influential internal causes of behavior. Thus, the behavior modification process concentrates specifically on the *observable* behavior that an individual exhibits.

The first step in changing a behavior is to make an accurate observation. The next step is to accurately describe the behavior using behaviorally specific statements that depict explicit actions or overt behaviors. *Overt behavior* is observable and measurable. Behaviors can be identified with the five senses. For instance, behaviorally specific terms that might be used to describe someone's explicit behaviors or actions include: laughs, runs, smiles, screams, cries, kicks, throws. If done correctly, the descriptors or labels used are not subject to different interpretations. In contrast, terms that are subject to different interpretations of behaviors or feelings include: lazy, polite, depressed, selfish, industrious, upset, indifferent, obstinate, angry, anxious, sad, apathetic. These terms are not applicable descriptors because they do not describe directly observable or measurable behaviors.

A critical next step in behavior modification is reinforcement, which was discussed briefly earlier in this chapter. Any object, event, stimulus, or condition that increases the frequency or duration of a behavior is **reinforcement** for that behavior. The reinforcement is positive if it involves the delivery or presentation of a consequence that is desired by the participant, after the participant has engaged in the appropriate positive behavior. In other words, something that is desired by the individual has been added to the situation. Reinforcement is negative if it involves the elimination or postponement of something from the environment after the participant has engaged in the inappropriate behavior. In either case, the behavior of the individual is strengthened.

Positive reinforcement can be practiced in many ways. For example, a counselor's reinforcement might involve smiling, winking, or using words of praise when a camper performs a task correctly. If the camper begins performing the task correctly more often, the counselor's actions would be identified as a positive reinforcer.

Wide individual differences exist in the reinforcers that are effective with different children, and the rewards used can take many forms. Achievement can be recognized through awards such as prizes or through a few words of praise or commendation for a task well done. Supportive statements such as "good work," "well done," "fine effort," and other praise often can be more meaningful than a tangible award. However, specific praises should be given for a specific action such as "good job on cleaning the cabin" or "you did a nice job in archery today."

Campers also can gain rewards from the satisfaction they get from carrying out a project from start to finish or from knowing that they have done something worthwhile. Regardless, alert counselors can do much to discover opportunities to give campers positive reinforcement.

A few additional ideas about the type of behavior to reinforce as well as the timing and frequency of rewards may be helpful:

1. Keep in mind that any type of behavior that is reinforced will likely be repeated. Therefore, concentrate on rewarding only good behavior or performance.

2. Appropriate behavior should be reinforced *immediately* or as soon as possible after the behavior takes place.

Immediate reinforcement is more likely to be associated with the appropriate behavior for which it is given. As noted earlier, the person receiving the reward must be able to recognize what performance warranted it.

3. Initially, desired behavior should be reinforced each time it occurs. Once established, however, the best method for assuring that the behavior is sustained is to provide reinforcement at variable intervals or intermittently rather than each time the behavior takes place.

4. When using positive verbal reinforcement, you should do more than simply offer praise alone. Your comments are of greater value if they contain language which comments on the child's experience: "You must feel so proud" (encouragement) vs. "I'm so proud of you" (praise). Further, the encouragement should be specific: "You kept going, even though you were tired" vs. "good job."

5. Consider offering praise in private. If encouragement takes place in front of peers, it can be embarrassing to the recipient. More importantly, peer response can be crippling. It has been shown that when two students perform the same task with the same effort and only one is praised, peers view the one given attention as having lower ability. Therefore, your best option may be to offer praise in private.

Punishment

Punishment is another behavior management technique that is used to weaken or eliminate an inappropriate behavior. Punishment is presenting a consequence that is considered aversive to the camper. Punishment may be in the form of scolding or reprimanding the camper, giving the person extra responsibilities, or doing some other activity that he or she does not like to do. For example, if Jeff is late to the flag-raising ceremony, the counselor may speak sternly or reprimand him. If Bobby is talking during group instruction time, the counselor may make him stay during free time to pick up all the equipment and put it away. If Jane uses profanity, the counselor may make her write a letter to her parents explaining what she said and why.

Punishment should be used sparingly and only after all other courses of action have been tried and have been found ineffective. Since punishment often results in a relatively rapid decrease in the target behavior, the possibility exists that it may become a procedure that is too readily applied when another procedure might be more appropriate. Nonetheless, although the punishment procedure has certain limitations and disadvantages, there are occasions where its use is justified.

Several useful techniques related to punishment can be used in camps and other programs. For example, *time-out* is the process of removing a camper from a reinforcing environment when he or she exhibits inappropriate behavior to decrease the future occurrence of that behavior. Time-out refers specifically to a fixed period of time that an individual is placed in an environment that is less reinforcing than the previous environment. For example, if Johnny exhibits unsportsmanlike behavior while playing volleyball, the counselor may make him sit on the sideline and watch for four minutes.

When using time-out, provide the individual with the opportunity to return to the program as soon as possible. Most successful time-out procedures do not need to last longer than five minutes since the length is usually not that meaningful to the child—what is important is that the time-out takes place. Keep in mind that the greater the contrast between the time-out and the original environment, the more successful the attempt at reducing a behavior. Consequently, make the environment used for time-out as nonstimulating as possible. Another suggestion is to reinforce the camper's appropriate behaviors once the youngster returns to the original environment.

In addition, time-out can be used as a warning. Address the child by his or her first name, state the unwanted behavior clearly, then state the warning about a time-out (Ditter, 1990). For instance, during a swimming lesson you could say: "Jim, if you keep splashing Sally, you might have to take a time-out." In follow up, if Jim stops splashing, it would be good to praise him for the right behavior.

Although no counselor wants to use punishment when dealing with behavior issues, situations may arise that warrant it. Make sure that you as a counselor remain calm and steady in all your interactions, and make sure communication continues between the camper and the counselor as behaviors are managed. Different approaches to behavior management may work to varying degrees with individual campers, but make sure you are fair in your deliberations. Also, if you run into problems, keep in mind that experienced staff members can often suggest helpful techniques. Since no one has all the answers to handle behavioral problems, it is also important to realize that in some cases you may not be fully qualified to deal with the predicament. When confronted with such a situation you should not hesitate to ask for help or make a referral to others within the camp organization who have more experience in handling behavioral problems.

An effective camp counselor must know as much as possible about campers and treat them as individuals. As noted earlier, information can be gained through parents, organizational records, health records, discussions with the camper, observations of the camper, and observations of the camper's peers. This information coupled with behavior management tools can help to assure a positive camp experience for all campers. Keep in mind that behavior management includes praising good behavior as well as finding ways to mitigate unacceptable behavior.

REFERENCES

Cohen, A., & Carlson, K. P. (2007). Developing positive behavior at camp: Contain-discuss-plan. *Child and Adolescent Psychiatric Clinics, 16,* 859–874.

Dattilo, J., & Murphy, W. D. (1987). *Behavior modification in therapeutic recreation: An introductory learning manual.* State College, PA: Venture Publishing Company.

Ditter, B. (2009, Jan/Feb). Martin and his friends: Counseling skills that effect change in camp. *Camping Magazine, 82*(1), 60–64.

Ditter, B. (1990, May). In the trenches. *Camping Magazine, 63*(4), 9.

Muchnick, B. S., & Bryan, P. S. (2010, May/June). Positive learning. *Camping Magazine, 83*(3), 64–69.

Schafer, E. (2004, Nov/Dec). The psychology of learning and behavior management: What it means for camp and staff training. *Camping Magazine, 77*(6), 18–24.

Tate, M. (2006, Jan/Feb). Sit & get won't grow dendrites. *Camping Magazine, 79*(1), 34–37.

PRINT RESOURCES

Leiken, J. (2006, May/June). Seven absolutes of camp counseling. *Camping Magazine, 79*(3). Provides seven tips for camp counselors in working with children.

Schottenfeld, A. (2001, May/June). Words of encouragement to the camp counselor. *Camping Magazine, 74*(3). Offers general tips for living and working with campers.

Thurber, C. (2010, May/June). Cracking children's secret code. *Camping Magazine, 93*(3), 56–59.

Wallace, S. (2010, May/June). Confessions of a disciplinarian. *Camping Magazine, 93*(3), 30–37.

9

Counselors as Group Leaders

Camp experiences can provide participants with benefits that come from working, playing, and living together in an outdoor setting. Nevertheless, these positive outcomes do not occur automatically. A camp's mission, philosophy, organization, and staff must create a favorable climate for desirable camper participation and positive growth. Therefore, counselors must make good use of the leadership opportunities provided. Leadership skills provide the tools for working with campers. Understanding what leadership is and how to develop leadership skills is necessary.

Leadership is defined in many ways. For example, Albert Schweitzer said, "Example is not the main thing in influencing others, it is the only thing." John F. Kennedy stated that "Leadership and learning are indispensable to each other." Bill Gates has suggested, "As we look ahead into the next century, leaders will be those who empower others." The common thread woven through most definitions is that a leader helps people move toward goals and facilitates change in their behavior. For purposes related to camp, a **leader** is someone who uses his or her influence to reach goals that address individual needs and desires while also achieving the aim of a group or organization.

Elements of Dynamic Leadership

Every group of individuals that acts together has a leader, either someone who spontaneously emerges as a leader or who is elected or appointed. Furthermore, the ability to exert positive leadership is not automatic by virtue of the position. Group members may feel they have to defer to a leader, but they actually may be influenced to a much greater extent by someone who has no official leadership status at all. This unofficial leader is often a member of the group who, because of personality and behavior, is able to bring the group together and influence its members' point of view.

As a camp counselor, you have a chance to demonstrate leadership by guiding your group into constructive activities. Although you will be teaching skills and performing many other duties, your most important contribution will be helping your campers develop a positive attitude and problem-solving abilities, and to appreciate the value of their camp experience.

Before becoming a good leader, you should learn to be a good follower. Even when you are a follower rather than the designated leader, you can do a great deal to assure the success of the group. Through practice, most counselors have already acquired the skills of living congenially with a group. This usually necessitates a spirit of cooperation and teamwork. Good group members work with their colleagues or peers and are willing to sacrifice their own wishes for the best interests of the group.

Whether in a camp setting or anywhere else, an ideal leader possesses the ability to mold a group into a well-coordinated team with each member contributing according to individual ability. In any group, however, personality clashes and conflicts inevitably occur, since many personalities and individual desires are involved. Nonetheless, a camp leader must create an environment in which a spirit of harmony and cooperation prevails most of the time. In a camp setting, group spirit should deepen and strengthen as goals are achieved and each successive project is completed. Group spirit, however, should never be allowed to reach a point where it creates an unfriendly rivalry with other groups or a willingness to sacrifice the welfare of the whole camp.

Developing excellence in camp leadership has challenges. Three specific challenges have been described by Shelton (2006). One is a lack of training. Leaders are not born, but are made. Therefore, the more you can learn about and practice effective leadership, the better you will become. A second challenge is personal leadership qualities. You must be able to evaluate yourself and look for ways to improve. The final challenge is feedback. Feedback is essential for improvement. Camp can provide a great way to gain training, experience, and feedback to improve leadership skills.

Shelton (2006) also suggests several additional strategies for leadership development. First, a counselor must establish a personal definition of leadership. Hopefully some of the examples in this chapter will help you consider your qualities and how you can use them to be an effective leader. The second is a formal feedback process, which ideally would include feedback from your supervisor as well as from your co-counselors and the campers with whom you work. Third, you need ongoing skills development; that is, learning as much as you can about leadership and practicing people skills such as self-awareness, empathy, and credibility. Finally, you will need to continually evaluate your environment and the opportunities you have for leadership. You are familiar with the idea that "practice makes perfect" but keep in mind that the better idea might be "perfect practice makes perfect."

As a leader, you will not only learn to understand and guide individuals, but also develop techniques to deal formally and informally with a group as a whole. Keep in mind that leadership and authority are not necessarily the same. For example, a boss drives people; a leader coaches them. A boss creates fear; a leader inspires enthusiasm. A boss says "I"; a leader says "we." A boss knows how something is done; a leader shows how. A boss says "go"; and a leader says "let's go."

Types of Leaders

Although leadership is a complex concept, three basic types of leaders exist: (1) **autocratic** leaders make all important decisions themselves as suggested in the boss example above; (2) **laissez-faire** leaders are almost the exact opposite; they are overly lenient and allow their groups to decide everything for themselves, doing whatever they wish with a minimum of interference; and (3) **democratic** leaders, who assume control and apply discipline on the few occasions when it is necessary. They ordinarily influence their followers through the respect and confidence they engender in the group. Democratic leaders motivate their followers through their personality and values, as well as by demonstrating skills in planning and working cooperatively with the group. Most leaders at camp fall somewhere between being autocratic and democratic.

The Autocratic Leader

Autocratic leaders single-handedly decide which activities, goals, and procedures the group will pursue, and then draw step-by-step instructions for others to follow. They seldom consider the opinions or desires of their campers or of staff under their supervision. Such leaders believe in their own judgments and decisions, and they seldom seek advice or help. They feel that they know what is best for everyone and are therefore justified in enforcing their mandates on the campers. These heavy-handed methods of control permit no lapse of discipline or questioning of authority. This leader may threaten punishment for all dissenters and nonconformists.

If used to extreme, autocratic tactics accomplish little permanent good since good behavior compelled by fear or force lasts only while the leader is present. Some people will respond to such a leader with passivity and subservience and may become so dependent that they lose the ability to make decisions for themselves. Others react by resisting or rebelling, and often develop an intense dislike for discipline and authority of any kind or from any source.

Under an autocratic leader, groups have a tendency to be more dependent and submissive and tend to show less individuality than those under other types of leadership. Although autocratic methods may sometimes be efficient or even necessary—such as during an emergency—they should not be used habitually since they reduce the initiative and creativity of those subjected to them.

Unfortunately, an autocratic leader sometimes assumes these dictatorial qualities unconsciously in a mistaken belief that such conduct is expected of a leader to indicate that he or she is forceful and strong. In reality, this type of leader could potentially be covering up deep-seated feelings of insecurity and inadequacy for which bossing others seems to compensate. For such people, the autocratic style often satisfies an unhealthy desire for power over others.

The Laissez-Faire Leader

Laissez-faire leadership is almost the exact opposite of the autocratic leadership style and consists of almost no authority or leadership at all. People who use the laissez-faire leadership style mistakenly believe that a group can become independent and self-reliant only through *complete* self-direction. These leaders realize that a group of campers should develop a friendly, cooperative spirit, but believe that such unity and happiness are produced only when people are entirely free to do as they please.

Counselors who subscribe to this method may (1) be trying to be popular by going along with whatever the group suggests, (2) lack an understanding of their leadership role, or (3) may be truly disconnected from the organization's mission and purpose. Although the laissez-faire individual initially may be liked, the group will soon lose respect for such a person when members recognize his or her weakness and lack of direction and leadership ability. Children subconsciously expect their appointed leader to be stronger and wiser than they and to act in a dynamic and positive fashion. Although they frequently protest against it, most children want and often need a certain amount of structure.

When campers are left entirely on their own to work out a program, their inexperience and limited awareness of possibilities can result in a pointless and fragmented approach that results in disappointment and boredom. Groups under the guidance of a laissez-faire leader often deteriorate, sink into indifference, and become apathetic. These groups often accomplish little unless a strong informal leader emerges from the group.

The Democratic Leader

The democratic style of leadership is often called *shared* or *participatory* leadership. Someone who uses this style of leadership has mastered the art of working *with, for,* and *in* the group without losing control of it. This person has successfully balanced the desire for fun and good times with the need to be firm and exercise control when necessary.

The democratic leader works cooperatively with the group by encouraging campers to express their views and to participate in planning the program to be extent that their ages and abilities permit. However, progress can be slow using the democratic process since explanations, discussions, and group action take more time than in an autocratic system. Even so, the democratic leader realizes that campers can grow and mature only by solving problems for themselves and that what campers learn is more important than the material things they accomplish.

The focus of a democratic leader is to develop a democratic group. A democratic group is one that has learned to work together cooperatively while initiating, conducting, and evaluating its own goals or program. This group is willing to accept and abide by the results of its own decisions. Citizens in a democracy must be willing to accept group decisions and do their share to carry them out. The democratic leader acts as an adviser and guide who helps when needed and ensures that responsibilities and privileges are distributed equitably.

Many counselors think they are using democratic planning with their group by holding perfunctory discussions with them but allowing them little real control over decisions. When real democratic procedures exist, all participants have a chance to express themselves and share in the decision-making processes of the unit, group, or camp either directly within the group, or indirectly through representatives on the unit council and all-camp council.

Which Leadership Style Is Best?

According to the definitions of leadership, the laissez-faire leader is not really a leader since few efforts are made to influence others or move campers toward common goals. Therefore, only two basic leadership styles exist: autocratic and democratic. These two styles can be used in a variety of combinations, and the decision as to what combination to use should depend on the situation or the need.

Involving participants in the democratic process is one of the major values of organized camping. Therefore, campers should be involved in the participative or democratic decision-making process as much as possible. On the other hand, sometimes a camp counselor must be fully in control by exerting total authority in decisions. At times a counselor may be torn between exerting *strong* leadership and *permissive* leadership. For example, sometimes knowledge and experience will push you in one direction (e.g., "I should really allow my campers to help make this decision"), but at the same time your experience may push you in another direction (e.g., "Time is of the essence. I'm more experienced and I really understand the problem better than the campers. Therefore, I should make the decision.")

A range of leadership approaches can be used by a camp counselor, and each approach may be appropriate depending on the situation. A successful leader learns to recognize the nature of the particular problem or situation with which he or she is dealing, and knows how to adopt the appropriate pattern of leadership to that situation.

Figure 9.1 presents a model of the range of possible leadership approaches and behaviors available. Each type of action is related to the degree of authority used by the counselor and to the amount of freedom available to the campers. The actions seen on the extreme left characterize the counselor who is more autocratic and maintains a high degree of control. Those actions seen on the extreme right characterize the counselor who uses the democratic process with campers by releasing an appropriate degree of control. Many possibilities exist along this range:

1. *The camp counselor makes the decision and announces it.* In this case, you identify a problem, consider alternative solutions, choose one of them, and then announce this decision to your campers for implementation. You may or may not give consideration to what your campers will think or feel about this decision. You provide no opportunity for them to participate directly in the decision-making process.

2. *The camp counselor "sells" a decision.* You take responsibility for identifying the problem and arriving at a decision. Rather than simply announcing it, however, you take the additional step of persuading your camp-

ers to accept it. In doing so, you recognize the possibility of some resistance among those who will be faced with the decision, and possibly seek to reduce this resistance by indicating what the campers have to gain from your decision.

3. *The counselor presents ideas, and then invites questions.* In this approach, you arrive at a decision and then seek acceptance of your ideas by providing campers with an opportunity to get a fuller explanation of your thinking.

4. *The counselor presents a tentative decision subject to change.* Before meeting with your campers, you think a problem through and arrive at a decision—but only a tentative one. This behavior on your part permits the campers to exert some influence on the decision, but the initiative for identifying and diagnosing the problem remains with you.

5. *The counselor presents the problem, gets suggestions, and then makes her or his decision.* Up to this point you have come to your campers with the ideas or decisions. Now, however, the campers get the first chance to suggest ideas or solutions. Your initial role involves identifying the project or problem. You might, for example, say: "We are faced with program options today, including work on our arts and crafts projects, a trip to the beach, a long hike, or possibly something else you would like to do. What ideas do you have?" From the list of alternatives developed by the campers, you as the counselor select the one activity that seems most favorable.

6. *The counselor defines the limits and invites the group to make a decision.* At this point you are passing the right to make the decision to the campers. Before doing so, however, you define the problem or situation to be dealt with and the boundaries within which the decision must be made. An example might be a decision on whether to allow your campers free time this afternoon, as opposed to requiring them to participate in the arts and crafts program. You might call your campers together and say: "This afternoon we are scheduled to participate in another arts and crafts lesson. However, since everyone has progressed so well in this activity, I am willing to cancel the lesson today and let you have free time instead. However, if you choose to have free time, you will need to use it constructively by either working on your individual special camp project or practicing your archery skills. What would you like to do?"

7. *The counselor permits the campers to make decisions within prescribed limits.* At this stage you are allowing your campers to operate in a democratic process, but you are still ultimately responsible for their productivity and overall welfare. Consequently, you should participate as part of the group in the decision-making process and should feel free to use your influence to persuade your campers to make appropriate decisions. From time to time you may need to intervene should the group decision-making process start to get out of hand or if an unsafe or unhealthy decision is made.

As illustrated by these approaches, decision making is done sometimes by the leader and sometimes by the group. Circumstances must be considered in deciding which leadership pattern to use at any one time. A good leader can first make a judgment based on a combination of factors including the leader's own background, knowledge, experience, and personality as well as the skills, knowledge, and experience of the followers. Each situation will be different. For instance, in certain emergency situations, time constraints may require rapid decision making. In other situations a more consultative participative style of leadership may be employed. The nature of the task to be performed by the group should also be taken into consideration prior to deciding what leadership style to use.

Further, a more open democratic style of leadership may be applied when certain conditions are present. For

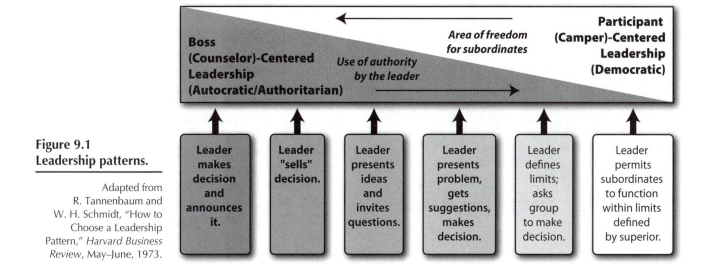

**Figure 9.1
Leadership patterns.**

Adapted from R. Tannenbaum and W. H. Schmidt, "How to Choose a Leadership Pattern," *Harvard Business Review*, May–June, 1973.

example, individuals should be allowed to engage in the decision-making process if they are ready to assume the responsibility and have the necessary knowledge and experience to do so. More freedom in allowing the group to make its own decisions can be effectively applied when working with individuals who are interested in and committed to the challenge or situation, and when the group members understand and identify with the goals and objectives of the program. Other factors to consider include how well the members work together as a group, and the complexity of the problem or situation to be addressed.

Characteristics of a Good Leader

Leadership involves influencing and motivating a group to act. Therefore, a good leader is someone who inspires a group to achieve goals that the group deems desirable and worthy. A leader must be capable of exerting positive influence on the group to help it conceptualize and formalize its goals and objectives, and also must serve as a motivating force in moving the group to meet those goals.

A leader is good at interacting and communicating with individual members of the group in order to persuade them to accept and move toward established goals.

One of the basic functions of leaders is to interact and communicate with individual members of the group to persuade them to accept and move toward the established goals. Other leadership functions involve organizing, directing, and coordinating efforts; helping to define situations and determine goals; and maintaining group happiness and cohesiveness. With these functions in mind, several suggestions may be helpful to the camp counselor in developing leadership skills (Kouzes & Posner, 2002).

Model the Way

Leaders should model the behaviors and exceed the expectations that they place on followers. By modeling the way, leaders are setting an example for their expectations, values, beliefs, and desires. Often, campers and staff members will mimic those characteristics that they observe in camp leaders. Thus, synthesizing your actions with your words will do more to prompt positive behavior than motivational speeches. Behaviors, not more words, influence others' behavior.

Inspire a Shared Vision

Leaders should have a holistic picture of goals and inspire their group members to achieve them. The mission and purpose of the camp should be the guiding vision for all counselors. By inspiring a shared vision among your fellow staff and throughout your cabin, counselors can work towards achieving the ultimate goals of the camp.

Challenge the Process

A natural leader does not simply wait to be placed in a position of authority. An inner motivation to guide, shape, and better the camp propels an individual to a more active leadership role. Maintaining the status quo is not the role of a leader. Raising the bar and attempting to achieve greater benefits for the campers is an example of successful leadership.

Enable Others to Act

By offering the opportunity for others to participate, to be empowered, and to execute self-determination, a leader establishes an environment of trust, evolution, and enhancement. Whether motivating campers or other staff members, a leader who enables others to act gains credibility, expands the diversity of ideas for problem solving, and helps perpetuate improvement in the entire camp.

Encourage the Heart

Acts of random kindness, concern for others, and honest encouragement do much to build cohesion, positive attitudes, and friendships. Often, praise and signs of appreciation are greater rewards than any tangible benefits. A counselor's genuine interest and caring will do much to build the leadership potential and dedication of campers and staff members.

In summary, consider these 10 ideas for becoming a good camp leader (Kouzes & Posner, 2002):

- Know who you are and what you stand for
- Lead by example
- Have a vision for the future
- Sell your vision to others and solicit their help
- Be opportunistic
- Don't be afraid to take risks
- Promote collaboration for improvement
- Enable others
- Award and applaud others for their achievement
- Celebrate the accomplishments as a whole

Group Development Stages

Leadership is necessary to provide positive camp experiences. Leadership by camp staff to promote group development begins the minute campers arrive at camp. When campers first arrive, they are assigned to a small group or unit that will operate under guidance of an assigned camp counselor. Since these individuals collectively make up what is known as a group, counselors need an understanding of the small group development process, which is a key part of organized camping.

Group development occurs in various stages. Awareness of these developmental stages can help camp leaders better judge when actions are needed to help a group function successfully. Different groups, however, progress through developmental stages at different speeds. Likewise, some people tend to progress more rapidly than other members of a group. The accuracy with which we can predict what will take place within a group depends on variables such as: the psychological background of each member and his or her ego needs; the amount of aggressive acts by the members; the stage of the group's development; how the group was formed; the way it handles conflict; the pattern of decision-making used; and forces such as the age, maturity, interests, history, and size of the group.

Depending on these and other factors, members of a group tend to locate themselves along a continuum that ranges from highly cohesive task-oriented groups to a completely loose-knit makeup of individuals who may never really become a group. Theoretical models help to explain what actually happens in groups as they evolve. Among them, the conceptual model of Garland, Jones, and Kolodny (1965) provides some information for anyone who works with camp groups. The construct of the model seems especially applicable because it was based

primarily upon observations of youths aged 9 to 16 years who had not been closely associated prior to formation into groups. The framework of the model identifies five central stages through which groups progress as they develop. These stages are pre-affiliation, power and control, intimacy, differentiation, and separation.

Pre-affiliation Stage

During this period of orientation and initial association, group members begin to become familiar with one another and their environment. Close ties have not yet developed. Relationships at this stage tend to include somewhat superficial and stereotypic activity as a means of getting acquainted. For protection, individuals often retain some social distance. It is common to witness some members' anxiety about participating in the group as they attempt to find ways within their framework of social experience to accomplish this process of affiliation. The basic struggle in this initial stage of group life usually is one of approach and avoidance. A hesitancy to get involved can be reflected in the group members' vacillating response to program activities and events. Leaders are likely to observe an on-again-off-again attitude toward such things as participating in games and activities together (versus choosing to play alone), and accepting responsibility (versus avoidance) in such activities like cleanup and planning.

During this stage, a camp counselor can work with his or her group to identify the expectations of members and organize preliminary program goals and objectives accordingly. To encourage individuals to relate to others in the group, activities should be organized to provide opportunities for the development of trust and positive group interaction.

Power and Control Stage

The power and control stage reflects the turmoil of change from a non-intimate to a close system of relationships. Once group participants realize that the group experience is potentially safe and rewarding, a brief power struggle may occur within the group. Members may lock horns on power and control issues such as individual status, group values, and making choices. The leader and other members may be tested in an attempt to define and formalize relationships and create a status hierarchy. Physical strength, aggressiveness, mental agility, and specific individual skills must be discovered. Cliques tend to form during this stage, and sometimes these initial alliances are made for common protection against others in the group. Also, attempts to exclude individuals from membership in the overall group may occur occasionally.

During this stage, a camp counselor wants to ensure that the group's atmosphere remains open and safe. Any individual power struggles within the group must not take place at the expense of other members, and the attempts of subgroups to jeopardize the goals of the whole group must also be prevented. Activities can be structured so that campers are able to express themselves openly, but it should be made clear to everyone in the group which decisions can be made by the group and which will be made by the counselor. Likewise, the counselor should not intercede in the group decision-making process unless necessary. A counselor who overrides group decisions risks lowering or invalidating campers' opinions of their decision-making abilities, and consequently a loss of group members' willingness to express themselves.

Intimacy Stage

The intimacy stage is characterized by an increase in personal development. Campers are more willing to express feelings regarding other members of the group, and cooperation is initiated by looking to one another for solutions. Deeper and more personal relationships are developed because of the desire to share experiences and become immersed in group life. Although groups in this stage exhibit greater proficiency in planning and conducting projects as a group, this proficiency will fluctuate as conflicts arise. Sibling-like rivalry tends to appear, as well as overt comparisons of the group to each individual's family life. Reference to siblings is prevalent, and discussions regarding what goes on at home tend to become more revealing and emotionally charged. As the closeness and level of involvement evolve, the group experience itself tends to be perceived as a family experience. This stage is critical because at this point campers either become a group or remain a collection of individuals. For the group to attain intimacy, a sense of cohesiveness must occur among members. To facilitate this process, the counselor should support positive achievements and also encourage campers to accept greater amounts of responsibility. Likewise, you can attempt to increase their dependency on one another.

The camp leader should serve as a resource in helping to clarify the group's identity as well as its relationship to other groups. You can act as a resource for group issues, but not as a "resolver" of issues. Attempt to diagnose problem areas and present them so that new perspectives may be seen. Also, explore possible ways in which individuals within the group can meet their needs without compromising the rights of others. By providing feedback and clarity when needed, a camp counselor will be helping campers take ownership of their behavior.

Differentiation Stage

A group that evolves to the differentiation stage has reached a "high community." These groups tend to be productive. They have fewer power struggles and more cooperative planning. The group is cohesive, yet able to identify both individual and group needs. Roles and status of group members tend to be less rigid as evidenced in the sharing of leadership and group functions. Individual differences are condoned, and members accept one another as distinct members of the group. Where needed, the group exercises control when individual behavior becomes group destructive. On the other hand, power problems and efforts to control tend to be minimized because group decision making is often done through mutual understanding and acceptance of facts. The group experience at this stage achieves a functionally autonomous character. As such, customs and traditions may be adopted and, if not already done, a group name and insignia might likely be developed. Due to this strong identity and affiliation, frequent comparisons of the group are made with other groups. It is also common to hear frequent complementary references made about "*our* group" or "*our* leader."

During this stage, the counselor can continue to help the camp group achieve its own goals. For instance, since there is great trust among group members during this stage, providing them with increased opportunity to take on initiative and responsibility in the group's functions is wise. To allow for personal needs, you can also support opportunities for campers to work independently.

A cohesive, task-oriented group works well together to plan and carry out activities.

Separation Stage

The final stage covers the period leading up to the termination or conclusion of the group experience. The termination of any group experience, including the windup of a camp session, tends to build up participant anxiety that can set off some negative reactions. In some instances, participants might deny or fail to recognize that an end will occur. Some group members may also regress to previous negative interpersonal behavior as the experience draws to a close.

A counselor can initiate structured opportunities to help bring the experience to a positive conclusion. One way for a counselor to do this is to provide opportunity for program review and recapitulation. By reflecting back, the campers have a chance to analyze the experiences that benefited them the most. Through discussion of past experiences, campers also have an opportunity to transfer this learning to other situations in their lives. This process is important because it will help them apply what they have learned to other situations.

Group Process Model

Another model of group processes that has become popular includes stages referred to as forming, storming, norming, performing, and adjourning (Garr, 2006). Although conceptually quite similar to the Garland et al. model just discussed, these five stages represent another way of thinking about group behavior.

Forming

Forming occurs as the group comes together. Campers tend to test one another as a means of learning about one another. They are busy gathering information and little conflict usually occurs.

Storming

This phase is characterized by conflict and polarization around interpersonal issues. Campers may resist group influence and may become impatient with one another. Minor conflicts may occur that can be addressed quickly. Campers need to have an understanding of the structure and rules of camp as well as an understanding of how a group should function.

Norming

In the norming stage, feelings of group cohesion and identity develop. Campers are willing to share with each other on a deeper level. This stage is when counselors often feel their group is fun to be with, especially if the conflicts of the storming stage have been resolved.

Performing

The performing stage gives campers and counselors a sense of pride in their group. Group members trust one another and feel interdependent. Common goals can be accomplished as group identity, loyalty, and morale are high. A great deal of creative energy exists.

Adjourning

As its name implies, adjourning is the separation stage. Group members often feel a sense of loss and campers may begin to disengage before the session is actually over. Counselors are challenged to help the group retain its cohesiveness, identity, and realize the accomplishments and achievements that were evident during their time together. Campers will likely have a sense of joy and sadness at the same time.

Working with a Group

Regardless of the group stage, effective camp counselors understand the phases of group development. Niepoth (1983) presented some generalizations about helping groups become more efficient and effective in carrying out their responsibilities. For example, it is important to remember that the group itself must take responsibility for its own actions and progress if it is to grow and become more efficient. Camp counselors who assume all of the responsibility for improving the effectiveness of their groups are actually denying the group members an opportunity to learn and to develop needed skills. Campers who become overly dependent on their camp counselors probably will never reach their full potential. Additional strategies to maximize group effectiveness include the following:

1. A leader who assists a group in clarifying goals or developing better ways of cooperating is actually enabling the group to become more effective.

2. A leader is helping the group if he or she assists individuals within that group to behave appropriately.

3. A leader who provides the resources needed by the group (e.g., ideas, supplies, or equipment) is adding to the group's effectiveness.

4. Since a group needs to know how it is doing in accomplishing its goals and objectives, a leader who helps the group develop and use communication techniques or feedback mechanisms is adding to that group's effectiveness.

A related aspect associated with group development is team building. Team building is a key way to encourage group development. Information about the use of initiative games and trust exercises for team building will be discussed in more detail later in this book. Effective communication also is a key aspect of leadership, and is discussed in more detail in the next chapter.

Developing Camper Leadership

Much of this chapter has focused on leadership styles and group dynamics. Counselors may also want to consider more specifically ways to facilitate campers as leaders. If you are a democratic leader and using a style that enables campers to make decisions, then you may be facilitating these opportunities. However, most counselors can do a better job by being more intentional about giving campers opportunities to show leadership. Too often campers become the objects or recipients of leadership rather than resources or partners in leadership (Thurber, 2009).

Thurber (2009) describes ways to maximize camper leadership based on ACA's research. The possibilities include:

- Choosing—campers get to choose from a menu of possible activities.
- Planning—campers design and plan new activities and events.
- Mentoring—campers serve as role models in activities for other campers.

- Presiding—campers lead some activities, including programs and discussions.
- Governing—campers help decide on rules and what to do when they are broken.
- Evaluating—campers assist in program evaluation (e.g., focus groups, questionnaire design).
- Envisioning—campers contribute to discussions about the camp's mission, vision, and values.

Sometimes obstacles prevent camper leadership and these limitations should be acknowledged. Some campers may not want leadership responsibilities and others may not be developmentally ready to assume leadership. Camp directors may be concerned about the liability of campers serving as leaders, although anyone in a leadership position must be supervised in some way. The mind-set of programming *for* campers rather than *with* them is a mind-set that may need to be changed. Many staff need training themselves in how to facilitate leadership among others. The bottom line is that any youth participation in a leadership role should be safe, congruent with the camp's mission, developmentally appropriate, meaningful rather than token, supported with training, and evaluated (Thurber, 2009).

REFERENCES

Garland, J. A., Jones, H. E., & Kolodny, R. L. (1965). A model for stages of development in social work groups. In P. Bernstein (Ed.), *Explorations in Group Work,* pp. 12–53. Boston: Boston University School of Social Work.

Garr, M. (2006, March/April). Understanding group processes. *Camping Magazine, 79*(2), 46–48.

Kouzes, J. M., & Posner, B. Z. (2002). *The leadership challenge.* San Francisco: Jossey-Bass.

Niepoth, W. E. (1983). *Leisure leadership.* Boston: Prentice-Hall.

Shelton, M. (2006, March/April). Developing excellence in camp leadership: 4 requirements. *Camping Magazine, 79*(2), 22–31.

Thurber, C. (2009, Sept/Oct). Youth as objects or partners? Advancing opportunities for camper leadership and decision-making. *Camping Magazine, 82*(5), 42–49.

WEB RESOURCES

Leadership (www.visionrealization.com) has information on behavior management, special days, rainy days, archery, at-risk youth, and self-esteem.

Mentoring (www.mentorcounselor.com) has articles on camp counseling and working with children.

PRINT RESOURCES

Colyn, L., DeGraaf, D., & Certan, D. (2008, March/April). Social capital and organized camping: It's about community! *Camping Magazine, 81*(2), 30–36.

Ditter, B. (2008, May/June). Top 10 tips for working with today's campers. *Camping Magazine, 81*(3). Offers tips for

working with campers; for example, getting to know each of your campers, keeping directions simple, getting into routines, etc.

Schafer, E. (2007, May/June). Training counselors to be role models: The basics and beyond. *Camping Magazine, 80*(3), 25–29.

10

The Counselor's Role in Guidance

The daily informal contacts of camp life give camp counselors unlimited opportunities to observe campers. By seeing campers as whole people and evaluating their individual strengths and weaknesses, you can gain a better understanding of them and why they are the way they are. This background will help you guide campers in developing their potential and becoming better people through their interactions at camp. Of course, be careful not to overestimate your capabilities in this area. If you do not use good judgment or lack adequate training and experience in the field of guidance, you can do harm through misguided attempts to help a young person during these formative years.

Camp counselors are not professional counselors. They must know their limits. However, camp counselors can observe campers' behavior and try to understand it through the lens of the normal processes of growth and development that have been previously discussed, as well as through consideration of the specific conditions that contributed to make them the sort of people they are. Under favorable conditions, camp offers a great way to provide positive guidance and help children and youth develop and grow.

All campers come to camp with preformed opinions of themselves as individuals, which are largely dependent on how they have been accepted by others in the past. If parents, teachers, or peers regard them as messy, lazy, or as troublemakers, they usually will consider these attributes to be true and probably will expect their new associates to feel the same way about them. Their self-concept may be so ingrained that they will attempt to live up to that reputation. If, on the other hand, children have been praised and are considered to be polite, friendly, and cooperative, they probably will behave that way at camp. However, if no one at camp knows of their previous char-

acterizations, they have the opportunity to reinvent themselves and be a different person.

As discussed earlier, when campers demonstrate bad behavior, punishing, nagging, or bribing them will do little good and may only make them worse. These children may be so accustomed to being blamed and scolded that they will pay no attention to you anyway. A better approach is to discern how children feel about themselves and what their true self-perceptions are. You will then be in a position to try to alter their behavior by giving them new and different ways to think about their self-identity.

Beneath a facade of indifference, a longing to be admired and accepted as a respected member of the group most likely exists. Therefore, try to reward campers with some token of approval each time they do something commendable. When occasions for positive reinforcement do not occur naturally, you may have to purposely create opportunities for individuals to do something praiseworthy. Nothing succeeds like success, and each time approval is won, children will be encouraged to try to win it again. Eventually these children may begin to think of themselves more positively and, hopefully, this new self-perception will carry over into their life after they leave camp.

Patterns of Guidance

The law of exercise previously discussed in chapter 8 states that people learn by practice since repetition develops habits. **Habits** are action patterns that have been repeated so many times that they are performed automatically with little conscious thought. People have a tendency to become set in their ways starting at an early age. Even young campers are likely to prefer to maintain the status quo unless something important or even catastrophic happens to shake them up and make them really want to change. Altering a pattern of life in even minor ways requires the expenditure of mental, emotional, and perhaps even physical effort. Also, people's egos cause them to resist change because admitting to any imperfection is difficult. People often hesitate to change because the well-worn path provides security, whereas venturing into the unknown produces fear.

You need to keep this law of exercise in mind when trying to influence others to change and equip yourself with patience, insight, empathy, and understanding. Be prepared for occasional backsliding and delays. Do not expect miracles overnight; even when people sincerely want to change, they will likely suffer periods of discouragement and impatience that tempt them to give up. At these times they need supporters to step in with encouragement and a pat on the back to remind them of the progress they have already made, even though only small changes may have occurred. Point out that their feelings are common to all who try to change their habits, and let them know that setbacks and frustrations are part of the process.

One of your basic aims in guidance is to help all campers respect themselves. As noted previously, campers can develop such traits as self-confidence, leadership ability, and social skills, and can learn the joys of group participation as well as cultivating and keeping new friends. They can also find acceptable ways to satisfy their fundamental needs or wishes by participation and achievement in camp life. No matter what specific activities campers do, their camp experience hopefully will teach skills and ways of living that provide immediate satisfaction and lay the groundwork for a well-balanced adult life.

At camp, children are the focal point and are fairly free to determine the role they will play. They can establish their own goals and then provide the momentum and drive to achieve them at their own speed. This opportunity encourages the development of self-reliance and emotional maturity. A camp counselor plays an important role in this development, applying a push in one direction or a restraining hand in another as the occasion demands. Encourage children to be as independent and self-reliant as they can, while you remain more or less in the background, ready to give them assurance, advice, and encouragement as needed. Doing your job well requires tact and skill in knowing when and how to assist, admonish, or help, and how to do it so unobtrusively that campers are barely aware of your participation.

Suggestions for Observing Behavior

Note Individual Differences

As you observe campers in their daily activities, you will note marked differences in individual reactions to the group and in the amount of interest and enthusiasm shown toward participation in camp activities. At home, children are usually accepted and loved just as they are, but at camp their acceptance will most likely depend on what they can contribute and the general compatibility of their personalities with others. Those who are outgoing might be quickly assimilated. They have probably been well-accepted in the past and have acquired enough self-confidence to approach a new group with friendly self-assurance and an easy, relaxed manner. Such children may never have had to deal with loneliness or rejection.

The majority of campers, however, may not stand out in any particular way and will remain more or less on the sideline while the group sizes them up and eventually decides what group status to accord them. Some individuals may remain on the fringe for a long time before being accepted, and a few others may be branded as unacceptable. No matter how much time a child spends with the group or the amount of effort he or she exerts to try to fit in, the ultimate outcome may be determined by intangible factors that are difficult for either the child or an observer to pinpoint.

Interpret These Differences

Campers' reactions to their peers can often reveal much about how they feel about themselves, especially to someone with the training and insight to interpret the message correctly. If unsure of themselves and afraid of being ignored, campers may try to disguise their discomfort by adopting an indifferent attitude or by demanding the spotlight and showing off. They may adopt a fearless attitude and brag about themselves so much that they come off as aggressive and conceited. Another tactic children employ is to retire into the background to be as inconspicuous as possible. They may be arrogant and quickly take offense when none was intended, or may become extremely sensitive and show signs of hurt feelings. They may adopt a self-deprecating manner, or attempt to get attention by telling tales of woe to anyone who will listen. Most of these reactions tend to repel others, and this rejection only intensifies the feelings of inadequacy and self-doubt.

Insecure people sometimes try to win acceptance and approval by being subservient; for example, eagerly running errands or performing little services for others. They may abandon all efforts to establish their own identity and win approval and respect by their own accomplishments. Instead, they are willing to accept any small signs of appreciation and attention they can get, no matter the cost.

Individuals who react in any of these ways may do so because of a lack of previous experience in informal situations with a peer group or because they are trying to protect themselves from a repetition of painful experiences in the past. They may be trying too hard to cope with a situation they don't understand or lack the skill to control. This behavior causes others to shy away from them. Whether campers react with aggression and assertiveness or by surrender and withdrawal, you can be sure that they feel frustrated, unhappy, and lonely. They may even want to give up and go home because of their innate desire to belong and be accepted. These children need someone like a camp counselor to help them find a way to connect with their peers. If they give up and run away now, it will only deepen their sense of inadequacy and make it harder for them to gain acceptance in the future.

Such individuals may have certain personality traits or habits that others dislike such as selfishness, bossiness, or even a reluctance to take a shower. Uncovering the possible reasons for these problems may be a challenge, and overcoming them may be even more difficult. However, a camp counselor must be alert to discover what forces are really at work, since an individual's outward behavior is often merely a camouflage to conceal underlying feelings and problems. What appears on the surface often bears surprisingly little resemblance to the turmoil underneath.

Guidance through Group Discussions

Every association you have with campers is a potential counseling situation. Everything you do—every word, action, gesture, or facial expression—sets a pattern or expresses an attitude that may influence them far more than you suspect. Each contact with a group or its individuals gives a camp counselor an opportunity to know

them better and perhaps influence them to some degree. A friendly and level-headed camp counselor can do a great deal to give campers the knowledge and judgment they need to make the right choices. However, you may not be able to solve every camper's problem, so do not hesitate to ask more experienced staff for help when dealing with guidance issues.

The foundation of your relationship with your campers should be based on a concern for each and every individual and an understanding of and willingness to accept them as they are. You should constantly seek to know them better; explore their personalities, their relationships with others, and their problems and help them examine and understand their emotions and ideas. With continued interaction, you should come to recognize them as unique individuals who differ from every other human being and whose individual patterns of thinking and feeling deserve your respect and acceptance.

You can get to know campers through many opportunities for communication. Everyone enjoys taking part in a discussion, and campers are no exception. Group discussions should be regarded as a valuable part of the camp counseling experience because the interchange of ideas and opinions is important to a camper's development as a person.

In addition to the usual spontaneous informal discussions, more formal opportunities can be planned either at your instigation or in response to requests from campers. At other times, you may want to introduce a topic in a casual way so that the ensuing discussion is more spontaneous. Unless a situation calls for an immediate discussion, such interactions may work better on rainy days, during

Group discussions provide a valuable opportunity to let campers exchange ideas and opinions.

an afternoon rest, while waiting for an activity to begin, or the period just before lights out or before campers leave day camp for the day. In the camp situation, a relaxed informal atmosphere is generally available.

People often engage in discussions to exchange opinions or acquire information. One of the most fascinating things about people of camp age is their insatiable curiosity and desire to know the how, where, what, and why of countless things not only in their own environment, but also in far-away places. Campers often enjoy discussing such diverse topics as college life, jobs, dating, love and marriage, religion, personal grooming, fishing, camping techniques, cheating, movies they've seen, current events, and world affairs. Through these conversations campers can acquire information, broaden their interests and insights, and learn to better communicate with and understand others.

Campers may also have problems or interests that they hesitate to discuss with anyone except a buddy or a few close peers. Questions of general morality, personal health problems, standards of behavior for self or group, intrapersonal relationships, camp rules or customs, the use of tobacco/ alcohol/drugs, or other campers who annoy or puzzle them often fall into this category. Campers may be somewhat embarrassed to talk about their interests or unsure of how adults or peers will react, so they will need assurance that you recognize their concerns as being perfectly normal and common. This aspect relates to the concept of validation discussed in the previous chapter. When these topics are brought up before the group, campers are often relieved to find that others share their interests and gladly enter into the discussion. The more relevant discussions are to the real problems and interests of campers, the more valuable they become.

Group discussion is also one of the best ways to clear up misunderstandings and solve problems such as how to divide cabin duties and thus avoid slackers and workhorses, how to deal with campers who spread gossip, or to explain the reasons for certain camp rules. When an insightful counselor detects undercurrents of tension that seem to be building, he or she should give the campers an opportunity to express their dissatisfaction and talk about it. Bringing controversial matters out into the open and discussing what is bothering people before tensions build up is usually best. An honest and open discussion often will be enough to solve the problem. Increased goodwill and mutual understanding usually results when well-meaning people learn how their thoughtless actions have been annoying others or find that their suspicions and distrust were based largely on imagination, idle rumor or gossip, or a chance act or statement that was misinterpreted. The usefulness of discussion applies to groups of staff as well as campers who may have misunderstandings during the course of the camp session.

The Role of a Counselor in Group Discussion

If you can gain enough of your group's confidence to be included in their discussions, you can give campers the benefit of your wider knowledge and more mature viewpoint and way of thinking. These discussions may also draw campers closer to you when they find you human and understanding. Do not avoid difficult issues and refuse to admit that your campers are curious about sex, drugs, and other moral and ethical topics. Whether or not these subjects are brought out into the open, your campers will discuss them. Make sure that your influence is for the good, and instruct, inform, and discuss as seems desirable. Some camps, however, do not want counselors to discuss personal issues with campers such as sexuality, so make sure you can lead a discussion that is appropriate. A counselor must be mature enough to demonstrate and pass on to others a balanced set of values.

Planned Discussions

The how, when, where, and what of a planned discussion are important considerations. A group of 6 to 8 individuals (never more than 15 campers) works best for a discussion so everyone can clearly hear and be heard, especially in an outdoor setting. A small group promotes a friendly climate in which each camper should feel free to speak frankly.

Either a counselor or a capable camper may serve as leader or chair of a discussion. When serving in this capacity, make sure to plan ahead with regard to time and place, notifying participants, and taking care of such details as lighting and seating. If participants are not already aware of what is on the agenda, you may want to inform them ahead of time so that they can come with well-thought-out ideas instead of talking off the top of their heads. You, as leader, may also want to prepare yourself by obtaining pertinent information and planning in some detail how to conduct the meeting. For instance, you may want to plan your opening remarks and outline the logical steps to follow in progressing to a meaningful conclusion to avoid having the discussion lag or become bogged down in digressions.

Discussion works best when everyone sits in a circle so that each can see everyone else. The leader should be part of the circle. If members are new to each other, have them introduce themselves and also have them supply a bit of pertinent information about themselves. A variation might be to pair them off to exchange information, each then introducing the other to the larger group.

An essential first step is to help the group define or arrive at a clear understanding of the exact topic or problem to be discussed and what should be accomplished. Everyone can then start on common ground. Someone may also be designated as secretary to keep a record of what's been decided. If several topics are up for discussion, you may want to ask the group to arrange them in the order of their importance, putting near the end those that could possibly be postponed until a later meeting. However, if discussion of topics cannot be postponed, draw up a schedule and allot the necessary time to each topic and make sure the schedule is followed.

Once the discussion has gotten started, the camp leader should fade into the background. The discussion should largely be between group members—not between the leader and the group. Your main function is to keep the discussion going in an orderly fashion, summarizing main points as they develop, and steering the group members on to the next step as rapidly as is feasible to reach a satisfying conclusion. Though it is occasionally a good idea to permit some digression from the subject, use good judgment regarding how much and how far digression should go before you tactfully but forcefully bring them back on course again. Be alert for signs of boredom or restlessness. Young children, in particular, have short attention spans and will likely grow impatient with purposeless monologues or repetition by group members.

One of the best ways to launch a subject, bring a wandering group back on course, or move them on to another topic is to ask a question. Express it as briefly as possible and choose your words carefully to clearly bring out your meaning. Ask open-ended questions that will require a thoughtful answer rather than a simple "yes" or "no." For instance, you might begin by asking, "Since our meeting is to decide what to do Wednesday night, what suggestions do you have?" List the suggestions on a piece of paper or blackboard and encourage discussion until they finally agree on two or three. Then, if the choice lies between items like going on an overnight stargazing trip or working on their outdoor cooking site, you can ask campers to speak for or against each idea. After discussion, call for a final vote. Once campers decide on a plan, ask what preparations will have to be made. Suggestions as to equipment, supplies, work committees, and duties can be recorded and then the details further discussed by the group.

Before concluding a meeting, summarize what was accomplished. You might do this by asking campers to state the most important things they gained from the discussion or by briefly restating important decisions reached or responsibilities assumed by individuals or the group, and when, where, and how they are to be carried out. Keep notes for yourself. To ascertain what progress is made, follow up at a later meeting or ask individuals to report on their progress.

Additional Hints for Group Discussions

If your group lacks experience or has drifted into bad discussion habits, plan an early meeting to consider with them how to prepare and carry on a good discussion. You might review rules of order and some of the courtesies and techniques of participation. For instance:

1. Each person should respect the rights of the one who has the floor and should listen with an open mind to what is said.

2. Campers should never interrupt rudely or be so focused on their own point of view that they do not listen to the good points others make.

3. Speakers should be brief and to the point and should avoid wasting time by restating points already made.

4. After the group has reached a decision, each member should accept it gracefully and wholeheartedly join in helping out.

With younger campers you will need to take quite a bit of the decision-making responsibility yourself, but you can and should let older campers gradually do more. They are increasingly resentful of being dominated by their elders and are eager to demonstrate their own ability to decide things and carry them out. Encourage them, even though they may make mistakes.

You can demonstrate your understanding of the meaning of democratic leadership. Campers often will surprise you with their good judgment and ingenuity when challenged and will take on projects they have planned with enthusiasm and determination. This *hands off*, but not laissez faire, policy is hard for many leaders to maintain; some will not be able to resist the urge to step in and suggest what should be done and how and by whom. The counselor's role should be one of standing by to prevent serious mistakes, instructing and assisting as needed, and exerting a restraining hand only when necessary.

Older campers can be introduced to the committee system, where committee members do certain parts of the job or perform preliminary work and then report back to the entire group. Ordinarily, the group should choose its own leaders and committee members. The group often knows their peers much better than you. When campers recognize the importance of selecting people who will be responsible and capable, they will usually choose wisely and will follow those chosen more willingly.

Strike a happy medium between letting a discussion drag and rushing through it. Stay in the background, yet maintain control by tactfully discouraging time wasters and monopolizers and encouraging the quieter campers to participate. Give all campers the feeling that you *want* to hear what they have to say. Listen respectfully and intently and thank them when they finish. Do not assume the role of judge or critic, and do not make sarcastic comments or make fun of others' ideas. Remember that your gestures and facial expressions convey impressions just as much as your words. If necessary, protect the members of the group from each other by immediately squelching rudeness, bickering, or derogatory remarks made by anyone to or about another's ideas. Set an example by showing respect for each individual with an attitude of courtesy and fairness. You are entitled to express your opinions like anyone else, but never take advantage of your position by forcing your ideas on the group or overruling majority opinion unless camp safety or policy demands it.

Methods for Prompting Discussions

Several useful techniques might be used to promote discussions.

Thorns & Roses.   This approach is an easy way for a counselor to debrief a situation, while also prompting ideas for further discussion. In a circle, members can share both positive and negative experiences that they have encountered throughout the day, during a trip, or over the course of the week. Counselors can ask campers to give both a thorn and a rose regarding their day. This approach might also be used in identifying the pros (roses) and cons (thorns) of a decision made by the group.

Pass the Torch.   The idea behind Pass the Torch is to allow every camper an opportunity to speak his or her mind by giving them the opportunity for discussion. Counselors can use a flashlight or candle and allow each person to pass the torch following her or his allotted time for sharing thoughts. The premise is for the person holding the torch to have the opportunity for adding comments and prompting further discussion.

Paper Airplane.   If campers are reluctant to initiate discussion, another tactic might be for them to write out their comments on a piece of paper, form it into a paper airplane, and for everyone to launch their airplanes into the center of a circle. At this time, campers should grab an airplane that does not belong to them and prepare to read it to the group. Discussion may be initiated following the comments of each airplane. This method may help promote anonymity among group members who are hesitant in initial or controversial discussions.

The Circular Response.   To overcome some of the limitations of the usual discussion method, arrange the group in the usual circle and choose someone at random to start the discussion. Then, proceed clockwise around the circle, giving everyone a specific amount of time, say one minute, to express themselves. No one may talk out of turn or speak again until the discussion goes around the circle. Someone acts as timekeeper, which could be a good job for someone inclined to talk too much. This person signals when the time is up. Continue around the circle as many times as seems profitable and then summarize the discussion as usual. When a person's turn comes, he or she may use the allotted time to add new thoughts or opinions, comment on previous remarks, elaborate upon previous remarks, pass with the understanding that another chance will be provided when the discussion returns to that person again, or ask that the person's time be devoted to a period of silence to give others time to summarize their thoughts. Be sure to spend time at the beginning making sure that all group members understand how this circular response method works.

Brainstorming.   This method is often used successfully to solve a problem or plan an activity. It is based on the belief that certain problems can best be solved by allowing the freest exchange of ideas possible. All involved are encouraged to share their thoughts on the subject at hand. Nothing is rejected as being too extreme. Even though a suggestion may have little value in itself, it may well stimulate someone else to come up with something of a more practical nature. After presenting a specific topic or problem to the group, members are asked to suggest in rapid-fire order as many solutions as possible, usually within a time frame of 5 to 10 minutes. Someone writes down all the ideas so that others can see. Initially, responses are not evaluated and all questions, criticisms, or other comments (including laughter) are out of order. Once this phase is completed, the ideas must be evaluated. During evaluation the group is asked to discuss and evaluate all solutions and ultimately select the best one. To accomplish this final task, the group first crosses out those ideas that are irrelevant or impractical. The remaining ideas are clarified, expanded, or combined. Finally, through consensus, the group prioritizes the remaining ideas and determines the one it wishes to consider further.

Sociodrama.   Another kind of discussion that is sometimes an appropriate group technique is sociodrama. It is actually a form of playacting in which individuals take on the roles of certain people, creating the dialogue as they go along or using a previously prepared script. Older campers often find this technique effective. It adds interest and variety to the program and can be useful as a teaching method and as a means of pinpointing and solving problems, especially when followed by a discussion of what took place and its implications. Sociodrama should be fun but should not drift into silliness or exaggeration. Some touches of humor can be allowed to creep in as actors inject their own personalities into the roles they are playing. Sociodrama can serve many purposes:

1. To instruct or get a point across. It may be particularly useful in working with a CIT group or regular counselors during training sessions. A hypothetical situation is presented with actors assigned to play roles. They may then act out proper (or improper) ways to behave on such occasions as visitors' day, in the dining hall, during rest hour, or in the hour before lights out. The group can then discuss and evaluate each presentation.

2. To solve a problem. The sociodrama may deal with a problem of campers, counselors, or both. Possible topics might deal with the person who talks after lights out, someone who shirks cabin cleanup duties, or who is bossy and always wants to run the show. This may provide a tactful way to allow campers to see themselves in a new light. However, be careful not to make the characterization so pointed that it hurts feelings. The problem may be a real or imaginary one. Each

person may act out his or her idea of the best solution followed by a general appraisal and discussion.

3. To develop empathy or attempt to put yourself in another's place. This purpose can help campers understand how someone else feels. This approach might be illustrated by acting out something like inappropriate table manners, the feeling of being teased or bullied, or the disappointment of never getting letters at mail call.

4. To learn desirable and undesirable ways to do something such as launch a canoe, build a fire, act as leader of a discussion, serve as camper leader to organize an overnight, carry on cabin cleanup, or wash dishes. The usual discussion and evaluation then follow.

5. To develop better communication within the camp and to provide insights or awaken new emotions in people. After participating in such activities, campers will probably mull over what happened and their own and others' feelings about it and, perhaps discuss it further with fellow campers or counselors.

Advantages and Problems with Group Discussions

Although the discussion method is slow and sometimes inefficient, it has the advantage of being democratic because it gives everyone a chance to express thoughts and feelings as well as hear thoughts of others. It minimizes the danger of letting the outspoken or more dynamic members exert undue influence. It also gives campers an opportunity to ask questions and obtain more information about unclear points. Participation gets people involved, keeps them aware of exactly what is going on and why, and makes them more willing to accept the decisions that result. Increased understanding and appreciation will result as campers learn to respect the opinions of others, even though not necessarily endorsing them, hopefully in the same spirit as Voltaire, who said, "I disapprove of what you say, but I will defend to the death your right to say it." Through discussion, you will often find that your campers have more insight and wisdom than you imagined. Sharing thoughts and ideas will help both you and your campers to gain a better understanding of each other.

As in every other camp activity, you will encounter problems in a group discussion. One or more campers may talk too much. Although these individuals may have good ideas, they often dominate the discussion, sometimes merely repeating what others have said, or just chattering on with words that apparently come from the mouth without benefit of having passed through the brain. Campers should be reminded of the importance of equal sharing of speaking time during one of your general sessions. You could also limit speaking to no more than a minute at a time. A talker might be made recorder to keep him or her occupied. You may occasionally have to be even more direct, asking someone to keep a record

of each person who speaks and the amount of time consumed, or possibly discussing the problem personally with the overly talkative individual. If you allow one person to talk too much, others may get bored or decide they do not need to contribute.

The opposite of the excessively talkative camper is the shy type who speaks too little and listens without contributing. You should ask yourself why this person does not enter into the discussion. One of the normal fundamental needs is to belong and fit in with the group and establish oneself as an individual. Perhaps this person lacks interest or fears making a mistake, being laughed at, or angering others. Some people "think to speak, while others speak to think." Thus, some people need time to formulate their ideas and may be slower to respond. You may need to invite these people into the conversation. Work hard to gain everyone's participation and then work even harder to maintain it.

Sometimes you may have one unpopular camper who is the butt of camp jokes or whose opinions are laughed at. You must try to change matters and keep others from negative responses or this person will soon stop trying to fit in and contribute.

Every group is likely to contain at least one opinionated person who thinks he or she knows all there is to know. These people look upon a discussion as merely a sounding board for displaying their own wisdom. They may attack any person who dares to differ. They should be reminded of the Chinese saying that getting angry is a sign that one has run out of arguments. As a counselor, you will want to keep control of the situation.

Guidance through Individual Discussions

Individual counseling or guidance also is an integral part of your job. You will have numerous personal encounters with campers as you seek out individuals or are sought out by them for a private chat or discussion. These informal conversations will provide some of your best opportunities to influence others. Since a warm relationship may already exist between you and the other person, both of you should be receptive to what the other has to say. Such a favorable climate is harder to achieve in more formal interviews or in appointments scheduled specifically for counseling. A formal situation may make a camper cautious and wary of free expression and thus less receptive to your comments or advice.

When the two of you are together, the camper may bring up topics that seem trivial to you but may be life and death matters to him or her. To establish good rapport, give that person your undivided attention and avoid interruptions if at all possible. The camper should feel that you want to hear everything said.

Through listening, counselors can play an important role in helping campers understand their feelings. Even adults need a confidant to talk out problems or lean on in times of confusion or anxiety. Talking with a good listener can be helpful in encouraging open, honest, and free expression and in gaining understanding, insight, and meaning in our lives.

A counselor can encourage campers to speak openly and say those things that are important to them. On the other hand, a counselor's responses can hinder or inhibit a camper's self-understanding if the response is judgmental or too full of advice. Therefore, when placed in the role of counselor, you should try to commend, praise, reassure, and encourage the person who is speaking. When appropriate, repeating or clarifying what you have heard shows that you understand and want to help the person gain insight into his or her problem and discover solutions.

A sense of closeness sometimes encourages campers to pour out their innermost thoughts and emotions. Offer encouragement and treasure these confidences, since these individuals need a sympathetic and understanding person. People who trust no one and do not talk tend to bottle up their thoughts and emotions until tension builds to such a degree that it may eventually explode in an uncontrolled outburst. By serving as a safety valve, you gain an opportunity to learn more about the campers. Learn to listen carefully and be observant regarding the camper's facial expressions, mannerisms, and gestures as they may reveal more than his or her words do. Body movements, facial expressions, and other indications of a camper's underlying emotions will help you discern what he or she cannot find words to express.

Develop the ability to sense when to be quiet and let the other person talk and when to enter into the conversation yourself. Good listeners are rare and thus, deeply appreciated. Talking about themselves may help campers organize their thinking or see things more objectively. Your main function is to help them think things through and eventually work out possible ways to handle whatever is bothering them.

Offer your own opinions and insights sparingly and refrain from either approving or disapproving of what is being said until you are sure you have a complete picture of the entire situation. Try to avoid the common mistake of telling anyone exactly what to do, which will only delay the process of learning to face up to problems and arrive at personal conclusions.

You should reassure your campers that whatever they tell you is strictly confidential. However, there may come a time when a camper seems to be on the verge of divulging information that your position requires you to reveal to a higher camp authority. Fairness requires that you warn the camper of your responsibility so that he or she will not continue unless willing to take this risk.

The Camper's Viewpoint

When an upset or worried camper comes to you, try first of all to get a picture of the problem or situation as he or she sees it. This process is not always straightforward since people sometimes falsely assume that they start on common ground with others and that their views are identical. On the contrary, more likely each person will have a different view that is determined by such factors as past and present experiences, mood of the moment, personality, general attitudes toward life, physical health, and self-concept.

An important point to remember is that people have a tendency to see what they are looking for or want to see in a situation. If a camper is thrown and painfully injured while riding a horse, he or she is likely to invent a dozen excuses for never attempting to ride again. If a child has been mistreated at home, he or she may not trust anyone and rebuff every effort you make to be kind and helpful. If a student's school course in nature study was presented in a bookish, boring fashion, the nature counselor will find it hard to stir up even a flicker of enthusiasm for nature study. When two people are confronted with an identical situation, they may each interpret it so differently that if you could read their minds you would not even recognize it as the same situation at all. Seeing a problem through the eyes of the campers is important; otherwise your reactions may not be of real help to them.

Changing a Camper's Viewpoint

Helping campers to look at situations from a different perspective may be useful. For instance, if a young boy or girl comes to you angry because the waterfront director will not allow him or her to practice diving off the dock after dark, you can try to help that person see the situation through the waterfront director's eyes. Chances are good that the waterfront director is not just trying to spoil campers' fun. That director wants campers to have all the *safe* fun they possibly can. However, undue risks and hazardous activities must be curtailed. When campers realize that the director is concerned only for their safety, they hopefully will see that the staff member is acting conscientiously.

In trying to broaden campers' viewpoints, encourage them to consider various aspects of a problem or situation. For example: Why did it happen? What is the motive or thinking of the others involved? They may want to consider alternative solutions to the dilemma and the probable consequences of each. By teaching campers to examine a problem from every possible angle, including others' viewpoints, you will help them avoid rash decisions and to choose a solution that will prove successful in the long run. This thinking process is used by individuals who act with maturity and good judgment.

A problem solving process that often works well involves the following steps, which you can modify to fit the situation.

- Determine exactly what the problem or dilemma is
- Determine possible solutions
- Evaluate the pros and cons of each potential solution
- Make a decision about the best approach
- Evaluate later whether the decision was best and use that information for future situations

Thurber (2009) outlined a specific approach to problem solving called *Collaborative Problem Solving* (CPS). CPS works well in camps as a way to defuse tension and promote positive behavior. In all stages of the CPS approach, the camper is asked, "What do you need right now?" This question will elicit how the camper views the situation. You may also want to ask the camper to backtrack in order to determine the triggers that set off problems within the group. Other questions used in this approach are, "What's the best way to get what you need?" and "What can I do to help?" The emphasis is on asking for collaboration: "What ideas do you have for working this out?" The final stages involve warning campers about the consequences if the problem continues, and, staying vigilant to assure that the collaboration continues.

Conflict Resolution

As suggested above, group issues that may arise in camp relate to conflict and its resolution, whether among campers or among staff. Conflict is inevitable when working with people. It can, however, be a way to also promote growth and creativity as well as clarify new options. Conflict occurs when the needs of others, our own needs, or the needs of a relationship are ignored.

People react to conflict in different ways. Some people try to avoid it always. The reality is that it usually never goes away and avoidance really means delaying conflict. Another common approach is to fight back, which often results in damaging relationships. Another strategy is to try to smooth things over and hope that the conflict goes away. Alternatively, a person may try to be authoritative and dictate how the conflict must be resolved. None of these approaches works well. The most productive way to handle conflict is to address it, talk about it, and move forward. If the conflict is not directly addressed, it can result in anger, blame, retaliation, gossip, or impasse.

Fee (2010) recommends six steps for resolving conflict that are similar to the steps involved in general problem-solving:

1. Show empathy. Seek to understand first and then respond. This step involves helping others feel understood or validated, reflecting their perceptions, and not arguing.
2. Clarify perceptions. Try to avoid assumptions. Note observable behaviors and provide your interpretation.
3. Focus on mutual needs. Identify what each party needs. Determine what is most important.
4. Generate options. This step should be done mutually so all parties have a say.
5. Create an action list. Determine what needs to occur as measurable behavior. Avoid saying that something will be tried. Be as specific as possible.
6. Focus on the future. Talk about what can be done today to make things better in the future.

Recognize that these six steps will become easier the more they are practiced. As a counselor, you may find them useful when working with campers who have conflicts with one another. The techniques may also be helpful if staff conflicts arise. Conflict cannot be avoided. But if handled appropriately, it can be a way to experience positive growth.

Be Aware of Your Limitations

The importance of remaining realistic about your own abilities to completely understand situations and guide people cannot be overemphasized. Going beyond your abilities can be dangerous. You cannot put yourself on a par with a professional guidance counselor who has studied extensively in such areas as mental health, group behavior, and psychology.

The purpose of this chapter has been to present some common-sense procedures to use when facing everyday camp situations. The aim has been to help you effectively solve those problems that you are able to handle and to recognize those that are beyond your capabilities. Limit your efforts to the commonplace problems of normal camp life and to those occasions when campers mainly want guidance and advice or someone to listen to them.

You don't want to overreact to quirky but benign behavior; but if you have any doubts, go immediately to a unit leader, head counselor, or camp director. And of course, never discuss a camper's problems with other campers or unqualified staff members.

REFERENCES

Fee, S. (2010). Conflict resolution skills. Retrieved from http://www.susanfee.com.

Thurber, C. (2009, May/June). Collaborative problem solving. *Camping Magazine, 83*(3), 58–63.

WEB RESOURCES

International Online Training Program on Intractable Conflict: Respectful Communication (http://www.colorado.edu/conflict/peace/treatment/civilcom.htm) has information on communication skills, anger, active listening; provides general information but can be geared toward children.

Teamwork and Teamplay (http://teamworkandteamplay.com) has a bookstore of free activity ideas and resources on team building.

PRINT RESOURCES

Garr, M. (2005, Nov/Dec). Looking for solutions, not problems. *Camping Magazine, 78*(6). Provides guidelines for working with unhappy campers or resolving conflicts.

Leiken, J. (2002, May/June). The difficult bunk meeting. *Camping Magazine, 75*(3). Discusses how to meet with a group that is having conflict or behavior issues.

Leiken, J. (2005, May/June). Exploring the true potential in thirteen-year-old boys. *Camping Magazine, 78*(3). Teaching boys how to feel good about themselves.

Leiken, J. (2005, May/June). Teaching thirteen-year-old girls a whole new way of life. *Camping Magazine, 78*(3). Teaching girls skills to feel good about themselves.

Nelson, D. C. (2000, May/June). Building bunk group buddies. *Camping Magazine, 73*(3). Creating a team and working together as a bunk group.

11

Potential Problems

People have many similarities and yet, they differ in numerous ways. They differ physically in such aspects as height, weight, musculature, hair coloring and texture, bone structure, complexion, facial features, and expressions. They also vary in body shape, speed and way of moving, voice tone and pitch, favorite expressions and word choice, and even ways of laughing. These features help you distinguish each individual. If someone recounts Jessie's remarks or actions to you, your immediate reaction is likely to be "that is just like Jessie." You have come to identify her with certain characteristic attitudes, emotional reactions, ways of thinking, likes and dislikes, abilities, and ideals that make up her particular personality. Human traits are numerous and the countless possible permutations and combinations rule out any chance of finding exactly the same combination in any two individuals.

These differences add variety to your associations with others, yet they also increase the difficulty of understanding different individuals and of establishing a mutually satisfactory relationship with them. Research in human behavior has provided generalities and probabilities that *usually* hold true, but each person is unique. People who have studied extensively in this area confess their inability to classify people with assurance or fully explain who they are, how they got that way, what they will do in certain situations, or how they will respond to a type of treatment. Therefore, those with relatively meager training and experience in human behavior should not attempt to diagnose and prescribe solutions or treatment in complex cases.

Fortunately, most campers seldom present serious problems since they are usually healthy individuals with mainly good qualities. Therefore, if camp counselors have some education, are well trained, and possess com-

mon sense, they should be able to cope with the kinds of problems they will likely encounter. However, it bears repeating that counselors should not hesitate to refer a matter to the proper person when they note signs of serious trouble. Bungling attempts to help, no matter how well intentioned, can do serious harm during these important formative years in a child's life. The purpose of this chapter is to provide general and nontechnical information designed to help you better understand and handle common problems and situations.

Appropriate Mental Health

Every society establishes types of behavior that its members consider acceptable, usual, standard, typical, common, average, conventional, or routine for given situations. This behavior is sometimes referred to as *normal*, although that concept is difficult to define since it is value-laden. What might be normal to one person may be highly atypical to someone else. Further, norms change with the passage of time, and also may vary by community, culture, or society.

When an individual's behavior follows along the accepted lines in a particular situation, he or she frequently receives the stamp of approval and is deemed normal. Conformity, or doing what is expected in a particular environment, is considered normal. Anyone who strays from the expected (ordinary) may be classified as exceptional, a genius, antisocial, weird, a failure, or whatever other term seems to describe the situation. If a young person's behavior bothers others, he or she may be labeled a *problem child*.

Good mental health and normal behavior are commonly discussed concepts. Most people have a general understanding of what they mean, but would probably be at a loss if asked to give an exact definition. Although measurable human traits vary in degree, rating a group of people by means of these traits would result in a *normal curve*. The majority of people would be clustered about a center or norm, and the relatively few found outside this area on either side would be classed as abnormal, outliers, or deviant. The exact point at which the abnormal begins would not be universally agreed upon since its location is a matter of opinion, and therefore would differ with each individual.

People with good mental health adjust well to others and find ways to solve their problems and meet needs that are mutually acceptable to both them and society. Their state of mind is in equilibrium in that they are at peace and on good terms with themselves and others. This state is hard to steadfastly maintain. As individuals attempt to satisfy their desires and needs they inevitably are confronted with conflicts and disappointments. These stressors and disappointments can cause temporary fluctuations in mood.

People with emotional maturity and good mental health have learned to adjust their own wishes to those of their associates and are willing to give as well as receive. They accept their disappointments and changing moods in stride without being overly upset or overreacting. Of course, even the most even-tempered person cannot always exercise perfect control and to act as others would like. Consequently, every person may be at one time or another a "problem child" to someone else.

Developing Insight

Newborn babies are entirely selfish and think only of themselves. They cry when they want something and are encouraged to continue the practice when it proves successful. As children grow older, those raising them recognize that desires must occasionally be denied, children must be taught to consider others, and they must be willing to sometimes yield their needs and wishes. People in society have effective and often painful ways of expressing disapproval of individuals who remain self-centered and insist on always having their own way.

Some children, however, manage to force others to give in to their wishes by crying, throwing temper tantrums, wheedling, cajoling, bargaining, blackmailing, begging, bullying, threatening, or making life generally miserable until they get what they want. Parents sometimes give into their children to keep peace or in a misguided attempt to show their love for the child. Whatever their motivation, these parents are effectively teaching their child that these tactics can be used to get what is wanted.

When these children come to camp, they generally continue to use these tactics to obtain material possessions, attain status, gain recognition or attention, or acquire anything else they want. Their methods may be so ingrained that they are barely aware of them and may be greatly surprised when their camp leaders ignore such immature behavior.

Although you will find such behavior annoying, remember that these children are immature and have problems that are largely the creation of others. You will need to help these children understand and overcome bad behavior patterns by learning to respect the rights and wishes of others. Otherwise, the other campers will avoid them and they will miss out on much that camp has to offer.

Children have wishes and needs they want to satisfy immediately, but often they can find no easy and direct way. In desperation, some children may take action that is counterproductive and seemingly unrelated to their desires. Neither they nor anyone else may understand exactly what they are trying to accomplish. For instance, a bully or braggart may be unconsciously demonstrating a need for status and attention. A counselor's natural reaction to this type of behavior might be to scold the camper in an attempt to take care of the problem. He or she may believe this action will discourage others from engaging in similar conduct, and thereby establish the counselor as the person in charge.

Looking at the problem more rationally, however, suggests that such actions only treat the symptom, not the underlying cause. Although the behavior might change temporarily, the net result may only be to intensify the situation and cause the camper to continue to have doubts about his or her worth as an individual. Unless you can find a healthy way to bolster this person's ego, his or her misgivings will continue to fester and likely break out again in a new direction.

As noted earlier, misbehavior often is merely an outward sign of underlying dissatisfaction, which is rarely overcome by direct treatment of the misbehavior. Repressing one type of undesirable behavior will often cause different and more severe problems. You need to probe beyond the symptoms until you can find the underlying cause and try to address it; only then will the symptoms subside.

Campers seldom understand why they misbehave or create problems. Although they may be aware of vague feelings of unrest and unhappiness, self-diagnosis is notoriously fallible. Behavioral difficulties have a cause that is real and often deep rooted. As emphasized throughout this book, everything a person does is for the purpose of meeting a need. When an individual's conduct is objectionable, camp counselors must have the patience and wisdom to analyze the problem and find ways to solve it. Solutions often are a real challenge since emotional pains are hard to diagnose. These issues apply to both campers and counselors.

So-called "problem campers" are often the products of problem environments and home situations. The problems accompany children to camp. For example, doting, overprotective "helicopter" parents can set up their children to expect the same attention in camp. A child accustomed to living in a household of adults who hover over the child, ready to offer help and support whether or not it is asked for, may be at a loss when placed with others of the same age, expected to contribute equally, and with a counselor who does not show favoritism.

In contrast, some children suffer from lack of love, may be jealous of the attention given to a brother or sister, or may feel that they were sent to camp just to get rid of them while the parents enjoy a trip or vacation. Such children will understandably appear "needy," craving the attention denied them elsewhere. Their difficulties sometimes arise for the first time in camp, or if already present, get worse when they participate in camp activities. Camps that have a highly structured program and that require each camper to participate in every part of it may find that some individuals react badly to such a regimen and become sensitive, irritable, or argumentative or rebellious. The child misbehaves as a reaction, causing discipline problems for the counselors, the entire unit, or even the whole camp.

Emotionally stable people can usually face their problems and disappointments honestly and work out satisfactory solutions. Emotionally unstable individuals meet problems in two ways: (1) *evasion* or *withdrawing*, or (2) *aggression.* The strategy exhibited by the subconscious mind covers up the real trouble, making it difficult for counselors to get at the source and help. Even after the cause is determined, there is seldom a sure-fire remedy since each situation is complex. Consequently, an unskilled counselor should seek assistance from a more experienced staff member.

Withdrawn or Evasive Campers

The need to help campers who are timid, apologetic, and withdrawn often is unrecognized. They cause little disturbance and are overshadowed by campers who are aggressive and create problems that demand the counselor's attention. However, a child's failure to demand attention and his or her apparent preference for solitude may indicate a developmental problem. The withdrawn camper, like the aggressive camper, usually has inner feelings of dissatisfaction, insecurity, or inadequacy. Instead of facing problems, these children may retreat into their own little world and adopt any of several automatic unconscious mechanisms to protect themselves from hurt and rejection.

Daydreamers retreat into a fantasy world to temporarily escape the stresses of everyday life. When kept under control, daydreaming can be relaxing and is often beneficial. Those who accomplish great things are usually great dreamers whose dreams stimulate them to action. However, when dreaming becomes an end in itself and provides complete satisfaction, it is problematic and interferes with the child's ability to satisfy real, tangible needs.

Wishful thinkers persist in believing what they want to believe despite all the evidence to the contrary. They escape facing unpleasant facts by simply ignoring them. These people may close their eyes to difficulty by simply refusing to worry about anything and expressing confidence that everything will turn out for the best. If any disaster occurs, they shrug it off by saying, "It might have been worse." This reaction frees them from guilt feelings or responsibility for neglected work or failure to recognize and correct their own faults. Although often happy and carefree themselves, their unwillingness to do their share leaves others with a disproportionate amount of responsibility to assume.

Sorry-for-themselves individuals indulge in a self-centered pity party where they can dwell upon how misunderstood and mistreated they are. Some want to run home when faced with the fact that others expect them to pull their own weight instead of demanding favors and pampering. Others develop a convenient illness to avoid unpleasant tasks, while still others become self-worshippers to compensate for their lack of status in the eyes of others. Some young people who have failed to secure affection and recognition from those of their own age become abnormally attached to an adult who has been kind or at least tolerant of them. They may claim to be bored with their age group.

Loners crowd out the unhappiness caused by inability to fit in with their peers by turning to strictly solitary pursuits such as reading or drawing. Thus, they eliminate the necessity of having to tailor themselves to group standards.

Yes-persons may have had their suggestions and remarks ridiculed or ignored. They may avoid further hurt by showing no initiative and retiring into the background to avoid calling attention to themselves.

Rationalizers try to avoid blame, either from their own conscience or the accusations of others. They will create a plausible excuse to make everything they do seem right and reasonable. A favorite form of rationalizing is projecting the blame (i.e., scapegoating) for what happens to other people or things. These campers may claim that they were late to breakfast because their counselor failed to wake them, that their team lost because the umpire was biased, or that they lost the tennis match because of their inferior rackets. They are afraid to face facts and admit that they, like all humans, have faults and weaknesses. Another form of rationalization is found in the *sour grapes* attitude of the fox that could not reach the grapes and so pretended they were so sour that he did not want them anyway. For example, a nonathletic student might speak of "dumb jocks" and a poor student might refer to good students as "nerds."

Self-repudiators are people whose feelings of insecurity about some trait make them fish for compliments by running themselves down with such remarks as "Oh, I'm stu-

A withdrawn camper may have inner feelings of insecurity or inadequacy that require a counselor's support.

pid" or "I'm ugly." They, of course, are hoping that you will quickly reassure them that just the opposite is true.

Compensators often fail to achieve success in a desired field so they redirect their efforts into another. For example, a girl who does not believe she has physical beauty may work extra hard to become an outstanding student or athlete. A boy without the coordination and physical stamina to excel in athletics may decide to become a great scientist or a famous writer. Obviously, substitution or compensation can be good when directed to a worthwhile goal. Some famous people experienced disappointments or feelings of inferiority in some area, which spurred them to achieve distinction in another field. However, when such feelings distort the personality and cause the person to compensate in a negative way—i.e., striving to be the biggest troublemaker, risk-taker, or lawbreaker—compensation is not good.

Aggressive Campers

Instead of trying to fade into obscurity, people with unmet needs sometimes try desperately to draw attention to themselves. Their behavior is represented in several ways.

The *braggart*, the *bully*, the *smarty*, and the *tough girl* or *tough guy* swagger around with an attitude of pretended fearlessness and assurance. They are likely covering up feelings of insecurity because of their failure to attract attention and gain status by legitimate means. Bullies usually attack those younger or weaker than themselves, or others who will not retaliate. Boastful campers are trying to convince themselves or others that they are actually the great people they inwardly fear they are not. Unfortunately, such attitudes repel others and cause them to ridicule, dislike, or ignore the aggressor, which only intensifies the problem.

Children who often swear and use foul language may be indulging in a misguided effort to relieve their pent-up emotions and gain status and recognition. Bossy, domi-

neering people exercise power in the only way they know—by making themselves so annoying that others would rather give in than resist. Children sometimes take out their frustrations by being arrogant or antagonistic, or resorting to acts of vindictiveness.

The show-offs and the girls or boys who go to extremes in dress or talking often would prefer to find their niches by other means if they knew how. People who are mimics, cutups, or practical jokers may get the attention desired, but do not know how to do so with regular behavior.

Constant talkers monopolize the conversation. Subconsciously they likely envy their quieter, more socially acceptable companions who can feel secure without constantly needing to occupy the limelight.

Unusual expressions of *individuality* such as people who eat the fastest, most, or least and those with numerous food dislikes or idiosyncrasies are often in the same category with those who bask in the individuality of an injury, or unusual ailment, or an artistic temperament.

People who cry easily or throw temper tantrums have probably found these methods effective in getting their own way in the past. They may continue the practice at camp.

Antagonistic, stubborn, or rebellious people might be unsure of themselves. They use loud or threatening words and violent action to drown out their own misgivings and discourage others from questioning them.

Intolerant people who "know all the answers" are in fact usually distrustful of their own beliefs and reluctant to listen to others who may point out their inferior reasoning. Similarly, *overcritical* people call attention to flaws in others to make themselves seem superior by comparison.

Campers who form *cliques* of two or more may be seeking comfort from each other because of their inability to make a place for themselves in the larger group. Forcibly breaking up the alliance may cause acute misery; a better solution for the counselor is to lead them gradually into general group participation so that they will no longer need the security of their clique.

Some campers resort to *regression,* or reverting to behavior of an earlier age. This may take the form of baby talk or complete dependence. They hope to be sheltered and excused for childish behavior and shortcomings as they were when at that age.

Other annoying ways of trying to draw attention are noisiness, getting in the way, asking innumerable questions, refusing to eat, deliberately running away, or constantly complaining of injuries and ailments. Although normal children and even adults sometimes use attention-getting devices, reliance on these immature methods should gradually diminish and disappear as children grow older and acquire more mature and satisfying ways to meet their needs.

Bullying

Bullying has received a great deal of attention in schools as well as camps over the past decade and deserves a separate discussion. The stereotypical image of bullying is the kind of physical bullying more common among boys. Far more common among both boys and girls, however, is verbal bullying, name-calling, and other forms of verbal harassment. Most school officials and bullying programs virtually ignore **relational bullying**, the systematic diminishment of a child's sense of self-worth through exclusion, shunning, and gossip.

The statistics about bullying are astounding. Every 7 minutes a child is bullied. About 85% of bullying episodes happen in front of bystanders. The level of aggression and abuse rises with each additional audience member. Adults intervene in only 4% of bullying incidents on the playground and 14% of bullying incidents in the classroom. Peers intervene in 19% of bullying incidents (NICHD, National Institutes of Health, 2001).

Storey (2010) has compiled information on preventing bullying at camp. She advocates that every camp should be a *bullying-free* camp. This type of camp requires that staff recognize bullying and intervene appropriately. Note that bullying can occur among staff as well as among campers. Sometimes the bullying between counselors may resemble sexual harassment.

Bullying is a form of emotional or physical abuse that usually has three defining characteristics: (1) it is deliberate, (2) it is repeated, and (3) it usually represents a power imbalance since bullies usually choose victims that they perceive as vulnerable (Storey, 2010). Several warning signs that might be evident are:

- Unexplained damage or loss of clothing and other items
- Evidence of physical abuse
- Loss of friends or lack of friends
- Reluctance to participate in activities
- Unusually sad, moody, anxious, lonely, or depressed behavior

- Problems with eating or sleeping
- Headaches, stomachaches, or other physical ailments
- Thoughts of suicide or revenge

One way to prevent bullying is to make clear that the camp will not tolerate bullying. These rules should be made clear to campers; that is, they should be told (1) treat everyone with respect, (2) help everyone feel safe and included, (3) bullying is not acceptable and will not be tolerated (4) if someone is bullying you, it is OK to stand up for yourself or ask for help from a friend or adult, (5) report bullying when you see it, (6) stand up for the person being bullied, and above all, (7) do not participate or laugh.

As a counselor, you have a moral obligation to prevent and stop bullying (Storey, 2010). You can assert this responsibility by:

- Promoting connections
- Building and communicating the shared vision of camp as a place where bullying is not tolerated
- Taking bullying seriously and being prepared to stop it
- Listening and talking to campers
- Intervening immediately when you see or hear about bullying
- Preventing cyber bullying both at camp and when campers return home

Homesick Campers

Some campers simply do not know how to handle being away from home and familiar surroundings when they first go to resident camp. They feel a sense of loneliness and homesickness upon first coming to camp. Fortunately, most of them adjust well and are soon having fun and enthusiastically joining in camp activities. However, some campers will resist any efforts to become part of the group and insist that they want to go home. Before you can help them, you will need to try to determine the root of their problem.

Children who have never been away from home before may be overwhelmed by strange faces and unfamiliar surroundings. They may have had little experience in associating with other children their age outside of school and may not know how to seek out or even accept friendships. Having to use a latrine or sleep in a room with others may be new and awkward for them. They may feel a vague uneasiness at the quiet strangeness of the woods, particularly at night.

This situation sometimes results from an overly dependent parent-child relationship, which may be mutual or one-sided. Parents, without realizing sometimes, come to depend upon the child to satisfy their own need to feel loved and important and therefore do everything they can to encourage the child's dependency. They may actually gain satisfaction in having their child express unhappiness at being away from them.

Communication from *childsick* parents may dwell upon how everyone—including playmates and pets—misses the child and how much fun they are having doing the things he or she used to enjoy. Parents may try to show their love and concern by frequent e-mails, letters, telephone calls, and boxes of goodies. Camp directors often counsel parents on the type of letter to write and ask them not to send packages or call (except in an emergency) or visit the camp unless a visitors' day has been structured for everyone. Most homesick campers will most likely be smiling and enthusiastic about what they are doing in a few days.

An opposite problem involves campers who feel that their parents do not love them and have sent them to camp so that the parents can enjoy a trip or an active social life without worrying about a babysitter. This feeling of rejection often leads children to believe that no one at camp will want them either. Counselors will need to provide reassurance and help the camper understand that he or she can become a part of a caring camp family.

Spells of homesickness normally reach their peak after a day at camp and are strongest at mealtime or in the evening around bedtime. These times are relatively inactive when campers have time to think about themselves. Homesickness has its basis in fear—fear of strangers, fear of unfamiliar surroundings, or fear of not being accepted. It is best forestalled by the methods suggested earlier to make campers feel welcome at their new temporary home. Talking it out may enlighten counselors and help campers. Assure campers that such feelings are perfectly natural and are experienced by nearly everyone when they first stay away from home. Allowing homesick campers to spend some time with an adult to whom they seem naturally attracted may be helpful in providing a substitute for their missed parents. It also helps to keep campers busy in cabin- or unit-planned activities or to involve them in an activity at which they excel, such as drawing pictures for the camp paper, helping with an outdoor fireplace, or decorating the tables in the dining room. Campers are less likely to feel homesick if they feel important and needed.

You cannot ignore homesick campers. Their misery is real and may only get worse if positive steps are not taken. Homesickness can manifest as real or imaginary physical ailments such as a stomachache or earache. If the nurse is sympathetic and gives the attention needed, the camper may seek excuses to go to the infirmary, which is fine. Other satisfying substitutes, however, need to be found.

Sometimes it helps to challenge a young person's pride. Convince him or her to stick it out for a certain period of time with the promise that he or she may go home after this time if the desire to do so is still strong. You should realize that you are fighting for more than just re-

taining campers on the camp roster. In dealing with homesickness, a counselor is contributing to children's welfare by guiding them to emotional maturity and gradual emancipation from home ties.

Sometimes the best efforts of a counselor fail, however, and if the camper shows no signs of improving, the camp director may want to consider letting him or her go home. In addition, homesickness is sometimes contagious and may spread to others who would adjust better if not exposed to it. Pointing out that parents can often reduce the possibility of their child getting homesick is important. Consider these helpful hints that can be conveyed to *parents* before they send their child to camp:

1. When saying good-bye to their child at camp, parents should not let the camper walk them to their car for one last hug. Parting farewells are best said in the child's cabin, where he or she will immediately be engaged by the counselor or cabinmates.

2. Parents can make sure the child receives written correspondence in the form of a letter the first day of camp. If permitted by the camp, an e-mail or text message would also be fine. A letter can be written and mailed before the child leaves home, or an e-mail or text message can be sent right after the parents depart for home.

3. In any communication with the child, either when saying good-bye or in letters or e-mails, parents should indicate how much they *love* their child and NOT how much they *miss* him or her. In addition to loneliness, many children actually feel guilty about going off to camp. In some cases, they think they have abandoned the family, especially if someone is sick. When a parent says, "I miss you," it sometimes makes the camper feel worse.

4. When sending letters or e-mail to a camper, parents should encourage their child to talk about the exciting experiences he or she is having at camp and about new friends and new skills. Parents can talk about what is going on at home but should minimize glowing details. If the child is already feeling lonely, the idea that he or she is missing out on something or is left out could exacerbate these feelings.

Here are some helpful hints for *counselors* with homesick campers:

1. Campers should say their good-byes to their parents while at the cabin so the counselor can begin immediately to foster the initial development of the group; counselors can encourage the group to support one another regarding the sad emotions of leaving parents.

2. Counselors should be prepared to have several short, fun activities that can be initiated during any lull in camp activity. These activities can be used in the period before or after meals, between activities, at night before bed, or while hiking across camp. For example,

team-building initiatives can prove invaluable for times such as these.

3. If campers insist on calling home, strongly discourage the action. Counselors might suggest that a phone call can be made only after a period of time has passed. Camps should strongly discourage, if not prohibit, the use of cell phones at camp to prevent immediate access to parents by homesick campers. Counselors should note that their behavior as a role model will either hinder or promote the use of cell phones by their campers.

Thurber (2006) has conducted extensive research on homesickness at camp. He concludes that camps that focus on homesickness prevention through a multi-modal approach report happier campers, calmer parents, higher enrollments, better retention rates, and a highly competent and confident staff who focus on fun and not homesickness. A focus on prevention will require less treatment and enable campers to get the most from their camp experiences.

Racism, Heterosexism, Sexism, and Other Prejudicial Behavior

Since camps are not disconnected from society, problems such as racism, heterosexism, and sexism are not absent from the camp experience. Counselors will need to address these issues whether they are raised through jokes told by campers or even comments by fellow counselors. These "isms" can be hurtful to individuals and promote intolerance. Camps should have policies about language and respect for all individuals at camp.

Like other negative behaviors, racism, heterosexism, and sexism are learned. When encountered and depending upon the severity of the situation, a counselor's reaction must be decisive. Protecting all individuals from acts of hatred whether aimed at an individual or a group of people is the responsibility of everyone at camp. Some specific steps that a counselor might take are:

1. Interrupt the action. Step in calmly and quietly. Ask campers to sit quietly for a minute, and take a moment to remind yourself to remain friendly, calm, and firm.

2. Remind children about rules: no hurting, no name-calling, no pushing, and no hitting. Disagreements are allowed, but meanness is not. Calling someone a name or making fun of a person or group of people is hurtful.

3. Listen carefully to all the children, one at a time, and help them talk about what is happening. Try to bypass the accusations and denials, and help them focus on what they feel.

4. Remind the young people that they have choices about their behavior. Ask them to think about how they might feel if they were the object of the joke or name calling.

5. Offer comfort if you know someone has been directly affected. Help that person realize that he or she is important and that others can be mean if they do not realize the consequences.

6. You may also need to explain that some grown-ups use negative words because they are not happy about themselves and they need to look down on someone else. Sometimes they do not even intend to be hurtful but say things without thinking.

7. Remind children to tell themselves that "just because someone says it doesn't mean it's true."

Involve campers in making a plan to avoid the behavior in the future. Help young people realize that they always have choices if something happens that they do not believe is right. They can walk away from the scene, find another person to talk to about what happened, stop what they are doing, or apologize (Teaching Tolerance, 2010).

Enuresis

Nearly all children suffer from *enuresis* (bed-wetting) at some stage in their growth. The cause can be physical, so children experiencing repeated occurrences should be referred to the camp doctor or nurse. Some cases, however, are manifestations of a child's inability to satisfy his or her emotional needs, resulting in anxiety and worry to which they respond by reverting to regressive behavior. Failure to get enough sleep or quiet time may be contributing causes, and the child with enuresis may have other symptoms of anxiety or emotional problems. An excessive state of anxiety may cause a child to be tense and poorly coordinated and consequently accident-prone. Additionally, sometimes bed-wetting occurs because the child is afraid to get up and go to the latrine alone at night and does not want to wake a friend or a counselor to accompany him or her.

If the health staff finds no physical cause and gives you the go-ahead, first set out to determine what is worrying or bothering the child and eliminate it if possible. Above all, do not add to an already fragile ego by shaming the child. Instead, be especially friendly and understanding, assuring the child that the trouble is not at all unique and that with his or her cooperation you feel sure that the difficulty can be overcome. In the meantime, use such precautionary measures as providing the camper with rubber sheets, limiting fluid intake after 5 PM, seeing that there is a visit to the latrine just before bedtime, and maybe again three or four hours later. Make sure the child has a flashlight and knows he or she can wake you to accompany him or her on night trips to the latrine.

Child Abuse

Child abuse is defined as non-accidental physical or mental injury caused by the acts or omissions of the child's parents or caretakers. It may include non-accidental injury, physical neglect such as the failure to provide adequate food or supervision, emotional mistreatment such as belittling or rejecting a child, and/or sexual abuse defined as sexual exploitation of a child for the sexual gratification of another person.

Child abuse is a form of violence and violence is something children are exposed to daily through video games, movies, and music. Some children are exposed to violent behavior on the playground, in the neighborhood, or at home. At camp, staff are responsible for safeguarding all children. Therefore, we must assure that child abuse NEVER happens at camp and that children who may experience abuse elsewhere are helped in all ways possible at camp.

If you believe that someone in camp has abused a camper, bring the situation to the director's attention immediately. Do not discuss the situation with others. The director will determine what action to take. Most camps have policies to help prevent any type of abuse; for example, requiring two counselors to be present in any activities with children. Men are more vulnerable to accusations of child abuse, whether founded or unfounded. Therefore, camps that employ males may want to assure that these rules are always followed. Each camp may determine specific guidelines based on the camp and the recommendations put forward by insurance companies as well as organizational policies.

All states have codes regarding the reporting of suspected cases of child abuse or neglect and circumstances which might reasonably result in abuse or neglect. Any person who willfully violates these reporting obligations can be prosecuted, so each camp should have specific policies and provide all staff with training so that there is complete understanding of staff responsibilities.

In general, when a counselor suspects abuse/neglect, he or she informs the camp director. The director determines that reporting is needed. Usually the camp director should make the report. A counselor reporting suspected neglect or abuse should not attempt to verify the facts. Reports should be made promptly, usually within one hour from the time it is known or suspected. Reports should be made to the social services department or police/sheriff department of the county of the child's residence. They will provide directions for how the report should be filed. Almost every state has a Child Abuse Hotline where many questions can be answered.

All incidents or suspicions should be kept confidential. Do not discuss in any specific way with anyone except the camp director. If you are contacted by anyone other than representatives of the agency to whom the incident was reported, do not discuss the situation. Do not expect to hear anything further about what happens or to be involved in what happens after you report. This is confidential between the agency investigator and the family. The agency will determine the appropriate action.

Sometimes a child may come to you to disclose that he or she has been abused. You should do several things: believe the child, find a private place to talk further, reassure the camper that he or she has done nothing wrong by telling you but also make it clear that you are *required* to talk to your supervisor and report the information to the proper authorities. Listen to the child, tell the child that help is available, report the incident immediately to your director, and seek out your own support system (e.g., a camp nurse or another medical professional) as this revelation may be highly disconcerting.

Above all, do not promise confidentiality, panic, or express shock. Do not make negative comments about the perpetrator. And, as noted, do not discuss the conversation with anyone but your camp director. Child and sexual abuse is very serious, and you should be aware of all the procedures that need to be followed in the event it is encountered at camp. More information can also be obtained from ACA (www.acacamps.org/child-health-safety/child-abuse).

Dietary Concerns and Eating Disorders

Campers may come to camp with *food allergies* and *dietary concerns*. Some examples include: vegetarian, vegan, lactose intolerance, celiac (gluten intolerance), nut allergies, tree nut allergies, citrus allergies, casein allergies, low carb (for diabetes), low sugar, low fat, high protein, and diets that conform to religious, family, or personal beliefs. The camp's health supervisor should let counselors know about any concerns for each session. Food allergies occur when the body thinks a food is harmful. The immune system tries to fight it off by releasing chemicals and histamine that trigger allergic symptoms. The most common symptom of a food allergy reaction is hives. Other symptoms can include tingling in the mouth and swelling of the tongue and throat. These symptoms should be immediately treated.

Eating disorders occur among campers of any age. They can also occur with staff. Staff should be aware of campers' eating habits. If you suspect any eating concerns, you should inform the health supervisor. Common eating disorders and their symptoms include bulimia—when an individual always tries to purge or vomit after eating. Anorexia occurs when an individual does not eat any food or eats very little. Compulsive eating occurs when an individual eats all the time and cannot control it. The health supervisor can talk with a camper, communicate with parents/guardians as needed, and can implement an "eating agreement/contract" with the camper. Rarely will a camper develop an eating disorder at camp. They often come to camp with an eating concern already present. Sometimes the stress of a new environment can trigger the behaviors.

Sexual Interest, Innuendo, and Sexual Identity

Since camps are interested in educating the whole child and meeting his or her physical, mental, emotional, and social needs, a counselor should be prepared to handle questions about sex. Although all children have a normal and growing interest in sex, present-day social pressures and practices sometimes push them into an exaggerated or premature interest in sex and dating. Girls physically mature approximately two years ahead of boys, but the interest in sex occurs at the same time.

If children cannot get their information from some legitimate source such as the home or school, they will seek it elsewhere—often from some equally uninformed or misinformed peer. Their discomfort and sometimes lack of knowledge may also result in inappropriate jokes. A camp counselor cannot ignore the presence of such interests and questions in every individual or group of young people. Instead, recognizing them openly is usually the better tactic but this issue must be handled carefully.

Group discussions sometimes are helpful, since they give campers a chance to ask questions and learn that their own anxieties and problems are common to others. When conducted by qualified leaders, these discussions provide a way to substitute sound information for half-truths and misinformation. Unless someone in authority asks you, do not voluntarily initiate this discussion as part of a program, particularly if you are unsure of your own qualifications for the task. Assess whether you are comfortable with and confident of your ability to handle such an assignment.

Children prefer associating with those of their own sex at certain stages. For the majority of individuals, this preference gradually changes into an acceptance of and then orientation to the opposite sex. Some individuals remain attracted to their own sex. In either case, people develop relationships with others that may eventually culminate in love and perhaps a lifelong partnership or marriage. In recent years, the topic of sexuality at camp has been discussed by many of the field's experts and practitioners. How a camp addresses sexuality is specific to each individual camp.

Regardless, sexual behavior is of great interest to campers and may be openly discussed (Wallace, 2007). Many adults are unaware of the pressures and choices young people face every day when it comes to sexual behavior. About one-quarter of middle school children re-

port engaging in sexual behavior, and about two-thirds of high school students. Sexual behavior among adolescents may not be new but the casualness and regularity in which this *hooking up* takes place is new.

If you have the opportunity and permission to talk to campers about sex, you may want to consider several talking points, according to Wallace (2007). Teens should recognize that social, emotional, and physical changes are going on in their minds and bodies. Sexuality and sexual decision-making are big issues. Young people are often pressured about sexual activity and they should realize that they always have choices since they are in charge of their bodies. Long-lasting consequences can be associated with having sex. Learning about one's sexual identity is a part of growing up, but it does not mean one has to have sex. Kids today are continually bombarded with media images of sexual behavior and must recognize that norms and expectations about behavior vary greatly. Each individual must decide when he or she is ready for sexual activity.

Always take a positive attitude toward sexual matters and do not be overly surprised by the sexually oriented attitudes, language, or behavior of your campers. However, if language or behavior becomes inappropriate, don't hesitate to intervene. If you believe that a problem exists concerning sexual relations at camp, seek the help of someone who is more qualified.

Strong Friendships, Hero Worship, and Crushes

For reasons that aren't always clear to us, we are strongly attracted to some people and just as strongly repelled by others. A well-adjusted person can usually get along fairly well with almost everyone. Nonetheless, most of us are fortunate to find a few people with whom we are almost always attuned and with whom doing almost anything is fun. Such mutual friendships provide life's most satisfying experiences and usually have positive benefits. Problems may occur, however, if these relationships absorb one or both of the participants to the point where they have neither the time nor the desire to carry on associations with other individuals or groups.

It is quite normal for young people to form strong attachments to someone they idealize, admire, and respect as a model or hero. This choice can have inestimable value if the model chosen is a positive one. It can provide a child with a powerful stimulus for his or her behavior.

Hero worship is most pronounced during the period when children prefer to be with their own sex. Consequently, the person chosen is often a particular pal, a member of a close-knit group, or someone of the same sex who is older. In camp, a counselor or another member of the staff is often chosen. If you become the object of your campers' admiration and respect, take pride in the compliment and recognize that it presents one of your greatest opportunities to steer campers as they develop to their full potential.

Occasionally a few campers may develop an overly strong attachment to another camper or counselor. The feeling may become so emotional and intense as to almost exclude normal relations with other individuals or the group. This *crush* is more likely to occur in individuals who have not received the warmth and affection they need from their family and friends. They may try to satisfy their emotional hunger by an abnormally close relationship with someone else. The feelings may or may not be mutual, and when extreme, the relationship may prove detrimental to one or both parties.

As a counselor, you should be aware of the possibility of becoming the object of such a crush. When it occurs, take steps to prevent it from progressing to undesirable stages. Maintain your normal friendliness with the camper, but avoid any show of favoritism or partiality. You might suggest that the camper participate in an activity led by other counselors, while checking in with the camper later. In time, with consistent behavior and understanding, your relationship will revert to a perfectly healthy and worthwhile counselor-camper relationship.

Immature counselors with unmet emotional needs might occasionally encourage this attention for their own gratification. Such a relationship has a bad effect upon both the camper and counselor. Others may notice and be critical, particularly if an older individual is selfishly satisfying his or her own needs by taking advantage of someone less experienced.

Do not mistake strong hero worship as a healthy friendship. Such misinterpretations are unfortunate and produce complications that will challenge your ability to do your job well. Most crushes at camp are examples of hero worship and the universal wish for mutual love and admiration. Handled properly, they can result in satisfying friendships later in life.

As noted earlier, it is impossible to avoid being more in sync with some children than with others, but counselors should keep such preferences to themselves by staying outwardly objective and impartial at all times. Children who are unattractive to you probably affect others in the same way, and consequently they are in the greatest need of your friendship and attention.

Substance Abuse

Drug and alcohol use and abuse by elementary, junior, and senior high school students is not uncommon. As a social problem, it can also occur in a resident or day camp setting. Everyone has to make decisions about tobacco use, drinking, or using drugs at some point in their lives. Experimentation with these substances is a part of growing up. Nonetheless, substance use is both harmful and illegal. Consequently, at no time should these substances be used by anyone in camp. Most camps have clear written policies pertaining to both staff and campers regarding smoking, chewing, drinking, and drug use.

Children need to be exposed to educational programs and healthy lifestyle alternatives so they are in a better position to make appropriate value judgments and responses. Camp is a place where value clarification can be discussed and where young people have many opportunities to observe and develop healthy values.

Nevertheless, substance abuse behaviors might occur at camp and must be addressed immediately. Because of the close associations and living arrangements at camp, counselors are in a position to closely supervise campers, and this should minimize any problems, but it won't prevent them entirely. Pills and other forms of drugs could be smuggled in and used without your knowledge. Consequently, counselors should remain observant to detect clues of any substance issues and respond correctly according to camp policy. If the policy is not evident, ask for clarification. Keep in mind that you are obligated to report any known use of drugs or alcohol to your camp director immediately.

Counseling Strategies and Advice

Recognizing problematic behaviors is the first step in determining what strategies to use in guiding problem campers. Ditter (2004) offered seven skills of highly effective counselors that may apply to situations described in this chapter (see exhibit 11.1 on the following page).

Remember that campers often are more likely to watch what you do rather than just listen to what you say. Keep your cool in all situations, and make sure your expectations are reasonable and realistic (Ditter, 2004). Always keep in mind that mastering the skills of working with campers takes practice and reflection.

In summary, camp is a positive experience for most campers and staff. However, some of the problems discussed in this chapter (as well as others that cannot be anticipated) may arise. No magic solutions exist and each issue must be addressed individually. However, the following advice may be helpful.

1. Learn all you can about campers, but do not take their previous records too seriously since a change in environment and maturity often produces a change in behavior. Children who have been labeled as problematic at home may completely change their behavior when exposed to the new personalities, influences, and activities of camp.

2. Help campers satisfy their fundamental needs and attain a feeling of security in their group. Vary the program so that each child's interests and abilities can be recognized, rewarded, reinforced, and satisfied in some way.

Exhibit 11.1

Seven Skills of Effective Counselors

1. Don't pick up the rope; or in other words, remain calm. Do not let campers push your buttons especially when the same behavior occurs time after time.

2. Enter their world. Most campers want an adult to take an interest in them. Therefore, the display of any type of behavior gives you the opportunity to gain a window into the camper's behavior and understand its origin.

3. State your expectations. Let the camper know what is expected and then let the camper try to work out the issue in his or her way.

4. Redirect. Try channeling a camper's energy in another direction away from the behavior being displayed.

5. Make campers right about what they are right about. Acknowledge the points a camper may have but explain why another approach might also be possible.

6. Separate a camper from his or her audience. If a camper is having a particularly difficult time, it may be appropriate to separate him or her from the group for a short time until the camper has settled down.

7. Create an atmosphere of respect. Talk with the camper to see what they have to say. Negotiate their needs as well as what you can offer in terms of assistance (Ditter, 2004).

3. Recall that misbehavior is usually a bid for attention, an expression of insecurity, or the result of feeling unloved and unwanted. Public scolding or punishment ordinarily only aggravates the situation.

4. Inconspicuously try to draw aggressive or retiring campers into activities that afford them a feeling of success and achievement. Their issues and problems often disappear if they are provided with socially approved ways to satisfy their needs and wishes.

5. Make a particular effort to get close to campers who seem to be creating a problem for themselves or others. This process may be tedious, since people who most need help are often too timid or proud to ask for it.

6. Cultivate the ability to be a good listener since most campers have a critical need for a trustworthy older person.

7. Seldom give advice. Instead, question the camper and offer suggestions that enable him or her to work out a personal solution. Making your expectations known, however, is important.

8. Do not heap blame on a camper for his or her misdeeds. Occasionally it may be necessary to strongly reprimand or punish campers who persistently refuse to recognize and accept their share of the responsibility, but use these methods only when all others fail.

REFERENCES

Ditter, B. (2004, Jul/Aug). Seven skills of highly effective counselors. *Camping Magazine, 77*(4), 12–13.

NICHD, National Institutes of Health. 2001. http://nichd.nih.gov/news/releases/bullying.cfm

Storey, K. (2010, May/June). Eyes on bullying: What YOU can do to prevent and stop bullying at camp. *Camping Magazine, 83*(3), 48–52.

Teaching tolerance. (2010). http://www.tolerance.org

Thurber, C. (2006, May/June). Essentials of homesickness prevention. *Camping Magazine, 79*(3), 38–42.

Wallace, S. G. (2007, March/April). Hooking up, losing out? The new culture of teen sex and how to talk to your campers about it. *Camping Magazine, 80*(2), 26–30.

WEB RESOURCES

Advocates for Youth (www.advocatesforyouth.org) advocates for positive adolescent sexual health.

American Diabetes Association (www.diabetes.org) has information on the basic types of diabetes, myths, common terms, tips, food, and fitness.

Bob Ditter (www.bobditter.com) is a social worker who works with summer camps; this site has links to his blog, resources, and other articles.

Child and Adolescent Coping Skills (http://coping.mhasp.org) provides tips and activities for children who are dealing with a family member's mental illness.

Childhelp (www.childhelpusa.org) identifies types of child abuse, signs, misconceptions, prevention, and statistics; site has helpful links, bookstore.

Coping Skills for Kids (www.copingskills4kids.net) has resources on how children develop coping skills.

Difficult Subjects (www.talkingwithkids.org) provides tips on how to talk to kids about difficult subjects; for example,

divorce, death, or other issues that might cause children to act out.

Eyes on Bullying (http://www.eyesonbullying.org) discusses interplay between bully, victim, and bystander and offers recommendations and strategies for adults for dealing with and preventing bullying.

Families for Depression Awareness (www.familyaware.org) has information about depression, support, resources, signs, and prevention for teens and children.

Homesickness (www.campspirit.com) offers tips on homesickness and additional resources.

National Eating Disorders Association (www.edap.org) identifies terms, prevention, contributing factors.

National Youth Advocacy Coalition (http://nyacyouth.org) is a social justice organization that advocates for young people who are LGBTQ; site includes resources, model programs, best practices, research articles, and publications.

Parenting Exchange (http://www.oh-pin.org/articles/pex-02–ways-to-teach-children-po.pdf) discusses ways to teach children positive coping skills during life changes.

Resilience (http://www.cyh.com/HealthTopics/HealthTopicDetails.aspx?p=114&np=122&id=1739) has information and resources on how parents can help children build resilience.

Respect U (www.respectu.com) describes the bully coach, offers tips and training to help prevent bullying.

Tanners Manners (www.tannersmanners.com) markets kits, training, resources, and publications on manners, social skills, bullying prevention.

PRINT RESOURCES

Alexander, R., & Kriesel, C. (2003, Nov/Dec). Don't assume I'm straight. *Camping Magazine, 76*(6). Discusses ways to make LGBTQ campers feel safe.

Coleman, M. (2000, May/June). "Don't laugh at me": Coming to camps. *Camping Magazine, 73*(3). Talks about creating a caring, ridicule-free environment for kids.

Ditter, B. (2008, Jan/Feb). New kids in the tent. *Camping Magazine, 81*(1). Discusses how overprotective parents and technology, among other things, are changing the behaviors of campers.

Evans, F. (2007, May/June). But words can never hurt me: The subtle power of language. *Camping Magazine, 80*(3), 42–45.

Garr, R. R., & Garr, M. (2006, Nov/Dec). Establishing clear limits. *Camping Magazine, 79*(6). Tips on establishing limits and providing structure for campers with poor behavior.

Grayson, R. (2001, May/June). Successful counseling. *Camping Magazine, 74*(3). Discusses five styles of counseling and behavior management.

Griffith, L. (1999, May/June). Creating new attitudes. *Camping Magazine, 72*(3). Nurturing the development of the adolescent soul.

Haber, J. D. (2006, Jan/Feb). Raising awareness to reduce bullying in summer camps. *Camping Magazine, 79*(1). Describes the types of bullying.

Haber, J. D. (2006, March/April). Successful bully prevention and management isn't rocket science. *Camping Magazine, 79*(2). Bullying prevention goals for camps and counselors.

Hairston, J. E., & Garst, B. (2004, May/June). Camp: A perfect place to address bullying. *Camping Magazine, 77*(3). How camp experiences can change behavior; the camp counselor's role.

Hanover, C. (2000, May/June). Camp safety basics. *Camping Magazine, 73*(3). Discusses violence at camp, what it looks like, prevention and control.

Kramschuster, J. K. (2007, July/Aug). Getting it, learning it, laughing at it. *Camping Magazine, 80*(4). Discusses the importance of the camp experience for kids with diabetes.

Pouton, L. E. (2000, Sept/Oct). Teenagers and sexuality at camp. *Camping Magazine, 73*(5). Talking about sex with campers.

Rothman, D. C. (2001, May/June). Discipline is not a dirty word. *Camping Magazine, 74*(3). Responding to challenging behavior.

Schafer, E. (2005, Sept/Oct). Children's mental health and camp: What is our role? *Camping Magazine, 78*(5), 18–24.

Schafer, E. D. (2006, May/June). Training your staff to manage the challenges of adolescence. *Camping Magazine, 79*(3). Dealing with the challenges adolescents bring to camp, like sexuality, eating disorders, and so on.

Shelton, M. (1999, July/Aug). Understanding anger. *Camping Magazine, 72*(4). The psychology of anger and steps camps can take to minimize it.

Shelton, M. (2008, May/June). Forced into manhood. *Camping Magazine, 81*(3). Discusses masculinity and homesickness.

Smieja, C. (1999, May/June). Coping with homesickness. *Camping Magazine, 72*(3). Prevention and ways to deal with homesickness.

Sorensen, B., & King, K. (1999, March/April). Play and healing. *Camping Magazine, 72*(2). Developing positive coping skills with therapeutic recreation.

Wallace, S. G. (2007, Jan/Feb). Epidemic: Translating drug prevention principles to camp. *Camping Magazine, 80*(1). Advice for camp counselors in helping youth make good decisions about drugs.

Winfree, C., Williams, R., & Powell, G. (2002, Nov/Dec). Children with cancer. *Camping Magazine, 75*(6). Benefits of camp for children with cancer.

Woods, A. (2002, Jan/Feb). Teenagers and risk-taking at camp. *Camping Magazine, 75*(1). Discusses negative risk-taking and how camp can provide positive-risk taking opportunities for teens.

Camp Activities

Come forth into the light of things,
let nature be your teacher.

—William Wordsworth

12 Planning the Program

Volumes have been written about program and curriculum development that can be applied to camp. The **program** is defined as the entire collection of activities that a camper encounters while at camp. The program includes structured activities, cabin interactions, special events, camp clean-up, and everything that occurs while a camper is at camp. Opportunities for positive development exist through all program activities.

One of the emerging trends in youth development, although not a new idea at all, is the idea of intentional or purposeful programming. This idea suggests that good things do not happen at camp just because it is camp. Positive outcomes occur because the camp has a program focused on addressing those outcomes. All staff recognize those goals and also communicate them with campers.

Each camp follows its particular mission. From that mission flow goals and objectives and then an appropriate collection of camp activities. The final element is evaluation of these programs to determine the value/benefit of camp to individuals and society. The American Camp Association has invested considerable resources in developing tools to be used by camp administrators and staff to conduct quality programming that produces developmental outcomes. Two of the best resources are *Creating Positive Youth Outcomes* (ACA, 2007) and *Designing Quality Youth Programs* (ACA, 2008). This chapter discusses components of camp program planning targeted to positive outcomes.

Program Mission, Goals, and Objectives

Targeting youth outcomes is a process that is based on seven steps (ACA, 2007):

1. Explore your readiness to evaluate youth outcomes.
2. Consider how to use the outcomes results.
3. Identify and be familiar with the camp's mission, goals, and objectives.
4. Learn to use a logic model to focus on camper change.
5. Complete a logic model.
6. Consider the youth outcome results.
7. Share the youth outcome results with others.

Being ready and eager to plan for and evaluate outcomes is the first step. This step requires that you and your camp colleagues target your camp mission and possible goals, objectives, and strategies.

All camps should have a mission statement. It should be clear and succinct and state why the camp exists. This statement should tell your camp's story in less than 30 seconds (ACA, 2007). It generally addresses such concepts as: target market, ethical/moral position, unique program focus, public image, and geographical domain. As a camp counselor, you should be able to quote that mission any time you are asked.

Specific goals and objectives in written form are a prerequisite for designing a camp program or preparing camp activities or events. Camp activities and programs should demonstrate direction, meaning, and purpose. These aspects are necessary for learning in any form, but society also demands that institutions like camps be accountable for performing adequately and furnishing evidence of positive results. Goals and objectives provide a necessary focus.

Properly developed objectives will provide the benchmarks or evidence to determine that positive changes in the campers have taken place. When campers can perform those activities they have set out to accomplish, you can be assured of the success of your program and leadership. Parents and sponsoring agencies also use these objectives to more adequately judge the potential values and outcomes of the camp's activities for those individuals they have entrusted to the camp staff. Finally, objectives are beneficial in that they provide a measure for the effectiveness of leadership, based on how well campers have progressed toward meeting the objectives.

Goals are broad general statements regarding the expected effect of the camp experience on the participants. These statements tend to be generalized such as: (1) developing the whole child, (2) aiding in character development, (3) developing leadership, (4) teaching good citizenship, (5) promoting good health and physical fitness, (6) developing appreciation of nature, and (7) encouraging independence and the ability to think for oneself. These are all goals worthy of camping, but they are not linked to developing specific programs and activities that can lead campers toward their achievement. Such broad statements are important but inadequate alone because they do not specify exactly what campers are to do or accomplish by the end of the camp experience. Therefore, goals should be developed as starting points followed by more refined functional statements or objectives.

Objectives are relatively specific statements of changes or learning expected to occur. An objective often is best expressed regarding a camper's outcome and includes a description of the behaviors expected to occur as a result of a learning experience at camp.

Behavioral objectives have become common practice among educational and recreational institutions including organized camps. With respect to camps, the clearest definition of behavioral objectives was made by Vinton and Farley (1979):

> **Behavioral objectives** are the foundation of the camp instructional program. They define specific behaviors based on the goals and philosophy of your camp. When clearly stated, they help the camp counselor select activities and materials, communicate what is to be learned, and evaluate whether or not learning has taken place. (p. 53)

SMART Objectives

A properly expressed behavioral objective has five main features that make it a SMART objective:

1. Specific
2. Measurable
3. Achievable
4. Relevant
5. Time-Bound

The Objective Is Specific

Avoid using vague expressions that can be interpreted in many ways since they do not communicate exactly what performance is expected or what is to be learned at the completion of the activity. Ambiguous objectives do not aid the counselor or leader in deciding on the proper methods. Further, they do not provide criteria by which to determine whether the camper has achieved the desired outcome. Here are some examples of nonspecific objectives:

EXAMPLE 1: The campers are to understand the principles of Leave No Trace camping.
Think about this objective. What is meant by "understand?" What are the campers to be able to do? What principles are emphasized?

EXAMPLE 2: The camper is to become acquainted with common western style equestrian techniques.
What is meant by the term "acquainted with?" What specific western style equestrian techniques are meant?

These objectives communicate little. They are too broad and vague as a basis for effective planning or for determining if a camper has successfully accomplished the objective.

The Objective Is Measurable

A well-written objective will address conditions such as when, where, and how the behavior will be completed.

The Objective Is Achievable

Examples of the behavior a camper might be expected to demonstrate and achieve may be described through such terms as: recite, demonstrate, write, assemble, define, repeat, do, complete, locate, identify, and name. Such terms define exactly what behaviors are expected of the camper.

The Objective Is Relevant and Expressed as a Camper Outcome

It is not difficult to express relevant objectives from the camper's viewpoint, although many counselors and staff members fail to do so and thereby place the emphasis in the wrong place. It is campers who must learn or perform the appropriate tasks—not the counselor. Therefore, it is best to use expressions such as "the camper will," "the child can," and "the participants are to be able to." On the other hand, avoid statements that emphasize the counselor's or leader's behavior, such as "to motivate the campers so they will," "to point out to the group," "to show the campers the importance of," or "to demonstrate to the campers." These expressions emphasize what the counselor is doing, not what the campers will learn or be able to demonstrate. Counselor or leader behaviors do not necessarily result in camper behavior.

The Objective Is Time-Bound

The objective should specify a time frame, such as "during the camp session," or "by the end of the first week."

By now you should recognize what comprises a well-written objective. Several examples of objectives containing appropriate behavioral descriptions follow. Note that they are SMART as described earlier:

EXAMPLE 1: By the end of camp, participants in the nature study program will be able to identify five trees in the camp area.

EXAMPLE 2: By the end of camp, campers will have at least two new friends that they did not have at the beginning of the camp session.

EXAMPLE 3: Campers will apply navigational skills by using maps and compass and a GPS system while on an overnight wilderness trip.

EXAMPLE 4: By the end of the second day of camp, the campers are to know three poisonous plants common to the area so that they can identify them by type and point them out to the rest of the group.

EXAMPLE 5: Prior to setting out on a three-day hike, campers will demonstrate knowledge of appropriate clothing to take along by gathering the correct items and packing them in a backpack.

These objectives provide the basis for measuring camp outcomes. Always keep in mind that outcomes go far beyond camp satisfaction ratings. Although campers should have fun, the most important aspect is the behavioral change that occurs because of camp.

Categories of Objectives

Statements of desired outcomes fall into one of three different categories, or domains, that generally relate to action, thinking, and feeling. These categories are: (1) psychomotor, (2) cognitive, and (3) affective.

Psychomotor Domain

This domain includes those objectives that deal with body movement such as muscular skill, manipulation or movement of materials or objects, or actions that include neuromuscular coordination. In a physical activity such as swimming or running you can determine how long it takes to travel a specified distance or how smoothly the task is performed. You can also determine how far or how accurately a ball is thrown or how easily a serve in tennis is performed. Similarly, the level of ability or performance in painting a picture or completing a crafts project can be measured. All are examples of performance of physical tasks.

Cognitive Domain

Objectives in the cognitive domain include factual knowledge, understanding, processes, and structures. These objectives emphasize remembering, reproducing a response that has been learned, or solving intellectual tasks and problems. Measuring objectives that require understanding facts, processes, or strategies is fairly easy to do. Such objectives commonly form the content of school subjects that require knowledge of names, dates, places, and facts. Although such information is important, most camping programs do not focus on facts, so the cognitive domain may only be used sparingly.

Affective Domain

Objectives in the affective domain deal with emotions and feelings, including attitudes, interests, and the degree of appreciation an individual has for what goes on around him or her. These objectives are often intrapersonal or interpersonal in terms of positive growth. Attitudes might include opinions and reactions to an idea, another person, or to the opinions of others. A person also may have feelings and appreciation for the aesthetic value of objects or events such as the beauty of a sunset, drops of dew on a leaf, the graceful flight of a bird, the music of the wind blowing through tall grass, or the sound of rain in the forest.

Of the three domains, objectives in the affective domain are the most difficult to express in behavioral terms and to measure—but are the most important. Many of these represent an internal experience that may not be expressed openly. The American Camp Association has made great strides in supplying instruments to measure some of these affective objectives. More outcome measures are developed each year, but currently available measures are listed in exhibit 12.1.

Exhibit 12.1

ACA Measurement Tools—Affective Domain

- **Friendship skills** (i.e., make friends and maintain relationships)
- **Independence** (i.e., rely less on adults and other people for solving problems and for their day-to-day activities)
- **Teamwork** (i.e., become more effective when working in groups of their peers)
- **Family citizenship** (i.e., encourage attributes important to being a member of a family)
- **Perceived competence** (i.e., believe that they can be successful in the things they do)
- **Interest in exploration** (i.e., be more curious, inquisitive, eager to learn new things)
- **Responsibility** (i.e., learn to be accountable for their own actions and mistakes)
- **Affinity for nature** (i.e., develop feelings of emotional attraction toward nature)
- **Problem-solving confidence** (i.e., believe they have abilities to resolve problems)
- **Camp connectedness** (i.e., feeling welcomed and supported at camp)

Camp Logic Models

A useful and popular way to develop a program and to evaluate the outcomes is to use a logic model. This model usually consists of:

- Program goals
- Program elements
- Desired short-term outcomes
- Desired long-term outcomes

Measures are available from ACA (2010) to determine if the goals have been met, such as the outcomes tools described above. Using the logic model requires assessing what inputs are needed to conduct programs as well as what possible activities might exist. The outputs relate to the actual events and opportunities that occur. The focus is on both the short-term and long-term benefits and results. Figure 12.1 shows an example of a logic model for a camp (ACA, 2007). If your camp uses a logic model approach, you should have ample opportunities to work to develop your own models relative to the goals of the camp (Molloy, 2006).

Although these models, goals, and objectives relate to positive human development and properly emphasize motor, cognitive, and affective outcomes, the program should always focus on addressing these outcomes in a fun and enjoyable manner. The recreational value of camp cannot be underestimated.

As noted earlier, play is a learning experience—although it differs from structured learning. Nevertheless, camp is a place where children can learn recreational skills and develop lifelong interests. Further, many children have structured and busy lives at home, so camp provides a place for them to relax and have time to be themselves without a focus on achievement. Camp is not a dichotomy between having fun and achieving behavioral outcomes. These elements must occur together if camp is to be meaningful. Thus, although developing a program that has positive outcomes is always important,

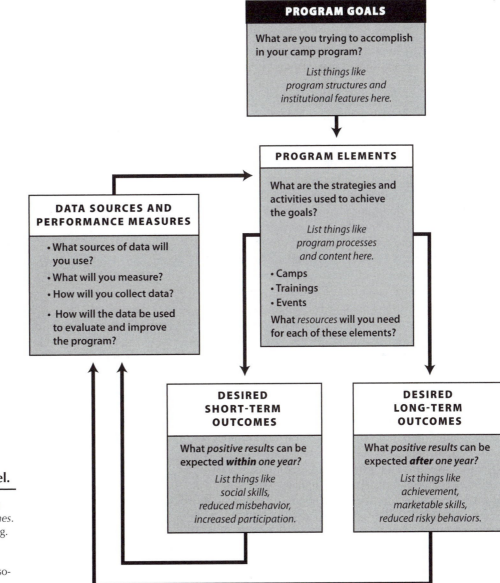

Figure 12.1   Logic model.

Source: Originally published in *Creating Positive Youth Outcomes*. Monterey, CA: Healthy Learning. Reprinted by permission of the American Camp Association. © 2007 American Camping Association, Inc.

While developing a program that has positive outcomes is important, planners cannot lose sight of the fact that the main reason children come to camp is for fun. (Photo courtesy of American Camp Association)

the enjoyment of campers is the main reason that children come to camp and should never be discounted.

Why Programs Differ

Camp programs are different in every camp. No two camps are the same, nor should they be. The reason these programs are quite diverse is because of the following kinds of variables that determine what will take place.

The activities chosen for the program will grow fundamentally from the mission of the camp or sponsoring organization and the goals and objectives of the particular camp. For example, a religiously affiliated camp will likely focus on activities of a spiritual nature; a school camp will emphasize acquiring information; and a not-for-profit camp will work toward the stated goals of the sponsoring agency. Special camps, such as those featuring dance, music, or activities for people who are physically challenged, obviously will have programs that concentrate on their particular specialty.

A camp program sometimes reflects the particular *philosophy, interests, or abilities of the camp or program director*. For instance, a person who loves music likely will emphasize related activities, while a person who participates in adventure/challenge activities may enthusiastically promote a strong sports program. Superior leaders, however, try not to overemphasize their hobbies and interests, but offer a well-rounded versatile program that is built around the organization's mission and the particular needs and interests of the campers.

Camps often reflect the *abilities of the staff*. Some camps hire a large number of specialists, whereas others hire mostly general counselors who bring with them a variety of more modest skills and interests. Specialists likely will provide better instruction in their fields, but when too many or their interests too limited, each could concentrate on promoting his or her own activity instead of cooperating as a team member to foster a well-balanced camp program. This is the exception rather than the rule, however. Broad-minded specialists not only do their own jobs well, but also promote the activities of others. A counselor who is good at geocaching (i.e., using a GPS unit to go on a treasure hunt) will soon have others joining in, and one who loves to sing will be surrounded by happy campers similarly engaged. A counselor who takes time on a hike to investigate some unusual plant life hopefully will be instilling an interest in nature in his or her followers.

The *nature of the camp site* will be influential in determining the program. A camp located near the mountains would be foolish not to take advantage of the opportunity for mountain climbing. No one, obviously, will be weaving honeysuckle baskets if honeysuckle does not grow in the camp environment. A remote unit in a decentralized camp can build its own council ring and outdoor kitchen right in its own backyard, whereas a day camp at a city park will often focus less on nature-based recreation and more on sports or recreation-center based activities.

Equipment and facilities will influence the camp program. A camp with an elaborate outlay of backpacking equipment is in a position to sponsor an extensive outdoor trips program. Although swimming and boating are almost synonymous with camp for some people, many camps without such facilities have quite successfully built a program around other worthwhile activities too often

Various activities are chosen to help meet the goals and objectives of the particular camp. Equipment, facilities, location, terrain, and the abilities of camp staff are some of the variables that enter into program design. (Lower left, middle left courtesy of Bradford Woods Learning and Outdoor Center; lower right, top courtesy of American Camp Association.)

neglected in camps, such as drama and archery. Imagination and a positive approach can turn a lack of equipment into a challenge for campers to make their own equipment or to substitute activities with less elaborate requirements.

The *location and terrain* of a camp can contribute to the camp program. When interesting historical sites abound in the vicinity, a camp should capitalize on this and visit them. Paul Bunyan country will call for storytelling and special events built around this favorite character. A seaside camp may plan visits to fish-processing plants and fishing vessels. In a camp with a steep hillside, campers might enthusiastically ski and toboggan on pine needles. In another camp, a babbling brook provides a place where campers could wade and discover the secrets of the animal and plant life.

Climate influences camp programs. Camps in hot, dry areas wisely plan campfire programs without benefit of fire and schedule an extra long siesta and quiet activities for the hottest part of the day. Camps with cool mornings and evenings will, on the contrary, lean toward vigorous activities, with swimming scheduled toward the middle of the day.

The *ages, previous experiences, skills, financial status,* and *social backgrounds of the campers* are influential in determining program components. A camper who likes to sing can lead others in songs. Another camper might demonstrate a particular craft learned from a relative. Children from rural areas may be ahead of their city peers in nature lore, but may lag behind in diving and swimming strokes.

Camps differ greatly in their *duration.* Campers who come for only a week will need fairly simple projects that they can complete in a short time. Campers from agencies such as Girl Scouts may attempt more advanced projects since they are putting into practice skills and knowledge already acquired under the sponsoring organization. In short-term camps, planning the program involves deciding on the number and types of activities that can be accomplished or mastered in the time available. Camp sessions that run from 4–8 weeks can offer more complicated plans that build up to a climax at the end of the session. A group of campers might build a log cabin to shelter their arts and crafts equipment or clear a vista and path through the underbrush down to the lake. These longer camps can also provide campers with progressive skills in such areas as swimming, canoeing, sailing, riding, and so forth.

A *high ratio* of counselors to campers is the ideal situation, since campers can be divided into small groups with each person receiving more personal attention. Small group work also may constitute a different program emphasis than in a centralized camp.

Changing Program Emphases

Years ago, camp staffs tended to keep participants busy every moment of the day. The entire day was planned out and campers followed a rigid schedule of activities and events. Activities were scheduled like school classes, with attendance carefully checked each day. Motivation was supplied by achievement charts, testing programs, intense competition between individual and groups, and elaborate systems of awards. In some cases, regimentation and scheduling were carried to a degree that almost obliterated the two things the camper most wanted—to have fun and to make new friends.

This period of regimentation was followed by a movement in the opposite direction toward openness and permissiveness. When carried to extremes, a camp might schedule no activities at all, leaving campers free to do whatever they chose the entire day. This practice was apparently based on the assumption that the way to teach children to make choices and to regulate themselves was to loosen the reins and let them learn by trial-and-error. Unfortunately, programs planned exclusively by campers often lacked continuity and were likely to degenerate into mere busy work and eventual boredom.

The best results in program development come from balancing the spontaneity and daring of youth with the influence of experience, knowledge, and greater maturity, which should occur when campers and counselors plan the program cooperatively.

To enact this cooperative program planning style, many camps use the first day or night to promote discussion between the campers and counselors regarding what the camp offers and what the campers hope to accomplish. Counselors can lead a discussion with the campers that will enable the staff members to plan out the week or session. When the staff meeting is held later that night or the next day, appropriate scheduling can take place to include those activities requested by the new campers.

The Conception of Program

The essence of a camp program was once considered to be only the activity periods, such as archery, swimming, outdoor living skills, and crafts, which children attended without question. This type of activity planning is termed a **structured program**. A program, however, is much more than just these activities—development does not begin with arts and crafts at 8:30, stop for lunch at 11:30, continue again at 1:30 with nature study, and then cease entirely after the final activity period. Camp program is, in reality, everything that happens to the camper throughout the day. Each single incident, no matter how trivial, is a potential influence for good or bad. Physical activities like tennis, swimming, or canoeing are important, but so are attributes like cooperativeness, punctuality, and friendliness. Campers are constantly learning something from every experience that takes place while they are at camp.

How a Camp Program Is Planned

As noted, camp programs may range from highly structured to unplanned or wide-open. Most camp programs lie somewhere in between as they focus on the outcomes they wish to address. The trend in program development is to let campers and staff cooperatively plan their own activities in what is known as an **unstructured** or **semi-structured program**. This approach allows enough flexibility to permit altering it as the days pass and needs and interests change. This flexible program provides variety and plenty of activity, yet is by no means haphazard and unplanned. Planning is certainly necessary to avoid conflicts over facilities, equipment, and the services of the specialists on the staff. Certain hours for rising, going to bed, eating, resting, and swimming that affect the whole camp must be scheduled or arranged to prevent groups from interfering with each other.

The program for an entire camp is usually coordinated by one person such as the program director, assistant camp director, or head counselor. Occasionally, particularly in small camps, the director serves in this capacity, but he or she more commonly acts as an advisor to someone else who has been delegated this particular responsibility.

In some camps, each camper may be allowed to decide his or her own activities during certain times of the day irrespective of what others in the unit are doing. Various methods for implementing this opportunity may be used. One is to have the program director announce at the end of a meal, such as breakfast, what activities are available for the morning. Campers then indicate by a show of hands or by sign-up sheets on the wall which activities they want to join. Duplicate lists are made up, one for the staff member in charge of each activity and the other for the camp office, so the location of each camper and counselor is always known. Better instruction occurs when participants are classified according to degree of skill, such as sailing lessons for beginners or advanced horsemanship for those who have passed their preliminary tests.

Another method of programming offers additional freedom of choice. In this case the program director opens the field for suggestions, and when someone requests an activity such as fishing, the program director asks how many would like to join in. This freedom of choice is usually more prevalent in long-term camps. Advocates claim as advantages that it focuses on the individual rather than the activity, widens a camper's circle of friends, allows campers to do what interests them, and prevents the possible conflicts that may occur when the same individuals eat, sleep, and do everything else together over a long period of time.

Many camps like to use an **indigenous program** approach. This approach is strictly personal to the camp and is based upon materials found in or near it. In arts and crafts, for example, native woods are used for whittling, native vegetation for dyeing, and local grasses and reeds for weaving. Nature specimens are the flowers, trees, and insects found on the camp grounds. Keep in mind that these projects are done only in accordance with good conservation practices. Music programs would feature folk songs, dances, and ballads of the region. Local folklore and legends could form the basis for stories, dramatics, and pageants. Information used for developing these activities could be obtained from local residents and the clippings, files, and other resources of the local librarian. No two indigenous programs are ever the same, since no two communities offer identical natural resources and historical backgrounds.

Short-term camps (i.e., one week) usually find unit programming more useful. Each camper will become better acquainted and feel more at ease if he or she spends time with only a small group of peers. In this small "family" the individual can gain recognition and have a better opportunity to voice opinions.

Under any programming plan, several all-camp events usually occur during the camp session. Their number and character vary with the particular camp. Many camps sponsor some sort of **camp council**, which consists of counselor and camper representatives from each unit who meet with the program director to plan such all-camp events.

The variety of activities depends to some extent on the camp facilities and talents of the staff. Hopefully all campers have a chance to develop their interests and abilities in several fields. One of the most important things a camp can do is to introduce children to hobbies and skills that may become lifelong pursuits or even financially profitable vocations or avocations.

How a Program Develops

When staff and campers join democratically in program planning, counselors act as consultants and advisors, not dictators. Counselors must be able to guide and control the situation so that wise choices are made without forcing their ideas on the group. Campers, however, should be clear about the types of outcomes the camp wishes to address. Campers need to understand what they should achieve. The method, strategies, or manner in which these goals are reached, however, can be determined greatly by the campers.

A counselor's ability to see opportunities, to select or reject, encourage or discourage, suggest, counsel, and use skill in changing directions will largely determine what both staff and campers get from a positive camp experience. Younger campers may need many ideas and suggestions. Many of them have unknowingly been dependent on their parents and on computers, movies, and television for entertainment, so they may find making decisions on how to spend their time difficult. Even older campers will often not be able to articulate what they *really* want to do. They are inclined to choose what they have already done, even if they have become somewhat bored with it.

Sometimes campers have too little experience or imagination to see other possibilities for camp programming. Camp offers a means to broaden their interests, and counselors may want to consider encouraging one of their own ideas initially. Suggestions from others will follow. Even when an idea is not accepted in its entirety, it may stimulate others until one idea finally captures the interest of the group for an exciting experience. An impractical or unacceptable suggestion often can be adapted into a more suitable variation.

When campers feel at ease and free to express themselves, many possibilities will emerge and the counselor's job will be to help campers settle on activities that hold priority with them. Encouraging them to look ahead and evaluate as they go along—foreseeing obstacles and planning how to overcome them—can give them valuable experience. You may, on rare occasions, have to come out with a flat "no" if what they are proposing is against camp policy or actually dangerous. At other times you may want to let them go ahead and learn by experience, as long as the consequences are not too serious. Above all, get them involved in all the planning.

Camps usually have a master calendar for all time periods during the camp week. This calendar can show days of the week, regular times such as when meals are served, special events, structured opportunities such as swimming times, and periods of time open for semi-structured planning.

The Test of a Good Program Activity

Campers can help evaluate whether an activity is good by asking themselves such questions as: What went well and what did not? What was learned from the experience and how can it be used in planning for the future?

Activities that hold up well under the following tests are likely to be good ones that make a contribution to the objectives of the camp experience.

1. Is the activity compatible with the idea of simple outdoor living? Does it further understanding and appreciation of the outdoors and is it in line with good conservation and ecological practices?

2. Does the activity develop the ability to live harmoniously with others, respecting their individual personalities and potentialities?

3. Are campers sometimes given the chance to do individual projects or activities of their own, or is everything always decided by the vote of the majority?

4. Does the activity address children's desire for fun and adventure? Do campers *want* to do it or are they merely acceding to the wishes of the adults? Is the activity interesting in itself without outside motivation such as awards or special privileges?

5. Does the activity challenge campers' initiative, resourcefulness, and creative expression, or is it merely a cut-and-dried process in which they simply follow instructions?

6. Does the activity broaden interests and appreciations?

7. Is the activity reasonably free from actual physical danger or have precautions been taken to minimize the risk without destroying the fun? Does it contribute to the greater health and well-being of the campers?

8. Could they do the activity just as well or better in their own home communities? Although campers certainly should have an opportunity to do some of the activities they do at home, the value of camp is in opening up new opportunities and allowing campers to explore opportunities that would not be available to them at home.

9. Does the activity have carry-over value for use at home or in later life? Not all activities can be done at home, but skills learned such as making friends, cooking a meal outdoors, or craft skills could be transferred home.

10. Does the activity fulfill fundamental needs (e.g., security, achievement) and contribute to the camper's overall mental health?

11. Is the activity a group endeavor in which each camper can feel he or she has made a contribution to the activity and its enjoyment?

12. Is some recognition given to campers who make great efforts or develop better-than-average skills? Keep this aspect in balance, however, and remember that it can be easily overdone. Every time there is a winner you also end up with several losers.

13. Most important, does the program result in positive human development outcomes?

Activities, Projects, and Events

Other chapters of this book present a number of program ideas under such general categories as waterfront, literature, outdoor adventure programs, ceremonies and special events, arts and crafts, nature and ecology, music and rhythm, and drama activities. Other special projects and activities can also become an integral part of the camp's program. For example, there are numerous activities that are well-suited for evening programs (see exhibit 12.2). In many camps an evening campfire program is a tradition that campers love. Make it varied enough so that it goes beyond mere routine and becomes one of the

---

Exhibit 12.2

Suggestions for Evening Activities

- Program of customs, costumes, and dances of other cultures
- Informal dramatics like charades or 1-minute skits
- Folk, square, or round dancing
- Themed parties—dances, pioneer, masquerade, the amazing race
- Progressive games (going from unit to unit to participate)
- Village night (invite the camp neighbors over)
- Barn dance
- Amateur night, talent show, American idol
- Hay ride
- Camp banquet
- Moonlight hike
- Star study
- Poetry, stories, music
- Shadow plays
- Discussion groups
- Liar's contest (see who can tell the biggest tale)
- Come-as-you-are party

Exhibit 12.3

Theme Celebrations

- Outdoor living day—hold demonstrations or contests in such skills as building fires, using knife and axe, and erecting a tent
- County or state fair conducted at camp
- Camp birthday
- Mardi Gras
- Dude ranch rodeo
- Backwards day
- Circus day
- Holiday of a foreign country (costumes, food, dances, games, songs)
- Staff day (when campers and staff interchange roles)
- Western barbecue day
- Regatta day
- Camp olympics
- Water pageant
- Local history day
- Celebrating the birthday of a famous person
- Clean-up, paint-up day
- Water balloon war games
- Storybook day (theme of Robin Hood, Paul Bunyan, Robinson Crusoe, or other story carried out through the day)
- Village day (when neighbors from the local community visit)
- Gift day (when campers or groups present gifts usually self-made to one another)
- International day
- Pioneer day
- Free choice day

---

most meaningful events of the session. These campfires may be inspiring when conducted in some secluded special place of beauty reserved for such events. Many camps have worked out elaborate fire-lighting ceremonies for such occasions. Physical comfort warrants attention too, since no one can sit in rapt attention during a fierce bombardment by voracious mosquitoes. Evening programs should taper off to a quiet sleep-inducing conclusion. Symbols such as a closing song or lullaby, no matter how simple, mean much to campers and serve to stimulate their imaginations and loyalties.

Many camps celebrate *special days* with activities that center around a particular theme. Exhibit 12.3 lists several possible themes that provide fun opportunities for campers and staff to exercise their imaginations.

Rainy days can present a problem to an unimaginative counselor, and a steady downpour of several days duration is enough to tax the ingenuity and resourcefulness of even the most creative leader. Nevertheless, keeping campers busy and happy is essential. Homesickness is more likely to emerge during periods of bad weather,

so counselors need to turn rainy days into an opportunity to try something new and fun. Wise leaders will keep the threat of rain in the back of their minds so that they are ready for those inevitable rainy days. Activity possibilities include those listed in exhibit 12.4 on the following page.

You will find other suggestions for programs throughout various chapters of this book as well as in the sources listed at the end of several chapters.

Exhibit 12.4

Rainy Day Activities

- Plan a carnival or puppet show
- Take a slicker hike in the rain—note the rainy day activities of wildlife
- Compose a cabin or unit yell, song, symbol, slogan, or the like
- Learn new songs and sing the old
- Work on scrapbooks
- Talent show in the dining hall
- Make candy or popcorn or serve "tea"
- Casino night with M&M's
- Play charades and other indoor games
- Plan an open house with simple refreshments for another cabin or unit
- Plan stunts for the next all-camp program
- Hold discussions
- Read or tell stories
- Write letters
- Listen to music
- Plan a future trip, a nature trail, or outpost camp
- Toast marshmallows
- Hold a contest to determine the Biggest Liar
- Compose a cabin or unit newspaper to be read at supper
- Organize a harmonica, comb, kitchen, trashcan, or kazoo band or other musical group
- Teach folk or square dances
- Plan a banquet (with candles or some little extra item of food and a program)
- Arrange a hobby show or other exhibit
- Plan a stunt night

- Make posters for the bulletin board
- Make puppets or work on a play
- Practice skills such as knot tying
- Make a model campsite or one of the entire camp layout
- Do plaster casts or nature crafts
- Carve or paint soap objects
- Do string art or bead work
- Whittle or carve objects
- Work on creating costumes for the next play
- Hold a spelling bee or quiz program
- Read or write camp poetry
- Write a dramatic production and prepare to produce it
- Make improvised camping equipment such as trench candles and waterproof matches
- Study weather, make weather flags and other weather instruments
- Study clouds as they change and move about with the storms
- Play active games to relieve tension and get exercise
- Work on repairing or maintaining riding tack, archery tackle, and so on
- Go pasture sliding in the mud
- Get extra sleep or rest
- Fish, boat, or swim in the rain (if no lightning)
- Spruce up living quarters with decorations
- Practice Red Cross first aid techniques
- Play indoor nature games or prepare for your next nature hike
- Study rules or techniques of such activities as tennis and horseback riding

REFERENCES

American Camp Association. (2007). *Creating positive youth outcomes*. Monterey, CA: Healthy Learning.

American Camp Association. (2008). *Designing quality youth programs*. Monterey, CA: Healthy Learning.

American Camp Association. (2010). Outcomes tools. Retrieved from http://www.acacamps.org.

Molloy, L. (2006, Mar/Apr). Strategic program planning: A recipe for success. *Camping Magazine, 79*(2), 39–45.

Vinton, D. A., & Farley, E. M. (1979). *Camp Staff Training Series, Module 3, Camp Program Planning and Leadership*. A joint publication of Project REACH, University of Kentucky; ACA; and Hawkins and Associates, Inc., 142 pp.

WEB RESOURCES

Kellogg Foundation Logic Model information: http://www.exinfm.com/training/pdfiles/logicModel.pdf

University of Wisconsin (Logic Models): http://www.uwex.edu/ces/pdande/evaluation/evallogicmodel.html

PRINT RESOURCES

Bialeschki, M. D., Halliday, N., & Fay, J. (2007). The role of skill building. *Camping Magazine, 80*(1), 60–65.

13

Spiritual Life, Ceremonies, and Special Events

One of the most significant outcomes of a camp experience is the development of spiritual feelings and values. The term *spiritual* as used here does not have an exclusively religious meaning, although camp is an ideal place for people to acquire religious values. Rather, the term connotes a belief in a power greater than oneself, an appreciation of nature, a sense of kinship with one's fellow campers, and an orderly universe. In the outdoors we have an opportunity to observe a nature over which humans have little control. The outdoors is a place where we can gain perspective, humility, understanding, and respect for the natural environment.

Spiritual Aspects of Camping

Spiritual experiences at camp do not always occur at formally arranged times or in specially designated places. Instead, these experiences may occur in times when thoughts and senses rise to unusual heights of perception. Sometimes a person may simply experience a deep appreciation of the goodness of a friend or the unselfishness of a stranger. Occasions for sharing deep and more serious thoughts with others sometimes come unexpectedly—sharing a brief time off with a fellow counselor, looking over the countryside from a vantage spot high on a hill, or when a small camper slips a hand trustingly into yours and confides some private thought. Other experiences may come in quiet periods of meditation while enjoying the beauty of a sky full of stars or the call of a lone whippoorwill in the distance.

Camps have different practices regarding the spiritual life of campers. However, most camps aim to further spiritual growth through an appreciation of the higher values of life. There is much that camps can do to heighten the spiritual aspects of life through camp programs, including worship services as well as special ceremonies or events.

Worship Services and Devotion

Many camps have daily or weekly all-camp periods of devotion or of time set aside for various cabin or unit endeavors to highlight a deeper sense of spiritual values. Note that these times can be religious in nature or may be quiet time for individual or group reflection about the universe.

Such supplementary experiences ordinarily consist of some combination of the following:

1. Grace before meals (oral, spoken in unison, sung, silence during an appropriate musical selection, or a period of silent prayer)

2. Outdoor vespers or inspirational programs such as campfires

3. Sunrise services or morning watch

4. Cabin devotions or meditations just before taps

5. Attendance at religious services in a neighboring church of the individual's choice or at services conducted by visiting clergy or camp personnel on the campsite in an indoor or outdoor chapel

6. Group discussions on religion, morals, and ethics

7. Singing of hymns and other appropriate songs

Interfaith Camps

Interfaith camps, compared to religiously affiliated camps, often include both counselors and campers of different faiths in the camp community. Religiously affiliated camps are typically associated with a particular faith

154

or denomination. The interfaith approach encourages living together in broad-minded acceptance of different faiths, as well as of those who profess no particular faith. These camps respect the right of each person to worship as he or she pleases. If you accept a position in such a camp, be sure you can support this attitude without trying to unduly influence anyone else. Rather, your efforts should be directed toward helping all campers become the best possible global citizens regardless of faith. Care should be taken not to force any child, either through rules or group pressure, to profess a particular faith unless religious development is central to the camp mission.

In various ways, many camps now actively try to foster this spirit of understanding. Encourage your campers to observe practices that they are accustomed to, such as a moment of silent grace before meals or an individual prayer before going to sleep. Your personal conduct, including consistent observance of kindness, tolerance, and fairness to and respect for every individual in camp, will best express your own spiritual convictions and their influence on your relationships with others.

In a large camp that runs for more than a week, camp officials may arrange separate services for the major religious groups (Catholic, Jewish, Protestant, and Islamic faiths). Each camp will approach these services differently and someone in camp should be responsible for ensuring that such services are done properly and according to the religion's doctrine. The Sabbath may be celebrated on different days and religions may have different holy days that could occur during the camp session.

Special Camp Services

Some camps hold inspirational opportunities during the week, which may or may not substitute for a regular weekly worship service. The most appropriate place for these services is in some special retreat, which the camp may refer to as its "wilderness cathedral," or "woodland chapel" in the outdoors. A site on a hilltop with a commanding view of the valley below, a natural amphitheater beside a gently flowing stream, or a sequestered nook surrounded by a forest are often most appropriate.

Inspirational programs planned jointly by campers and staff are usually the most meaningful. The activity can be built around some central theme of general interest such as friendship, giving 100 percent, what harmonious camp living means, tolerance, patriotism or love of country, beauty, the wonders of nature, the ideals and motives of the organization sponsoring the camp, humility, empathy, inspirational people who achieved much in spite of difficulties, or the application of the Golden Rule to camp life.

Adjust the language and nature of the inspirational service to those attending it. Adopt an informal spirit of sincerity, dignity, and reverence but avoid sanctimoniousness or undue piousness. Unless there is an outside speaker, let some staff member or camper give a short talk, bringing out the main thought of the service. A short story or anecdote usually promotes interest and understanding.

Set the stage for the proper mood as the audience enters the area. To avoid the midday heat in summer, you may prefer to hold the special activity in the early morning or evening. A blazing campfire can provide light for a night meditation, which also lends itself nicely to a possible candle lighting service. Appropriate music helps, and having campers meet at a distance and file silently down to their seats is also effective. Counselors and older campers can be stationed along the path with flashlights, lanterns, or lighted candles to show the way.

Encourage all participants to use their creative abilities to furnish poetry, prose, songs, or art for the occasion. Music often plays an important part, with individuals and groups furnishing vocal and instrumental numbers. The service should last only 30 to 45 minutes, since most people will get restless and attention wanders if they have to sit still much longer.

Sabbath in Camp

For campers who observe their special day of worship or Sabbath in camp, the regular daily program is usually more relaxed and campers are often given free time to engage in quiet activities, although tennis courts, boats, waterfront, and other facilities are available to those who want to use them. For longer term camps, having a break from the regular schedule may be useful and a designated Sabbath day may be enjoyable. Breakfast may be served a little later than usual and some variation to the routine may be incorporated, such as eating in a special place or being served cafeteria style. The day can focus on spending time together as a cabin group, listening to music, singing, holding discussions, telling stories, or writing letters. It might be designated as Visitors' Day, with the camp playing host to parents and friends. A cold supper or cookout for small groups is customary to give the kitchen staff extra time off. This day might also provide an opportunity for small groups to take their meals to a special location. Campers generally will appreciate the designated Sabbath as a change-of-pace day to renew strength of mind and spirit for the coming week.

Special Events

Special events may be planned for the beginning or end of each week of camp and usually involve the entire camp community. A variety of themes and ideas can be used depending on the nature of the camp and the creativity of the staff. Several examples are described below.

Camp banquets can be festive dress-up occasions with special menus and a candle lighting service: the director lights the candles of the staff and unit heads, who in turn

Special events are often planned for the beginning or end of each week of camp and usually involve the entire camp community. (Photo courtesy of Bradford Woods Learning and Outdoor Center)

pass the light on to the campers. A unit or committee can plan a program of songs, poems, short talks, skits, or other activities around a central theme. Inspirational talks, the presentation of awards and certificates, and the reading of selected poems, plays, and stories written by campers can also take place.

A *dedication ceremony* may be arranged to recognize a new camp acquisition, especially a project campers have completed such as a newly laid trail, a site for an outdoor chapel selected and furnished by them, or a new outpost camp. Plan a serious but brief program with appropriate songs and a special speech of dedication, with praise for those who donated their time and efforts to create something of benefit both to present and future campers.

On the *Fourth of July*, the camp can hold a special flag ceremony and stress the day's history and traditions as well as reasons for celebrating it. Serve special food with table decorations in a patriotic motif of red, white, and blue. More elaborate outdoor games or a parade might be planned. If a fireworks display is occurring in a nearby community, campers might have an opportunity to view them.

Campers appreciate having some notice taken of their *birthdays*. A party for those having birthdays within the month with a special "unbirthday party" for the rest handles the situation nicely. Serve everyone with a special lighted birthday cake, with cake and ice cream for everyone. Use favors, sing a birthday song, and hold a brief program. Some camps also set aside a special day to celebrate the camp's birthday.

The *last campfire* can be a memorable event starting with a processional to the fire, which may be lighted by one of the special methods discussed later on in the chapter. The mood should be light, but also reflective. End on a note that emphasizes the beauty of nature and the affirmation of friendship. If the philosophy of your camp sanctions awarding honors, badges, and certificates, they might be given at this time.

If the last campfire program is held near water, a memorable closing event consists of having each unit bring a "boat" fashioned from a piece of cardboard or other material that will disintegrate quickly. It can be tastefully decorated with leaves, flowers, and other elements of the environment. Be sensitive to not littering in the water. After a brief ceremony, each unit affixes a small lighted candle to their boat, and as it is set afloat, each camper makes a wish and watches it disappear into the distance. All then form a *friendship circle* (cross hands to clasp the hand of the person on either side) and sing "Taps" or a good-night song or repeat a prayer or quotation in unison, perhaps ending with your own special camp or unit hand squeeze.

Flag Ceremonies

A flag-raising ceremony may be held at the opening of the first camp day, or it may take place every morning during the camp session. A flag-lowering exercise may occur at the end of each day or may be a special event at

A flag-raising ceremony is a great way to start the camp day. (Photo courtesy of American Camp Association)

can be solicited for a special camp project, and announcements about the daily or evening activities can be voiced.

Evening Outdoor Programs

Most resident camps hold at least one outdoor program for the entire group each week and sometimes something special each night. When well planned, such programs are impressive and tend to be remembered by campers long after camp is over, which can influence their attitudes and character more than almost any other event of the camp session. These programs usually are held in an area reserved especially for this purpose. The very act of sitting closely with friends in a muted light that shuts out the surrounding fringe of darkness can make even the shyest of campers feel they belong. Most camps have developed certain traditions and customary ways of doing things that returning campers love and eagerly look forward to each new year. Like any program, evening outdoor programs require careful planning.

Some camps do not allow wood fires for safety reasons. Alternative methods of providing light include the familiar device of using crepe paper or thin plastic in shades of orange, yellow, or red to camouflage such sources of light as camp lanterns, flashlights, or electric light bulbs. Candles placed upon flat stones can produce a cozy and pleasant atmosphere, although you may need a windscreen if there is a breeze. The direct light from flashlights, electric lights, or camp lanterns may be used, although it is usually more effective to at least partially conceal them. If a wood fire is used, all precautions for safety should be taken. In addition, creative ways to light the fire might be explored.

the end of the particular camp session. Such occasions offer a chance for campers to learn proper demeanor around the US flag as well as how to handle and care for it. They also provide an opportunity both to learn about the history of the flag and its importance as a symbol of a way of life and the principles under which the US functions. The complete rules and customs for the care and display of the American flag are contained in a Flag Code, which is readily available from many sources. Most camps that conduct flag ceremonies have procedures established for the ceremonies.

Flag ceremonies also offer an opportune time to communicate information to campers. During the raising or lowering of the flag, most if not all of the camp is in attendance. Special announcements can be made, a team-building activity can take place before dinner, volunteers

A blazing campfire provides a contemplative atmosphere for evening programs.

As always, let the campers accept a major role in planning and carrying out the evening program, since it should provide entertainment *by* them, not *for* them. Plan it to last no longer than an hour. A good master of ceremonies moves the program along and assures that it is finished in the allotted time. Vary the activities and provide for active audience participation. After lighting the fire, follow with something lively and gradually taper off into more serious and quieter activities. End on a quiet note such as singing peaceful songs, reading poetry, or storytelling. The final campfire program may be one aspect that will linger with campers as they return home.

WEB RESOURCES

Blue Tree Resources (www.bluetreeresources.org) offers resources for those who lead and create programs for outdoor ministries; it also provides a good book list.

Center for Spiritual Development in Children and Adolescence (http://www.spiritualdevelopmentcenter.org/) is a global initiative to promote spiritual development as an aspect of human development.

Kid Spirit Magazine (http://kidspiritmagazine.com) is a magazine for kids focusing on big questions and meaning of life.

National Study of Youth and Religion (www.youthandreligion.org) offers current research, articles, books, videos, and links to other youth religion websites.

Search Institute (http://www.search-institute.org/spiritual-development) includes research on spiritual development in youth, including camps.

PRINT RESOURCES

Ferguson, N. (2007, March/April). Camps and spirituality. *Camping Magazine, 80*(2), 18–24. Discusses the difference between spirituality and religion in camp, and the spiritual development of children.

14

Music, Rhythm, and Drama Activities

Rhythm has played an important part in people's lives since the beginning of time. Nearly all studies of primitive peoples show that they created chants and ceremonial dances to use on special occasions. Some expressed joy after a successful hunt while others lamented a misfortune such as the death of a loved one. Throughout history, workers have sung to relieve the tedium of their long hours of labor, and armies have incorporated songs as well as bands and drum and bugle corps to lessen marching fatigue and to raise morale and patriotism. Humans are, and always have been, lovers of rhythm of all types. Campers are no exception.

Singing in the Camp Program

It is quite natural for happy campers to sing—at any time and any place. Singing can make waiting for meals or the beginning of any activity more enjoyable. Good music is a great leavening agent. Most people love a catchy tune, a strong rhythm, or the beauty of a soft melody. No camper or counselor should return home without a new repertoire of songs. In addition to musical expressions during free moments, music can enhance life in camp each day, at the beginning and ending of the day, at mealtime and in campfire programs, during spiritual occasions, for talent shows or special musical concerts, when taking a trip on the camp bus, or while on the trail.

Songs Types and Occasions

Most songs can be divided into four general types, with each having a definite place in the camp program: folk songs, rounds or canons, art songs, and pop songs.

Folk songs cannot be traced to any one composer. They originated at some time in the past and were passed down orally from generation to generation with some modification along the way. These old folk songs came from the emotions and everyday experiences of those who sang them. *Ballads*, for example, tell a story, while *sea chanteys* boosted the spirits of sailors working on the vast seas. Many of the so-called folk songs sung at camps today are of recent origin and by a known composer and so are not true folk songs. Nevertheless, there is a story behind all folk songs, whether they are singing games, spirituals, cowboy songs, or mountain ballads.

Rounds or *canons* are sung with the group divided into two or more sections with each singing the same melody but starting at different times. Many camps have traditional rounds that they sing. Rounds have been favorites for a long time (e.g., "Three Blind Mice" appeared in print as early as 1609). Sometimes campers like them because they offer a mild form of group competition. A song leader can also provide common examples of rounds.

Art songs were composed by the masters and may merit a special place in the camp program. Their sheer beauty makes them a pleasure to sing; moreover, they help develop a taste for good music. A few of these art songs are based on old folk songs or on hymns.

Pop songs, such as Steve Miller Band's "Dance, Dance, Dance" and the Indigo Girl's "Closer to Fine" are quite common around the campfire or on a camping trip. Songs from modern pop and rock musicians such as John Prine, Phish, the Grateful Dead, the Tokens, Indigo Girls, and the Beatles are increasingly finding their way into camp. A genre of music called Christian Rock is also highly popular among some young people. As the generations of campers and counselors change, so does the music they listen to. Today, more than ever, finding the lyrics and music to songs is quite easy via the Internet.

Songs can be appropriate for almost any time or place. They serve well as ice breakers to thaw out a group of new acquaintances. Singing in front of a blazing fire in an indoor fireplace banishes gloom on a cold rainy day. Singing in close harmony develops a spirit of camaraderie and togetherness as voices blend to produce the total effect. Songs can welcome newcomers, express regret at someone's leaving, or even quiet hunger pangs while waiting in front of the dining room for the signal to enter.

Music relieves tension and frazzled nerves, and singing during a rest break on the trail helps to reduce fatigue. Quiet music can induce a particular type of mood. Music can furnish a background for writing letters, reading, cleaning equipment, or working on an arts and crafts project. Fitting songs can help with rowing, canoeing, horseback riding, hiking, or almost anything else on the camp agenda. Songs help to maintain campers' spirits when an activity is disrupted temporarily. Camp offers numerous opportunities for song.

Leading Songs

Although camps usually designate one or more staff members as official song leaders, anyone can lead songs in appropriate times and places. Almost everyone has a sense of rhythm. Just watch a group listening to a catchy rhythm and note how many unconsciously sway their heads or tap their feet. After a little instruction and some practice, almost anyone with a good sense of rhythm can do a creditable job of song leading. Formal musical training undoubtedly helps; just don't let it curb your spontaneity. The main aim in camp singing should be providing enjoyment and satisfaction.

Many good song collections are available on the market, including some inexpensive paperbacks with songs selected especially for their appropriateness to the camp setting and their appeal to those of camp age. Words to many songs can be downloaded from the Internet. If you have no songbooks, but want to provide words and music to the singers, use an LCD projection or print large characters on poster board.

As previously mentioned, singing may spring forth spontaneously at any time and place. At other times you may want to plan a special song festival or use singing as a purposeful component of another program. Plan to have the singing last no longer than ten to fifteen minutes—it is better to stop while everyone is still enthusiastic and wanting more. As with any successful program, a good singing session does not just happen. Such preparation brings confidence and an ability to be relaxed and informal. In addition, sometimes knowing the background of a song can help campers appreciate it more. When did it originate and on what occasions did people sing it? Little anecdotes about the composer or the song add great interest. When you can convey to your group the mood of the people who sang the song, they will enjoy it more and sing it with more meaning and spirit.

Promote friendly, informal competition between groups occasionally, basing it on harmony, depth of feeling, and best interpretation of the song, never on loudness and just plain noise. If campers tend to sing too loudly and with little feeling for the song, have them sing it progressively more softly, dying away into a final pianissimo. Encourage campers who are especially interested to try their hand at leading, or ask them to help you to plan the songs to be sung. Although the aim of camp singing is enjoyment and the satisfaction that comes from doing it well, you may want to do serious numbers as well as songs sung just for fun. Include songs that are slow, fast, happy, catchy, sad, rollicking, thoughtful, and sentimental.

Individuals may want to form duets, trios, or quartets and sing just for their own amusement or for some special occasion. A choir group can add immeasurably to a vesper or Sunday service. Songs at camp are often done *a capella* (without instruments) but some camps use guitars and a piano to accompany the singing. Some camps also use drums to accompany singers.

Singing has long been a much-loved component of camp life, whether breaking forth spontaneously or as part of a special event. (Photo courtesy of Bradford Woods Learning and Outdoor Center)

Campers might also compose tunes to reflect their experiences at camp. The lyrics of favorite songs can be changed to reflect the campers' experiences. Original songs or words can be made quite personal and can recount funny little happenings and private jokes known only to the composers. Regardless of whether old favorites, traditional camp songs, or new harmonies or words, singing has long been an important part of camp.

Singing Games and Dances

Singing games and dances are popular in some camps. Many of them are quite vigorous and may include round, square, and folk dances. The accompaniment can be done by simple instruments, but often recordings are used as the background. You may find dance callers on your camp staff or in a nearby community, or you can use CDs that are available both with and without calls. A good way to begin is with simple steps and figures. This approach gets everybody out on the floor and builds confidence as they gradually progress to something more complicated.

An *international night* might feature the native costumes and dances of one or more countries and is often well received, especially if the camp has international campers and/or counselors. This cultural event may be an all-camp project, one sponsored by one or two units, or each unit or cabin may be responsible for preparing one number and teaching it to the others. Additionally, this special event might assist campers and staff from abroad to feel comfortable with their new surroundings and give their fellow campers a deeper understanding for international customs.

Rhythmical Instruments

Many camps encourage campers to bring their own instruments so they can play in combos and other special groups, or perhaps even in an all-camp band. Rhythm bands are also popular, comprised of instruments that are easy to play and can be rented or made from materials around camp. Percussion instruments are easily made and fun to use.

A *drum* (figure 14.1) can be improvised from a tin can, an oatmeal box, a round wooden box, the bottom of a plastic bleach bottle or plastic bucket, or even a round wooden bowl. The name "drumstick" for the leg bone of a chicken probably comes from the practice of some indigenous groups of beating their drums or tom-toms with the leg bone of a wild fowl. Drumsticks can be made from sticks of any type. The drumsticks and the sides and heads of the drum can be painted or decorated in some way if desired.

Make *rhythm sticks* to beat together by whittling them from round sticks and sandpapering them smooth, then

Many camps encourage campers to bring their own instruments to camp so they can play in combos, rhythm bands, or even an all-camp band.

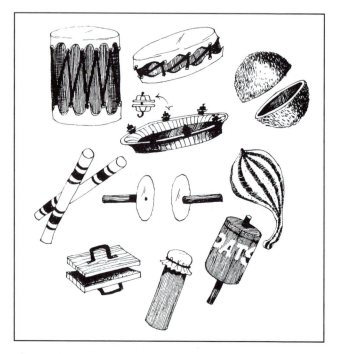

Figure 14.1   Percussion instruments campers can make.

shellacking and painting them. To make *sand blocks* glue or tack heavy pieces of sandpaper to the bottoms of wooden blocks to use as you "swish" them together as a rhythmical accompaniment. *Shakers* and *rattles* can be made from a hollow object such as a gourd, tin can, cardboard cylinder, or wooden box, partially filling it with pebbles, beans, hard seeds, bottle caps, or small nuts. Try varying either the container or the materials inside to get different sound effects. Use a large nail or other metallic object to tap a resonant piece of metal such as a horseshoe for use as a *triangle*. A *kazoo* can be made by using a rubber band to fasten a piece of waxed paper tightly over one end of a mailing tube. Hum through the open end of the tube.

Drama Activities

Children are born imitators. To them, such imitation is not really acting at all. They often throw themselves so wholeheartedly into their roles that they *become* what they portray. This advantage frees them from the self-consciousness and fear of ridicule that hamstrings many adults. A child can transform with ease from one character to another without losing a sense of reality.

Formal plays with elaborate scenery and costumes are generally too involved for most camp programs. Such productions violate at least two criteria of good camping: (1) they could be done just as well if not better at home, and (2) they consume a disproportionate amount of time from activities more indigenous to the camp environment. Formalized dramatics should be left to camps that specialize in that field—and a number of specialty camps do. However, several types of informal dramatics fit with the spirit of general camping and provide children with an outlet for their natural instincts to pretend and imitate.

Short, informal productions are recommended. You can cut long plays or use some of the one- or two-act plays and skits available for campers that can be rehearsed quickly so that they do not consume too much time. If time to learn parts is not available, use an off-stage narrator or let the players familiarize themselves with their lines and act them out as they read them.

The improvisational plays concocted by staff and campers are usually quite entertaining and very much enjoyed. Use either the whole group or a committee for planning. As soon as the general theme has been decided, ideas and suggestions will probably flow freely. In fact, the real chore will be weaving them into a practical activity or production. Counselors have the job of reining in ideas that are in poor taste.

Since children love all kinds of animals, you may want to work several into the script, giving them anything from walk-on parts to starring roles. Shy children often lose their timidity when concealed behind a mask or walking about on all fours as some animal. Don't be afraid to exaggerate both the action and the plausibility of the plot. You can incorporate appropriate dances and songs and let the audience join in on a chorus. The main purpose of drama is enjoyment and the true measure of the results is what happens to the participants.

Ideas for plays can come from many sources such as nursery or Mother Goose rhymes, or well-liked stories such as those of Dr. Seuss or the poetry of Shel Silverstein. Other possibilities are historical or current events, Bible stories, the local history of the community or camp, or events that have transpired during the current camp session.

Try to maintain a brisk pace so that there are no lulls in the action. End each act with a semiclimactic touch of humor or excitement. Make sure the characters are exaggerated so that the audience can enjoy booing the villain or rooting for the hero. Such audience reactions are fine in moderation but should not be allowed to get carried away.

Some camps provide a proper stage. This, however, is not necessary with informal productions. For indoor staging, use a corner of the room with the chairs arranged diagonally across it, or place the audience in a circle around the actors to create a theater-in-the-round. An

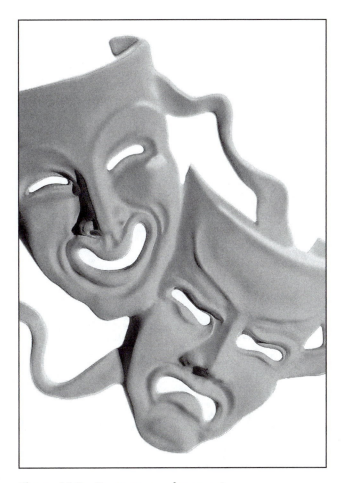

Figure 14.2   Everyone can be an actor.

outdoor setting may be more in keeping with the camp ideal. Since children's voices do not carry well, place the audience close to the action, and avoid locating the stage in front of a body of water, since it will absorb sound and make hearing difficult.

Background scenery should be simple—children's imaginations will supply the details. Props can be made from everyday items. For example, an inverted tablespoon can serve as a telephone, a large towel or blanket as a rug, while a cardboard, crescent-shaped moon can be dangled from a fishing pole held by someone standing on a ladder behind the scenes. Colored sheets, tent halves, tarps, or blankets can be fastened over ropes or wires to serve as curtains.

Costuming can include odds and ends. Many camps have a costume box with an odd assortment of discarded apparel for use when the need arises. Campers' personal gear will provide boots, hats, raincoats, PJs, and other possibilities. Crepe paper comes in a large variety of shades and is helpful for costume-making and other purposes.

Paper bags just large enough to fit over the head make good animal or human masks when ears and noses are pasted on and holes are cut for eyes and mouth. You can improvise beards and false wigs from pipe stem cleaners, frayed rope, shrubbery, or an old mop head, and feathers, grasses, or branches make good hat decorations.

You can use recorded music before the show, between acts, or to set moods during the action. Sound effects can be made by all kinds of items as well as with human voices.

Some children may not have parts in the play either because they do not want them or because there are not enough to go around. But there are many non-acting chores to keep everyone involved, including director, prompter, properties, programs, sets, costumes, lighting and sound effects, seating, ushers, publicity, and superintendent of clean-up.

Productions need not always be for an audience. Some of the most fun and successful dramatic activities are those that arise spontaneously simply to pass the time on a rainy day or programless night. However, the initial effort may prove so successful that it stimulates the group to put a little more work into the production and to stage it on some special occasion such as a council fire or visitors' day.

The most popular productions are often built around camp personalities and local events, as when campers lampoon their counselors or the staff depicts the campers as seen through counselors' eyes. Campers can usually see the funny side of their own experiences when viewed in retrospect and with a little humor.

Activities Related to Dramatics

Several activities, although not really dramatics, are related in that they contain some elements of make-believe and dramatizing. *Play reading* may serve as a satisfying substitute for those who like plays but do not want to go into them extensively enough to memorize lines and actions.

Stunt night is a traditional fun night when campers and staff display their talents in almost any area: demonstrating feats of magic, putting on a skit or play, or performing on a musical instrument. Let a counselor or responsible camper act as master of ceremonies and hold a preview of the numbers to see that they are suitable.

In pantomimes, actors take parts as someone reads a ballad, story, poem, folk song, or original skit. In one version, each person takes a part such as a horse, crow, or freight train. Whenever that character is mentioned, he

Stunt night is a traditional fun night when campers and staff display their talents. (Photo courtesy of Bradford Woods Learning and Outdoor Center)

or she makes the appropriate noise. An activity like this can also be done with the whole audience taking part.

Charades is a familiar game in which one team or individual selects a word and pantomimes the syllables while the others try to guess the word. You can use such categories as movie titles, book titles, songs, story book or television characters, advertising slogans, famous people of today or yesterday, or different professions.

A variation called New Orleans is somewhat more active. Each team has a baseline that it must stay behind while the other team takes a turn at coming close and acting out a chosen occupation such as pushing a lawn mower, chopping wood, or rowing a boat. The team behind the line tries to guess the occupation and as soon as successful, tries to tag as many of the acting team as possible before they can run back to safety behind their own baseline. Any member tagged must transfer to the other team who does the acting next.

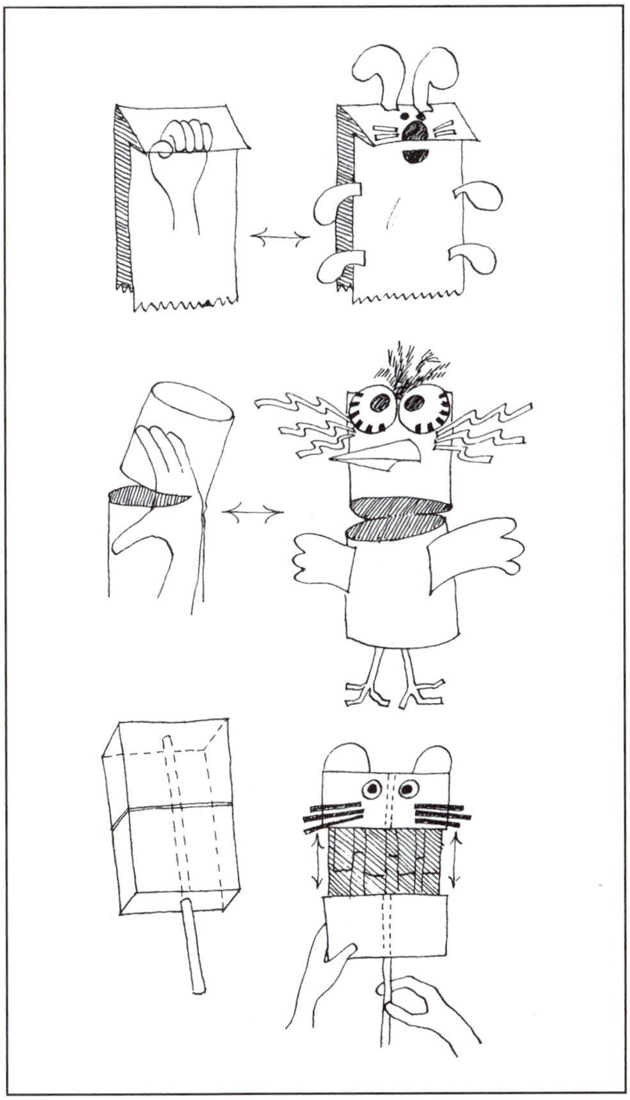

With *paper-bag dramatics*, each group receives a paper bag of simple props. Group members must then use these props to present a skit.

Sealed orders is an activity similar to charades. A number of humorous or serious situations are written on slips of paper and placed in a hat. Each individual or group draws a slip and must then act out the situation while the others attempt to guess what it is. Categories such as those mentioned previously in regard to charades may also be used, or each group may be given a list of characters to work into a skit.

Shadow plays are another quasi-dramatics activity. Stretch a sheet (preferably wet) tightly to serve as a transparent curtain with the stage directly behind it and bright lights (auto lights, flashlights, or spotlights) set far enough back to make the actors stand out in silhouette. Turn off all other lights and keep the actors close to the curtain so that their silhouettes will be sharp and clear. Have the campers act out a skit, story, or ballad; these can be accompanied with music if desired.

Puppets (figures 14.3 and 14.4) are designed to slip over a child's hand so that they can be manipulated with

Figure 14.3 Bag and box puppets campers can make.

Figure 14.4 Puppets made from natural materials.

the fingers; marionettes are more elaborate, and are manipulated by using strings that are attached to control sticks held by the operator. Puppets can be fashioned quickly from sacks, bags, boxes, socks, groves, wooden spoons, or other materials. Campers can also make "nature puppets" by using materials found in the wilds such as seaweed for hair, shells for mouths, and driftwood for noses. Stories and tales can be told around the campfire with these creatures made of natural materials.

The possibilities for music, dance, and drama at camp are abundant. The fun lies in the kind of improvisation done. Remember that these activities are generally done for fun and entertainment and that focus should be kept in mind.

WEB RESOURCES

Campfire Skits (http://www.weknowskits.com) offers more than 400 brief, youth-oriented skits.

Campfire Songs (http://www.weknowcampfiresongs.com) provides lyrics (and in some cases video links to hear the melody) for more than 1500 campfire songs for all occasions, arranged alphabetically by title.

Song lyrics (http://lyrics.com) provides lyrics of artists from the 1960s through today.

Songs for Teaching (http://www.songsforteaching.com) features a compilation of songs suitable for teaching, broken down into different categories.

Zeise, A. (1997). *A to Z home's cool homeschooling.* http://home-schooling.gomilpitas.com/explore/drama.htm

PRINT RESOURCES

ACA (2006). *Sing.* Martinsville, IN: ACA.

Cain, J. (2002, May/June). The evening dance program at camp. *Camping Magazine, 75*(3). Provides several activity ideas.

Evans, F., & Sanborn, J. (1998). Drama can be full of surprises. *Camping Magazine, 71*(3), 20–21.

French, C. (2008, Nov/Dec). Add some music to the mix. *Camping Magazine, 81*(6). Describes an example of a camp with a strong music program.

Maddox, I., & Cobb, R. (1998). *Campfire Songs.* Guilford, CT: Globe Pequot Press.

Ozier, L. (2008, Nov/Dec). The sound of music. *Camping Magazine, 81*(6). Talks about implementing a music program, MAP—the Music Ascension Program.

Weintraub, J. (1995). Percussion programming. *Camping Magazine, 67*(6), 16–17.

15

Literature
and Writing

Many people of all ages have never learned to appreciate good literature. Literature is a depository of accumulated wisdom of humankind, and also serves to transport the reader into a world of entertainment, excitement, or beauty that allows a temporary escape from everyday life. A well-stocked camp library, judiciously used, can help campers see literature as a source of knowledge, adventure, and fun instead of merely a chore to complete for a required school assignment. Learning to appreciate good literature is a habit that may well prove contagious when a few campers give it their seal of approval.

Literature fits in well with many phases of the camp program. Some camps schedule reading as one of the choices available during an activity period, especially on bad-weather days. Though reading is not an activity unique to camp, it does have its place. Reading can provide a way to enjoy oneself in front of a blazing fireplace on a gloomy day or in a group that gathers for storytelling, reading aloud, or simply curling up individually with a favorite book. Moreover, literary selections can add to an evening program, vesper, or spiritual service. A brief appropriate "Thought for the Day" or proverb may be posted on the bulletin board or read at a set time such as before or after a meal, at the beginning of rest hour, or in a cabin gathering just before taps.

Camp Reading Programs

Many camps have camp libraries where they have a collection of books and magazines available for both campers and counselors. The library might also have "how-to books," although in this Internet age, most "how-tos" can be found through an online search as indicated by many of the references in this book. As in any public or school library, the camp library should have a method for checking out hard-copy library material and returning it prior to the end of the session. Books can be accumulated by borrowing from libraries, asking campers to bring along a favorite book to donate, or by conducting a community book drive. The books to be included in the library, however, should be carefully chosen, keeping the interests and reading levels of campers in mind.

A new emphasis on reading opportunities at camp has emerged recently, prompted in large part by concern among educators that children are experiencing learning loss over the summer if they are not exposed to programs that stimulate them to think and learn. Since camp programming by its nature encourages thinking and learning, camps are in a position to help address this learning loss. In fact, some camps have expanded upon informal reading opportunities (e.g., during free time and quiet periods) by adopting more purposeful reading programming.

A more formal activity instituted by the American Camp Association in 2011 is the *Explore 30 Camp Reading Program.* This national program addresses summer learning loss by providing youth with at least 30 minutes of reading time per day. The Explore 30 program aims to increase camp reading by assisting with access to books and children's magazines as well as online reading resources. The program offers activity ideas for developing a camp reading program along with incentives for reading completion. It also provides information about how to advocate for the potential of camps to address literacy and the reversal of summer learning loss. The Explore 30 program enables camps to incorporate academic enrichment into their program by introducing young people to the joys of reading and learning during the summer (ACA, 2011).

Storytelling

The art of storytelling is probably almost as old as human beings. History reveals that from the advent of speech, primitive peoples clustered around one of their most respected members, the storyteller. For centuries, people loved to gather to listen to the oft-repeated tales of courage and adventure told by a skilled narrator. To this day, everyone from the toddler to the older adult loves a well-told tale. Though television, the Internet, and movies may have somewhat lessened the interest and ability of both teller and listener in the home, summer camp may be the exception. Most campers are still excited when a member of the staff or a known speaker steps up to the campfire to share a story. Storytelling does not typically occur in their lives. You may need to encourage some campers to participate the first few times since it may be an entirely new experience for them. A few sessions usually will convert them into avid listeners.

No counselor should fail to have a few good stories for that inevitable moment when nothing else quite fills the bill. Almost anyone can learn to be a *good* storyteller.

Numerous reasons exist for telling stories. Hearing a good story is fun, and that is important enough to warrant its inclusion. Stories are a means for enjoying good literature since not all great literature can be read. Storytelling also provides a means for reliving great moments. The adventures of pioneers and heroes like Joan of Arc, Robin Hood, Johnny Appleseed, or Robinson Crusoe can be of great interest. Campers also can become much more interested in and appreciative of their camp community after learning about the customs and history of the area. You usually can gather such information from local historical associations or the clipping files and catalogued books of the local library. Although most people were not privileged to know famous people like Juliette Low, John Muir, Rachel Carson, or Abraham Lincoln in person, people can be introduced to them through a storyteller. Further, stories can be a way to communicate virtue and values. Since youth is the age of hero worship, teaching about virtue through good stories is interesting and painless.

Almost any time can be story time, but some occasions at camp are ripe for a story. A campfire, a hilltop at sunset, or a circle of listeners rolled in their blankets under a starlit sky form a perfect setting for storytelling. A rainy day seems less boring with an open fireplace and an exciting tale. A well-chosen story can keep restless children relaxed during the rest hour or put them in a mood for going to sleep quickly at night.

A few sure-fire stories appeal to almost everyone but, in general, the group dictates the story. What would be lapped up by one group may fall perfectly flat with another. You should size up your group and pick your story for *them.* Suit it to their general age, background, gender, and personalities. For example, boys and girls ordinarily

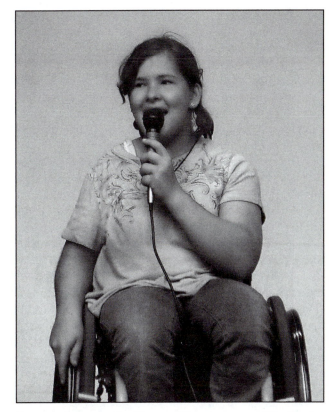

Everyone loves a well-told story. (Photo courtesy of Bradford Woods Learning and Outdoor Center)

like the same stories until they are about ten years old. Tales of explorers, pirates, airplanes, battles, sports, and science generally appeal more to boys. Small children like stories containing alliteration and nonsensical jingles as well as those about animals and people. Older children demand something that challenges their developing judgments a bit more. They prefer to draw their own conclusions from well-constructed but more subtle plots. Teens are more discriminating, but these campers might be more interested in hearing real-world stories that a counselor can tell from personal experience. Campers of all ages have a good sense of humor.

For the novice at choosing stories, many lists are available that classify stories according to type and age appeal. You can find many of these on the Internet. Another safe way to pick a story is to recall your own childhood favorites or note stories that would be good for telling as you read for your own pleasure.

Stories may be quite brief or can be longer. Books containing long stories are often more successfully read than told. To read a story effectively, however, familiarize yourself with it in advance so it can be read with real expression, using appropriate gestures, and frequently glancing up at your listeners.

The inevitable cry, "Tell us a ghost story," sometimes poses a problem. Some campers may find them seriously upsetting. However, there are some *good* ghost and mystery stories that might be used to entertain your group. You should be selective of the story based upon your audience.

One possible consideration for campfire stories would be the retelling of events from the week. If your cabin has had a unique experience or you led a camp activity such as an out-of camp trip, gather the group of campers to compile an exciting and worthwhile story to share with the group.

After you have selected your story, read it carefully for general plot and action and decide upon the best method of presentation. Read it again several times until it is almost memorized. Practice telling the story to yourself until you are positive of every character and bit of action. Gather your group and seat yourself where all can see and hear you clearly—a semicircle is usually best. Place yourself in the firelight or suspend a lantern on a post or tree so that all can clearly see your facial expressions and gestures. Towards the end of a campfire is an opportune time to share a story. Campers are winding down and should be ready to listen. Arouse interest by pausing a moment before you begin and choose a first sentence that compels immediate attention and curiosity as to what will follow.

Since your voice is the center of attention, make it pleasant, enunciate clearly, and avoid mumbling. Keep your tone low to demand close attention yet loud enough to be audible to those on the outskirts. Check by asking if campers can hear you. Talking too loudly is irritating and distracts listeners. Vary your tone and rate of speed. Get excited when the story calls for it, and talk in a tired or dispirited tone if that best expresses the mood of the action or character of the story. Appreciate the value of a pause in arousing anticipation. Elicit active participation from your listeners by asking them to guess what will happen next or what they would do in this situation. Your enthusiasm, facial expressions, and gestures will make it much more enjoyable for your listeners. Watch their faces for reactions, making a mental note for future use of those techniques that are most effective. If one or two of your audience seem inattentive, look and talk directly to them to bring them back into the fold.

A good storyteller paints a vivid mental picture of what is happening in the story and of the locality and surroundings in which the action takes place. If your story has a moral, do not overstress it. Ask your listeners to point it out or let them draw their own conclusions. When you reach the climax, end the story quickly. If they ask if the story is true answer them honestly.

Storytelling has no secret formula. Each good storyteller develops his or her own techniques. Observe skilled performers and practice whenever possible. You can learn from each experience.

Creative Writing

To be *creative* you must generate a new idea, or take something that is familiar and rework it with your own imagination and personality into a new and unique product. When your goal is to encourage creativity in others, you should proceed cautiously, particularly with suggestions and guidelines. Your role as a counselor is to encourage and give aid where needed. Writing is simply putting words together to show how you think and feel. Writing involves three simple steps: (1) see it, (2) feel/experience it, and (3) write it down.

In other words, instead of talking about an experience, a person writes.

Many campers enjoy keeping a journal or diary as a technique of self-expression.

Campers often are inclined to dismiss the idea that they compose a poem or do a piece of creative writing. Some have been discouraged by insistence in school upon such mechanical details as neatness, legibility, spelling, and punctuation. These techniques are important, but original thought and self-expression are the paramount objectives in creative work.

Encourage campers to jot down their thoughts for their own benefit, if not for sharing with others. Many campers enjoy keeping a journal or a diary as a technique of self-expression, which campers may or may not be interested in sharing. Encourage everyone to write poems, plays, diaries, letters, and accounts of things seen and done. They always should have the option of sharing if they would like. They can also be illustrated with simple line drawings. Any written document allows the author to review his or her thoughts and reflect on memories at a later time.

When it comes to *journal writing*, remind your campers of the following tips. These can guide campers as they create their personal record of events. All it takes is paper, pencil, and a little time each day.

1. The journal can be made up of notes of details to reinforce the camper's memory. Lengthy essays are not needed, nor are they necessarily desired.

2. It is useful to establish a routine of making journal entries; for example, during rest time after lunch or right before campers go to bed.

3. Campers should write only what they know. For instance, attention can be given to basic data such as: times, weather, activities, people, distances, weights, smells, feel, location, view, taste or flavor, and so on. All five senses can come into play. The journal writer may also want to make notes on specific topics such as plants and animal sightings, teachings or leadership ideas, characteristic statements or gestures, and personal or group goals. Surprises and problems can be noted as well as memories and dreams.

A *group log* is a variation of the personal journal that seems to work well with campers. Individuals can be assigned the rotating responsibility of making the journal entry on specific days. By having one person include essential data in the group log, it frees other individuals from the task of recording that information separately in their own personal journal. Group logs also encourage

some campers to try journal-keeping when they would not otherwise be inclined. At the end of the camp, the journal can then be duplicated as a memento that reflects everyone's contribution. Here are a few more suggestions for making a group journal:

1. Give the campers a step-by-step format, listing specific kinds of information to be recorded.

2. Suggest a specific topic for each entrant such as descriptions of group characteristic phrases or gestures, memorable incidents, or the entrant's physical surroundings as he or she writes.

3. Make the first few entries yourself, but have everyone eventually participate.

4. Go over the log with the group periodically to ensure that entries are to everyone's satisfaction.

Some camps have a *camp newspaper* that encourages and recognizes creative writing, keeps campers and staff as well as parents and friends informed of the doings of the whole camp, fosters good camp morale, and serves as a souvenir to recall happy memories of the camp session. Camp papers vary greatly in frequency of publication. Some camps put out a page or two every week or a paper at the end of the session. Computers enable the papers to be put together and made available quite easily. The endeavor is usually a shared camper and counselor activity.

Today, more than ever before, the experience of handwriting or receiving a handwritten letter is infrequent. Encourage campers to write a letter to their family members or friends, not just an e-mail, to share their camping experience and to keep their loved ones posted on the summer's events. If necessary, provide campers with paper, writing utensils, envelopes, and postage to complete this process. Offering a "letters home" activity during a rest period is a way to relax and get campers to reflect about their experiences at camp. Encourage this activity earlier in the session rather than later. The post needs to have time to make it home before the campers' scheduled departure.

Another activity is to have the campers write a letter to themselves describing their camp experience. The letters can be put in self-addressed envelopes and sealed. The counselor can then mail them to the campers in a month, two months, at Thanksgiving, or whenever the campers would like to read what they wrote about camp.

REFERENCES

American Camp Association. 2011. Explore 30. Retrieved from http://www.acacamps.org/explore 30

WEB RESOURCES

Book List Websites
- American Library Booklist (http://www.ala.org/ala/booklist/booklist.htm)

- 101 Out of this World Books for Kids Ages 8–13 (http://als.lib.wi.us/MRList.html)

- Lots of Lists: Everyone Has an Opinion about What Kids Should (or Shouldn't) Read (http://www.ucalgary.ca/~dkbrown/lists.html) contains an extensive variety of recommended book lists targeted to different reading audiences.

Choral Readings Websites

- Classroom Strategies: Choral Reading (http://ww.readingrockets.org/strategies/choral_reading/) contains links to example choral readings and a list of children's books to use with this learning strategy.
- Welcome to Lois Walker's Scripts for Schools (http://scriptsforschools.com/) offers links to a variety of literary products for reading learners.

Folklore and Storytelling

- American Folklore (http://www.americanfolklore.net) contains retellings of American folk tales, myths, legends, tall tales, ghost stories, and many other genres.
- American Folklore Society (www.afsnet.org) has general information on folklore, history of folklore, resources.
- Native American Indian Legends and Folklore (www.native-languages.org/legends.htm) includes a collection of folktales and traditional stories.

- Nature Writing (http://naturewriting.com) offers general information, examples, stories, ideas, and books.
- Storytelling Tips (http://www.campfirestory.com) provides storytelling tips, campfire tips.

Poetry Websites

- Casa Poema—Famous Poems, New Poetry, Photos, and Quotes (http://judithpordon.tripod.com/poetry/index.html) contains collections of poetry covering a variety of topics.
- Poetry (www.poetryteachers.com) offers teaching ideas, activities, poetry theater.
- Poetry Forge (www.poetryforge.org) provides online tutorials for writing poetry, as well as other resources.
- Poetry Foundation (www.poetryfoundation.org) includes an online learning lab, sorted poetry topics, children's poetry, and a newsletter.
- Poets.org (www.poets.org) has information about poets and poems sorted by topic.

PRINT RESOURCES

Evans, F. (2008, Nov/Dec). Put poems in your pockets. *Camping Magazine, 81*(6). Provides poetry tips, sample poems, benefits of poetry.

Grayson, R. (1999). Evening embers. *Camping Magazine, 72*(1), 14.

Pickle, M. (2008, March/April). Letting campers make their mark. *Camping Magazine, 81*(2). Includes numerous writing activity ideas.

Weintraub, J. (1996). Ghost-story telling. *Camping Magazine, 68*(6), 11–12.

16 Arts and Crafts

Arts and crafts constitute an important segment of the overall camp program. These activities contribute to the accomplishment of major camp objectives. The arts and crafts program allows all campers to experience the personal satisfaction of handling materials and learning new skills that provide an outlet for self-expression. The camp program should not duplicate the child's school art activities, which may be conducted in an equipped room, under the direction of a specialist, and are sometimes geared to people of unusual talent and interest. Instead, it should include something for everyone—from the gifted to those who claim to be too inartistic to even draw a straight line.

A wide range of arts and crafts projects can be incorporated, including utilitarian activities like repairing or making camping equipment. Scrap lumber can be recycled by building tables, chairs, shelves, and other items for the camp living quarters and decorating them according to each individual's particular taste and personality. Arts and crafts projects can range from making souvenirs to activities carried on just because of the satisfaction of creating something interesting.

Good programs can be conducted without any special crafts center. Some camps have a central area with at least one staff member especially trained and skilled in this field who acts as consultant or instructor. The center may be elaborate or quite simple with only a well-lighted room, comfortable chairs, tables, outside picnic tables, workbenches, and a few simple tools and raw materials.

Programs are conducted in a variety of ways. In a more *formal* programming situation, each living unit is scheduled for a session at the crafts center at a designated time, or individuals may choose to come during a regular activity period or in their free time. In *informal* programming, living units may be supplied with basic materials and can check out special tools and materials for a crafts program.

The arts and crafts center may be kept open for those who want to spend extra time on a project, with staff either present during open hours to give help and advice or available on call when needed. This latter arrangement makes sense, since activities like sandpapering and waxing a piece of driftwood require painstaking, time-consuming work that can be done at odd moments.

Arts and crafts are an important component of the overall camp program, providing an outlet for self-expression and creativity.

174

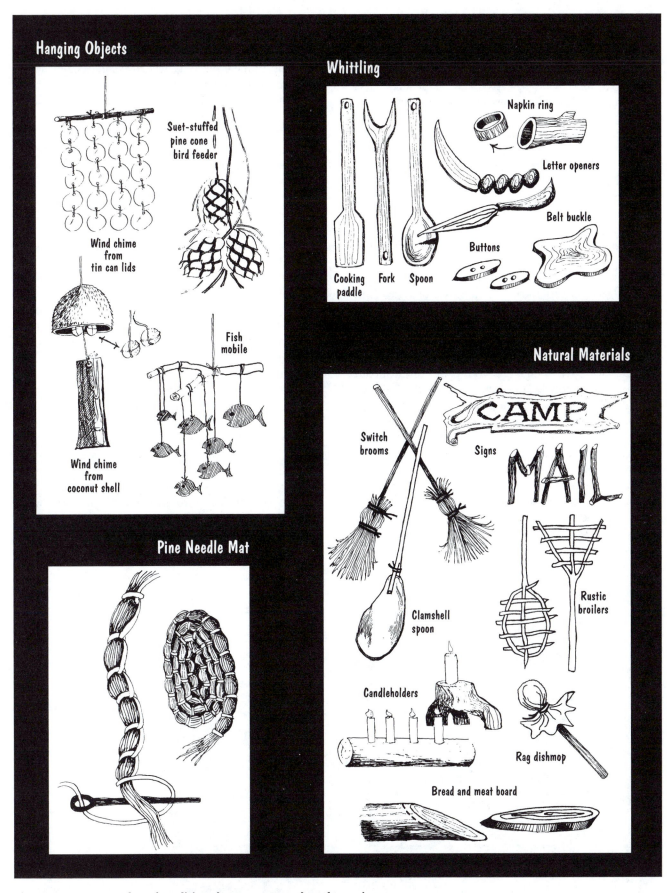

Hanging Objects

Wind chime from tin can lids

Suet-stuffed pine cone bird feeder

Wind chime from coconut shell

Fish mobile

Whittling

Napkin ring

Letter openers

Belt buckle

Buttons

Cooking paddle

Fork

Spoon

Natural Materials

Switch brooms

Signs

CAMP

MAIL

Clamshell spoon

Rustic broilers

Candleholders

Rag dishmop

Bread and meat board

Pine Needle Mat

Figure 16.1   Examples of traditional camp arts and crafts projects.

An Indigenous Program

Like all phases of camp programs, arts and crafts should supplement rather than duplicate the camper's home or school activities by capitalizing on the uniqueness of the camp setting and the raw materials and inspiration from nature available there. This approach does not completely rule out kits or preparing models by merely following directions. However, using natural materials can stimulate campers' imagination and creativity, not to mention the satisfaction of producing something with their own hands out of materials they have gathered and prepared.

Activities carried on with native materials, gathered and prepared on the camp site, constitute what is called an *indigenous* program. An indigenous program is distinguished from the type of program in which the materials are purchased from a supply house in a prepared or semi-prepared state. One of the prime objectives of many summer camps, although not all, is to better acquaint campers with an affinity for nature. Crafts using indigenous materials are a way to combine nature study and art. For example, when campers become absorbed in searching for materials to weave into a basket, plants or flowers to provide natural dyes for a grass mat, or wood suitable to cut and sand into a tie rack or a photograph album, they unconsciously learn about nature in an enjoyable way.

A broad arts and crafts program exposes campers to a panorama of possibilities for self-expression and encourages them to dabble in many activities. Campers should be free to explore and experiment to expand their knowledge of nature and the arts. An additional advantage is that campers learn that there are ways to entertain themselves that don't cost anything, since indigenous materials are free.

Counselors, however, need to make sure that campers are not destroying the natural world as they scavenge for materials to complete their projects. Let them gather materials for the projects as needed as long as they do not violate the principles of good conservation and minimum impact. No camper should needlessly destroy or damage a living thing, especially if it would deplete the supply so that not enough remains to quickly replenish. As a general counselor, you will want to work with your campers in this area as in all other phases of their program.

Conducting the Program

Arts and crafts programs can be conducted in many ways. If natural materials are the focus, campers may need to develop awareness and knowledge about what the natural world has to offer. An observational tour might be the starting point—with the campers encouraged to notice contrasts and blendings of colors; graceful curves and shapes found in grasses, trees, or shrubs; the contours of hills, valleys, and water lines; the movements, formations, and coloring of clouds; and the speed and grace of animal, bird, and insect movements. With practice, the campers will develop an awareness and sensitivity to their natural surroundings.

In presenting new information, a new technique, or the use of a new medium, it is best to demonstrate by using the actual materials as you explain what you are doing and why. You will need to use discretion in determining just how much help to give an individual and when and how to give it. Some campers prefer to be left alone and are frustrated and irritated when someone stands over them giving unsought suggestions and advice. Oth-

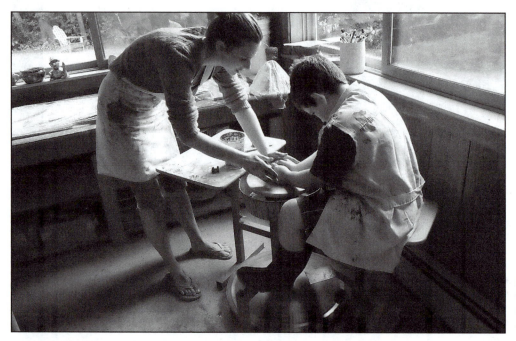

Learning to use a potter's wheel to shape a clay pot. (Photo courtesy of American Camp Association)

ers may lean on you too much to the detriment of their own creativeness and originality.

If you search the Internet, you can find hundreds of ideas for nature craft projects. You may want to let campers determine which kinds of projects they would like to do. Examples of native materials that lend themselves to arts and crafts projects are listed in exhibit 16.1.

Exhibit 16.1

Native Materials

Acorns	Growths of bamboo
Bird feathers	Hickory and other nuts
Bones	Horns/antlers
Cattails	Moss
Discarded birds' eggshells	Native clay
Dried pods	Pine cones and needles
Ears of corn	Sand
Fallen birch or other bark	Sea or clamshells
Fish scales	Seeds
Fungus	Weeds and grasses
Gourds	

Although the camp's arts and crafts program may emphasize nature, many recycled materials often can be used to supplement individual projects. Recycled art is an area with numerous resources available on the Internet. Staff and campers may want to be aware of the potential for using commonly discarded items such as those listed in exhibit 16.2.

Exhibit 16.2

Recycled Materials

Aluminum foil	Eggshells
Bags and sacks	Empty cereal boxes and
Bits of cardboard	other cartons
Bottle caps	Feathers
Bottles (glass or plastic)	Ice cream sticks
Buttons	Linoleum or rugs
Cans and can lids	Magazines
Cellophane wrappings	Milk cartons
Chicken wishbones (fine for	Mop and broom handles
making bow-legged	Newspapers
cowboys)	Old boards
Coat hangers and odd bits	Old drapes and sheets
of wire	Old furniture
Coconut shells	Old inner tubes
Cord and rope	Paper cups
Corks	Sewing scraps
Corn Husks	Spools
Corrugated cardboard	Straws
Discarded clothing	String
Discarded toothbrushes	Toothpicks
Egg cartons	

Both natural and recycled materials can be supplemented with readily available supplies like those listed in exhibit 16.3. These items might be routinely stocked in the crafts center, or can be easily obtained.

Exhibit 16.3

Common Arts and Crafts Materials

Brushes	Paste and glue
Cellophane tape	Pins
Colored thumbtacks	Pipe cleaners
Colored toothpicks	Popcorn
Compass	Poster paints
Construction paper	Ribbon
Craft foam (Styrofoam, etc.)	Rubber bands
Dowel sticks	Rubber cement
Enamels	Shellac
Gumdrops	Stapler and staples
Inks	Thread
Marking pens	Unshelled peanuts
Needles	Various types of paper
Oil paints	Wallpaper samples
Paper clips	Wax crayons

Let individuals use what they have gathered, or compile all the materials in one location for common use. Have campers sort it into piles of related items and place them on shelves or in boxes and bins where everyone can see what is available.

Possible Projects

Typical camp activities have included basketry, making pixies or other imaginary creatures, mobiles and wind chimes, driftwood sculptures, woodcarving, collages, sand painting, papier-mâché, clay modeling, dyeing with natural dyes, weaving, and tin can craft. The possibilities are limited only by the campers' imagination.

As noted earlier, hundreds of ideas for arts and crafts projects are available on the Internet. Many of these projects have specific directions, so we offer a list of just a few of the possibilities in exhibit 16.4. Directions for these ideas may be available online or in books in the camp or public library.

Exhibit 16.4

Possible Arts and Crafts Projects

Baskets	Games	Mosaics	Scrapbooks and memory books
Belts	Greeting cards and stationery	Murals	Soap sculpture
Birdhouses and feeders	Hiking sticks	Musical and rhythm	Table decorations
Bookbinding	Indian costumes, rattles,	instruments	Three-legged stools
Bookends	tom-toms	Napkin rings	Tie racks
Bookmarks	Jewelry	Nature displays and trails	Totem poles
Bows and arrows	Kachina dolls	Paperweights	Toys
Camping furniture and	Kites	Party favors and place cards	Trinket boxes
equipment	Knot boards	Photography	Vases
Candle holders	Lamps	Picture frames	Wall plaques
Candles	Lapel pins	Plant boxes	Wastebaskets
Coasters	Letter trays	Pot holders and hot plate	Whistles
Coin purses	Marionettes and puppets	pads	Winter bouquets
Costumed dolls	Masks	Relief maps	Wooden buckles
Doorstops	Mobiles	Rustic signs	Wooden buttons
Fishing equipment	Model campsites	Sand candles	Yarn animals and dolls

---

WEB RESOURCES

Basket and Fiber Arts

- (http://www.allfiberarts.com)
- (http://www.beebes.net/basket/)
- (http://basketmakers.org) offers tips, tutorials, and materials for different types of baskets.
- (www.nationalbasketry.org) provides links to relevant sites as well as an online bookstore.
- Boy Scout Merit Badge in Basketry (http://www.meritbadge.com/mb/027.htm)

Beads

- Beading Daily (www.beadingdaily.com) contains a glossary, free projects, a magazine, and a bookstore.
- Beading Times (www.beadingtimes.com) offers free, archived beading projects with step-by-step directions, pictures, and material list.
- Beadwork (www.beadage.net) provides step-by-step tutorials, as well as a material and tools list.

Ceramics and Pottery

- Basic Instructions (http://42explore.com/pottery.htm)
- Ceramics Monthly (www.ceramicartsdaily.org) includes a bookstore, techniques, tools, and project ideas.
- JH Pottery (www.jhpottery.com) has tutorial pages for coil pots, pinch pots, slab pots, throwing on a wheel, and adding handles.
- Newton Abbot Adult Education Centre Pottery (http://www.abbotpottery.com/aec/potterycourse.html) has instructions for projects, safety tips.
- Out of the Fire Studio: How to Make Pottery (www.howtomakepottery.com) contains step-by-step instructions and videos for various stages of pottery making.
- Pottery Magic (www.pottery-magic.com) provides instructions for projects, tips and techniques, and tools.
- Teach Pottery (www.teachpottery.net) has instructions on how to create basic clay forms.

Crafting

- Friendship braids and knots (http://www.wikihow.com/Make-a-Cross-Knot-Friendship-Bracelet)
- Home Schooling Arts Activities (http://homeschooling.gomilpitas.com/explore/artscrafts.htm) describes how art brings out good qualities in kids.
- Imagination Factory (www.kid-at-art.com) has a collection of project ideas.
- Jewelry Making Headquarters (www.jewelrymakinghq.com) contains book list and free patterns/directions.
- Jewelry Making Professor (www.jewelrymakingprofessor.com) provides online videos and patterns for beading, at a cost.
- Leather Braintanning (http://www.braintan.com/)
- Leather Factory (www.tandyleatherfactory.com) offers patterns, books, and tools.
- Leathercraft Guild (http://iilg.net/)
- Metal Craft (http://www.craftsitedirectory.com/metal/index.html)
- Needlepoint (http://www.needlepointers.com/ShowArticles.aspx?NavID=669) contains information on different kinds of crafts, including weaving activities for kids with directions.
- Weaving (http://www.hallnet.com/weave.html) provides instructions on how to build and weave on a simple frame loom.

Mosaics

- Institute of Mosaic Art (www.insituteofmosaicart.com) offers resources and supplies.
- Mosaic Art Supply (www.mosaicartsupply.com) has instructions, a tile calculator, and frequently asked questions.
- Mosaic Mercantile (www.mosaicmercantile.com) offers a tile calculator, help, and an online bookstore.
- Mosaic Patterns (www.mosaicpatternsonline.com) provides tips, techniques, and patterns.

Papier-Mâché
- (www.ultimatepapermache.com) has recipes and tutorials.
- (http://www.dltk-kids.com/type/how_to_paper_mache.htm)
- (www.papiermache-art.com) provides step-by-step instructions, recipes, other tools, project samples.

Wood Carving
- (www.woodcarvingillustrated.com) has tips and archived magazine articles.
- (www.carvingpatterns.com) free patterns, online video tutorials, glossary, tools, tips, and techniques.
- Scouts Woodworking (http://www.scouts.caincreek.com/)
- Totem Poles (www.chainsawsculptors.com/totem_poles.htm) describes totem pole history, meanings, and types.

PRINT RESOURCES

Clark, S. (1997). ABCs of working with younger campers. *Camping Magazine, 70*(4), 18–19.

Foster, E. (2003, Nov/Dec). Art matters. *Camping Magazine, 76*(6). Discusses why kids need art at camps.

Kravitz, L. R. (2004, May/June). A practical approach to pottery at summer camp. *Camping Magazine, 77*(3). Provides tips and steps to implementing a pottery program.

Pick, D. (1997). Earth art. *Camping Magazine, 70*(4), 28–29.

van der Smissen, B., Goering, O., & Brookhiser, J. (2005). *A leader's guide to nature-oriented activities* (4th ed.). Martinsville, IN: American Camp Association.

Wallace, S. (2008, Nov/Dec). The art of camp. *Camping Magazine, 81*(6), 22–24.

17

Nature, Ecology, and Science

Learning about the outdoors is sometimes called outdoor education, nature study, ecology, conservation education, environment-based education, or interpretation. No matter what term is used, the objective should be to enable campers to think reasonably and with understanding about their environment—to see patterns of cause and effect and to relate these patterns to other aspects of their lives. However, to gain a sense of awareness about the environment, people must first develop a better understanding of it.

Not all camps make extensive use of the outdoors. However, the traditions of camp have been built on the outdoors, so some emphasis should be evident in all camps. Since human health and well-being depend in large part on the quality of our environment, concerns about its conservation should be emphasized to all campers.

Sometimes new camp counselors feel that teaching about the environment should mimic educational experiences from their academic life. Although information is conveyed and learning occurs, the structure and method of education at camp can and should be quite different than the traditional education methods employed in schools. You are not expected to be an authority on all things natural, but rather you should be interested in nature to some extent and willing to use whatever knowledge and ability you have to learn alongside campers. You may often find yourself saying, "I don't know, but let's find out."

Nature study and developing an affinity for nature can occur in unexpected places. When campers are alert to their natural surroundings, a hike may end a hundred yards from the cabin when a fascinated group stays to watch a spider weave its web. A trip to gather materials for arts and crafts may turn into a study of different woods and their uses. These are *teachable moments*!

The qualities you need to instill an interest in and respect for nature in your campers are curiosity, enthusiasm, and insight into the possibilities for integrating nature with other camp experiences. However, the most important quality is interest in and love of *human* nature. Your attitude is important, so show enthusiasm and an eagerness to learn—campers will take their cue from you. Every undertaking should be done in a spirit of fun and adventure, although sometimes for a specific purpose such as catching minnows for bait, searching for wild strawberries or blueberries for a pie or cobbler, visiting an old lumber mill, or learning about the measures a neighboring farmer is taking to prevent erosion. A leisurely pace and a receptive attitude can turn an outdoor excursion into an opportunity to explore nature. With the hectic pace of modern life, not enough time is taken to develop this appreciation for nature.

Such equipment as microscopes, pocket magnifying glasses, butterfly nets, binoculars, and nature books can help stimulate campers' interests. Learning is enhanced when hands and imaginations are occupied in making equipment, arranging bulletin boards, mounting displays, and planning museums and nature trails.

Understanding the Ecosystem Concept

Ecology is the study of the interrelationships and interactions between individuals, organisms, and their environment. Ecology includes the interactions that humans have with the environment as well as the way that organisms in the environment interact with one another. In the camp setting much can be observed about ecologi-

The study of ecology is an interesting camp activity because it takes place in nature's own laboratory.

cal relationships when campers begin with the principle that every living organism is related to other organisms (i.e., plants and animals) and the basic substances (e.g., sunlight, air, water, and soil) in its environment. In other words, the individual members of a natural community interact to further the welfare of the whole just as is done by the members of a human community.

Many books, articles, and website sources describe this complex and sophisticated subject. The discussion in this book is designed to give a brief introduction to some of the major concepts that might be used at camp. The ultimate goal of a nature and ecology program is to invite campers to ask questions about how the natural world works. With the ongoing conversations about nature-deficit disorder (Louv, 2005), the importance of young people connecting to nature cannot be overemphasized. To address this goal, a camp counselor does not need extensive background in biology or wildlife management. A basic understanding of the elements of the ecosystem and access to resources is a good point from which to start.

The Ecosystem

The word *ecosystem* combines two words: *ecology* and *system.* It connects the idea of *eco,* the natural world, with that of *system,* a set of interactions over time among living and nonliving elements in the environment. **Ecosystem** can be further defined as an ecological community functioning as a unit with its environment. The entire planet is an ecosystem. An ecosystem also can be as small as a lake or pond, or it could even be represented by a jar containing pond water and a few small aquatic animals and plants. Thus, an ecosystem may be viewed as a set of elements, living and nonliving, interacting over time within a defined locale.

All living things are ultimately dependent upon plants. Every animal—including humans—either dines directly upon plant life or upon other animals that consume plant life. Each is simultaneously engaged in a struggle to secure its own food and to avoid becoming the food of another. In addition, every animal has a way of protecting itself. For example, deer can outrun most of their enemies, and cats climb trees to evade dogs. Nature, if left to its devices, usually will keep all species in balance so that they neither die out nor become so numerous as to overrun the earth. Every single form of life has its own role in maintaining this equilibrium, which is called the *balance of nature* or *equilibrium.*

Almost everything people do affects plant or animal life in some way. For example, picking berries in the fall reduces the supply of winter food for some bird or animal as well as the number of seeds that might sprout and grow into new plants. Spraying trees with insecticides kills the insects and grubs that provide food for certain birds, and it may leave residues harmful to bird and animal life, including people. Killing squirrels will eventually mean fewer trees, since dead squirrels cannot bury nuts to sprout and grow into future forests. Humans have cut down the trees and shrubs and cleared the fence rows that used to provide food and shelter for animals and birds. These acts, along with the massive development of rural lands, the draining of wetlands, and urban sprawl in general have fragmented plant and animal habitats, decreasing the ability for movement, and diminishing food supplies for a number of the nation's animals.

For campers to acquire an understanding of ecology, they need to develop an awareness and understanding of natural interrelationships. Campers can realize that the removal of just one small component from the ecosystem can have major consequences. Fortunately, a variety of educational games and activities are available to help campers develop an awareness of these relationships. The Internet contains many ideas for nature study and a few examples of possible topics will be presented in this chapter.

Nature Appreciation and Learning Activities

Nature hikes can be great fun as well as a learning experience for campers. A group should seldom be in too big a hurry that it cannot stop and watch the antics of a squirrel or listen to a noisy blue jay. Campers will learn best through hands-on experiences using techniques of inquiry, discovery, problem solving, and personal observation.

Campers can develop an awareness of all the facets of nature as they encounter the natural world through all of their senses—including sight, sound, smell, touch, and even taste. In his classic work, Van Matre (1972) used the term *acclimatization* to describe this feeling for the environment. Specimens can be found everywhere—whatever lies beside the path, under rocks or old logs, in trees, or at the bottom of a creek or pond. With the aid of such inexpensive pieces of equipment as a homemade butterfly or dip net and a little pocket microscope, the field of exploration is unlimited.

As a counselor, you should encourage learning through *inquiry* as often as possible. To illustrate the use of the inquiry technique as a learning tool for campers, consider this example using the beaver. What is the beaver's role in nature? Where is the beaver's home? What organisms and substances in its environment does the beaver depend upon for survival? How does it use these organisms and substances? How does the beaver affect other organisms and substances? What organisms and substances in this environment depend upon the beaver? How do these organisms and substances use it? How do other organisms and substances affect the beaver? Where does the beaver fit into the food cycle in its environment? How does the beaver reproduce? How may the beaver be affected by climatic conditions and change? What adaptations has the beaver developed to suit itself to this environment? Discover the answers to these questions with your campers.

Conservation Projects

Conservation is the appreciation, understanding, and wise use of natural resources for the greatest good for the most people for the longest time. Camp provides an ideal climate for instilling in young people an appreciation for conservation. It is hoped that campers who are exposed to nature will return home with a greater commitment to protect the natural environment for future generations. After all, campers will be voters someday and will determine the policies of the future. True conservation is based upon an appreciation of the value of each living thing in maintaining the balance of the whole.

One of the best ways to familiarize campers with nature and good conservation practices is to involve them in projects of their own choosing to improve the camp or a nearby area. Be sure to discuss any plans with your camp director before proceeding. It is also wise to confer with such experts as the camp caretaker or manager, county agent, conservation officer, park superintendent, or forester, since ill-advised efforts by amateurs some-

Campers' natural curiosity will lead them to spontaneous discovery of the natural world around them.

Figure 17.1   Conservation pledge.

This pledge originated in a national competition conducted in 1946 by *Outdoor Life Magazine* and is reprinted through their courtesy.

times do more harm than good. Here are some sample ideas for conservation projects:

1. Take your group on a tour of the camp, noting any areas that show the results of violations of good conservation practices. Make a list of what needs to be done and arrange it in the order of priority. Let each group decide which issues, if any, it would like to undertake. Involve your campers in all proceedings. Remember, do *with*, not *for*, them.

2. Make and erect birdhouses. Numerous guidelines for making simple birdhouses can be found on the Internet.

3. Help forest development by thinning out places where trees are too thick for any to grow well. Weed out less desirable species or trees that are crooked or diseased. Clear out grapevines or other invasive species that are choking younger native trees. Remember that it is sometimes wise to let dead trees stand. They furnish homes and nests for certain birds and animals and will eventually rot away, returning their substance to enrich the soil as nature intended.

4. Promote a conservation, anti-litter, earth, or ecology day at camp with appropriate activities and learning opportunities.

5. Hold a scavenger hunt, awarding varying points for bringing in such unwanted debris as bottles, cans, and loose paper. Make a wire enclosure to display the haul, and recycle when possible.

6. Volunteer for community service in cleaning up adjoining roads, a public beach, or park.

7. Clean up the banks of a lake or other body of water and improve living conditions for its surrounding wildlife.

8. If trails begin to show signs of wear or overuse, repair them. Trails that go up steep slopes should have switchbacks or zigzags to prevent erosion. Make "Stay on the Path" signs and post throughout camp to discourage careless destruction of tender vegetation growing along the paths. Campers may also want to outline main paths with small rocks.

9. Stress good principles of conservation, such as cutting no living trees unless absolutely necessary and choosing wisely when you cut. If you build wood fires, prepare safe fire sites and put out fires completely. Depending upon your geographic location, soil type, and climate, you may want to seriously consider using stoves and fire pans instead of wood fires on barren ground. Choose materials for arts and crafts judiciously, and use sparingly.

10. Study the helpful roles played by commonly despised creatures such as bats, ants, skunks, worms, spiders, snakes, bees, wasps and the like. All of them play an important role in nature's master plan. Educating campers about these roles will encourage them to develop a more tolerant attitude toward these creatures.

11. Make a compost pile at some distance from the main camp, placing on it grass cuttings, excess leaves, food waste, and the like. Keep it damp, and stir it up occasionally. This provides excellent humus to mix with soil in a flower or vegetable garden or other area where you want growth to occur.

12. Discuss the environmental effect of some camp activities such as campfire rings, cookouts, games and sports, trips, fishing, arts and crafts, and hiking. Does the camp need to reevaluate any procedures?

Sensory Awareness Activities

Having campers refine the use of their five basic senses (taste, smell, touch, sight, and sound) to the greatest extent possible can help them develop a greater appreciation and understanding of nature and become more aware of their physical environment.

Although most people have *sight*, they may not notice some of the interesting aspects of the outdoors. To illustrate just what is possible, have your campers stand or sit quietly in the woods to concentrate upon the trees around them. How do they vary in size, shape, limb arrangement, and leaf structure? How many can they identify? Do any show signs of disease or pests? Are there birds' nests or signs of animal homes? You might also have the campers lie on their backs looking up with their feet pressed against the base of a tree like spokes in a wheel. From this location they can gain yet a different perspective of the natural world.

To improve your campers' awareness of *smell*, have them take a deep breath: What odors can they detect? How does the smell of a swamp, bog, or pine forest differ from that of the city? Why? As your group walks along a trail, have them note any change in odors and try to find out what causes them. Many animals have a much keener sense of smell than people do and thus, detect our presence long before we are even in their sight. For this reason, you will need to keep an animal downwind when trying to approach it. Select some familiar substances such as moss, a wild onion, and a crushed mint leaf and pass them among the campers while blindfolded to see how many they can identify.

Beware of indiscriminately *tasting* things in nature with which you are unfamiliar. However, have campers try out such items as a leaf of wintergreen, a sassafras twig, a juniper bush, and other substances that you know to be harmless.

Encourage campers' sense of *touch* by having them feel the texture of things in nature and note the differences. Try this with a circle of blindfolded persons to see how many "mystery objects" collected from outdoors can be identified. With the loss of sight people become more aware of the sense of touch. Another idea might be to blindfold the members of your group and direct them to put their left hand on the shoulder of the person in front of them. Follow a trail around the area, stopping to touch any objects within reach. Ask individuals to use three different words to describe what they feel. This same activity can be repeated with smelling, listening, and tasting.

To help campers develop their *hearing* skills and become more aware of the sounds around them, have them sit down, close their eyes, and listen. They should make a mental note of everything they hear in a period of five minutes and then have them compare their perceptions with one another. This activity can be performed at various times of the day and night to bring into focus the changes in frequency, pitch, and intensity of sounds in the natural environment.

Collecting Materials

Although collecting natural materials still has its place in camp, it should be done judiciously. Before picking a flower or other specimen, apply good principles of conservation by being sure that ample quantities are left to carry on the species. Collections of rocks, minerals, flowers, leaves, seeds, insects, shells, ferns, and mosses that are correctly identified can add to a nature program. Usually collecting is best done as a group project rather than as an individual effort. Each mounting can be accompanied with the item's name, place found, and any data concerning its life or place in the balance of nature.

Reproducing specimens by painting, sketching, or photographing them rather than collecting them is just as meaningful and more in accordance with good con-

servation practices, since it leaves the specimen intact. Keep in mind the principles of "leave no trace" and "minimum impact."

Even though your state may be one of the few in which it is not illegal to keep wild animals in captivity, the best advice is not to do so. Many wild animals die from lack of proper food and care, and those successfully kept for some time often lose their ability to fend for themselves when turned loose. When you find a young animal in the woods or on the prairie, it is best to leave the animal alone and not intrude upon its territory. Often seemingly deserted babies have only been left temporarily while their parents go out searching for food.

Making a Nature Trail

Laying out a nature trail is a great learning experience and also provides an educational experience for other campers and visitors. These trails can be laid out in many ways, but the focus is to identify various aspects of nature that can be keyed to a sign or specific location. A trail about one-half to a mile long arranged as a loop or figure-eight takes about an hour to wander through and brings the traveler back to the starting point. Short side trails or spurs can be indicated to show interesting sights such as an unusually large tree or a deserted bee's nest. If a trail already exists at camp that can be used as both an interpretive trail and a hiking trail, it would be advantageous to double up on the existing trial and not promote further development.

A nature trail provides opportunities for self-conducted tours using signs or labels instead of a human guide. Pick out the features you want to showcase along the way and ask for volunteers to look up information about them. Although each situation varies, 15 to 18 features are about the right number for a half-mile trail. Campers can select the content and presentation of the information for each feature. In general, brevity should be the keyword. These trails can be designed in numerous ways; there are several good sources related to developing such trails at camp. Remember that a nature trail must be maintained to assure that it is kept in good condition.

Studies in the Environment

Numerous aspects of nature may be studied in more depth, depending on the interests of your campers. *Bird study* is one of the most popular nature activities. Here are just a few of the activities that might be undertaken:

- Bird walks are best done in early morning or early evening, when the birds are most active.
- Contrast the bills and feet of birds to see how they are adapted to their diet and habits. Listen to the bird's song and watch its pattern of flight.
- Make a bird scrapbook of pictures, stories, anecdotes, and poems.

Such equipment as binoculars, pocket magnifying glasses, microscopes, butterfly nets, and nature books can help stimulate campers' interests.

- Make plaster casts of tracks in mud or at the beach.
- Construct a bird sanctuary somewhere near camp with protective cover and other items to attract birds and provide a bulletin board with identifying pictures.
- Construct bird houses and hang them in the area to increase the bird population from year to year.

Examples of nature activities that focus on *plants* include the following:

- Draw or paint pictures of wild flowers, adding name, date, where found, and such information as native country, seeds and their dispersal, pollination, and uses.
- Study seeds and their dispersal by barbs, parachutes, wind, animals, and other means.
- Make a plant gall collection.
- Study lichens, mosses, and ferns. Look at them through a microscope.
- Identify nut-bearing bushes and trees. Learn when the nuts ripen and what animals eat them.
- Study flower arrangement for indoor decoration.
- Identify poison ivy, poison oak, and poison sumac.
- Identify different types of mushrooms, particularly the morels, which are safe to eat. Do not trust other kinds, since even experts have difficulty in distinguishing the poisonous ones.
- Determine which flowers open at different times of the day, and devise a flower clock.

Trees can be identified by contour, color, leaf, bark, flower, seed, and wood and branch structure. Help campers learn all they can about them such as what they are used for by wild animals and people, and how they burn.

- Press and mount leaves.
- Photograph trees. Make sketches or watercolors of them.
- Learn how individual trees serve as shade, beauty, soil conservation, firewood, or commercial products.

- Study stumps to learn the life history of the tree such as its age, injuries, insect damage, favorable and unfavorable seasons, and the like.
- Learn the uses of different kinds of woods in fire building (tinder, kindling, heat, light, fire dogs, and others).

Almost a million varieties of identified *insects* exist in the world. Learn the distinguishing characteristics of spiders, bees, wasps, grasshoppers, beetles, flies, moths, butterflies, and others. Watch them in their native habitat. Learn their habits, food, life cycles, and use or destructiveness.

Butterflies and other insects are fascinating to inquisitive campers. (Photo courtesy of American Camp Association)

Learning how to distinguish between *rocks and minerals* can be interesting. You might visit a quarry, an outcrop, a fresh road cut, a dried-up stream bed, or a mine opening. You can gather specimens using a geology hammer (an ordinary hammer will serve) to prepare uniform sizes (about 1½ by 2½ inches) for collections.

Have campers make their own poles, baits (flies and lures), and lines to go *fishing*. They can catch or dig their own live bait. Help them learn to recognize the different species, and even how to clean fish (good opportunity to study their structures). You also will enjoy eating them!

Animals offer several fascinating opportunities for study:

- Take close-up photographs. Use the portrait setting on your digital camera.
- Make plaster casts of tracks (see figure 17.2).
- Play stalking games.
- Look for traces of animals such as droppings, tracks, dens, burrows, bits of fur, and homes.
- Find out which animals can see, hear, smell, or taste more acutely than humans.
- Stalk animals with a camera. Lie or sit still and watch them.

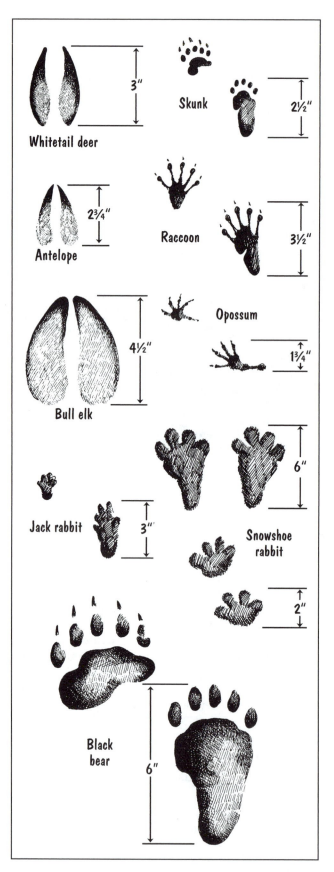

Figure 17.2   Animal tracks.

Astronomy is an activity that many people enjoy. The stars are a source of comfort as well as a source of information (Jackson, 2004). Unfortunately, many people rarely see the stars because of the glare of city lights. On a clear night in the best conditions, far from the smog, haze, and artificial lights of cities, about 2,500 stars are visible in our own galaxy. In a camp setting, the night sky can be exciting. Learning about the cycles of the moon and the importance of the sun can also be of interest to campers. Many good resources about astronomy are available. You may wish to explore topics such as constellations, the Milky Way, navigation using the stars, the Big Dipper (see figure 17.3), star mythology, meteors, comets, aurora borealis (northern lights), and techniques for star gazing.

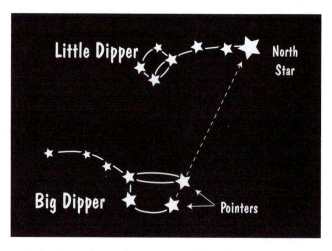

Figure 17.3   Big Dipper and Little Dipper.

Nature Games

Nature games are not only fun and educational for the participants, but also can sharpen campers' observation skills. Numerous ideas and guidelines can be found on the internet. Here are some possible ideas:

- Wild edibles hike

- Nature treasure or scavenger hunt

- Leaf relay (Give each team a list of trees. The first one in line runs to get a leaf of the first tree on the list, returns, and gives the list to the second in line, who then reads the second kind of tree and runs to get a sample, and so on. The first group finished wins.)

- Identification (The first person to identify the picture correctly receives the card.)

- Touch, taste, smell identification

- Upside down hike (Turn over rocks, decaying logs, and large sticks to see what is living underneath them—be sure to restore them without harming any inhabitants living under them.)

Program Resources

As noted throughout this chapter, many educational resources are available to explore the interrelationships between living and nonliving things. Although some of these materials were initially designed as learning activities for the elementary or secondary school classroom, their use is not limited to formal educational settings. *Project Learning Tree* and *Project Wild*, for example, are two environmental learning programs with educational content that is adaptable to the camp setting.

To summarize, here are some of the projects that you might consider that have been successfully used at camp. Directions for all can be found on the Internet.

- Making microsystems in jars
- Predator and prey games
- Using tree or flower guides to identify the plant life at camp
- Soil conservation
- Making birdhouses
- Making bird feeding stations
- Make a compost pile
- Camp gardens
- Tracking wildlife
- Night hikes
- Identifying medicinal plants
- Making a plant (leaves and flowers) press
- A fernery or wild flower garden
- An aquarium for water life
- A terrarium for things that live on land
- Making nature prints
- Casting animal tracks

The prose in exhibit 17.1 aptly describes the importance of meaningful connections between children and nature.

Exhibit 17.1

The Birthright of Children

All children should know the joy of playing in healthful mud, of paddling in clean water, of hearing birds sing praises to God for the new day. They should have the vision of pure skies enriched at dawn and sunset with unspeakable glory; of dew-drenched mornings flashing with priceless gems; of the vast night sky all throbbing and panting with stars.

They should live with the flowers and butterflies, with the wild things that have made possible the world of fables.

They should experience the thrill of going barefoot, of being out in the rain; of riding a white birch, of sliding down pine boughs, of climbing ledges and tall trees, of diving headfirst into a transparent pool.

They ought to know the smell of wet earth, of new mown hay, of sweet fern, mint, and fir; of the breath of cattle and of fog blown inland from the sea.

They should hear the answer the trees make to the rain and the wind; the sound of rippling and falling water; the muffled roar of the sea in storm.

They should have the chance to catch fish, to ride on a load of hay, to camp out, to cook over an open fire, tramp through a new country, and sleep under the open sky.

They should have the fun of driving a horse, paddling a canoe, sailing a boat. . . .

One cannot appreciate and enjoy to the full extent of nature, books, novels, histories, poems, pictures, or even musical compositions, who has not in his youth enjoyed the blessed contact with the world of nature.

—Henry Turner Bailey

REFERENCES

Jackson, E. (2004, May/June). Innovative astronomy programs for camps. *Camping Magazine, 77*(3), 20–26.

Louv, R. (2005). *Last child in the woods.* Chapel Hill, NC: Algonquin Press.

Van Matre, S. (1972). *Acclimatization.* Bradford Woods, IN: ACA.

WEB RESOURCES

Birds

Audubon (www.audubon.org) is one of the leading organizations regarding environmental issues affecting birds; site features additional resources and a kids' center.

Bird Watcher's Digest (www.birdwatchersdigest.com) provides an identification guide, gear, tips on conservation, and photos.

Bird Watching (www.birdwatching.com) has tips, stories, frequently asked questions, and a bookstore.

- (www.birding.com) discusses how to begin bird watching, identification, fact sheets, photos, songs, and more.

- (www.wildbirds.com), (http://www.whatbird.com) and (http://www.birdingguide.com) offer bird-watching tips.

Birder's World Magazine (www.birdersworld.com) provides archived issues, tips, identification guides, and a bookstore.

Cornell Lab of Ornithology (www.allaboutbirds.org) provides a bird guide, basics of birding.

The Feather Atlas (www.lab.fws.gov/featheratlas/index.php) has images, glossary, and frequently asked questions.

The Science of Birds (www.ornithology.com) has information on bird watching, books, facts, feathers, and more.

Winston's Bird Field Guide (www.birdfieldguide.com) provides a comprehensive list of birds by alphabetical order, including pictures.

Butterflies and Moths

Butterflies (www.thebutterflysite.com) has facts, gardening tips, houses, links, and activities.

Butterflies and Moths of North America (www.butterfliesandmoths.org) includes taxonomic groups, maps, species search, and image gallery.

Butterfly gallery (www.butterflywebsite.com) has articles, photo gallery, checklists, conservation, stories, videos, and frequently asked questions.

Butterfly School (www.butterflyschool.org) has information on behaviors, identification guide, butterfly houses, arts and crafts, photos, and more.

Fish and Shells

Fish (http://www.landbigfish.com/fish/default.cfm). Check your state's DNR Department of Natural Resources website for information about fish in your area.

Shells (http://vt.essortment.com/seashellscoll_rvwj.htm)

- (http://www.schnr-specimen-shells.com/CollectingIntro.html)
- (www.seashell-collector.com) offers photo gallery, articles, book reviews, beginning tips, and identification tips.
- (www.seashells.org) has information on identification, cleaning and preserving, legends.

Water Life (http://www.projectwet.org)

Insects

Amateur Entomologists' Society (www.amentsoc.org) discusses insect identification, care sheets, facts, and conservation.

Bug Bios (www.insects.org) offers bug descriptions and resources.

Dragonfly Society of the Americas (www.odonatacentral.org) has checklists, maps, photos/identifications, and other resources.

Insects (http://bugguide.net/node.view/15740)

- (http://www.insectguide.net)
- (www.insectidentification.org) has pictures and descriptors of common insects.

Miscellaneous

Edible Wild Mushrooms (www.ediblewildmushrooms.com) offers a virtual wild mushroom field guide.

Man and Mollusc (www.manandmollusc.net) provides articles, images, and a kid's section.

Mushrooms (http://www.gardenbythesea.org/about/mushroom/)

- (www.mushroomexpert.com) discusses preservation, collecting, identification, odor and taste.
- (www.rogersmushrooms.com) has a glossary, identification tips, keys.

Recycle Works (www.recycleworks.org) has facts and information on recycling, composting.

Nature/Outdoor Education

Association for Experiential Education (www.aee.org) offers publications and resources on experiential education.

Cary Institute of Ecosystem Studies (www.caryinstitute.org/publications.html) has lesson plans and discusses ecosystem literacy.

Children and Nature Network (www.childrenandnature.org) provides news and research on connecting children with nature.

Environmental Protection Agency, Teaching Center (www.epa.gov/teachers/index.htm) has teaching resources, publications, kids' page.

Environmental Stewardship (www.environmentalstewardship.org) provides general information on stewardship.

Greenhour (www.greenhour.org) features an activity center, information for educators.

Learning to Observe (http://www.princeton.edu/~oa/nature/naturobs.shtml)

Leave No Trace (www.lnt.org) promotes responsible enjoyment and active stewardship of the outdoors.

Louv, R. (www.richardlouv.com) discusses children and nature deficit disorder.

National Environmental Education Foundation (www.neefusa.org) includes a variety of environmental education topics and resources.

National Wildlife Federation (www.nwf.org) provides wildlife resources, information on climate change, and outdoor activities.

Nature (www.enature.com) provides field guide to species including insects, spiders, wildflowers, and more.

Nature Games (http://www.bbc.co.uk/sn/games/)

- (http://www.ultimatecampresource.com/site/camp-activities/nature-games.page-1.html)
- (http://www.inquiry.net/outdoor/winter/activities/games/nature.htm)

North American Association for Environmental Education (www.naaee.org)

Project Learning Tree (http://www.plt.org/)

Project WILD (http://www.projectwild.org/)

Sierra Club (www.sierraclub.org)

Tread Lightly (www.treadlightly.org) promotes responsible outdoor recreation through ethics and stewardship.

U.S. Department of the Interior, Bureau of Land Management (http://www.blm.gov/wo/st/en/res/Education_in_BLM.html) provides learning landscapes, teaching resources, activities.

U.S. Forest Service (www.fs.fed.us) provides a kids' section, regulations and manual, recreational activities, safety tips.

Wildlife Habitat Council (www.wildlifehc.org) provides wildlife management tools, links, and publications.

Plants

Flowers (http://www.enature.com/fieldguides/intermediate.asp?curGroupID=11)

- (www.wildflowerinformation.org) allows you to search flowers by features, and provides detailed information on wildflowers.
- (www.mywildflowers.com) allows you to search for wildflowers, provides identification tips.

Natural Resources Conservation Service, Plants Database (www.plants.usda.gov) provides classification, links, threatened and endangered list fact sheets, and plant guides.

Reptiles and Amphibians

Adult Amphibian Identification Page (http://imnh.isu.edu/DIGITALATLAS/bio/amph/main/aamphid.htm) has information on identification, larval amphibians, and eggs.

Reptiles and Amphibians (http://animal.discovery.com/guides/reptiles/reptiles.htm)

Reptile Channel (www.reptilechannel.com) has a kid section, information on snakes, lizards, turtles, frogs, and other reptiles, care sheets, videos.

Rocks and Minerals

Mineral and Gemstone Kingdom (www.minerals.net) has information on gemstones, photo gallery, glossary, minerals, and resources.

The Paleontology Portal (www.paleoportal.org) offers a photo gallery, resources, kids' section.

Rocks and Minerals (http://www.stf.sk.ca/teaching_res/ library/teach_mat_centre/tmc/e10625/e10625.htm)

- (www.rocksforkids.com) provides tips on identification, experiments, glossary, formation, and more.

- (www.fossil-facts-and-finds.com) has lesson plans, detailed information on fossils.

Sky

Google Sky (www.google.com/sky/) is an interactive site to explore the sky, moon, constellations, solar system, and other sky features.

Sky and Telescope Magazine (www.skyandtelescope.com) has stargazing tips, specific to date, glossary.

Sky Map (www.sky-map.org) allows you to browse different features of the sky.

StarDate (www.stardate.org) offers lesson plan, stargazing tips specific to date, resources, beginner's guide.

Trees

Arbor Day Foundation (www.arborday.org) includes a tree guide, discusses benefits of trees and other basic information.

Bark Identification (http://www.hsu.edu/default.aspx?id=7544) includes pictures of various types of bark.

Trees (www.oplin.org/tree/) has information on tree identification by leaf, fruit, or name.

- (www.tree-identification.com) has tips for identification by topics including bark, leaves, type and more.

- (www.growingnative.org) offers resources, games, identification, curriculum.

PRINT RESOURCES

Bordeau, V. (2005). Nature is the program. *Camping Magazine, 78*(3), 1–3.

Forster, G. (2005, March/April). "This old camp" goes green. *Camping Magazine, 78*(2). Discusses green initiatives put forth by camps such as lighting, heating, and composting.

Henchey, K., & Carvajal, M. (2000, Sept/Oct). Building environmental awareness. *Camping Magazine, 73*(5). Provides activity ideas for teaching campers the importance of minimizing their impact on the environment for ages 6 to adult.

Jackson, E. (2004, May/June). Innovative astronomy programs for camps. *Camping Magazine, 77*(3). Discusses teaching astronomy at camp during the daytime.

Lieberstein, T. (1997). Hands-on, Minds-on. *Camping Magazine, 70*(2), 20–22.

Louv, R. (2005, Jan/Feb). Camp revival. *Camping Magazine, 79*(1), 28–33.

Marion, J. L., & Bates, D. (2005, May/June). Implementing leave no trace at camps. *Camping Magazine, 78*(3), 54–57.

Molloy, L. (2006). Strategic program planning: A recipe for success. *Camping Magazine, 79*(2), 1–6.

Montgomery, H. (2005, Nov/Dec). Food for thought! *Camping Magazine, 78*(6). Discusses a camp program teaching a sense of responsibility for the natural world, wasting less food.

Murphy, R. (2004, Jan/Feb). Ambassadors of the environment. *Camping Magazine, 77*(1). How to teach campers to have a positive view of themselves, to respect the outdoors, teach sustainability, and life skills.

Parry, J. (2005, Jan/Feb). An editorial on the nature of things at camp. *Camping Magazine, 78*(1), 22–28. Integrating "green thinking" into the camp setting.

Thompson, Z. (2005, May/June). Licking banana slugs, poking at scat. *Camping Magazine, 78*(3). Provides teaching suggestions for introducing kids to the environment.

18

The Waterfront

Water holds a certain fascination for almost everyone, and camp aquatic activities rank high in popularity. All types of swimming and boating are enjoyable and nearly every other camp activity can be integrated at one time or another with the waterfront. For instance, a beautiful waterscape provides an almost perfect setting for a campfire or spiritual program, storytelling, sketching, discussions, painting, or photography. Singing is particularly beautiful when performed by a group on the opposite shore or out in boats, with sound resonating over water.

Near water, campers can study an entirely different assortment of plants and animals. Water goggles are helpful in studying underwater life and some camps provide glass-bottomed boxes and boats for this purpose. Almost any type of boat, from a canoe to a raft, will furnish transportation to explore the water.

Even a small stream provides fun and opportunities for learning, Campers can study wildlife, catch minnows with their hands, construct bridges and dams, and make and sail miniature boats. Beachcombing is a favorite activity in camps located near a seashore.

Water Safety

According to the Centers for Disease Control's National Center for Injury Prevention, there were 3,443 unintentional drownings (nonboating related) in 2007, averaging 10 deaths per day. More than 20 percent of victims were children 14 and younger. Many drowning deaths are preventable with proper supervision and safety procedures (CDC, 2011).

Activities in or near water are popular throughout the United States, whether in coastal areas, rivers, or inland lakes. Everyone should have instruction in correct swimming and boating techniques. Safety as well as pleasure increases in direct proportion to the skill and confidence of the participants. The following safety precautions will help to minimize hazards and prevent accidents.

Teach Children to Swim

It is important to teach children to swim and feel confident in the water at the earliest age possible. More important than learning to do advanced swimming strokes is developing the ability to do one or two dependable strokes. Still more essential is developing children's sense of comfort in the water, so that they can relax and stay afloat by treading water, doing a face or back float, doing the bobbing jellyfish float with its accompanying travel stroke, or, best of all, using the technique of *drownproofing*. Drownproofing is a simple water survival technique that utilizes natural buoyancy and gentle breathing movements rather than relying on physical strength or intensive training (www.drownproofing.com).

One factor that contributes to tragedies in the water is that weak swimmers tend to panic in an emergency and become tense or struggle frantically. They soon wear themselves out or dip below the surface, ingest water, and become even more frightened. However, a human body with air in the lungs simply cannot sink. Staying calm gives a swimmer in trouble an opportunity to capitalize on his or her natural buoyancy.

Camps should join with the American Red Cross, American Canoe Association, youth organizations, schools, recreation and park departments, and other organizations that offer swimming classes and water safety instruction. If you are interested, inquire about the first aid/CPR, swimming, lifeguarding, water safety, and re-

The best way to keep children safe around water is to teach them basic swimming strokes and how to relax and tread water. (Photo courtesy of Bradford Woods Learning and Outdoor Center)

lated courses conducted each year by the American Red Cross. The classes are offered at various locations and at minimal cost to the participants.

Never Leave Children Unattended

Counselors responsible for children should never leave them unattended near water. Further, counselors unskilled in handling boats should practice in safe water and receive instruction before taking them out. Swimming should be done only at supervised beaches or swimming pools. Campers should never go swimming without a companion or "buddy."

Campers without good swimming skills should never be allowed in water over their heads even if using such artificial supports as water wings, inner tubes, noodles, swimming boards, or air mattresses. Many deaths result when weak swimmers rely on air-filled or foam toys for support, only to fall off or have them slip out of reach.

Train Staff in Water Safety

All counselors regardless of their direct responsibility at the waterfront should perfect rescue and water safety skills—not only for their own benefit but to be able to help someone in trouble. Do not allow running or horseplay while in or near water. Although night swimming might appear to be adventurous, it is also highly dangerous because finding a lost swimmer would be nearly impossible.

Don't Swim in Unknown Waters

Often times campers on a canoe or boat trip like to cool off by jumping into the lake or river. Take extra caution when swimming in these situations. Explore what might lie beneath the surface, and take note of upcoming rapids or waterfalls. Generally speaking, a calm clear body of water is generally safer than faster moving water, water near bridge abutments, or muddy water with high turbidity.

Finally, the danger that comes with *diving head first* into a body of water is extreme. The diving end of a swimming pool is generally the safest place for such activity. Diving into lakes, rivers, and ponds is extremely dangerous and should be discouraged. If water recreation is planned for such waters, swim the area first, checking for underwater rocks, the depth of the area, and logs/debris that may be lying beneath the surface.

Program Trends

Paralleling the increased public interest in water activities, camps have shown a corresponding increase in their offerings. In addition to the usual forms of swimming, diving, lifesaving, and boating, such accessories as flutter boards, water skis, wake boards, swim fins, surfboards, and wind surfing boards are increasingly being used. Some camps include such activities as snorkeling,

Expanded program offerings at some camps include snorkeling, scuba diving, surfing, and sail boarding. (Photo courtesy of Bradford Woods Learning and Outdoor Center)

scuba diving, surfing, and sail boarding. Increased participation has placed more emphasis on such related events as water pageants and water carnivals, synchronized swimming, competition in swimming and diving, water polo, water basketball, and many other water games and contests. Many camps offer canoe and kayak trips.

Rowboats remain popular at camp but outboard motorboats are also available for lifesaving and water skiing, and provide transportation for fishing and camping trips. Canoes and kayaks are classic camp boats used for both day and overnight trips. An increasing number of camps are offering sailing experiences. Many camps, though possessing natural bodies of water, also use swimming pools for their instructional and free swim programs.

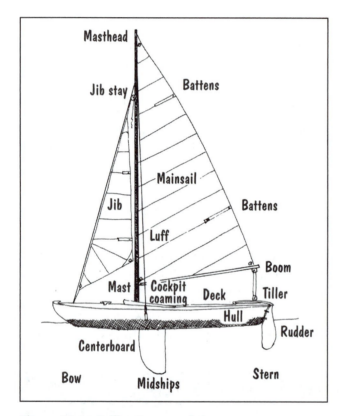

Figure 18.1   Sailboat nomenclature.

The Waterfront Staff

The Waterfront Supervisor

The aquatics supervisor is in charge of all waterfront activities and, according to ACA Standards (PA-1), should be at least 21 years old and currently certified in lifeguard, swim instructor, or boating/watercraft certification training from a nationally recognized certifying body.

In addition to the certified lifeguards who are required to supervise swimming, any camp staff (i.e., lookouts) assigned to guard swimming activities should have

training in elementary forms of nonswimming rescue (PA-3). Those staff involved in teaching swimming should be certified as water safety instructors. Likewise, if the camp has a recreational boating area, it should be under the supervision of the aquatics supervisor. Also, waterfront staff involved in teaching boating activities should hold the equivalent of an American Red Cross instructor rating in the appropriate craft of canoeing, kayaking, or sailing.

The aquatics supervisor is responsible for assigning duties to his or her assistants and for seeing that they are utilized in carrying out a well-planned program that is coordinated with the entire camp program. The supervisor also sees that campers are tested and classified and that minimum skill levels are established for aquatic activities. He or she trains and supervises the aquatic staff, which may include instructors in such waterfront activities as swimming, diving, lifesaving, scuba diving, water skiing, canoeing, rowing, outboard boating, and sailing. He or she makes sure that all equipment is adequate in quantity and quality and that safety precautions are strictly observed. The supervisor also makes appropriate seasonal reports and recommendations for the following season.

Although these many duties usually exempt the waterfront supervisor from cabin responsibilities, he or she should be aware of the full range of camp activities in order to see the waterfront in its proper relation to the total program. The supervisor has one of the most demanding jobs in camp and is at one time or another likely to be responsible for the safety of every person there. He or she must have presence of mind, sound judgment, and the ability to remain calm in an emergency.

The supervisor also is responsible for staff use of the waterfront. Usually during precamp training he or she tests and classifies all staff members according to their swimming and boating abilities and sets up procedures and schedules for their instruction and use of equipment. The supervisor also acquaints them with swimming hazards and safety measures and the general rules and procedures for camper and staff use of the waterfront. ACA Standards (PA-16) require that a lifeguard be present at all staff water activities.

Waterfront Assistants and Counselor Duties

The camp should have a policy about the number of lifeguards and lookouts required for supervision of campers in the water (ACA Standard PA-4). These members of the waterfront staff may or may not have cabin responsibilities, and their waterfront duties are determined by the aquatics supervisor in accordance with their abilities in swimming, diving, or boating. All waterfront personnel should be trained and interested in the whole camp program and should consider their activities as integral components of it. All should cooperate willingly to help with the general camp program on rainy days and as their duties at the waterfront permit.

A cabin counselor usually is expected to accompany her or his campers during their periods at the waterfront and may be asked to help as needed. Also, those staff with appropriate skills may be asked to help out during the peak periods of the day. Waterfront rules must be obeyed at all times and counselors should set a good example themselves as well as make sure that their campers follow the rules.

The Swimming, Diving, and Lifesaving Program

Early in the camp session where water activities are involved, all campers should be tested and classified as nonswimmers, beginners, intermediates, swimmers, or lifesavers (ACA Standard PA-10). Swimming periods (ordinarily 30 to 45 minutes in length) are usually scheduled to teach swimming lessons or as free swim periods. In decentralized camps, campers usually go to the swimming area as a unit and separate according to classification upon arrival at the dock or pool, each going to his or her respective area for instruction.

Waterfront supervisors must remain vigilant. One accident during a summer can cause untold grief, seriously damage the reputation of the camp, and even do a great disservice to the whole field of organized camping. Three special safety techniques are in common use.

The *buddy system* provides each camper with a companion of similar ability. The two campers enter and leave the water together and stay near each other at all times. Thus, the chance that one of them can disappear under water or get into difficulty without this immediately being known to the other should be impossible. When the signal for "buddy call" is given (about every ten minutes), the buddies quickly join hands and raise them in the air.

Some method should be used to keep track of every swimmer in the water. For example, as swimmers enter the water they turn over a tag bearing their name or an assigned number on the *check board* so that the red side is uppermost. As each leaves the swimming area, he or she turns it back to expose the white side again. A counselor should be stationed near the board to see that no one forgets. Some camps use pegs with the camper's name on them to insert into a peg board in a similar manner.

Some programs require that every swimmer wears a *colored cap* or some other large symbol denoting his or her swimming ability so that waterfront staff immediately can spot campers out of their proper area or those engaging in activities too hazardous for their abilities. The following color system is suggested:

Nonswimmer—red (danger)
Beginner—yellow (caution)
Intermediate—green
Swimmer—blue
Lifesaver—white

Waterfront counselors must keep their eyes and attention on swimmers at all times. Chatting, reading, or basking in the sun are definitely not allowed. When on duty, lifeguards never enter the water except to rescue a swimmer or when necessary for some particular phase of teaching.

Sunburn is a danger for both campers and staff. A broad-spectrum sunscreen with an SPF of at least 15 should be applied regularly. Staff might want to wear hats and long sleeves, at least during a portion of the hours on duty. Research shows that constant exposure to the sun and heavy tanning can cause skin cancer, premature aging of the skin, and damage to the body's immune system.

As in all camp activities, informality and fun are of great importance, but waterfront rules must be rigidly enforced. Too much is at stake to overlook even minor breaches of the rules. Waterfront staff must be businesslike when on duty and see that every instruction is obeyed.

Campers and counselors should never go swimming alone or at times when the waterfront staff is not on duty. They should never swim when overly tired. Remember

Water activities rank high in popularity among campers.

that overestimating one's own ability and taking chances are among the major causes of swimming catastrophes. Unexpected fatigue and muscle cramps can incapacitate even experienced swimmers.

On trips away from camp, campers and staff should swim only in approved areas and when at least one lifeguard is on watch. Never allow diving into unknown waters that have not been thoroughly investigated for sufficient depth and hidden hazards. Visitors should use the waterfront only under the same regulations as staff and campers.

Thunderstorms are a particularly serious menace to people near water. Everyone in the water or out in boats must immediately head for shore.

Distance swimming can be allowed at the discretion of the waterfront staff and only if each swimmer is accompanied by qualified staff in a rowboat.

Boating

The popularity of boating almost equals that of swimming. It not only gives pleasure in itself but also provides transportation to outlying regions for fishing or camping. Boats are also a means of rescuing campers in distress.

Properly constructed and maintained boats do not capsize when used with common sense and some degree of skill. Most incidents result from using boats in poor condition or from such misuses as improper loading or overloading, traveling in dangerous or rough water, fooling around, standing up, rocking the boat, or changing positions improperly. All small craft should be tested for seaworthiness and steadiness. They should be used only by those persons who have passed appropriate tests (including actual practice in shallow, safe water) in recovering from capsizing and swamping.

The Federal Boating Safety Act of 1971 requires that *every* passenger in *any* boat on federal waterways must have a U.S. Coast Guard approved life preserver, technically known as a personal flotation device or PFD. ACA Standards (PA-22) state that PFDs must be worn at all times by all staff and campers when on the water. Today's life jackets are comfortable and do not interfere with the wearer's activity. Campers become accustomed to them and regard wearing them as a normal part of small-craft boating.

When canoeing, it is important to keep the center of gravity low in the craft. Always step, sit, or kneel in the exact center of the canoe to keep your weight balanced. When changing seats, do so only in shallow water and keep your weight as low as possible and exactly in the center of the canoe, grasping a gunwale with each hand as you proceed slowly and deliberately.

Of all small craft, rowboats are least likely to tip over, canoes are the second safest, and kayaks and sailboats are probably the trickiest. Tipped boats, even if submerged, will not sink to the bottom. Therefore, anyone thrown into the water should swim to the boat and hang on until help comes, rather than attempt to swim for the shore. Endurance and the ability to tread water and float occupy a prominent place in boating tests for this reason.

The popularity of boating almost equals that of swimming. (Photo courtesy of Bradford Woods Learning and Outdoor Center)

Before venturing far from shore, boaters should learn to interpret weather signs. Head for the nearest land at the first signs of an approaching storm. Stay near shore on trips in large bodies of water, even though it means traveling greater distances.

Neither visitors, counselors, nor campers should use boating equipment until they have passed appropriate tests and secured specific permission from the waterfront staff and given their exact departure time, destination, and expected time of return. Boating after dark is permissible only in an emergency or for an occasional moonlight cruise under the immediate supervision of the waterfront staff.

REFERENCES

Centers for Disease Control and Prevention (CDC). (2011). *Unintentional Drowning: Fact Sheet*. Retrieved from http://www.cdc.gov/HomeandRecreationalSafety/water-safety/waterinjuries-factsheet.html

Drownproofing: Introduction. Retrieved from http://www.drownproofing.com/

WEB RESOURCES

American Red Cross (http://www.redcross.org/services/hss.aquatics/lifeguard.html)

Water safety (http://www.safekids.org/safety-basics/safety-resources-by-risk-area/drowning/)

Sun Safety (http://pediatrics.about.com/od/summersafety/Summer_Safety_and_Health_Tips.htm)

PRINT RESOURCES

Kantor, J. (1995). Ready-made sailing. *Camping Magazine, 68*(1), 31–32.

Kauffman, R., & Mason, D. (1995). Using gates to enhance your paddling program. *Camping Magazine, 67*(6), 13–15.

McConnell, S. (1996). Is your waterfront safe? *Camping Magazine, 68*(5), 43–44.

19

Outdoor Adventure Programs

Outdoor adventure programs are an important aspect of some organized camps. Most activities are so specialized that entire books have been devoted to them. Therefore, this chapter attempts only to familiarize camp counselors with some general considerations and ideas on those programs most suited for camp use. To really understand and master the required skills, however, you will need to consult other sources as well as gain personal experience under competent leadership. Some of the better sources for review are noted at the end of the chapter.

Everyone, particularly youth, dislikes monotony. Teens especially crave excitement, new experiences, and a chance to test their maturity, skills, and ability. In recent years many organized camps have expanded their programs to include activities that meet this need through intensive, thrilling, and physically challenging outdoor adventure pursuits. This shift toward adventure programming allows campers to seek and meet challenges through self-imposed obstacles that test their abilities. Adventure programs have been particularly effective in helping youth develop leadership ability, social skills, and a sense of responsibility as well as gain appreciation for the strengths and weaknesses of themselves and others.

Characteristics of Adventure Programs

One of the characteristics shared by almost all adventure programs is the role of the natural environment in posing challenges to the participants. Air currents, gravity, height, water, ice, snow, rocks, mountains, rivers, and caves all pose challenges. Although usually a natural outdoor setting is used to carry out these programs, artificial structures such as climbing walls and ropes courses may also be used.

Activities commonly associated with adventure programs are wide ranging. For some camps, trip camping (sometimes called pioneering, tripping, or backpacking) provides the means for adventure. Tripping allows a group of individuals to travel from one site to another over an extended period of time. Travel might be by foot or by horseback, canoe, raft, kayak, sailboat, or bicycle. Other activities that can be included in adventure programs include mountaineering or rock climbing, scuba diving, spelunking (i.e., cave exploration), canyoning, orienteering, winter camping, and cross-country ski touring. Whatever the activity, adventure programming features direct experiences and methods and settings that are generally unfamiliar and exciting to the participants.

Some camps may not have a geographic setting or other resources that allow programs such as those just mentioned. However, as a segment of their regular camp activities, a camp might be able to offer adaptations that include activities such as initiative games and trust exercises, aerial ropes courses, or wall climbing. These activities, which will be described later, can be stand-alone events or can serve as introductions for other adventure programs. Further, some camps provide out-of-camp tripping programs to offer adventure activities that might not be possible in the camp setting.

Values of Adventure Programs

In addition to those values mentioned at the start of this chapter, other values might be gained by providing campers with opportunities for participation in adventure programs. One is the development of a good self-concept (including self-image, self-respect, self-satisfaction, and self-realization) that can come about by successfully meeting new challenges and overcoming personal fears.

Another value of adventure programs is that campers can improve their physical fitness from the sustained and strenuous activity. A moderate amount of psychological or physical stress can help a camper gain personal insights as well as insights about others and encourages self-evaluation and reappraisal of one's relationships with others. Such opportunities can also develop determination, tenacity, and self-reliance. Campers also learn to cooperate with others by identifying conflicts, making decisions, communicating, solving problems, and sharing responsibilities under stress conditions. Through adventure programs campers can gain an increased appreciation for the balance of the natural world and can put this awareness into practice by showing respect for the environment and having minimum physical impact on it.

Outdoor adventures, especially tripping, build confidence. Someone who is popular with his or her peers at home because of ample free time, spending money, and material possessions but who cannot build a fire or keep up on the trail may be less popular among trail mates. A camper is judged solely on his or her own merits and parents cannot run interference. Following a trail by foot or canoe and making camp is hard work and the boy or girl with the stamina and know-how to do it successfully can be rightfully proud of the achievement.

Helping to plan and carry out a trip successfully encourage lifelong skills. Campers must learn to anticipate and plan ahead as they make checklists and use them for packing. They must work and cooperate closely with others, accept responsibility, and carry their own loads. The vigorous activity and self-prepared meals promote independence, good health, and physical fitness.

A love of nature can best be instilled by living intimately with it 24 hours a day, as occurs in most outdoor trip opportunities. Living amid nature can underline the importance of practicing good conservation. Attitudes and skills acquired can influence a lifetime of family camping, boating, picnicking, hunting, or fishing.

When well-informed youth become an integral part of planning an exciting trip, they enjoy it the most. Deep and lasting friendships can form as a small group lives in its own world for a period of time. Sharing inside jokes, laughing together over funny incidents, and working and struggling together toward a common goal all develop an appreciation of "one for all and all for one." Although each person in the group learns to be self-reliant and independent, he or she must also learn to fit in as part of the group, which eventually develops the spirit of "we-ness" and cooperation.

Inevitably, occasional frictions and misunderstandings will arise. Some campers may display selfishness, thoughtlessness, or a tendency to rationalize and blame others for their mistakes. However, they likely will be subjected to what is generally considered to be the most effective punishment—the disapproval and lack of acceptance by peers.

The important point is that a wide variety of human needs can be satisfied through well-developed camp programs that contain elements of challenge and adventure. You, as a counselor, will never have a better opportunity than using adventure programs of all types to get better acquainted with your campers and exert a subtle influence on them.

Core Components

The core components of outdoor adventure programs include activities that are both intense and sustained and that demand the best from the participant. *Intense* aspects (often called stress components) might consist of activities that include challenging natural and artificial obstacles and various elements of uncertainty. *Sustained* aspects (e.g., endurance components) can include hiking long distances or taking on tasks that cannot be completed quickly. Typical of intense and sustained components are mountaineering expeditions, rock climbing, survival camping, initiative tests, and endurance

Many organized camps have expanded their programs to include activities that are intense, thrilling, and physically challenging.

training. These activities help people understand their potential and limitations, and reveal to them that difficult and sometimes frightening situations can be overcome regardless of personal limitations. Since cooperation is important to successfully complete many of the tasks, participants quickly learn the requirement of dependency, trust, and close interaction with others.

To develop a program with sound content, a blend of physical and recreational activities that contain structured exercises in leadership, self-discovery, group dynamics, and teamwork are needed. Like most other programs in camp, the emphasis on small peer groups is important. Whatever the activity, its purpose is to allow each participant to experience success and a sense of accomplishment. The magnitude of the challenge should be matched to the skill of individual participants.

Risk Versus Challenge

Some outdoor adventure programs might at first glance seem to have high levels of risk associated with them. Yet, if the programs are planned properly and good equipment is used under careful supervision and direction, they can be every bit as safe as other types of camp activities. Leaders and supervisors always have the moral obligation to be reasonable and prudent in choosing the activities in which campers will engage. Participants can be challenged physically and psychologically without confronting a *real* risk, even though they may *perceive* the activity to be risky. In other words, one's fear or anxiety may be irrational, since the danger or risk may be perceived rather than actual.

The focus of adventure programs should be on the word *challenge*—challenge through stress and adventure, not challenge through risk. These activities should also allow for *challenge by choice,* which means that an individual should always be able to choose how much risk he or she wishes to take. Regardless, all campers should be encouraged to participate at least once in adventure activities. Sometimes campers are fearful because these activities are unfamiliar to them.

What must be understood by the program leader is that challenging activities need not necessarily be risky. What may be exciting and challenging to an unskilled or inexperienced camper may actually be routine and unchallenging to the leader. Elements of challenge or stress can be regulated to assure that the penalties for failure are not too high. The type of challenge can be adapted to all levels of skill and risk. For example, activities should be structured in a sequence of progressive difficulty so that success is achieved by building upon previous successes. As skill is acquired, participants will be able to successfully meet more difficult tasks.

To justify programs containing elements of challenge, adventure, and stress, camps must be able to guarantee that the danger involved is at a reasonably low baseline level. The instructor or leader must ensure that any danger is mitigated rather than real and that the exposure to danger involves minimal personal risk while keeping the stress and excitement level high. The key is the use of controlled or disciplined adventure that is based on the participant's level of skill and ability. A participant's involvement in any adventure program should be geared by the leader at a level commensurate with his or her competency and experience, just as it would be with any other camp activity.

The level of control, diversity of situations, and variety of resources used can be moderated by competent instruction. The leader's efforts should concentrate on providing the proper program content, activity sequencing, and safety measures. The leader must take positive steps to reduce the degree of hazard without removing or diminishing the excitement-producing elements. Therefore, as far as leadership and responsibility are concerned, a fine balance must be struck between challenge and risk.

In addition to a concern for reducing the potential for physical harm, the leader must also see to it that adventure programs are not psychologically harmful. Emotional trauma can result when a camper is forced into situations for which he or she has not been adequately prepared. No one should ever be forced to do anything that could possibly result in this sort of psychological injury.

The Role of the Leader

The key to the development of an adventure program is competent leadership. Potentially dangerous activities such as whitewater canoeing, kayaking or rafting, caving, mountain biking, and mountaineering demand competent and responsible staff. Leaders must be thoroughly familiar with the equipment and skills needed as well as possess other strong leadership abilities like general knowledge of the outdoors, actual experience in the activity, and sound judgment and decision-making skills. Among these attributes, the ability to make sound judgments is probably the leader's most important trait, since skill alone does not make a good leader.

The staff responsible for conducting adventure programs is different from other staff in the camp. The adventure staff needs to be more qualified in terms of safety and must have advanced training and experience in outdoor leadership. The program director should have certification in advanced first aid, as well as hold the appropriate certification in the specific adventure activities he or she is responsible for supervising or leading.

Camps should not sponsor adventure activities unless they have enough experienced personnel and the necessary equipment to do it safely. Fortunately, those interested can acquire such training in a variety of ways. The American Camp Association is increasing its efforts to improve and expand counselor training, and some institutions of higher learning now also provide leadership training courses. The National Outdoor Leadership School (NOLS), Outward Bound, Project Adventure, and the Wilderness Education Association (WEA), for example, sponsor myriad outdoor learning opportunities and leadership training.

Project Adventure has played an important role in providing adventure-based experiential programming for the academic and physical education curriculums of public schools. The concept emerged from the Project's efforts to incorporate various aspects of Outward Bound with ongoing school activities to help students develop confidence and competence. The program uses initiative games, ropes course activities, and other outdoor skills designed to develop confidence and problem-solving skills. The Project also offers workshops and technical assistance to schools and other groups throughout the country.

Outward Bound, Inc. is an action-oriented program of self-discovery that uses challenges found in a natural setting. Depending on location, activities might include sailing, mountaineering, backpacking, skiing, canoeing, kayaking, whitewater rafting, or dogsledding. Special seminars and training programs are designed for teachers and instructors. Recently Outward Bound has designed a number of urban programs that address outdoor learning.

A key to the development of an adventure program is competent leadership. (Photo courtesy of Bradford Woods Learning and Outdoor Center)

The *National Outdoor Leadership School* is a private, nonprofit educational institution dedicated to teaching people how to enjoy and conserve the outdoors. Leadership courses are conducted in a variety of geographic settings and range from 10 days to a full semester in length. Skills are oriented around wilderness expeditions and instruction in the areas of mountaineering, snow and ice climbing, ski touring, winter mountaineering, horsemanship, sailing, and whitewater and ocean canoeing and kayaking. The school offers an outdoor leadership certification program for its students.

The Wilderness Education Association was founded in 1977 with the central notion of teaching individuals how to be outdoor leaders while embracing the "role of education in the preservation of this country's wild land areas." Today, the WEA offers courses in outdoor leadership, Leave No Trace instruction, and the 18-Point Curriculum. With affiliates in over 40 locations, access to a WEA certified course is widely available.

Initiative Games, Trust Exercises, and Ropes Courses

Learning to make and accept decisions, work together, and trust one another is necessary to accomplish goals and objectives, whether on an extended trip or in camp. This trust does not necessarily happen automatically since any group consists of individuals with varying backgrounds, skills, and personalities.

A good way to unify a group and develop useful physical skills is to employ initiative games, trust exercises, and ropes courses. These activities can help shape an aimless collection of individuals into a cohesive, efficient unit by breaking down individual inhibitions, introducing campers to one another, enhancing each member's ability to interact and serve effectively in the group, and increasing each person's awareness of and need for mutual support. In addition, problem-solving competencies are refined and feelings of trust, responsibility, and competence are enhanced. Much more detail about these activities is available from Project Adventure and the other sources listed at the end of this chapter. A few examples are provided here.

An *initiative game* is a group problem-solving task that requires mental and sometimes physical effort to resolve. Usually teamwork and cooperative planning by the entire group are necessary to complete the task. The counselor or leader presents a clearly defined question or problem and the group is required to solve it. There are no right or wrong ways to perform the task as long as the problem or situation is resolved within the guidelines and restrictions imposed by the leader. The goal is for the entire group to participate as a unit.

A *trust exercise*, on the other hand, is an activity that requires the participants to place trust and confidence in the hands of either one other person or a whole group of people. The activity usually takes a bit of courage to perform, such as falling backward from a low platform into the waiting arms of fellow campers. With proper instruction and training the activity is really quite safe. Such ac-tivities are great confidence builders. As individuals learn to cope with uncertainty they also begin to understand the importance of sensitivity, cooperation, responsibility, and reliance on others.

A *ropes course* is essentially an obstacle course de-signed to present a series of graduated challenges to par-ticipants as they climb, swing, jump, and balance on rope

A good way to unify a group and develop useful physical skills is to employ initiative games, trust exercises, and ropes courses. (Lower left, lower right, upper right courtesy of Bradford Woods Learning and Outdoor Center)

and log structures. Ropes courses are usually designed as low ropes or high ropes. The *low ropes* activities usually focus on group problem solving. The *high ropes* courses aim to develop individual abilities to negotiate some type of challenge. The various structures are built at progressively higher elevations to develop individual and group confidence. As with initiative games and trust exercises, the ropes course requires both individual and group effort and support.

Initiative and trust activities can be performed at just about any time and in any place. The various tasks can be performed individually or they can be combined into a series of progressive events. They can vary in their level of difficulty with some that are simple to solve and others that are more complex. The leader must always give special consideration to factors such as age, fitness, and maturity when deciding which activity to choose.

Leadership Considerations

Several leadership techniques must be followed when working with campers on initiative, trust, and ropes-course activities.

Participation should always be *voluntary*. No one should ever be forced to take part in any of the activities. The courage and willingness to participate must come from the individual alone. This does not mean, however, that the leader and the group should not attempt to encourage those who are reluctant. If someone decidedly chooses not to take part, respect should be shown for his or her rights and decisions.

Use only those activities that are *appropriate for the age, ability*, and *number in the group*. In cases where you have a large number of people, it may be advisable to split the participants into several smaller groups. Be sure to use only those activities that provide every individual with an opportunity to succeed.

Some activities require good *spotting* technique to help break potential falls. Spotting is essential when someone is jumping, balancing, or attempting other maneuvers from several feet off the ground. As a general rule, spotting is mandatory for any activity taking place above the ground. Spotting involves having an individual (or a whole group, if necessary) ready to help support someone who is falling to reduce his or her impact. A spotter should be attentive, and should stand a few feet away with hands up ready to support the upper part of the person's body.

Following completion of each activity, it is important to *debrief* or take time to discuss with the group what has happened. How was the problem solved? What were the group's strengths and weaknesses? What other methods could have been used? Who took the leadership role? Was there group cooperation and involvement? What analogies can be made between the campers' solution and real-life situations? Asking these and other questions during the debriefing can help to focus on the values of the exercise and can draw the group's attention to their own actions and behavior.

Types of Activities

To provide variety and to reduce monotony, offer a good mix of activities. The examples of initiative games, trust exercises, and ropes-course activities that follow are among the more popular ones and have been used successfully for years. Many more ideas are available from outdoor education resources and on the Internet.

All Aboard

Construct a platform, locate a flat rock, or find a stump several feet tall and ask everyone to get on it at the same time. They must hold the position for at least 8 seconds, with everyone's feet off the ground. Pick a platform that has *just* enough room for everyone, requiring that they hold on to each other and work cooperatively. Ten or so people should be able to fit on a space 12 to 15 inches in diameter. This activity can also be done by laying a T-shirt on the ground and giving the same instructions.

Human Knot

Ask a group of 10 to 15 people to stand in a tight circle facing inward. Each person then raises his or her right arm and grabs someone's right hand. The same is done with the left hand, being sure it belongs to someone different. Without letting go, the group must now untangle the human knot to form a circle. On most occasions the group will unwind to actually form the circle, but sometimes they end up in a figure eight, which is also fine. If the group is unable to solve the problem within a reasonable period of time, you can help them out by breaking one pair's handhold and rejoining it in a different position.

Four Pointer

The object of this activity is to get seven cooperative people to travel together for a distance of 30 feet using only four simultaneous points of contact (hands, feet, or whatever) with the ground at any one time. If your group is large, divide it into several teams.

Get Up

Have everyone sit in a circle with their feet touching. The group then has to stand up together by working out a system of grabbing hands and pulling or whatever other method they may choose. Let them figure it out.

Circle Stand

As a follow-up to the previous exercise, have everyone turn around and sit with their backs to the circle, interlocking arms with the person on each side. Again, the object is for the entire group to move from a sitting to a standing position together. After the group has worked out a cooperative method of succeeding, have them try to do the same thing without locking arms.

Boil Water

Working in groups of four, or whatever number seems appropriate, provide each team with one match and a pot of water. They are then given 15 minutes in which to search out wood, start a fire, and bring the water to a boil. To add interest, campers can pretend that one member of their party is coming down with hypothermia and they must treat him or her with a hot drink as soon as possible.

Trust Circle

Everyone sits shoulder to shoulder in a tight circle with knees bent and feet touching. One at a time each takes a turn at standing in the middle of the circle and performing a trust fall. The person who falls is instructed to stand erect and stiff with arms folded in front of the body. The group forming the circle serves as catchers, holding their arms up with palms out. When ready, the person in the middle falls stiffly backward onto the outreached hands of a catcher, who then passes the faller on to another person. The object is to see if the faller can be passed all the way around the circle at least once.

Chaos

Blindfold members of the group; without talking or using hands or arms, they must line up by height along a wall.

Blind Pitch

Blindfold every member of the group. Then ask them to set up a tent.

Higher Elements of Ropes Courses

In addition to these activities, group members can be challenged by a number of low and high ropes courses. Because of the height involved in high ropes courses, participants are required to be on a belay to stop a fall. For the belay, one end of the rope is attached to the person performing the activity while another person braces the rope around his or her body or a fixed object such as a tree, boulder, or artificial aid. Specific techniques are involved and require specialized training. Anyone who is responsible for either constructing high ropes courses or conducting activities that require a belay should first consult the appropriate certification sources to become familiar with and skilled in these techniques.

Trip Camping

Many organized camps use a trip camping program as a means of providing adventure. Anyone involved in organizing these trips must have extensive training. For our purposes, a brief description of some of the components will suffice.

Trip camping involves overnight travel and may include hiking, bicycling, boating (e.g. canoeing, rafting, sailing, or kayaking), or any other appropriate form of transportation. Such an opportunity allows campers to put into practice what they have learned about finding their way with map and compass, using tools, cooking outdoors, pitching a tent, packing, and carrying equipment to make themselves safe and comfortable in a "home away from home."

No matter what mode of travel is used, trip safety and comfort require at least a minimum of special equipment and supplies. Camps must usually invest enough to supply such necessities as tents and cooking equipment, and they, or the campers, must provide whatever personal gear is needed. Usually expensive outlays are unnecessary, and good care and handling will lengthen the life of whatever equipment is on hand. The last section of this book provides more detail about many aspects of trip camping.

A trip can include a variety of experiences, but should *progress* from simple cookouts and overnights to longer outings that make full use of expanding skills and knowledge. For young inexperienced campers, the first excursion may be a simple lunch or supper cookout. Next may come an overnight, perhaps not far from camp, but it will involve packing up a few belongings, getting the provisions for a simple meal or two, and sleeping under the open sky or out in a tent. A new camper will gain valuable experience as he or she helps plan what supplies and equipment will be needed and uses a checklist to see that nothing is left behind. A good trip program will provide for progressively longer and more exciting outings as the session progresses and with each succeeding summer.

Some camps are fortunate enough to have several possibilities for trip camping within their own camp and the surrounding environment. Picking out a suitable route and destination and perhaps establishing a more permanent *outpost* or *primitive camp* is an option in some camps. It is best to have several alternate destinations that vary in distance and difficulty. When a camp has only limited acreage available, you may find it advisable to look for other places to go such as a park or other public area. Traveling by canoe, sailboat, rowboat, or even raft or kayak to a distant shore where sites are available for overnight stops may be possible. Avoid the more popular areas, especially during their peak seasons, since they offer little privacy.

No trip should degenerate into an endurance contest or a race against time. Distance travelled should depend on the activity itself and the age and experience of campers. Allow plenty of opportunity for seeing, exploring, and having fun along the way. Before taking a group over a proposed route, the trip leader should survey the route or collect as much information as possible from others who may have used the route, in order to find good places to stop overnight as well as locate sources of water and firewood.

The best number for a trip group is six to ten campers, with at least one counselor for every five campers

Trip camping provides adventure and gives campers the opportunity to practice what they have learned about outdoor living.

(depending on their ages). No group—no matter how small—should ever start out without at least two leaders, which is required by ACA Standards (PT-4). All leaders should hold a current First Aid and CPR certificate. Trip campers should be of approximately the same age, strength, and experience.

Every person going on a trip should be screened by the camp health staff just prior to departing (and upon returning; ACA Standards PT-9). It is a good idea to provide campers with progressive skills-training opportunities before going. The list can be brief and easy for first trips, with additional skills added for succeeding, more difficult excursions. A set of tests might cover the following:

- Demonstrate responsive interaction with the natural environment, including "leave no trace"
- Use and care of knife, hatchet, and saw
- Selection and use of appropriate forms of fuel
- Conservation and proper extinguishing of campfires, if used
- Outdoor cooking
- Knowledge of trip equipment and proper packing of duffel
- Camp sanitation and proper disposal of garbage
- Knowledge of weather and weather prediction
- Lashing and tying useful knots
- First aid and safety
- Experience with one-meal, all-day, and overnight trips
- Paddling, horseback, or bicycle riding skills, if the trip involves such methods of transportation

The Trip Counselor

Many camps appoint one person—known by some title like "trip counselor"—to take charge of the entire trip-camping program with one or more assistants to help as needed. These staff members can set up a program of progressive skills to prepare the campers as noted above. The trip counselor should be a mature person who knows trip camping through experience as well as through instruction and certification. He or she should be level-headed, resourceful, completely dependable, a good organizer, and a good communicator.

One of the main responsibilities is to make sure that equipment is adequate and of the right type and that it is well maintained and replaced when necessary. The trip counselor must arrange for storing equipment efficiently and safely in the equipment room and must keep lists as group equipment is checked out and in. He or she must know how to care for and perform routine maintenance on stoves, tents, and other gear to keep them in top condition.

Planning the Trip

Much of the pleasure of a trip consists in planning and anticipating it. Decisions must be made about where to go, how to get there, what to take, and how long to stay. These decisions will depend upon such factors as:

- Ages and experience of those going
- Probable temperature and weather conditions
- Means of transportation—e.g., canoe, hiking, horseback, bicycle, pack animal, and so on
- Possibilities for restocking along the way
- Ruggedness of the terrain—hills, density of underbrush, altitude

- Means of cooking and facilities for camping along the way
- Availability of safe water for drinking, cooking, and washing. Will you need to purify it?
- Amount of time to be devoted to cooking and the type and variety of cooking utensils available
- Number and length of stopovers desired to take side excursions or do special activities such as supervised swimming, if it is allowed on trips
- Ability to acquire permits (if necessary) to camp, build fires, or fish
- Navigating ability with good maps/compasses or GPS units (no one should venture along an unmarked or poorly marked trail unless at least one person in the group is thoroughly versed in way finding)
- Emergency preparedness—how would you reach the nearest physician or forest ranger in case of an emergency? Is there cell phone coverage in the area? The person in charge should have complete information about this.

Start planning well ahead of time and elicit input from campers. Let it be *their* trip, not *yours;* they will be more invested in the trip if they have been involved in planning, decision making, and problem solving. How much responsibility they can handle will depend somewhat upon their ages and experience. Ask campers for their preferences but recognize that the camp staff is ultimately responsible. The ability to guide followers into making wise decisions is the mark of a good leader, but when it becomes a question of violating principles of good judgment, safety, or good camp practices, you must have the ability to say "NO."

Menus must be compiled and lists of food items and quantities turned in far enough in advance to allow time for assembling stock items and ordering food. Each camp usually sets up its own procedures for doing this menu planning. Consider what cooking utensils will be required. The number can be reduced by planning to cook one-pot or aluminum foil meals. Also consider how much time will be needed for cooking. Some foods require elaborate preparations and long cooking times, while others are quite simple.

Make a list of what group equipment you will need such as:

- Tents or tarps for sleeping shelters
- Cook stove and food preparation gear such as pots and pans
- Serving utensils, fillet knife, forks, spoons, and so on
- Trowel for digging latrines or catholes
- First aid kit
- Matches and lighter in weather-proof container
- Compass, maps, GPS, and other necessary navigation equipment
- Soap for sterilizing and cleaning up
- Extra rope or cordage

Using the detailed lists and information in chapter 31, help campers make out their own checklists of personal equipment. Certain items are mandatory for everyone. Further, a common error in packing is to assume that the weather will stay just as it is at the moment. Help campers plan for it and be prepared.

Your mode of transportation may influence what gear is taken and how much. More items can usually be taken in watercraft than when backpacking. Different types of trips will require different planning. As long as you and the campers have everything you need, the lighter the pack the better. Some camps minimize the problem of transportation on long trips by sending heavy materials like food, clean clothing, and bedding ahead by car, van, or pack horse. You may also be able to replenish food supplies at stores along the way or by shipping supplies ahead by parcel post. Clean clothing can be supplied in this way and the soiled returned to camp.

Work out a complete itinerary of just where you expect to be at any given time and leave a copy at the camp office so that they can locate you if necessary. Give some thought to things to do for recreation during down times along the trip and take suggestions for games, songs, and so on to use as they fit.

You should impress upon the group the importance of sticking together at all times so that no one gets lost. Counselors should have whistles, with perhaps a few extra for campers who must temporarily leave the group for water or firewood. Agree upon an exact procedure for both the group and the camper if someone should become separated.

Leave No Trace

Whether you are taking campers on an extended outdoor trip or conducting activities around the camp, campers must understand how to interact with the environment. For this reason, *Leave No Trace* (LNT) and minimum impact principles have been developed and are widely used by the majority of leaders in outdoor recreation. The general premise of LNT principles is to promote responsible interaction with the natural environment. These principles include:

- Plan ahead and prepare
- Travel and camp on durable surfaces
- Dispose of waste properly
- Leave what you find
- Minimize campfire impact
- Respect wildlife
- Be considerate of other campers

More information on LNT principles can be found on the Internet.

Many other aspects must be considered when on the actual trip. Trained and experienced trip leaders know to think about looking for a good campsite well before sundown; assigning duties to campers such as setting up tents, cooking, stove starting or fire building, cleaning up and sanitation, locating a latrine area for disposing of human waste, garbage disposal, dish washing, and storing food overnight. All of these duties have specific procedures, which the campers should learn prior to the trip, while time can be spent on the trip discussing situational modifications.

Before leaving a temporary campsite in the backcountry, be sure that the area is in better condition than it was when you arrived. Unless the site had a permanent campfire area, you should see that all traces of the fire are eradicated. Make every attempt to restore it so that no one will know that you have been there. Take a last look around to see that nothing is left behind.

Trips by Watercraft

Trips by canoe, kayak, raft, or other kinds of watercraft are exciting and especially suited for older campers. Long distances can be covered on water, particularly when traveling with the current of a river. To safely undertake extended trips, however, campers must be excellent swimmers and skilled boaters. Camps should have rigid standards or tests that campers must pass before they can qualify for water trips. All campers should be familiar with the type of watercraft that is being used. Canoes require different skills, for example, than do rafts.

Several general planning considerations apply to all extended trips by water. Some alterations may be needed depending on the type of craft used and the type of water traveled. What may be appropriate equipment or procedures on calm lakes or streams may not suffice. Regardless of the type of water, every person should wear an approved life jacket at all times. Sunglasses should be worn to protect against glare, and a safety strap to hold them on is a smart idea. Campers and staff on water should always beware of sunburn and use sun block every day regardless of how sunny or cloudy. Additional clothing, gear, and food can be stored in waterproof bags or containers that are securely tied or strapped in the craft. Be sure to pack things on top that you might want in a hurry.

Find shady places to stop for lunch and take plenty of time to rest. Keep campers well hydrated. On extremely hot days, it may even be necessary to confine travel to the cool of early morning and evening. When taking long voyages it is best to plan layovers every three or four days for rest and relief from the constant physical strain.

When putting in to shore and disembarking, make sure your craft is properly fastened by its painter to a tree, rock, or stake so it will not be washed away or lost. On large bodies of water, stay close to shore. Learn to anticipate changes in the weather and get off the water if a storm is approaching. In some circumstances you might want to carry a small weather radio. The general rule when capsized is to stay with your craft.

Another general rule is never boat alone. There should be a minimum of three boats, and boaters must maintain a visual communication system. An experienced and prudent person should be in the lead craft and another in the sweep position in the rear boat. All other craft should stay between these two boats.

The leader should know the body of water (i.e., river, lake, ocean) or obtain the services of an experienced guide. It is also wise to walk the bank to determine how to run difficult rapids that may be encountered. When in doubt, do not gamble. Carry craft around the rapids. Respect the river. Know river classifications and learn why

Trips by canoe, kayak, raft, or other kinds of watercraft are exciting and especially suited for older campers. (Photo courtesy of American Camp Association)

and how rivers are classified. It cannot be stressed too strongly that beginners and novices should learn and practice basic paddling skills under competent supervision prior to a trip camping excursion.

Much more information specific to particular kinds of trips is available in published resources and on the Internet. The material included in this chapter provides a general framework for planning overnight trips.

WEB RESOURCES

Adventure Cycling Association (http://www.adv-cycling.org)
Bicycle Touring 101 (http://www.bicycletouring101.com)
Boat and Canoe Camping (http://www.canoecountry.com) and (http://www.canoecampfish.com)
Ken Kifer's Bike Pages (http://www.kenkifer.com/bikepages/touring)
Leave No Trace (http://www.lnt.org)
National Outdoor Leadership School (http://www.nols.edu/)

Outward Bound (http://www.outwardbound.org/)
Project Adventure (http://www.pa.org/)
Wilderness Education Association 18 Point Curriculum (http://www.aai.cc/pdf_download/WEA_18_point_curriculum.pdf)
Wilderness Education Association (http://www.weainfo.org/)
World Wide Bicycle Tour Directory (http://www.bicycletour.com)

PRINT RESOURCES

Bennett, J. (1999). *The essential whitewater kayaker.* Blacklick, OH: Ragged Mountain Press.

Bunting, C. (1988). Group initiatives: Make a game out of problem-solving. *Camping Magazine, 61*(1), 26–29.

Eschen, M. (2003). *River otter: Handbook for trip planning.* Boise, ID: Anotter Press.

Fleming, J. (2002). *Staying found* (3rd ed.). Seattle, WA: Mountaineer Books.

Gullion, L. (1996). *Kayak and canoe games.* Birmingham, AL: Menasha Ridge Press.

Hutchinson, D. (2002). *Sea kayaking* (4th ed.). Guilford, CT: Globe Pequot Press.

Jordan, D. (1998). Getting to know you. *Camping Magazine, 71*(3), 24–25.

Judson, D. (1995). *Caving practice & equipment.* Birmingham, AL: Menasha Ridge Press.

Long, J. (2004). *How to rock climb* (4th ed.). Guildford, CT: Falcon Publishing.

Marion, J. L. (2005, May/June). Implementing leave no trace at camps. *Camping Magazine, 78*(3), 54–57.

McGivney, A. (2003). *Leave no trace* (2nd ed.). Seattle, WA: Mountaineer Books.

O'Bannon, A. (2001). *Backpackin' book: Traveling and camping skills for a wilderness environment.* Helena, MT: Falcon Publishing.

Rohnke, K. (1977). *Cowstails and cobras.* Boston: Project Adventure.

Rohnke, K. (1984). *Silver bullets: A guide to initiative problems, adventure games, stunts and trust activities.* Boston: Project Adventure.

Rohnke, K. (1989). *Cowstails and cobras II.* Dubuque, IA: Kendall/Hunt.

Webster, Steven E. (1989). *Ropes course safety manual.* Dubuque, IA: Kendall/Hunt.

20

Physical Activity and Other Camp Opportunities

As emphasized throughout this book, one of the values of camp is that it is NOT like many of the experiences that children, youth, and adults have back home. Physical activity and sports are widely available options for many individuals through schools and other organizations. However, camp is a place where kids of all types can participate—not just the elite athletes. In addition, camps provide creative opportunities for young people and adults to get exercise while they are having fun and trying activities that they might not have access to at home. The purpose of this chapter is to describe briefly some additional camp activities that might be part of an organized camp program.

Physical Activity in Camps

A particular social concern today is the epidemic of obesity among both children and adults. People gain weight when an imbalance exists between caloric intake and caloric expenditure. As described earlier, food services at camp strive to offer nutritious meals and efforts have been made in many camps to offer healthy snacks. The other side of this issue relates to the amount of physical activity that campers get each day. Most people would assume that camps are places where campers are always physically active. However, camp staff need to make a sustained effort to assure that children are getting enough exciting and enjoyable physical activity while at camp.

This epidemic of physical inactivity has contributed to an increasingly unhealthy and disease-susceptible population. Children are of specific concern since the current generation is one of the most inactive and unhealthy in history. A national study conducted by the Centers for Disease Control and Prevention (CDC) reported that 62% of children aged 9 to 13 did not participate in any physical activity during nonschool hours and 23% engaged in no daily physical activity (Duke, Huhman, & Heitzler, 2003).

To promote physical development and prepare children for a healthy future, the United States Department of Health and Human Services (USDHHS, 2008) recommends 60 or more minutes of moderate to vigorous physical activity daily. For children, meeting recommended physical activity guidelines can result in leaner bodies, increased muscular strength, endurance and flexibility, healthier cardiovascular and blood lipid profiles, reduced blood pressure, development of higher peak bone masses, and greater musculoskeletal health.

Some researchers have found that children may be more susceptible to weight gain during the summer months. Summer breaks from schools may result in less structured days for children, leading to less physical activity and a less healthy diet. Researchers and youth development specialists have suggested that structured summer opportunities such as youth summer camps could provide an opportunity for children to be physically active. Most camps feature an array of experiential settings including outdoor open space, indoor sports courts, playing fields, trails, and lakes that should facilitate fun, physical opportunities.

Hickerson (2009) conducted an exploratory study to examine the physical activities of kids aged 8 to 12 in resident and day camps to determine correlates of their physical activity participation. Campers at resident camps took an average of almost 20,000 pedometer-recorded steps during full camp days, while day campers took 12,000 steps during the time they were at camp. These step counts exceeded the recommended daily steps. Hickerson found that positive correlates for day-camper physical activity were males, nonminorities, individuals with average weight for age, high peer-group and counselor step counts, and larger and more activity facilities. For resident camps, he found similarly that boys, nonminorities, average weight, high peer-group step counts, and more physical activity facilities contributed to more steps. He also found in resident camps that campers were likely to be more active with greater camp acreage, longer walking distance between programming areas, low camper-staff ratio, and with intentional physical activity programming. Although some individual characteristics influenced activity, this research clearly showed that social, physical, and organizational environments can impact campers' physical activity. Therefore, camps can do much to assure that children and youth are as active as possible at camp.

Physical activity at camp should be omnipresent. Camps can employ several strategies to assure that campers are active. Spain, Bialeschki, and Henderson (2005) offered some specific recommendations for encouraging greater physical activity in camps.

- Intentionally emphasize physical activity each day by programming an *active* hour as well as a *rest hour.*
- Encourage campers to walk across camp by using pedometers and converting the steps to miles. When campers see how the steps add up they may be motivated to continue walking when they return home.
- Make physical activity fun with contests and games.
- Campers will be as active as their counselors, so counselors should be role models of healthy living.
- Try new activities at camp (see next section) that will be fun and get young people moving.
- Get campers involved in a nearby community walk or race.
- Choose games, sports, and activities that do not require a great deal of equipment.
- Encourage having walking teams or walking buddies at camp.
- Do not emphasize winning or being the best.
- Above all, focus on making physical activities FUN.

Children sometimes spend a good deal of time standing or waiting when they might be active. In addition to the regular camp program of aquatics, outdoor skills, arts and crafts, hiking, horseback riding, and so forth, staff may want to consider active games and participatory sports that can be played to encourage more physical activity among all campers.

Physical activity at camp should be omnipresent.

Sports and Physical Activity

So far we have not addressed sports as camp activities. As noted, one of the values of camp is the opportunity for people to participate in activities not available at home. If a child wants to play baseball, for example, he or she is likely to join a community baseball league and may not come to camp. Nevertheless, not all campers have access to organized sports in their communities, so camp can be a place where they have opportunities to learn new sports skills or practice what they already know.

Camps often have access to sports areas. Many camps have open spaces where campers might play softball, soccer, or Frisbee. Some camps have basketball courts or hoops set up for campers to play during their free time. Tennis courts are available at some camps. Volleyball is a fun activity that can be played on grass or sand. All of these examples can provide fun physical activities for campers.

Other sports may be available at camp that may not be possible to do at home. Shooting sports are one example. Many camps offer archery or riflery. Since there are numerous safety concerns that must be addressed, these sports are always offered under the direct supervision of staff and often are situated at a site where few campers go except to participate in these activities. Counselors who work with shooting sports must have specific training and certification to lead these activities properly. In addition, equipment must be kept in good repair and be appropriate for the age of the campers participating.

Other sports and physical activity that might be offered for instruction or as a special activity at camp might include: golf, street hockey, billiards, ping-pong, miniature golf (putt-putt), lacrosse, field hockey, Frisbee golf, tetherball, trampoline, fencing, kite-making and kite-flying, slip sliding, mud wrestling, skateboarding, roller-

Camp is a place where children have opportunities to learn new sports skills or to practice and improve upon what they already know. (Photo courtesy of American Camp Association)

blading, wrestling, flag football, dodge ball, foosball, kickball, cheerleading, rope swings, cricket, weight lifting, juggling, sling shooting, tree climbing, 4-square, soap box derby, and badminton. Some camps have playgrounds available for younger children.

A key focus of any sports activity is participation. Counselors should keep campers active and design activities so that campers are not sitting or standing around for long periods of time waiting for their turn. All campers, regardless of skill and ability, should have an opportunity to participate. Subramaniam (2005) advocated a quality sports program that caters to the needs of all campers, offering the following tips:

- Ensure that athletic programs are developmentally appropriate. Developmentally inappropriate activities are likely to lower camper self-esteem rather than raise it.

- Provide plenty of practice time.

- Keep in mind that campers need to experience success regardless of skill level.

- Create a positive learning climate when teaching activities.

- Emphasize positive values and cooperation among campers.

- Strive to appropriately increase the physical activity level of all campers.

- Positively engage campers of ALL ability levels in your athletic programming.

- Consult some of the excellent resources available about the best way to *coach* youth sports.

Horseback Riding

Although not as active as some program areas, a number of camps offer equestrian programs that are highly popular among campers. A riding program requires a sizable investment in equipment, purchase or lease of horses, and barn upkeep. Both Western and English riding opportunities are possible, often dependent on the geographic location of the camps. Counselors working in the riding program, often called wranglers, need great skill in taking care of horses properly, choosing the appropriate horse for a rider's needs, and helping campers have a positive riding experience. Certification opportunities are available for these counselors.

Horseback riding is usually done in arenas or corrals as well as on trails. Campers learn to ride in an enclosed space so they and the counselors have almost complete control over the horse. When a rider feels more comfortable, he or she may have the opportunity to go on a trail

A number of camps offer equestrian programs that are highly popular with campers. (Photo courtesy of Bradford Woods Learning and Outdoor Center)

ride. Some camps offer horse trips to areas where riders can camp overnight. Some camps also offer pony rides for younger campers who may not want to ride a full-size horse.

Camps that can offer horseback riding are popular. This activity is one that many urban campers do not have access to unless they go to camp. Safety standards such as requiring helmets, long pants, and boots are necessary to help prevent injuries.

Other Opportunities for Physical Activity

The possibilities for activity are almost endless at camp. Some camps offer bicycling, for example. These camps make bicycles—which may be designed for the road or trail/mountain use—available to campers. Some camps offer bicycle trips as part of the tripping program. Counselors working with a bicycle program need some knowledge of bicycle mechanics and must assure that bikers have bikes that fit their size, that campers wear head protection at all times, and that rules of the road are followed. Some camps have BMX or dirt bike courses set up for campers.

Gymnastics are offered at some camps. Equipment is required and staff need training, but campers often enjoy learning and practicing these physical opportunities.

Some camps offer walking, running, or other fitness groups for campers. These may be formal groups or simply opportunities to use the camp's trails for personal fitness. Some campers enjoy opportunities to participate in aerobics or yoga or in martial arts or defense skills like karate or judo. Counselors leading these exercise activities will need proper training in order to provide the best instruction.

Outdoor activities such as fishing and bird watching are available at some camps, while gardening and animal care are gaining popularity. These opportunities allow for some physical activity while immersing campers in nature.

Other Innovative Program Opportunities

Not all activities at camp need to be physically active. Opportunities such as arts and crafts, music, dance, and drama have previously been discussed. Other creative opportunities include photography and movie making. Campers enjoy the opportunity to be creative and to produce projects that others can also enjoy. Rocketry is another area of interest, as is woodworking. Some campers form bands, playing the usual instruments, while others form rhythm bands using instruments made from available materials.

Nearly any activity can be adapted for camp. Campers may even want to create new games and activities that they can do while at camp. The possibilities are limited only by campers' imaginations.

Photography is just one of the many creative activities available at camp.

REFERENCES

Duke, J., Huhman, M., & Heitzler, C. (2003). Physical activity levels among children aged 9–13 years—United States, 2002. *Morbidity and Mortality Weekly Report, 52*(33), 785–788.

Hickerson, B. D. (2009). *Individual, social, physical environmental, and organizational correlates of children's summer camp-based physical activity.* Ph.D. dissertation from North Carolina State University.

Spain, V. K., Bialeschki, D., & Henderson, K. (2005, Sept/Oct). Kids and healthy lifestyles. *Camping Magazine, 78*(5), 26–33.

Subramaniam, P. R. (2005, July/Aug). Fostering quality athletic programs in camps to promote lifetime physical activity. *Camping Magazine, 78*(4), 52–55.

U.S. Department of Health and Human Services. (2008). *2008 physical activity guidelines for Americans.* Washington, DC: U.S. Government Printing Office.

WEB RESOURCES

Coaching

(www.wecoachkids.com) offers fundamentals for coaching, practice principles, and links to additional resources.

(www.y-coach.com) provides links to sport-specific coaching instructions.

Sport Coaching (www.guidetocoachingsports.com) offers sport specific tips and drills/activities.

Disabled Sports

Disabled Sports USA (http://www.dsusa.org/) has detailed information about making various sports accessible for people with disabilities.

National Center on Physical Activity and Disability (http://www.ncpad.org/) includes information about disabilities and creating inclusive physical activity opportunities for people with disabilities.

North American Riding for the Handicapped Association (www.narha.org) features articles and listservs.

Games

(www.gameskidsplay.net) has an index of games including ball games and mental games.

(www.mrgym.com) lists and provides directions for games including cooperative, small space, and dance/rhythmic activities.

(www.group-games.com) includes a database of group games sorted by type or age.

General Activity

Action for Healthy Kids (http://www.actionforhealthykids.org/) provides programs and information for family, school, and community partnerships to improve nutrition and increase physical activity.

America on the Move (http://aom.americaonthemove.org/site/c.krLXJ3PJKuG/b.1524889/) is an online community to promote healthy lifestyles for individuals and groups.

American Heart Association (http://www.americanheart.org/presenter.jhtml?identifier=3007589) offers tips about exercise for children.

Camp Resource (www.ultimatecampresource.com) includes art projects, games, skits, songs, stories, icebreakers, ropes course activities, team-building activities, field trips, articles, and suggestions for theme days.

CDC's Guide to Community Preventive Services: Physical Activity (http://www.thecommunityguide.org/pa/) has reviews of literature on the most effective physical activity programming practices.

CDC's Recommendations and Reports: Guidelines for School and Community Program to Promote Lifelong Physical Activity among Young People (http://www.cdc.gov/mmwr/preview/mmwrhtml/00046823.htm) provides comprehensive guidelines for physical activity programs in communities and schools including specific population preferences for physical activity.

MacScouter (http://macscouter.com) offers ideas for cooking, skits, games, stories, campfire, ceremonies, gear, themes, and more.

PE Central (www.pecentral.org) features a database with a broad range of physical activity lesson plans and activity ideas.

President's Challenge Physical Activity and Fitness Awards Program (http://www.presidentschallenge.org/) includes activity logs, ideas to get active for people of various ages and ability levels.

Resources-UK (www.campresources.co.uk) has ideas for games, arts and crafts, bunk activities, ice breakers, evening programs, performing arts, rainy day activities, water activities, homesickness, getting a job, and more.

SPARK—Sports, Play and Active Recreation for Kids (http://www.sparkpe.org/) is a school-based program to promote physical activity.

Take10! (www.take10.net) offers a set of lessons available for purchase for elementary school teachers to integrate 10-minute intervals of physical activity into the school day.

U.S. Dept. of Health and Human Services' Small Step (Adult & Teen) (http://www.smallstep.gov/index.htm) provides diet and exercise advice, obesity statistics, activity log and graphs to monitor performance and other resources.

Wilderdom, A Project in Natural Living and Transformation (www.wilderdom.com) offers suggestions for group activities, outdoor education, experiential learning, quotes, bookstore, and youth development.

Horseback Riding

American Association for Horsemanship Safety (www.horsemanshipsafety.com) features a bookstore and information on riding clinics.

American Riding Instructors Association (www.riding-instructor.com) provides resources through its bookstore and magazine.

Certified Horsemanship Association (www.cha-ahse.org) features books, videos, posters, magazine, articles, and information conferences.

Christian Camping Horsemanship International (www.instructors4christ.org) provides resources for a biblical approach to horsemanship.

Equine Law and Horseman Safety (http://asci.uvm.edu/equine/law/) provides resource materials on equine law and horsemanship safety.

Meredith Manor International Equestrian Centre (www.meredithmanor.com) provides a large list of articles for riding and training.

United States Pony Clubs (www.ponyclub.org) has lesson plans, publications, and rules.

Miscellaneous

All-American Soap Box Derby (http://aasbd.whitespace-creative.com) provides introductory information, history, and rules.

National Alliance for the Development of Archery (www.teacharchery.org) includes archery instructor information.

USA Archery (http://usarchery.org)

USA Fencing (http://usfencing.org)

USA Water Ski (www.usawaterski.org)

Sports and Exercise

American Academy of Pediatrics (http://www.aap.org/healthtopics/physact.cfm) focuses on youth sport participation and safety.

American Alliance for Health, Physical Education, Recreation, and Dance (www.aahperd.org) provides links to associations, and other informative newsletters and publications.

American College of Sports Medicine (http://www.acsm.org/AM/Template.cfm?Section=Brochures2) features printable brochures on topics such as equipment use—pedometers, stability ball, resistance band, and weights.

American Council on Exercise (http://www.acefitness.org/ofk/) provides information and resources for practitioners and educators involved with youth sports.

American Running Association (www.americanrunning.org)

National Youth Sports Safety Foundation (www.nyssf.org) contains information on preventing injuries in sports.

PRINT RESOURCES

James, V. L., & Hohnbaum, C. L. (2002, Jan/Feb). Kids camping takes the challenge. *Camping Magazine, 75*(1). How to increase healthy eating and activity opportunities.

Lorimer, R. (2004, Jan/Feb). Success with horses = success with life. *Camping Magazine, 77*(2). Describes the benefits of having a horse program at camp.

Mann, D. (2008, March/April). Developmentally appropriate sports skills for three- and four-year olds. *Camping Magazine, 81*(2). Provides an explanation of psychomotor skills for three- and four-year-olds.

Stanger, A. M. (1999, May/June). Rainy day fun. *Camping Magazine, 72*(3). Provides ideas for rainy-day activities with an emphasis on outdoor activities for rainy days.

IV

Outdoor Living, Camping, and Trail Skills

Earth and sky, woods and fields, lakes and rivers, the mountain and the sea, are excellent schoolmasters, and teach some of us more than we can ever learn from books.

—John Lubbock

21

Safety and Emergency Skills

This final section of the book focuses primarily on specific outdoor activities that may occur at camp. Some of the issues presented apply to various dimensions of all camp activities while others relate mainly to outdoor living skills. The following chapters provide an overview of some of the specific issues related to a variety of camp activities.

Many people are wary of camping and outdoor adventure because they are unskilled or inexperienced, and concerned about potential dangers. With proper knowledge, training, and supervision, however, campers and staff can experience a wealth of benefits from working, playing, and living outdoors. Most people are much safer in camp than they would be in a city environment.

Throughout the text, we have stressed safety. This chapter covers emergency situations that might arise in camp. Risk management means being aware of potential problems and taking steps to avoid them, rather than trying to remedy problems after they occur. The nature of the safety issues may depend upon where a camp is located. For example, if dangerous animals live in the environment where a camp is located, staff will need to be far more knowledgeable than the brief overview provided here. Each camp's risk-management plan should identify issues that might occur and how to address them.

Common Health and Safety Problems at Camp

Camps are not free from accidents or illness. Having an awareness of the most common health problems occurring in a camp setting will alert counselors to possible symptoms so they can more effectively assist campers. Some of the more common ailments include:

Animal and snake bites
Blisters
Conjunctivitis (inflammation of the eye)
Constipation
Contact dermatitis
Diarrhea
Drug sensitivity/ allergic reaction
Earache
Foreign object in eye or ear
Headache
Heat exhaustion
Homesickness
Lice
Minor lacerations and abrasions
Nausea and vomiting
Nosebleed
Painful menstruation
Skin fungus infections
Sore throat: strep and viral
Sprains and strains
Sunburn and sun poisoning
Upper respiratory infection

Of all the ailments to confront campers, *blisters* on the feet are usually the most common. Although they may first seem to be a relatively minor problem, they can lead to incapacitation if not treated. Blisters are caused by the friction of the skin rubbing against a rough surface such as a boot. Moisture, temperature, and friction are the three major factors in blister formation. To prevent problems, shoes should fit well. For chronic blister problems, potential blister areas may be covered with moleskin or adhesive tape prior to beginning an activity. Equipment for treating blisters should be in the first aid kit.

Sunburn can be a serious as well as painful condition. The use of a good sunscreen with a sun protection factor (SPF) of 15 or higher is recommended. When going out for long periods, like a canoe trip or hike, the best protection is clothing—a wide-brimmed hat, long sleeves and pant legs, and a turned-up collar. Sunglasses also should be worn to protect the eyes. After a sunburn occurs, keep the exposed area covered. Aspirin and over-the-counter local anesthetics can be used for pain. Severe sunburn with blisters may require a doctor's attention.

When people participate in vigorous activities, especially during the heat of hot summer days, they must be wary of *heat exhaustion*. Its symptoms are extreme fatigue, nausea, headache, and faintness. The skin becomes clammy and moist and the eye pupils dilate. Treatment is relatively simple and includes allowing the victim to rest quietly in a cool area. Also, lightly salted water or an electrolyte replacement should be swallowed in moderate amounts at frequent intervals.

Dehydration can be prevented by consuming adequate amounts of liquid throughout the day. A loss of 1½ quarts of water without replacement will result in a 25% loss of stamina. To avoid dehydration, remind campers to drink often.

Digestive disturbances can be upsetting and usually account for campers' stomach problems. Observing the principles of moderation and good nutrition will go a long way toward preventing this discomfort. Make sure dishes are thoroughly washed and sterilized. Additionally, dehydration is a common variable in stomach ailments. See that campers use their own individual drinking cups and water bottles rather than pass them among friends. Prevention also includes treating all unknown water either chemically, with a water purifier, or by boiling it. If conditions get worse, seek medical help.

Dealing with Emergencies

Because of the adventurous and challenging activities offered in many camp programs, there is a potential for more serious injuries. These are far less common than those mentioned above, but must be considered. They include:

Acute abdominal pain	Hypothermia
Altitude sickness	Near drowning
Fractures	Severe bleeding
Head injury	Spinal injury

Many of these health issues are the result of accidental injuries that must be dealt with under emergency situations.

Training in first aid and CPR and up-to-date certification should be required for all camp personnel. A well-stocked first aid kit should be available in every program area. The health care director should assemble first aid kits and they should be available at every activity area of camp. Some injuries result from failure to identify problems in time and to take appropriate action. Consequently, a camp counselor must be familiar with common safety concerns and emergency situations. He or she also should know how to use the supplies in a first aid kit.

Although first aid kits can be purchased, many camps prefer to assemble their own. The supplies included will depend on local health personnel and would likely include the items listed in exhibit 21.1.

Altitude sickness (or mountain sickness) can result from a rapid ascent to altitudes over 7,000 feet, especially for people who are not accustomed to being this high. The sickness caused by climbing too high in altitude without allowing one's body to acclimatize can be quite uncomfortable and in some cases, very serious. Symptoms can include headaches, loss of appetite, nausea, vomiting, nosebleeds, and even insomnia. The best treatment for altitude sickness usually is rest, although people who are more seriously affected probably should descend to a lower elevation for a day or so. A good rule of thumb is that you should not go *up* until the symptoms come *down*. Be sure that the person drinks at least 2 or more quarts of liquid daily as this seems to help.

Perhaps the most dangerous problem facing inexperienced campers on outdoor trips is *hypothermia*. This problem is caused by the loss of one's body heat at a rate greater than it can be produced, which causes a drop in the body's internal temperature. If a person's internal temperature is lowered far enough, it can result in mental and physical collapse. Hypothermia often occurs well above freezing temperatures, and even in summer months. It is

Make sure dishes are thoroughly washed and sterilized to kill the germs that can potentially cause upset stomachs.

Exhibit 21.1		
Typical Items in a First Aid Kit		
Absorbent cotton	Disinfectant	Safety pins
Ace bandages	Eye ointment	Small scissors
Adhesive bandages and band-aids	Gauze squares—roller gauze	Snakebite kit
Adhesive tape (2″ roll)	Insect repellent	Sunburn ointment/aloe
Alcohol swabs	Instruction book or reference material	Sunscreen with sun protection factor
Antihistamine	Latex sterile gloves	Treatment for burns
Aspirin	Mild soap (biodegradable)	Treatment for poison ivy or oak
Baking soda—for bites, stings, indigestion, or sunburn	Moleskin—for preventing blisters	Triangular bandage (a clean bandanna will do)
	Needle	Tweezers—sharp pointed

aggravated by moisture (e.g., wet clothes), wind, and exhaustion. Someone who is tired and who has already depleted most of the body's energy is in poor condition to fight off hypothermia. Symptoms may come slowly but often include lapses in memory, error in judgment, clumsiness, and loss of body coordination. Because of the victim's mental state, he or she is unaware that these things are happening. The three sequential stages of hypothermia are: (1) uncontrollable shivering of the body, (2) loss of judgment and reasoning power resulting from cold numbing the brain, and (3) stupor or collapse and death.

Immediate treatment should commence at the first signs of hypothermia. Get the victim out of the wind or rain and remove all wet clothing. The person should be placed in warm clothes and a warm sleeping bag. If the victim is in a semiconscious state or worse, it may be necessary to place him or her in a sleeping bag with another person. At this stage, the victim is no longer capable of generating body heat to warm the bag. If the person is able to eat, administer foods containing high levels of carbohydrates and sugars. If untreated, hypothermia can result in death.

To prevent hypothermia:

- Dress appropriately to ward off cold, wind, and wetness
- Get plenty of rest and consume energy foods (e.g., carbs) and water
- Wear non-cotton clothing, layer clothing, and remove extra layers prior to sweating
- Use rain gear before it rains
- Monitor the weather, pack and dress accordingly
- Monitor fellow participants for hypothermia
- Avoid fatigue and overexertion

Making Drinking Water Safe

The only way to be absolutely sure a natural water supply is safe for drinking, cooking, or washing dishes is to have it tested by qualified personnel. If this testing has not been done, you must sterilize it, no matter how clear or sparkling it looks. Water may carry serious diseases such as typhoid fever and viruses such as Giardia. Even in remote wilderness areas, giardiasis has now become a serious problem caused by drinking infected water from streams or lakes in the high mountains. Use one of the following methods to purify water:

1. Boil it until it rolls. An old camping dictum indicates that water should be boiled for five minutes to make it drinkable. Giardia dies within a minute, and bacteria and viruses die after a minute at 180 to 190 degrees.

2. Use an approved water filter designed for this purpose. A variety of light portable water filters have become available on the market. A general rule of thumb is to have a few sealable plastic bags to keep the inlet hose and outlet hose separate to avoid self-contamination.

3. Use iodine, Potable Aqua, or Halazone tablets according to the directions printed on the container. Let treated water stand for 30 minutes. A few drops of lemon juice will improve the taste.

4. Use household chlorine bleach (5.25 percent sodium hypochlorite, Clorox, or Purex), adding 8 drops to one gallon of raw water. Mix thoroughly and let it stand 30 minutes before using. Be sure to purify the mouth of the bottle just as you would do with iodine or Halazone tablets.

When water is available at an outpost or frequently used campsite, it is worthwhile to send a sample to the state board of health for testing so that you will not have to sterilize it. Directions for doing this can be secured from your state or county board of health or the camp director.

Plant Hazards

Poison ivy, poison oak, and poison sumac cause much distress. At least two out of three people are allergic to at least one of these plants, and they are so common and widespread that campers always run the danger of encountering them. All three have common characteristics.

The allergic reaction results when urushiol, the oily substance from these plants, comes in contact with the skin. Symptoms may appear from within an hour or two up to several days after exposure, beginning with redness, burning, and itching in a localized area that may then spread. A rash, swelling, and watery blisters with possible fever, major itching, and general discomfort follows.

Susceptible persons vary in the severity of their reactions to these poisonous plants. The greatest concentration of the toxin causes the quickest and most severe reaction. Although poisoning is ordinarily caused by direct contact with the leaves, it is also possible to contract it from contact with the stems, roots, or even soot and smoke from burning plants in a brush fire or campfire. People can also get the oil on their skin indirectly by contact with things on which the oil has been deposited, such as clothing, tools, or even the hair of dogs or other animals that have been running through the brush. Poisoning is possible at any time of the year, but it occurs most commonly in spring and summer when the sap is more abundant and people are more likely to be outdoors.

Poison Ivy

Poison ivy is probably the most widespread of the three with some variety found in almost every area of the United States. All varieties have the same characteristic arrangement of leaves, which always grow in clusters of three on a single stem, as shown in the accompanying photo. Thus the old saying, "Leaves of three, let it be" is still a good rule to follow, although it may make you unduly suspicious of certain harmless plants. The plant growth takes many forms including appearing as a vine twining about trees, fences, houses, and even rock piles or as a low, leafy shrub, growing out in the open. As it matures, it sometimes resembles a small tree with a trunk several inches thick. It sometimes grows along the ground, blending with other plants to form an attractive green carpet.

Poison ivy.

Poison Oak

Poison oak is a misnomer since it is not a member of the oak family but simply another form of poison ivy whose characteristic three-leaf clusters are lobed somewhat like oak leaves (see photo). It is most commonly found in the states of California, Washington, and Oregon and ordinarily grows as an upright shrub, although it sometimes climbs on other objects like a vine.

Poison oak.

Poison Sumac

Poison sumac is found chiefly in swampy areas east of the Mississippi River. It never grows as a vine, but rather as a coarse, woody shrub or small tree from 5 to 25 feet tall that is frequently asymmetrical, often leaning to one side. It is commonly confused with certain harmless varieties of sumac that serve useful purposes such as furnishing tannin for treating leather, controlling erosion on waste hillsides, or growing as ornamental plants.

Poison sumac. (Troy Evans, Great Smoky Mountains National Park; Bugwood.org)

Treatment

Since it is usually impractical—and improper—to try to eradicate the plants over all areas where campers live and hike, campers and staff should learn to recognize them and keep an eye out to avoid direct contact. It is a good idea to post warnings along well-used trails and paths where poisonous plants have been identified. When hiking, protect skin areas by wearing long sleeves, long pants, and even gloves. If you think you have been exposed, immediately remove clothing when you return to camp and avoid touching it until after it has been laundered. Several commercial products are available for scrubbing the skin if you think you have been exposed.

Posted warnings along well-used trails and paths can help campers avoid contact with poisonous plants.

Relief from minor itching can be obtained by applying wet compresses. If itching is intense, antihistamine tablets can provide relief. If you are without common commercial applications, the itchiness can be lessened by applying the juice from crushed jewel weed or plantain.

If the rash weeps or blisters, wash the lesions with cool water, blot dry and apply a drying agent such as calamine lotion. Repeat this procedure two or three times per day. Your camp health center may have other remedies available. Rashes on the face, mouth, eyes, groin, or covering more than 25 percent of the body should be evaluated by a physician as soon as possible. Resources on the Internet may also be useful in preventing and treating rashes caused by poison plants.

Creature Hazards

Few dangerous animals will be found at camp. Although many of nature's creatures can prove bothersome or possibly even dangerous on occasion, most merely want to live and let live as far as humans are concerned. Nonetheless, it is wise to learn something about them and their habits.

The probabilities are that you can spend weeks or months in the outdoors without seeing a poisonous snake or dangerous animal. If they are present, they are usually shy and even less anxious than you to foster a close acquaintance. An animal's senses are keen and they are often aware of people's presence long before people are aware of them. An animal will not usually bite or otherwise cause harm unless surprised or frightened. It may fight back in self-defense.

Bears

The black bear is the smallest, most common bear in the United States. Its range includes sparsely settled, forested areas of the upper Northeast, the northern Midwest, the Rocky Mountain region, the West Coast, and Alaska. The larger, more aggressive Alaskan brown bear and grizzly bear live only in Alaska, western Canada, and portions of the Northwestern United States; thus they are not as likely to be an issue for organized camps as are black bears.

All bears should be considered potentially dangerous. However, you can prevent bear-human conflicts by taking a few precautions. Since bears are creatures of habit, they will return to any area where food was once found. One of the best ways to deter bears, and other animals, is to keep a clean campsite. When traveling by foot or other means in bear country, place food in a commercial bear canister or hang food in a bag from a tree branch at least 10 feet above the ground and four feet out from the tree trunk. *Do not* store food in tents and keep items such as candy, toothpaste, and deodorant away from the sleeping quarters. When hiking, stay with the group and watch for signs of bears. Generally, however, bears will try to avoid people, so make your presence known by singing, talking, or making other noises. Bears have poor eyesight, so they may approach you simply out of curiosity. If suddenly confronted by a bear that is

Black bears are the most common bears in the United States.

standing ground, you probably should back away slowly. Don't run, since this may excite the bear into pursuit. If a black bear actually does attack, the recommended action is to fight it off.

Snakes

Snakes are widely feared and despised. Yet of the several hundred varieties in the United States, only four are poisonous—the coral, the rattler, the copperhead, and the cottonmouth (water moccasin). Few people are bitten by snakes and very few die from snakebites.

Snakes play an important part in the balance of nature and are especially useful because they eat large quantities of insects as well as rats and mice. Snakes want to be left alone and will rarely bite unless they are surprised or provoked. A snake's usual reaction upon detecting human presence is to slither away to safety or to lie still to avoid being noticed. Hence, for every snake you see, there are probably countless others that detected you first and crept silently away. To minimize the chances of an encounter, watch where you step, sit, and place your hands. Although snakes have no ears and cannot hear, they are quite sensitive to ground vibrations.

If someone gets bitten by a poisonous snake, seek prompt medical treatment. The most helpful treatment is an injection of antivenom (antivenin) to counteract the poison and minimize pain and discomfort. Keep the victim quiet and at rest, since any physical activity will speed up the person's circulation and spread the poison more rapidly. Fright and shock often do almost as much harm as the actual bite, so try to keep the victim calm. More information about the four types of poisonous snakes as well as nonpoisonous snakes can be found in tables 21.1 and 21.2 (on pp. 230–231) and on the Internet.

Insects

Insects can be a nuisance since their bites can cause discomfort. More serious complications can occur in some people if they are particularly allergic to stings. About 60% of all deaths from venomous animals in the United States are caused by insects, with flying insects accounting for 40% of the total. A snakebite victim can

Table 21.1 Common Nonpoisonous Snakes

Garter Snake

Garter snakes are one of the most common snakes. Garters are generally striped against a plain or checkered background, with subtle coloring that blends into the background. Garters are generally 18–26 inches long, but larger varieties can reach 4 feet.

Kingsnake

Common kingsnakes are usually between 2–4 feet long, with different species exhibiting a variety of colors and patterns. The scarlet kingsnake and the Sonora Mountain kingsnake resemble the venomous coral snakes, but the kingsnake's red rings are bordered by black rings, and the coral snake's red rings by yellow rings. Remember the old saws: "Red touches black, you're okay, Jack," and "If red touches yellow, you're a dead fellow."

Table 21.2   Poisonous Snakes in the United States

Copperhead (Northern Moccasin, Pilot Snake)

The copperhead (also called the Northern moccasin or pilot snake) is usually 2–4 feet long and of a hazel or pinkish-brown color with cross markings of darker reddish-brown blotches that are shaped somewhat like an hourglass or a short-handled dumbbell. The name "copperhead" comes from the distinctive copper coloring of its head. It usually prefers rocky, wooded terrain.

Coral Snake

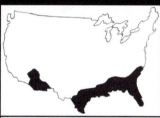

The coral snake is southern and exists in several varieties, each potentially quite dangerous, since their venom is the most toxic. Coral snakes prefer darkness and tend to stay burrowed beneath the soil in daytime. You are not likely to encounter one except at night or after a flood or hard rain. They have short fangs that are permanently erect. Instead of striking to inject their poison in one or a few quick jabs, they try to catch hold and hang on to chew and thus inject their venom in a number of places.

The coral snake is long, slender, colorful, and attractive. It closely resembles some harmless varieties of the king snake and the milk snake. The only sure way to distinguish between them is to note the color of the nose and exact arrangement of the red, yellow, and black bands. The coral snake has a black nose and its broad red bands are next to the yellow bands. The black bands lie between the yellow bands.

survive 6 to 48 hours before receiving medical treatment, while the victim of a flying insect (e.g., bees, wasps, hornets, and yellow jackets) can die within an hour if severely allergic.

A number of commercial products are quite effective in repelling insects. Repellents containing adequate amounts of "DEET" protect effectively for several hours against a large number of pests, such as leeches, spiders, ticks, chiggers, biting flies, gnats, and mosquitoes. Such repellents can be applied directly to the skin or sprayed on clothing and around the tent for sleeping comfort as well as for protection when on the move. If "buzzed" by such insects as hornets or bees, walk slowly away. Avoid moving rapidly or slapping at them frantically, since this makes them more likely to bite.

When insects bite or sting they usually inject an acid that causes redness, itching, swelling, and pain. Avoid scratching the bite and apply an antiseptic to minimize the danger of infection. Several over-the-counter agents can be used to minimize and neutralize the irritation caused by insects. For individuals allergic to many insects, a sting can cause a response known as *anaphylactic shock*. This occurs rapidly, usually within a few minutes. Such persons should always carry a doctor-prescribed insect sting allergy kit that contains antihistamine and an epinephrine adrenalin-loaded hypodermic.

Mosquitoes

In addition to being intensely annoying and inflicting itchy bites, mosquitoes are vectors of several serious

Table 21.2   Poisonous Snakes in the United States *(continued)*

Cottonmouth (Water Moccasin)

The cottonmouth is usually found in swampy territory or in the trees and bushes overhanging streams and marshes in southern states. It is 3–6 feet long and has a dark muddy or olive-brown color with eleven to fifteen inconspicuous darker bars on its short, thick body. It is inclined to stand its ground and fight rather than retreat when threatened. Several varieties of harmless water snakes resemble it and are often mistaken for it. It usually threatens before striking by opening its mouth wide to show the white interior; this explains its name, "cottonmouth."

Diamondback Rattlesnake

It is estimated that there are 16–26 varieties of rattlesnakes in the United States, with at least one variety in nearly all 50 states. They range in size from the 8-inch pygmy rattlers to the giant diamondbacks. They are variously marked and colored, but all have one common characteristic—the rattles on the end of their tails with which they usually warn their victims before striking. The tail and rattles vibrate so rapidly that you can scarcely see them and they make a unique sound somewhat like the ticking of an alarm clock or the sound of a locust.

diseases. The most common of these in the US and Canada is West Nile Virus. The vast majority of cases are mild, producing flu-like symptoms that persist for a few days. In its most serious form (less than 1% of cases), West Nile Virus causes a fatal inflammation of the brain.

There were 620 cases of West Nile Virus reported to the CDC in 2010, with 23 deaths (Nadakavukaren, 2011). The best way to avoid mosquito bites at camp is to use mosquito repellent and to eradicate mosquito breeding sites; that is, standing water.

Chiggers (chigoes, jiggers, or red bugs)

Chiggers are orange-red spiderlike creatures that are the larvae of a tiny mite. They are so small that they cannot be seen without a microscope. They come into contact with you while you walk through grass, and they often wander about a person's skin for an hour or more until they find a suitable place to bite. They can best be avoided by using insect repellents and covering yourself with clothing.

Ticks

Ticks are blackish or reddish-brown parasites that cling to tall grass or shrubs and transfer themselves to people and animals as they pass by. They cause discomfort and are vectors of several serious diseases. Fortunately, ticks tend to wander around on the body before settling down, and usually are attached to the carrier several hours before feeding. They usually can be removed before any harm is done.

Inspect campers for ticks at least twice a day when in tick country, paying particular attention to the head and back of neck. When undressing for the night, campers should also check areas providing good concealment, such as the genital region. Tick bites can best be prevented by wearing clothing that keeps them from your skin, particularly clothing that fits tightly at the wrist, ankle, and waist. If a tick attaches itself to you, try to make the tick detach itself by applying a bit of alcohol, kerosene, gasoline, Vaseline, or fingernail polish to it. An antiseptic should always be applied to the bite as with any open wound. Individuals who have handled ticks should wash their hands, since tick secretion may be infective.

If attempts to remove the entire tick fail, or should there be any other problems, it is important that the person see a physician. Similarly, if a person experiences general malaise with fever, headaches, and muscle pain within two weeks after tick removal, consult a physician immediately. The most common tick-borne disease in the US is Lyme disease, the most characteristic symptom of which is a circular, spreading red rash that may resemble a "bulls-eye." The rash may be accompanied by headache, fever, chills, joint pain, and fatigue. If Lyme disease is not treated promptly with antibiotics, it can progress to nervous system dysfunction and arthritis (Nadakavukaren, 2011). Some of the other serious diseases transmitted by ticks include Rocky Mountain spotted fever, tick paralysis, and anaplasmosis.

Spiders

The bites of several spiders are quite painful, but few are actually dangerous. One bite that is dangerous is that of the female *black widow spider* (see figure 21.1). If you are bitten, seek professional medical treatment promptly. While waiting for medical attention, follow the same measures recommended for snake bite. The venom of the black widow spider acts as a nerve poison, but bites are seldom fatal. The first symptom is acute pain at the site of the bite, though for some there may be only minimal local reaction. For those who experience a severe response, localized pain may be followed by muscle cramps, abdominal pain, nausea, vomiting, dizziness, and chest pain. Small children and the elderly are more seriously affected than young adults (emedicinehealth.com). Black widows are primarily outdoor spiders, typically found around piles of wood or other debris or in dark corners or crevices of outbuildings. These spiders are nonaggressive and usually bite only when disturbed (nationalgeographic.com).

Another dangerous spider is the *brown recluse spider* (figure 21.1), which can be recognized by the dark brown fiddle-shaped area on the front portion of its back. The brown recluse tends to hide during the day in obscure places such as under rocks, in woodpiles, in decayed logs, or in dark closets or other dry remote areas in buildings, coming out only at night to feed. Like the black widow, it bites only when provoked. Its bite causes severe pain that may be delayed as long as one-half to two hours. The poison injected by the bite of a brown recluse is a cytotoxin, causing tissue death in the area of the wound. It can result in large, open ulcerations that leave an ugly scar. Get professional help as soon as possible to prevent serious complications and minimize scarring.

Centipedes and Scorpions

Centipedes and scorpions live in the warmer areas of the world, and they are particularly numerous in the southwest United States. The scorpion stings with its poisonous tail and the centipede bites with its poisonous fangs. Many campers have been asleep when they were stung or bitten and attributed the symptoms to the flu or even bad drinking water. These creatures are nocturnal, so be sure to thoroughly inspect your bedding before retiring and your shoes and clothing before putting them on in the morning. If someone is bitten, give first aid treatment as for a spider bite and get the patient to a doctor as soon as possible.

Brown Recluse Spider
has dark brown
fiddle-shaped area
on its back

Black Widow Spider has
bright red hourglass
on underside

Figure 21.1   Poisonous spiders.

REFERENCES

emedicinehealth.com. *Black widow spider bite symptoms.* Retrieved from http://www.emedicinehealth.com/black_widow_spider_bite/page2_em.htm

Nadakavukaren, A. (2011). *Our global environment: A health perspective* (7th ed.). Long Grove, IL: Waveland Press.

nationalgeographic.com. *Black widow spider.* Retrieved from http://animals.nationalgeographic.com/animals/bugs/black-widow-spider

WEB RESOURCES

American Academy of Pediatrics (www.aap.org) includes children-specific health topics.

American Association of Poison Control Centers (www.aapcc.org) offers tips for children and adults, first aid, and frequently asked questions.

American Heart Association (www.amhrt.org) has information on CPR, children's health, and warning signs.

American Lyme Disease Foundation (www.aldf.com) includes frequently asked questions, prevention products, related links, and general information.

American Mosquito Control Association (www.mosquito.org) includes frequently asked questions and provides information on mosquito borne diseases, repellents, traps, and West Nile Virus.

American Red Cross (www.redcross.org) has information on training skills, preparedness fast facts, CPR, and first aid.

Association of Camp Nurses (www.acn.org) provides job postings, bookstore, research, and references.

Centers for Disease Control and Prevention (www.cdc.gov) provides resources and general information on all health topics.

Food Allergy and Anaphylaxis Network (www.foodallergy.org) contains specific information about food allergies at camp, specific food allergies, and other helpful information.

NC Department of Transportation Reference Guide to Poisonous Snakes, Insects, and Plants (http://www.ncdot.org/doh/operations/division6/pdf/fieldguide.pdf) has information specific to North Carolina but excellent pictures and first aid tips for snakes, spiders, and plants.

Poisonous Plants
- (http://www.cdc.gov/niosh/topics/plants/) provides an overview of poisonous plants, geographic distribution, identification, symptoms, and first aid.

- (http://aggie-horticulture.tamu.edu/Plantanswers/publications/poison/poison.html) includes a chart of poisonous plants and their toxic parts, and symptoms.

Snakes
- (www.venomoussnakes.net) has information, pictures, videos, tips, and bite symptoms.

- (www.venomous.com) gives an overview of types of venomous snakes.

Wilderness Medicine Training Center (www.wildmedcenter.com) provides information on backcountry first aid certification courses.

U.S. Department of Health and Human Services (www.hhs.gov) has general resources and information about a variety of health topics.

Utah State University Wildlife Damage Management Series: Venomous Snakes (http://extension.usu.edu/files/publications/publication/nr_wd_008.pdf) is specific to Utah, but contains good information on snake bites and first aid.

Wilderness First Aid (http://wfa.net) offers a wilderness first aid certification course and provides links to online resources.

Wilderness Medical Associates (www.wildmed.com) has course offerings, gear, links, and frequently asked questions.

Wilderness Medical Society (www.wms.org) offers publications, research, conferences, and curriculum development for wilderness medicine education.

Wilderness Survival (http://www.wilderness-survival.net/Appd.php) offers survival references and features pictures, descriptions, habitat, and distribution of dangerous insects and spiders.

World Health Organization (www.who.int/en/) provides resources and information on a variety of health topics.

PRINT RESOURCES

ACA. (2003, March/April). Lyme disease: Prevention and control. *Camping Magazine, 76*(2). Discusses the signs and symptoms, protection tips, and steps for tick removal.

Allen, R. A. (2001, May/June). Snakes have feelings too. *Camping Magazine, 74*(3). Explores the techniques for keeping snakes at camp and the benefits of having a snake program.

Castillo, G., & Yerkes, R. (2006, May/June). The pros and cons of administering epinephrine to campers who are experiencing anaphylactic shock. *Camping Magazine, 79*(3). Discusses the training, policies, and procedures for administering epinephrine.

Friese, G. (2004, May/June). Emergency response drills for camps. *Camping Magazine, 77*(3). Discusses the types of drills to practice and how to execute them.

Garst, B., & Erceg, L. E. (2009, March/April). Ten ways to reduce injuries and illnesses in camp. *Camping Magazine,* 82(2). Offers tips on knife safety, reducing fatigue, and maintaining hygiene.

Piper, C., & Rebull, H. (2002, July/Aug). Allergies galore. *Camping Magazine, 75*(4). Discusses dealing with allergies at camp.

Ratner-Connolly, H. (2003, March/April). Poison ivy: A primer for prevention. *Camping Magazine, 76*(2). Covers poison ivy prevention.

Scholl, M. (2004). *Wilderness medicine.* Philadelphia, PA: Saunders.

The Food Allergy and Anaphylaxis Network. (2004, July/Aug). Campers with food allergies. *Camping Magazine, 77*(4). Provides information and tips to ensure campers with food allergies are safe.

Tilten, B., & Hubbell, F. (1994). *Medicine for the backcountry* (2nd ed.). Merrillville, IN: ICS Books.

Wilkerson, J. (2001). *Medicine for mountaineering and other wilderness activities.* Seattle, WA: Mountaineers Books.

22

Knots and Lashing

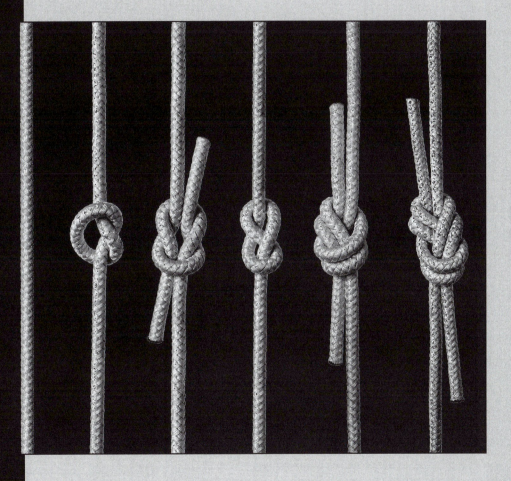

From their earliest existence, humans have needed to fasten things together. They have used such natural materials as vines and thin strips of bark or hide to fulfill this need. Some Native Americans used thongs or dried strips of leather from the skins of animals, applying them wet so that they would contract into tight fastenings as they dried.

The use of knots and lashings for various constructions can be part of the overall program of organized camps. However, when doing this activity, staff and campers must act responsibly and should understand and follow sound environmental practices. Campers should understand when and where it is appropriate to build structures and that it is inappropriate to damage trees and other vegetation. Of course, anything that is constructed should always be disassembled after use unless it has been constructed as part of a larger more permanent project such as a new camp outpost.

Ropes

Ropes are used for knot tying and lashing. Rope traditionally was made of such natural materials as jute, cotton, sisal, manila, or hemp. These original sources of rope have now been largely replaced by synthetic or artificial materials. These newer ropes are stronger, easier to handle, not as easily damaged, float on water, and are available in a number of colors. Their one major disadvantage is that they are often slick, and therefore fail to hold well in some knots.

Ropes are useful in dozens of ways around camp: pitching tarps, flying a flag, hanging laundry to dry, or mooring a boat. Ropes made from nonsynthetic materials will be weakened by dampness. Such ropes also shrink and swell when wet. Avoid walking on a rope or otherwise grinding dirt into it since the particles will gradually cut the fibers. Sharp bends and kinks weaken the rope, so untie knots when you are through with them. When your rope is not in use, arrange it as shown in figure 22.1 by gathering it up in even loops, circling the loops with an end, then passing the end through one of the loops (called *hanking* it).

It is useful to know the following rope terms:

- *End*—short part of the rope
- *Standing part*—remainder or long part of the rope
- *Bight*—formed when an end is laid back parallel to its standing part (figure 22.2)
- *Underhand loop*—made by crossing one end *under* its standing part
- *Overhand loop*—made by crossing one end *over* its standing part
- *Overhand knot*—made by pulling an end through a loop
- *Hitch*—used to fasten a rope to something, such as a post or ring

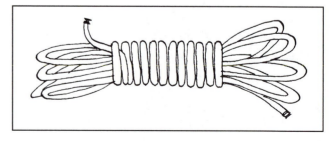

Figure 22.1   Hanking a rope.

236

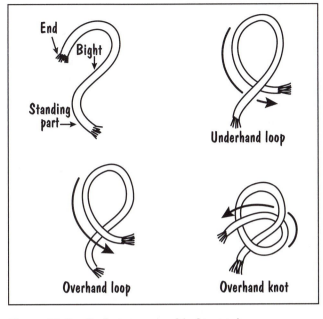

Figure 22.2   Basic terms used in knot tying.

The ends of a rope will untwist or fray unless they are fastened in some way. If the rope is made of synthetic material, fuse the fibers at each end by applying heat from a match or candle. Two simple methods of fastening the ends of a rope made of nonsynthetic material are tying an overhand knot in each end or wrapping the ends with electric tape.

Knots

Knots can be made in hundreds of ways, but a few knots can meet most ordinary needs in camp. Learning to tie these knots and knowing what each is used for will be useful. You will need two ropes of the same or different length to practice some of the knots, but most of them can be tied with the ends of the same rope. When teaching others how to tie knots, it helps to give each end a different appearance by dipping one or both in ink of contrasting colors or by painting them. You can then instruct by saying, "Now cross the red end over the white," or "Pass the blue end under its standing part." Characteristics of a good knot include:

- It is simple and easy to tie
- It performs well in the job for which it is intended
- It will not jam and is easy to untie

To Enlarge the End of a Rope

Stopper or *end* knots are used to enlarge the end of a rope to keep it from pulling through a ring such as a tent grommet, or to provide a good hand grip on the end of the rope.

Overhand Knot

This knot tends to jam after stress has been applied so that it is hard to untie. To make it larger, double the end or pass it through the loop several times before tightening it (see figure 22.2).

Figure Eight Knot

This knot is slightly larger and easier to untie. Among other uses, you can attach a fishhook to a line with it. Make an underhand loop and bring the end over around the standing part and pull it up through the loop. Now pull it tight (see figure 22.3A).

To Join Two Ropes

Square or Reef Knot

This knot requires two ropes of equal size or the two ends of a rope. Form a bight with one rope and bring the end of the other rope up through it, around behind both the end and standing part, and down through the bight again. Pull it tight. To untie it, give a hard pull sideways on both the end and standing part of one rope and pick it apart (see figure 22.3B).

It is easy to tie a *granny* instead of a square knot, but it is not effective since it will pull apart when stress is applied. Note in figure 22.3C that this knot results from bringing the end of the white rope around in such a way as to have the end and standing part on *opposite* sides of the bight in the black rope instead of on the *same* side as in the square knot.

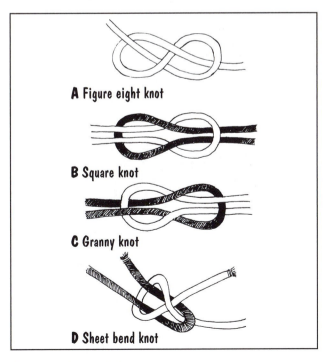

Figure 22.3   Basic knots.

Sheet Bend (Weaver's Knot or Becket Bend)

A square knot will not hold when joining two ropes of unequal size, but a sheet bend will. Make a bight in the black rope and bring the end of the white rope up through it, around behind both the end and standing part of the black rope, across and around under its own standing part and pull it tight (see figure 22.3D). Be sure to leave both ends somewhat long so that the knot will hold. For greater security, after bringing the end of the white rope across and under its standing part, take two or more turns around its bight and pull it under its standing part again (not shown). To untie it, pull on the end of the black rope and its standing part to loosen the knot and then pick it apart.

To Attach a Rope to an Object

Taut Line Hitch

This knot can be used to anchor a tent guy rope, to secure a rope to a ring, or for lifesaving purposes. This knot will not slip, yet you can tighten or loosen the rope by pushing the knot up or down on the standing part. Pass the end of the rope around the peg, and, starting away from the peg and working back toward it, take three turns around the standing part and finish with an overhand knot around the standing part above the turns (see figure 22.4). Pull it tight.

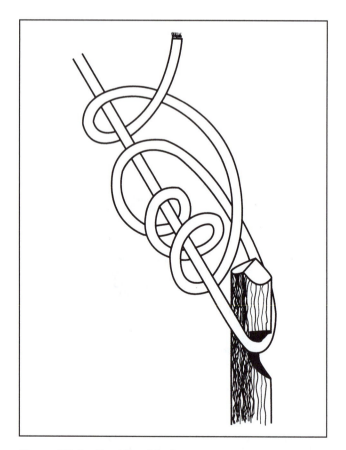

Figure 22.4   Taut line hitch.

Clove Hitch

This knot is used to start and finish lashing, put up a clothesline, or anchor a rope to a tree or other object. Do not use it for anything that moves about, such as a horse or boat, since movement may loosen it. Bring one end of the rope around the post in an overhand loop and continue around the post again and tuck it under the turn just made (see figure 22.5B). Pull it tight.

Half Hitches

This knot is used to attach a rope to a post (for example, when stringing a clothesline), or to a ring (like in the painter of a boat). Use two or more hitches for greater security. Wrap the end of the rope once or twice around the post in an overhand loop and tuck it up through the loop (one half hitch). Then make a second half hitch by making an overhand loop and bringing the end up through (see figure 22.5A).

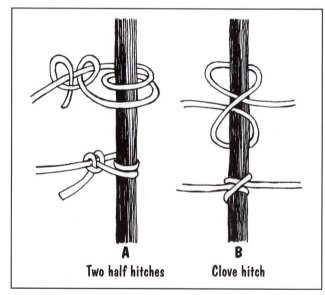

A
Two half hitches

B
Clove hitch

Figure 22.5   Two half hitches and a clove hitch.

To Make a Loop in a Rope

Bowline

This knot is used to make a permanent loop in a rope that will stay the same size even when stress is applied. It is useful for anchoring a boat, when tied in the end of its painter or bowline (hence the name) and slipped over a post, for emergency use like lowering a person from the window of a burning building, and also for making a bedroll, tying around the waist of a mountain climber, leading or tethering an animal, or to throw to someone in trouble in the water.

This little saying may help your campers remember how to tie this knot:

The rabbit jumped out of its hole,
Ran round the tree, and
Jumped back in its hole again.

Make a small overhand loop with the standing part far enough down to allow for the size noose you want (see figure 22.6A). Bring the end up through the loop (rabbit jumped out of its hole), around behind the standing part (ran around the tree), and down through the loop again (rabbit jumped back in its hole again). Hold onto the end as you pull the standing part to tighten the knot.

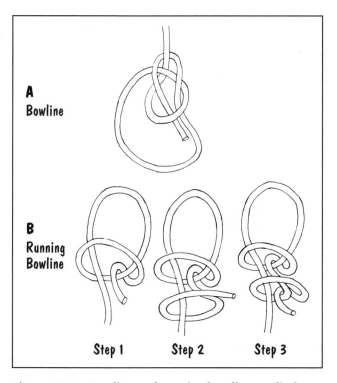

Figure 22.6   Bowline and running bowline or slip knot.

Running Bowline or Slip Knot

This knot forms a noose that pulls tight when stress is applied. Therefore, it should never be used on a person or animal. Use it to retrieve an object floating in water, tie up a package or bedroll, suspend an object from a tree, or whenever you need to fasten a rope tightly around an inanimate object (see figure 22.6B).

Step 1   Use the end to tie an overhand knot around the standing part.

Steps 2 and 3   Use the end to tie a second overhand knot around the standing part and pull the knot tight. Note that since both overhand knots are tied around the standing part, they will slip up and down on it and so adjust the noose tightly about the object.

To Shorten a Rope or Bypass a Weak Spot

Sheep Shank

Step 1   Fold the rope twice as shown to get the length you want or to bypass the weak spot (see figure 22.7).

Step 2   Use each end to tie an overhand knot around the folded portion adjacent to it.

Step 3   Tighten the knots. For more permanency, pass each end down through the loop next to it.

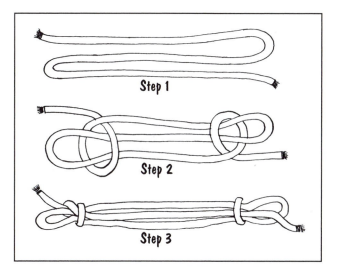

Figure 22.7   Sheep shank.

To Suspend an Object

Barrel Hitch

This knot can be used to suspend a handleless object (see figure 22.8 on the following page).

Step 1   Place the object on the rope, leaving one end long enough to complete the hitch. Bring that end and the standing part of the other up above the object and complete a half knot.

Step 2   Pull the half knot open sideways to form two bights.

Step 3   Pull the two bights halfway down on opposite sides of the object and bring both the end of the rope and the standing part up above the object.

Step 4   Use the end to tie a slip knot about the standing part. Draw the slip knot tight around the object and suspend it by the standing part.

Lashing

Lashing is used to join sticks or poles together using cord or light rope. Lashing is very secure when properly done and can be applied and removed without damaging

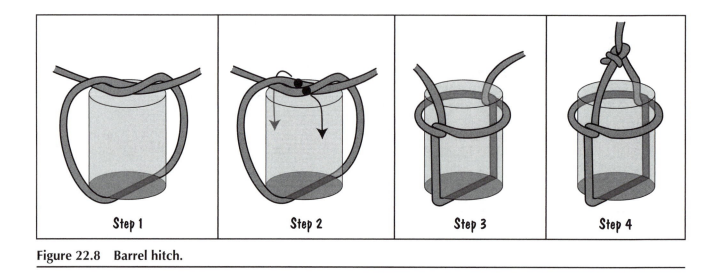

Figure 22.8   Barrel hitch.

either poles or cord. It substitutes well for nails, which can inflict permanent damage if driven into living trees.

Lashing can be useful in many camp projects, such as constructing tables, benches, racks to hold cooking gear or tools, rustic bridges, tripods for supporting a washpan, or drying racks for bathing suits or towels. The same sticks and poles should be used repeatedly to preserve the trees in the camp. If dead and fallen wood from trees is unavailable at your campsite, you can substitute old broom and mop handles, metal bars, and such.

Practice in lashing, using string and lead pencils or small sticks, provides a good activity for rainy days or at night, and campers can later transfer the skills mastered to actual camp situations. The secret of a tight, solid job of lashing is found in the final step, *frapping* (see figure 22.9). Wind the cord tightly between the sticks and the turns previously made. It is customary to use the standing part of your cord when lashing instead of the end as done when tying knots.

To Join Sticks at Right Angles

Square Lashing

Step 1   Cross two sticks at right angles and use the end of the cord to make a clove hitch around one of them, leaving enough of the end to complete a square knot when you have finished (see figure 22.10).

Step 2   Bring the standing part down across the horizontal stick, around behind the vertical stick, up across the horizontal on the other side and then around behind the vertical stick again.

Step 3   Continue this process until you have made at least four or five complete turns around both sides of each stick.

Step 4   Frap with four or five tight turns between the lashing and the sticks.

Step 5   Tie a square knot or clove hitch with the two ends, then cut off any excess twine and tuck the ends in under the lashing.

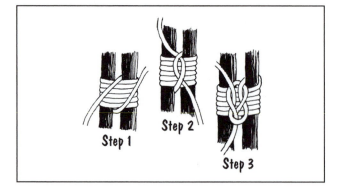

Figure 22.9   Round or shear lashing.

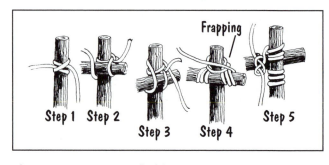

Figure 22.10   Square lashing.

To Join Two Sticks at an Angle

Diamond or Diagonal Lashing

Step 1   Anchor one end of the rope with a clove hitch around both sticks, leaving enough of the end to complete a square knot when finished (see figure 22.11).

Step 2   Use the standing part to make three to five turns around both sticks.

Step 3   Repeat the same process in the opposite direction.

Step 4   Frap tightly and finish with a square knot (not shown) with the ends of the rope.

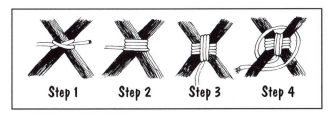

Figure 22.11   Diamond or diagonal lashing.

To Join Sticks into a Base

Tripod Lashing

This type of lashing is used to join three sticks that can then be spread apart and stood upright to form a base.

Step 1   Lay the three sticks parallel and tie them together with a clove hitch.

Step 2   Weave the cord over the first stick, under the second, over the third, etc., until you have made four or five turns around them.

Step 3   Frap somewhat loosely between the sticks, allowing enough slack to stand the sticks up and spread them apart as a base. Finish with the usual square knot or clove hitch.

To Join Parallel Poles or to Lengthen a Pole

Round or Shear Lashing

This lashing is used to join two poles together side by side or to make one long pole by lashing two poles together (refer to figure 22.9). To lash two poles together:

Step 1   Using a clove hitch, anchor one end of the rope to one of the poles. Place the two poles parallel and wind the rope around them five or six times, as shown. Leave the ends long enough to make a square knot when completed.

Step 2   Frap at least once tightly between the poles and tighten with a single knot.

Step 3   Finish off by tying a square knot with the two ends. Lash in at least two other places along the joining.

To lengthen a pole by splicing another to it, lay poles with their ends overlapping and do shear lashing with tight frapping at three or four places along the overlapping parts.

To Make Table Tops and Other Objects

Malay Hitch

This hitch is used to join sticks or boards together to make a shelf or table top. You can also use it to convert wisps of long grass, straw, or other suitable materials into a mattress, a mat for your cabin floor, a fence, or a screen in front of a latrine or outdoor shower.

Step 1   Use a cord slightly more than twice as long as your completed object is to be. Space out the sticks or portions of grass at appropriate distances. Loop the middle of the cord around the stick and continue by tightly bringing one end of the cord alternately over and under each succeeding stick or wisp of grass. Then circle the top stick and bring the cord down again, passing on the opposite side of each stick until the end is down where you started. Join the two ends with a square knot (see figure 22.12).

Step 2   Repeat this process as many times as you wish at various places along the length of the sticks. You can gain extra security by circling each stick with the cord before going on to the next one.

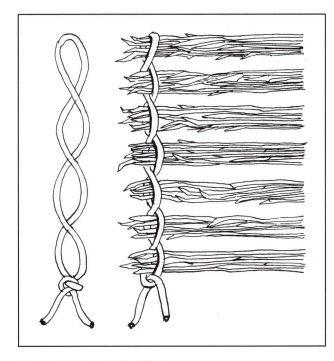

Figure 22.12   Malay hitch.

Continuous Lashing (Paling Hitch)

This technique is used to lash several small sticks, lengths of bamboo, or laths along one long stick or pole or between two or more sticks. You can use it for making a table top that can be rolled up for easy storing or transporting, a tie or belt rack, or a ladder for a climbing plant.

Step 1   Although not absolutely necessary, it will add more stability if you notch both long poles and crosspieces to make them dovetail snugly together. Elevate the long poles by resting their ends on objects such as rocks or chair seats so that you can work freely.

Step 2   Use a piece of string or cord about four times as long as one of the long poles and use a clove hitch to fasten the middle of the cord near the end of one of the long poles.

Step 3   Place the crosspieces at desired intervals along the long pole, then bring both ends of the cord tightly across the top of the first crosspiece, then around behind the long pole, and bring them up over the next crosspiece. Continue on to the end. Keep the cord just as tight as possible. Now make a few

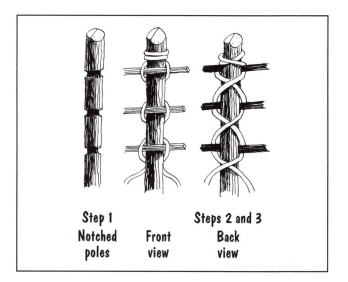

Figure 22.13   Continuous lashing.

turns with each end around the long pole and join them with a square knot (see figure 22.13).

Step 4   Fasten the other ends of the crosspieces to the other long pole in the same manner.

WEB RESOURCES

Animated Knots by Grog (www.animatedknots.com) demonstrates knots for boating, climbing, fishing, scouting, and so forth as well as terminology.

International Guild of Knot Tyers (www.igkt.net) offers a wide array of subjects from beginner to advanced.

Knots Gallery (http://www.tollesburysc.co.uk/knots/knots_gallery.htm) provides interactive tutorials on knot tying.

Knots on the Web (http://www.earlham.edu/~peters/knotlink.htm).

Lashing (www.bsatroop780.org/skills/Lashing.html) provides step-by-step instructions on lashing skills.

Scouting Resources (http://www.scoutingresources.org.uk/knots_books.html) offers a variety of resources and helpful content.

Scouts South Africa (http://www.scouting.org.za/resources/pioneering/) provides diagrams of basic knots and lashing.

Tying Knots (www.2020site.org/knots/) offers descriptions and illustrations on tying over 35 knots.

23 The Weather

Weather plays an important role in our lives. Usually our interest is only casual; other times, we are riveted by accounts of extreme weather events like tornadoes, blizzards, and hurricanes. We consult the Internet, radio, television, or daily newspapers to determine how to dress or whether to go ahead with plans for a picnic or trip to the golf course. However, the weather is also of vital interest to campers. When on a trip away from the main camp, a group leader may bring a weather radio; but often your group will have to depend on members' weather knowledge and powers of observation to forecast what is in store and what should be done to prepare. If a group is on the water, individuals' lives as well as the safety of boats and gear may depend on heading for shore in advance of an approaching storm. Many lives are needlessly lost each year because of lack of weather knowledge and proper respect for such hazards as rough water, mountain storms, lightning, and flash floods.

Studying the basics of weather prediction and the conditions that cause and forecast weather changes can be interesting as well as instructive. Many people are fascinated by weather, particularly the spectacular changes that clouds undergo in the build-up of a storm. In this chapter, we present general information on how weather may influence activities at camp.

Weather Forecasting

Amateur weather forecasters cannot equal the long-range forecasts of the National Weather Service with its highly trained personnel and elaborate equipment for observing and measuring conditions and collecting data. However, even the most sophisticated methods do not produce 100% accuracy. Many of the forces affecting the weather interact in unpredictable ways, necessitating constant revisions and liberal use of terms like *probabilities* or *possibilities*.

As a camp activity, campers can—after some study and with the aid of a few simple instruments—do a creditable job of forecasting weather on a short-term basis of from 2 to 12 hours. Although a summer storm may give as little as an hour's warning of its approach, campers will enjoy seeing how accurate their predictions are. Campers will need to learn how weather is *made* by the interaction of such factors as temperature, pressure, moisture, and wind, which can be observed or measured. When these observations and measurements are interpreted properly, they can help campers make useful predictions.

The study of the air or atmosphere is called **meteorology** and those professionally trained in this area are known as *meteorologists*. Weather features like air currents, air pressure, humidity, temperature, water condensation, cloud cover, and precipitation are components of most professional forecasts. A great deal of information on these elements can be found on the Internet and in science books. For our purposes, we will focus on clouds and precipitation.

Precipitation and Related Weather

You have no doubt noticed minute bits of dust floating about in the air when a ray of sunshine strikes them in a certain way. Similar dust particles are distributed throughout the atmosphere and on a clear day they make the sky look blue. When especially numerous, they give the sky a gray or hazy appearance. These dust particles are the nuclei around which moisture collects as droplets when rising air cools to the *dew point;* that is, the temperature at which the water vapor in the air begins to condense. As the air continues to rise and cool, it squeezes out moisture in the form of droplets that eventually take on electrical charges that attract them to each other. As they unite into larger droplets, they eventually become too heavy to be airborne and fall to earth as *raindrops.*

Snow results when the droplets freeze into tiny ice crystals in the cold, upper regions of the atmosphere, with hundreds or thousands of them uniting into the beautiful designs of single snowflakes. *Sleet* occurs when snow partially melts as it falls through a layer of warmer air just above the ground. If the half-melted snow freezes just as it hits the ground, it is called *glaze.*

Hail results when rain from a low-lying cloud is caught in a strong updraft of air and tossed back up into a high, freezing area where it is coated with snow and ice. It then falls back down through the low-lying cloud, acquires more moisture, and again falls down into the strong updraft that may throw it back up to acquire another layer of ice and snow. This process may be repeated several times until the ice-covered pellet finally becomes so heavy that it pierces the updraft and crashes to earth as hail.

Frost happens when the temperature drops below freezing under conditions that would ordinarily produce dew.

We see a *halo* or *ring* around the sun or moon when we see its light shining through ice crystals in the atmosphere. Rain may be possible in a day or so.

Mythology explained *lightning* as bolts of fire sent by the War God, Thor, to paralyze the earth's people. Lightning, however, is actually a form of electricity. Electrical charges in the atmosphere usually pass harmlessly from one cloud to another, but a bolt of lightning occasionally comes down to earth with enough power to kill humans or other animals, start fires, or uproot trees. Lightning follows the line of least resistance as it leaps from one handy electrical conductor to another on its way to the ground. Therefore, to prevent it from striking you, you must avoid becoming the most convenient conductor in its path by making sure you are not the most prominent object in the area or near something else that is. Some of the most dangerous places to be are near a fence or clothesline, at the top of a hill, in a boat, on the beach, riding a horse or bicycle, on a golf course or meadow, or under an especially tall tree or one standing alone. Among the safest places are in a car (the metal body conducts the bolt to the ground), in a ravine between two hills, or in a grove of trees. If you are caught out in the open, lie flat on the ground or in a ditch. If you are indoors, stay away from plumbing and electrical appliances and don't use the telephone or take a bath. Since water is a good conductor of electricity, anyone swimming or boating should get on land as quickly as possible.

Thunder, although often alarming, is harmless. It is caused by the rapid expansion of the air as it is heated by the passage of lightning through it. To roughly estimate the distance of lightning in miles, count the number of seconds between the time you see the bolt and hear the thunder and divide by five. (You can roughly estimate seconds by counting one-thousand-one, one-thousand-two.) Sound travels at approximately 1/5 mile per second. Therefore, a thunder interval of 5 seconds would indicate that the lightning was about a mile away.

A *rainbow* occurs when the sun's rays are seen through rain that is falling opposite the sun. The water, like a prism, breaks the rays into the colors of a rainbow.

Clouds

The sky, nature's roof, forms a backdrop for the clouds, whose names are of Latin derivation. There are four basic types of clouds.

Cirrus

Cirrus clouds are high-level clouds (5 to 10 miles) with a thin, wispy appearance. They are composed entirely of ice crystals and are white. They are sometimes called "mare's tail" because the wind often blows them into long streamers. If the sky is bright blue above and the wind is from the north or northwest, cirrus clouds indicate fair weather for 24 to 48 hours. However, if the sky is gray-blue and the clouds are moving swiftly, especially from the west, they will likely turn to *cirrostratus* clouds and rain or snow may follow.

Stratus

Horizontal layers of gray stratus clouds may look like a fog that doesn't reach the ground. These clouds are a uniform gray in color and are sometimes dark enough to practically conceal the sun or moon. Rain usually follows.

Cumulus

Cumulus clouds are the billowy, puffy clouds with flat grayish bottoms that rise to a high dome shaped mass of white. They can look like floating cotton balls. They are low clouds, only about a mile above the earth. They are often quite active and usually indicate fair weather, except on a hot, muggy day when, if massed near the horizon or increasing in size, they may indicate rain.

Nimbus

Nimbus clouds are the low-lying "umbrella" clouds. They are dark, with ragged edges and no definite shape. They usually indicate steady rain or snow. *Scud* clouds are the small, ragged pieces frequently seen traveling rapidly across the sky below the nimbus clouds.

Many variations of these four basic cloud types exist, as well as combinations like cirrostratus, altocumulus, stratocumulus, and cumulonimbus (see figure 23.1).

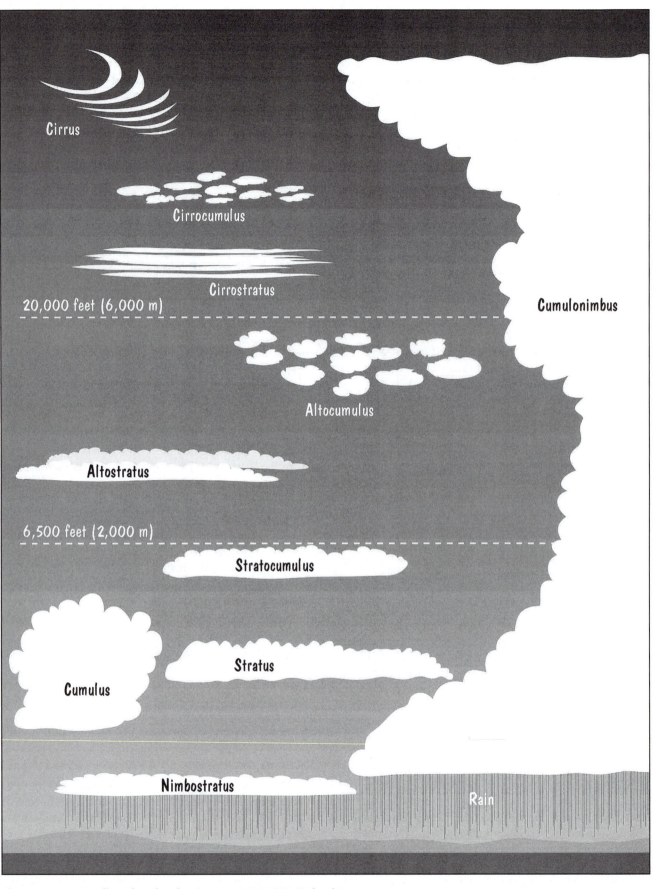

Figure 23.1   Reading the clouds. (Source: NASA/JPL/Caltech)

Weather Instruments

If campers want to assemble a weather station, they can purchase commercially made instruments or might try making some of their own.

A *barometer* is used to measure atmospheric pressure. It can measure the pressure exerted by the atmosphere by using water, air, or mercury (see figure 23.2). Air becomes more and more compressed and consequently heavier as it nears the ground owing to the continuing attempt of the atmospheric gases (primarily nitrogen, oxygen, and carbon dioxide) to expand, the pull of gravity, and the weight of all the air above pressing downward. When the atmospheric pressure is rising, weather is usually good. When it begins to fall, stormy weather is likely on the way.

Air contains moisture in the form of invisible *vapor*. The amount of moisture in the air is expressed as its *humidity*. Most of the moisture comes by evaporation from rivers, lakes, oceans, soil, and trees and other forms of vegetation. A perpetual interchange of moisture takes place between the earth and the atmosphere: the air draws or evaporates moisture in the form of vapor from the earth's surface; this vapor forms clouds and the moisture is eventually returned to the earth as rain, snow, or some other type of precipitation.

A barometer measures the amount of moisture in the air by determining the amount of weight or pressure it exerts. By taking successive readings, you can note not only the amount of humidity in the air but also whether it is increasing or decreasing and how rapidly. Dry air (low humidity) is heavier and hence exerts more pressure than moist air (high humidity).

One of the oldest weather instruments is the *weather vane* or *wind vane*. It can be built very easily (figure 23.3). Use light wood or a large tin can flattened into a sheet and cut into any form desired, such as an arrow, rooster, fish, or boat. Make the tail large and broad enough to catch the wind so that it will always keep the longer, lighter head pointing directly into the wind. Place a pole out in the open where the wind has free access to it and fasten on direction indicators as shown, lining them up with true, not magnetic, north. Find the balance point of the vane and drill a hole just in front of it and glue one end of a round shaft or dowel into it. Drill another hole in the top of the pole deep enough to hold the other end of the dowel securely and large enough to let it turn freely when used with a pair of washers.

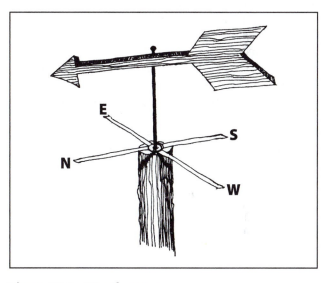

Figure 23.3   Weather vane.

Although you may prefer the conveniences of a commercial *thermometer,* you can estimate the temperature when it is between 45° and 80°F by counting the chirps of a cricket. Count them for 15 seconds and add 35. The sum will closely approximate the true temperature, because a cricket varies its rate of chirping with the temperature.

An *anemometer* measures wind speed. To make an anemometer, cross two sticks at right angles (figure 23.4) and fasten four lightweight cups or cones across them parallel to the ground. Paper or plastic cups can be used temporarily, but for more permanent cones, plug the ends of small funnels with tight-fitting pieces of cork or whittled wood, or make a paper pattern and cut the cones from flattened tin cans or other light metal and solder them together. Give them a coat or two of paint for protection, making one a contrasting color to make it easy to count the number of revolutions as they spin around.

Figure 23.2   Aneroid barometer with the dial pointing to rain.

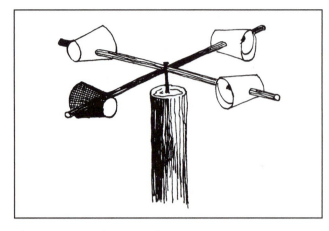

Figure 23.4   A homemade anemometer measures wind speed.

A camp weather station. (Photo by Joel Meier)

Mount the crossed sticks on a dowel, then make a hole in a pole deep enough to hold the dowel securely and large enough so that the dowel can turn freely. Insert the dowel into the pole using a pair of washers. Place the anemometer out in the open where even a slight breeze will turn it. To roughly estimate the wind speed in miles per hour, count the number of revolutions in 30 seconds and divide by 5.

Weather observations should be made early in the morning and about 12 hours later. Observations can be recorded on a form such as that found in figure 23.5. Keep in mind that practically no weather signs universally hold true for every area of the United States. Many factors such as the topography of the country and the presence of lakes, hills, and woods cause variations. If you study weather observations over a period of time, you and your campers can often detect a consistent pattern of causes and results.

In addition to weather forecasting via observation and measurement, there are countless proverbs that describe the weather. Some are based on superstition. Others, however, have value since they describe atmospheric conditions that actually "cause" the weather they are predicting. Some of the more reliable proverbs are contained in exhibit 23.1. Observable indicators of bad and fair weather are listed in exhibit 23.2. While no single indicator is infallible for predicting weather, such observations can be useful and fun for campers and staff.

Date	Rel. Hum.	Wind		Temp.	Clouds		Other Signs	Forecast	What It Was
		Dir.	Vel.		Type	Move-ment			

Figure 23.5   Form for recording weather data and predictions.

Exhibit 23.1

Weather Proverbs

- Red sky (or rainbow) in the morning, sailors take warning.
- Red sky (or rainbow) at night, sailor's delight.
- Evening red and morning gray, sets the traveler on his way; evening gray and morning red, brings down rain upon his head.
- A red sky has water in its eye.
- Rain before seven, clear before eleven. (Rain seldom lasts longer than five hours anyway.)
- When dew is on the grass, rain will never come to pass.
- When grass is dry at morning's light, look for rain before the night.
- When the stars begin to huddle, the earth will soon become a puddle.
- Sound traveling far and wide, a stormy day will betide.
- The higher the clouds, the finer the weather.
- Mackerel scales and mare's tails make lofty ships carry low sails.
- When the wind's in the south, the rain's in his mouth.
- When the smoke goes west, good weather is past. When the smoke goes east, good weather is next.
- The weather will clear when there is enough blue sky to make a pair of Dutchman's breeches.
- Ring around the moon, rain by noon, ring around the sun, rain before night is done.

Exhibit 23.2

Weather Indicators

Indicators of bad weather

- Rainbow in the morning
- Cows bedding down or standing in one corner of a field
- Wind lacking to moderate, and from southeast or east
- No dew at night
- Atmosphere muggy and sticky
- Temperature 70°F or above, especially if rising
- Falling barometer
- Smoke not rising straight up in the air
- Crickets, birds, and other noises seem extra loud
- Odors are especially noticeable
- Breeze causing underside of leaves to show
- Rapidly moving cirrus clouds, especially from the west
- Dark clouds gathering on the horizon to the west
- Stratus, nimbus, altostratus, cirrostratus, or cumulonimbus clouds
- Clouds moving in different directions at various heights
- Clouds becoming more numerous and nearer the earth
- Red or rosy morning sky
- Gray or dull sunset
- Insects are especially obnoxious and hang about screens, tents, etc
- Smoke drifts downward

Indicators of fair weather

- Rainbow in late afternoon or evening
- Gentle winds, especially from the west or northwest
- Heavy morning dew, fog, or frost
- Temperature below 70° F, especially if falling
- Steadily rising barometer
- Smoke rising straight up
- Cloudless skies or only clouds high in the sky
- Cumulus clouds or stationary cirrus clouds
- Night sky full of bright stars
- Stratocumulus, altocumulus, cirrocumulus, fractonimbus, fractostratus, or fractocumulus clouds
- Red sunset (sun goes down like a ball of fire)
- Spiders spin long, widespread webs and scurry busily over them

WEB RESOURCES

National Weather Service Lightning Safety (http://www.lightningsafety.noaa.gov/outdoors.htm)

NOAA's National Weather Service (http://www.weather.gov/)

Research and investigation experiences for middle school science students and teachers (http://www.oar.noaa.gov/k12/html/forecasting2.html)

Tips for forecasting the weather (http://eo.ucar.edu/webweather/forecasttips.html)

Weather Channel (http://www.weather.com)

Weather Concerns
- (http://www.noaa.gov/)
- (http://www.nols.edu/resources/research/pdfs/lightningsafetyguideline.pdf)

- (http://www.redcross.org/services/hss/tips/coldweather.html)
- (http://www.weather.com/safeside/)

Weather forecasting activities (http://weathereye.kgan.com/cadet/forecast/index.html)

Weather forecasting—online meteorology guide (http://ww2010.atmos.uiuc.edu/(Gh)/guides/mtr/fcst/home.rxml)

Weather safety (http://www.weather.com/safeside/)

Web weather for kids (http://eo.ucar.edu/webweather/)

24

Finding Your Way in the Outdoors

ampers or hikers often travel off the beaten path on trails or poorly constructed back roads with no signs to point the way. Much of the satisfaction gained from hiking and backpacking is the feeling that you are where others seldom go and seeing things others do not see. However, for such voyaging you will need to develop special skills, such as being able to find your way using a Global Positioning System (GPS) as well as a compass and *topographic* maps (often referred to as "topos" or "quads"). Many campers enjoy an activity known as *orienteering* in the woods. A popular new activity that also can be done at camp is *geocaching*.

Navigation Aids

GPS

The Global Positioning System is a space-based system of 24 satellites orbiting the earth at a very high altitude. The satellites send radio waves that are picked up by GPS receivers, providing location and time information. GPS receivers are able to determine time through decipherment of a code that is sent by both the satellite and the receiver at the same time. GPS units are commonly found in cars, but can also be hand-held units. The two primary ways to use a GPS receiver are to store longitude and latitude coordinates, called waypoints, when moving from one location to another, and to enter waypoints into the unit to obtain travel directions (Bourdeau, 2007).

Compass

Even if you and your campers have GPS receivers, you should also know a little bit about maps and compasses. Compasses come in several different types. How-

ever, compasses that you will use at camp usually have three main parts: a magnetic needle, a revolving compass housing, and a transparent base plate. Working together they make an efficient and highly practical instrument. The plastic base plate has a *direction-of-travel arrow* imprinted on it that points in the direction you want to go. The base also has a metric scale along one side and a scale in inches across one end for measuring distances on maps. The transparent base lets you see the map through the compass. Just above the base is a freely moveable circular *housing* containing a circle called the *azimuth circle*

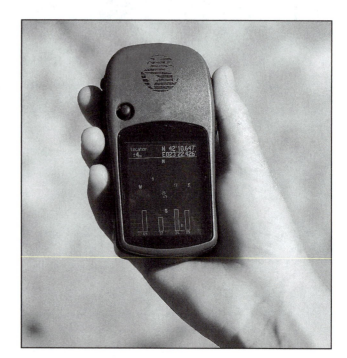

A hand-held GPS unit.

252

on which 360 degrees or *azimuths* are marked in a clockwise direction. The circle is divided into *quadrants* with N (north) at 0° or 360°, E (east) at 90°, S (south) at 180°, and W (west) at 270°. The letters for the quadrants and the degrees are engraved on the top of the plastic housing.

Printed inside the housing is a stationary *orienting arrow* that points to N (0° or 360°) and a *magnetic needle* that is mounted on a pin so that it moves freely. The end of the needle is painted red and is magnetized so that when you hold the compass level so the needle can move freely, it always points to magnetic north, no matter how you turn the compass.

Since the tip of the compass needle is magnetized, metal or steel will deflect it, resulting in an inaccurate reading. Therefore, avoid using the compass near metal such as a belt buckle, knife blade, hatchet, outboard motor, metal bridge, or telephone or power line.

To read directions from a compass, you must first *orient* it, or turn it so that the magnetic needle is aligned with north as printed on the dial. Turn the dial so that the orienting arrow (N) is pointing in the same direction as the direction-of-travel arrow. Hold the compass level about waist high so that the needle will swing freely. Now turn yourself around until the needle lies along the orienting arrow and the red end points to N (0° or 360°). You are now facing magnetic north. Your right shoulder is toward the east, south is behind you, and west is at your left shoulder.

Now, suppose you want to travel in a certain direction—let's say 60°. Orient your compass and set it by turning the dial to bring the figure 60 directly above the direction-of-travel arrow. Hold the compass level and turn yourself around until the red end of the needle is lined up with the orienting arrow and pointing to N on the dial. The direction-of-travel arrow is pointing in the direction you want to go. To take a *bearing* or *azimuth reading* on some distant object, point the direction-of-travel arrow toward it, and turn the dial until the needle lines up with the orienting arrow. Now read your bearing in degrees where the direction-of-travel arrow intersects the dial.

To follow a compass direction, pick out two conspicuous landmarks such as trees or rocks in line with the arrow and start out, picking out another landmark in line with the arrow as you approach the first so that you always have two landmarks to walk toward. This technique frees you from having to keep your eyes glued on the compass. Stop occasionally to recheck the compass bearing to make sure you are still on course.

Maps

A map is a vertical view of an area as it would appear from the air. Maps range from detailed printed ones to basic, hand-drawn sketch maps for guiding a person through relatively simple terrain.

The most useful maps for someone in the outdoors are topographic maps that are published by the United States Geological Survey (USGS). They are inexpensive and are excellent for anyone traveling on foot, on horseback, or by canoe. They give a graphic picture of what can be seen on a particular trip. Each of these maps covers a relatively small area in great detail. Contour lines indicate where hills are located and how steep and high they are (figure 24.1). Such maps show streams and may show canoe routes and places where it will be necessary to portage. Marshlands are indicated so that you can avoid camping near them and their mosquito inhabitants. Timber areas, valleys, and lakes are depicted, as well as "improvements" like houses and bridges. Topographic maps usually can be purchased in local sporting goods stores or map shops. You can find other places to purchase them on the Internet.

A map usually contains a *legend,* or summary of information, in the lower right-hand corner that includes such items as the following:

1. *Name* or *title* of the region depicted.
2. *Name of the person or firm* who made the map and *date* made. The date is important, particularly for maps of well-settled regions where construction and land use or disuse may entirely change the appearance of a locality within a few years.

Figure 24.1   Topographic map with contours.

3. *Compass direction.* Maps are ordinarily laid out with north at the top, but the particular contour shown or the shape of the area sometimes makes it more convenient to do otherwise. Most maps use two arrows to indicate true north and magnetic north, and the arrows are joined to form the angle of declination.

4. *A scale of distances.* A map is drawn to a certain *scale*, which is the proportional relationship between the distance as represented on the map and the actual distance over the ground. The scale may be given as a ratio or fraction, and usually also as a graphical scale or measuring bar, which is convenient because you can readily measure it off on paper for use in measuring distances between points on the map.

5. A *key* to the meaning of the various symbols used on the map (see figure 24.2).

Certain map symbols are in general use and enable one person to understand maps made by others. These symbols are of four types:

1. *Culture symbols*, or human-made features such as bridges, houses, and dams, are shown in black. However, red is used to emphasize important roads or to show urban areas.

2. *Relief symbols*, or relative elevations and depressions above or below sea level (hills and valleys), are shown in brown. Hills are indicated by *contour lines*. All points on a single contour line are the same elevation, or height, above sea level. Thus, if you walked along the line you would not go up or down. Contour lines are often arranged in groups of five with the fifth index line somewhat heavier and with the height printed along it. Each line indicates a rise or fall of a certain number of feet (from 5 to 250 feet, as stated in the map legend). Widely spaced lines indicate a gradual slope; those close together, a steep one. Lines falling practically on top of each other represent a cliff or steep mountainside. Contour lines spread widely over the countryside signify that the whole region is rolling. It may help you to better visualize the actual appearance of the land if you think of the contour lines as rings left by water that once covered the hill and slowly receded, leaving a ring at each stopping point.

3. *Water features* such as lakes or rivers are shown in blue.

4. *Vegetation symbols*, such as woods or crops, are shown in green, with black or blue overprints sometimes showing type.

Using a Map and Compass

Although skilled map readers may not need to use a compass for navigation, they should always have one with them and know how to use it. Compass skills may become important, especially if you become disoriented or caught in a situation where visibility is poor.

A typical compass features a magnetic needle, a revolving housing that contains the 360-degree azimuth circle, a transparent base plate, and a direction-of-travel arrow.

When using a map and a compass to plan a trip, first locate your present position and intended destination on the map. Study the symbols of what lies between and try to form a mental picture of the intervening terrain. Remember that the shortest route is not always the best since it may lead through difficult or even impassable terrain. Plan your route carefully, making appropriate *doglegs* around obstacles, and trace on the map or a sheet of paper the exact route you plan to follow.

To take an azimuth or bearing on the first leg of your trip, you must first orient your map by laying it flat on a table or the ground, placing your compass above it, and turning the map until the magnetic N–S lines you have drawn lie parallel to N–S as indicated by the needle on your compass. Now place the bottom of the base of your compass at your present location and rotate the base so that the direction-of-travel arrow lies parallel to the path of the first leg of your route. Read off the azimuth or bearing where the direction-of-travel arrow intersects the housing. Measure the length of the line, and using the distance scale on the map, estimate the length of the first leg. Determine the directions and distances of other legs in the same way and record the information on your map. Note which landmarks on the map you can use as check points as you follow the trail.

When you are ready to start out, place the direction-of-travel arrow at the degree reading of the first leg and orient your compass. Then place yourself directly behind the arrow, pick out two distinct landmarks ahead, and start toward them. Once the first leg has been completed, determine the new direction and pick out landmarks to walk toward as before.

Using similar principles, you can use the *triangulation method* to find out where you are on the map when out in the field. Pick out two visible distant landmarks that can also be located on the map. Orient the map, take a bearing on the two landmarks, and draw lines through them

BOUNDARIES

National	
State or territorial	
County or equivalent	
State forest, park, reservation, or monument and large county park	

BUILDINGS AND RELATED FEATURES

Building	
School; house of worship	
Well (other than water), windmill or wind generator	
Tanks	
Located or landmark object (feature as labeled)	
Campground	
Picnic area	

COASTAL FEATURES

Coral or rock reef	
Group of rocks, bare or awash	
Exposed wreck	

CONTOURS

Topographic

Index	
Intermediate	
Depression	

CONTROL DATA AND MONUMENTS

Horizontal control

With checked spot elevation	△ 1012

Vertical control

Third-order or better elevation, with tablet	BM ✕ 5280

GLACIERS AND PERMANENT SNOWFIELDS

Contours and limits	

MINES AND CAVES

Quarry or open pit mine	
Mine tunnel or cave entrance	

RAILROADS AND RELATED FEATURES

Standard guage railroad, single track	

RIVERS, LAKES, AND CANALS

Perennial stream	
Perennial river	
Intermittent stream	
Intermittent river	
Perennial lake/pond	
Intermittent lake/pond	
Dry lake/pond	
Wide wash	

ROADS AND RELATED FEATURES

Primary highway	
Secondary highway	
Light duty road, gravel*	
Trail	
Trailhead	

SUBMERGED AREAS AND BOGS

Marsh or swamp	
Wooded marsh or swamp	

TRANSMISSION LINES AND PIPELINES

Power transmission line; pole; tower	
Aboveground pipeline	
Underground pipeline	

VEGETATION

Woodland	
Shrubland	

Figure 24.2 **Common topographic map symbols.**

at these degrees. You are located at the point where the lines intersect.

You may want to have your campers make maps just for the fun of it as well as for the learning experience. They can make a rough sketch of a map or even make a map out of papier mâché. A person who draws or makes maps is known as a *cartographer.* Knowledge of mapmaking also allows you to plan and participate in many enjoyable orienteering games. Directions for making a map can be found at various places including books and on the Internet.

Do Not Get Lost

Studying brief treatises about GPS units, compasses, and maps will not make you an expert. You will need to practice many hours with the available tools. A miscalculation of just a short distance or a few degrees can have harrowing consequences. Always tell some responsible person at camp where you are going, the exact route you plan to take, who will be in the party, and when you expect to return.

Never start without your compass, and if possible, take along a detailed map of the region on which to mark your trail. Jotting down walking time as well as distances between various points is a good idea. Two essential things to do are to *look back* occasionally to see how things will look on your return and to *write things down* instead of relying on memory. A compass is not much use when you are lost.

Although some people claim to have a sixth sense of direction, experiments have shown that it simply is not true; even those who are experienced in the outdoors become disoriented when blindfolded and told to walk in a straight line. A person's seemingly uncanny ability to find his or her way without using a compass or map can probably be attributed to a highly developed habit of observation. Such people unconsciously note things like the position of the sun, the direction of prevailing winds, details about the terrain, and distinguishing landmarks along the way. Make a conscious effort to improve your observation skills.

If you are hiking in a group, stay together. You may want to give each member a whistle to use if he or she inadvertently becomes separated from the group. A whistle blast carries a long way through quiet woods.

If you realize that you are lost or stranded, do not panic. Stay calm and think back over past events to see if you can retrace your route. Chances are that you are not far off the route and no real emergency exists. Climb a tree or hill to get a long view and to try to spot some landmark that is familiar or that can be located on your map. Try to remember the exact route traveled since you were last oriented.

If none of these actions help, it may be best to just sit down, conserve energy, and wait for someone to find you. If conditions are suitable, it might even be appropriate to build a fire. This will keep campers busy with a familiar activity and help ease any worries, plus the smoke may also attract attention. Camp staff will either come looking for you, or perhaps alert law enforcement officers if they are not sure exactly where you are. The chances are that you will be found within a few hours.

Even if your group has to stay out overnight, the experience will probably not amount to much more than an inconvenience. If you have brought the minimum essentials including a knife, matches, and flashlight, you should be fine for a short time. If night is approaching or a potential storm is brewing, the first priority is to find the best shelter possible. Clear a space and build a fire for warmth. Remember that even warm days are often followed by uncomfortably cool nights, so have campers gather enough wood to keep the fire going as long as needed. If you leave the site for any reason, such as to look for water or more fuel, be sure to mark the path so that you can readily find your way back.

If it is fairly early in the day and you decide to look for a way out, keep in mind that every unguided person tends to travel in a more or less circular path, usually to the right but occasionally to the left. Unless precautions are taken to prevent it, you will probably travel in a wide circle that will eventually bring you back very close to where you started. It is best to choose one direction, then pick out two landmarks in line with it and start walking. Pick out another landmark as you near the first, as previously discussed. If you have a compass, use it to maintain a consistent direction of travel.

It is wise to mark your path so that you can return if you wish and so searchers will know the trail. Tear off strips of cloth and tie them at eye level at intervals or use one of the methods for marking a trail discussed later on in this chapter. A railroad track, a telephone or electric line, or a wall or fence will eventually lead you to civilization. Also, it is usually best to travel downhill along water drainages rather than uphill. Listen for human sounds and look for signs of smoke.

Placing three items together has long been recognized as a signal of danger or distress. Three rocks placed on top of each other, three clumps of grass tied in knots, three blazes on trees, three smudge fires, three whistle blasts, or three gunshots are examples. Note that the Morse code applies this principle in its call for help, SOS, which consists of three dots, three dashes, and three dots.

Telling Directions without a Compass

Using Mother Nature's signs to tell directions is not very dependable or consumes too much time to be practicable. However, the following methods are helpful, although they should not be considered as routine substitutions for the compass that should always be a part of your standard gear.

The stars are the oldest and most faithful guides to direction. The *North Star* (also called *Polaris* or the *Pole Star)*, is an accurate guide to direction because it never varies more than one degree from true north no matter where you are in the United States. You can locate the North Star by finding the *Big Dipper* and the *Little Dipper* in the sky. The two stars opposite the handle that form the front edge of the Big Dipper are known as the *pointers* because they point directly to the North Star in the tip of the Little Dipper's handle. Although the Big Dipper circles around the Little Dipper every 24 hours, the pointers never cease to point to the North Star. The bowls of the two Dippers constantly face so that they always seem to be pouring into each other.

To navigate during daylight hours when the stars are not visible, you might want to make a *shadow* compass. To make a shadow compass, select a place where the sun is shining and drive a stick (2 to 5 feet tall) into the ground. Place a stone or other object at the tip of the stick's shadow. Wait at least 15 minutes, or until the shadow has moved to a new location, and again mark its tip. If you have time, do this several times. Connect the tip marks with a line; it will lie roughly true east–west with the first mark pointing west. A line exactly perpendicular to the east–west line will consequently lie approximately north–south. This method is most accurate around noon and decreases in accuracy the further away from noon the time. When your own shadow is so short that you can almost step on the tip of it, you can be sure it is about noon.

Way-Finding Games

Many activities can be done at camp to teach the use of GPS units, maps, and compasses. Many more examples are available on the Internet, but here are some possible ideas.

Map Symbol Relay

Teams of 4 to 10 players line up in relay formation. Each team has a set of cards bearing map symbols stacked in front of it and a similar set with names of what the symbols stand for spread out nearby. On signal, the first player on each team runs forward, picks up the top symbol card, places it on top of its matching name card and runs back to touch off the second player who repeats with the second symbol card, and so forth. The first team placing all of its cards correctly wins.

Compass Change

One player is "it" while eight others distribute themselves around the circle in the positions of the different directions (N, NE, E, and so forth). A prominent sign marks N on the circle but no other positions are marked. "It" calls out two directions (for example, NE and S) and these two players try to change places before "it" can slip into one of their positions. The person left out is "it" and the game continues.

Beeline or Crow-Flight Hike

Pick out a compass bearing and follow it as closely as possible on a map or outdoors to find out where it will lead and make a note of what you see along the way.

Buried Treasure

Give each person a card with a set of directions, such as "Go 25° for 75 yards, then 120° for 100 yards, and 75° for 150 yards." Each participant uses a compass and estimates distances to try to find the correct destination. Sets of directions can vary as long as all participants end up at the same spot. The person most nearly correct wins the buried treasure. This can also be a "trip" over a topographic map.

Progressive Supper Hike

Half of the group takes food and equipment for a cookout and lays a trail, distributing themselves at four spots along the trail. Campers at the first spot prepare the first course, the second the main dish, the third dessert, and the fourth presents the evening program. The rest of the group follows the trail with their eating utensils and enjoys a progressive supper.

Orienteering

Orienteering is a sport that originated in Sweden many years ago and still flourishes there, providing fun, exercise, and valuable experience in navigating with map and compass. Orienteering is now an international sport. Many variations accommodate everyone from the beginner to the expert.

In the most common type of competition, called *point-to-point*, the object is to cover an unfamiliar route in the shortest possible time using a map and compass and good judgment to pick out the best way. The route can cover from 1/2 to 10 miles and includes at least five or more landmarks or *control points* that are each prominently marked in the center by a 10″ × 10″ nylon bag so that they are clearly visible to anyone coming reasonably near. Individuals or pairs start out at several minute intervals, trying to find each of the control points and complete the course in the least possible time. Each is given a clue sheet describing the controls and is allowed a certain amount of time to study the clues and the map to determine the best way to go. To ensure that a contestant passes each control point, a hole-punch or marking device is attached to the control bag for marking a card carried by the contestant.

Point-to-point or cross-country orienteering, as just described, is the classic form of orienteering. Each participant must visit a set number of controls or checkpoints in a prescribed order, and winners are determined strictly on a time basis, providing they have completed the course properly. This is the form of orienteering used in all major championships.

The object in *score* orienteering is to accumulate points by visiting as many control points as possible in the time allowed. The event area contains more controls than could possibly be visited within the allotted time. Control points nearest the start have a low point value while controls farther away or which require a higher degree of skill to find carry a higher point value.

In cross-country orienteering the control points are given out at the start and route choice is left to the individual. However, in *line* orienteering, no control locations are given to the competitor. Instead, the exact route is shown on a master map and the individual must copy the route onto his or her own map and then follow the course. The winner is determined on the basis of time and mapping accuracy. When the participant finds a control point along the route, the exact spot must be marked on the individual's map.

In *route* orienteering, speed and accuracy again determine the winner. Route orienteering is actually a simpler version of line orienteering, since participants simply follow a course already marked out on the ground with flags or some similar device. The location of the control markers must be marked on the map when they are found.

Team and relay orienteering involves teams of two to six members. Everyone starts and finishes at the same place, but each individual in succession must complete the course. An alternative to this is to have all team members compete simultaneously over different sections of the course. In both cases the combined times of all persons on each team are added together to determine the outcome.

Geocaching

Geocaching is a game played by people who use GPS units to participate in a scavenger hunt. A geocacher can place a geocache anywhere in the world, pinpoint its location using GPS technology, and then share the geocache's existence and location online. Anyone with a GPS device can then try to locate the geocache. Geocaches vary in size and appearance. A basic geocache is a container that holds a logbook. Larger geocaches might contain a variety of items. Participants who take an item from a geocache must leave something of equal or greater value for the next person to find. The general idea for camp would be to place caches with interesting artifacts/rewards around the camp property, marking the coordinates for each. The participants then use a GPS unit to find the cache/reward, and replace it with something else for another group to find. Much information about geocaching can be found on the Internet.

REFERENCES

Bourdeau, V. (2007, Nov/Dec). Teaching GPS: Technology in nature education programs. *Camping Magazine, 80*(6), 48–52.

WEB RESOURCES

Geocaching
Geocaching (http://www.geocaching.com)
Geocaching with Kids (http://eduscapes.com/geocaching/kids.htm)
Geocaching—Garmin Style (http://www8.garmin.com/outdoor/geocaching/)

Navigation with Map and Compass
Kjetil Kjernsmo's Illustrated Guide on How to Use a Compass (www.learn-orienteering.org/old/) provides directions on how to use a compass.
Reading Topographic Maps (www.map-reading.com)
(http://www.geocities.com/Yosemite/Falls/9200/navigation_map_compass.html)
Search and Rescue Service of British Columbia—Map and Compass (http://www.sarbc.org/m&c.html)
The Compass Store (www.thecompassstore.com) offers advice on how to use a map and compass, and answers frequently asked questions.

Use a Compass (www.buckskin.org/Resources/Outdoor/compass1.htm) provides directions on how to use a compass.
USGS Map and Compass (http://rmmcweb.cr.usgs.gov/outreach/gps.html)
USGS—Finding your way with map and compass (http://egsc.usgs.gov/isb/pubs/factsheets/fs03501.html)
Web Skills Map Basics (http://www.mscd.edu/~cra/webskills/map_instruction/WS_map_instruction.htm#Top)
Wilderness Backpacking (www.wilderness-backpacking.com) offers wilderness tips, navigation advice.

Orienteering Skills
(www.us.orienteering.org/OYoung/Skills.html) provides an overview of orienteering.
(http://www.orienteering.org)
(http://www.navigationgames.com/)
(www.4orienteering.com) discusses the history of orienteering, skills needed, and general overview.
International Orienteering Federation (http://www.orienteering.org/i3/index.php?/iof2006)

25

Hiking and Trail Skills

iking is a popular activity for many people—including campers. Thousands of miles of footpaths and trails exist and more are being developed each day. Many hiking trails now exist in urban areas. Often, resident camps have opportunities on their property for hiking or have public or private lands available nearby. This chapter introduces basic information anyone needs to know before heading into the backcountry or nearby trails.

Care for Your Feet

Nothing is as important to a hiker as footwear. Blisters or foot pain will quickly dampen enthusiasm for a hike. Sturdy footwear such as athletic shoes or boots is recommended for many types of hiking.

Hundreds of brands and models of boots are available. One of the myths about hiking boots is that they must be heavy monstrosities in order to hold up under rugged conditions in the woods and mountains. Although heavy boots might be needed in some cases, many people wear running shoes and lightweight boots for hiking. New varieties of trail running shoes and lightweight hiking boots on the market may be quite satisfactory for counselors as well as campers. To meet the demand for these shoes, bootmakers are trimming their models while running shoe manufacturers are coming out with reinforced shoes that work well for day hiking and even for extended trips in moderate terrain. In addition to shoes made of leather, lightweight synthetic materials such as nylon, Gore-Tex, Klimate, and Thinsulate are used for added comfort and weight reduction.

Boots or shoes that reach above the ankles with cleated or corrugated soles are recommended. Well-fit-

A sturdy boot that reaches above the ankles is recommended for many types of hiking.

ting, sturdy work boots with cleats or corrugated soles give good support and work well for most people. *Trail boots* are tougher and stiffer and preferable for the hiker who follows longer trails or travels cross-country, where running streams or rock slides will occasionally be crossed. *Mountaineer boots* are heavier and more rugged and have thicker soles. Although they are too heavy and stiff for general hiking, they may be desirable for expeditions into heavy brush or where the user is likely to encounter rocks, ice, or snow. For those who will be sloshing around in very wet areas, there are boots with rubber bottoms and leather tops.

Soles should be sufficiently thick and hard to protect the feet on rough terrain and are usually made of corrugated synthetic rubber that provides good traction. The most rugged soles have lugs that are strategically placed for traction, stability, slip resistance, braking, and kick off. Softer soles offer less protection from rough surfaces

Boots with corrugated rubber soles provide good traction.

Lightweight, flexible trail shoes are a good option for day hiking in easy to moderate terrain.

and wear out rapidly. Further, boots should have as few seams as possible because they are difficult to waterproof; any seams should be double or triple stitched. Boots that reach just above the ankle give good support and protection from rough underbrush and outcroppings along the path. Retail outlets that sell outdoor gear can advise you on the best boots to fit your situation.

Boots should be suitable for the type of travel you and your campers will undertake and should fit well. As a general rule, the more rugged the travel conditions, the sturdier the boot should be. However, choose the lightest shoe that will do the job—each pound carried on your foot is estimated to be equivalent to 5 pounds carried on your back. A fairly light, flexible shoe that fits comfortably and is reasonably priced will, for ordinary purposes, give all the protection the average hiker needs. The important thing is to choose what's right for you and the situation.

Getting good hiking boots for children is sometimes difficult. However, there are now strong work shoes and athletic shoes widely available, and manufacturers now make regular hiking boots in children's sizes. One drawback to buying an expensive pair is that children's feet grow so rapidly that the shoes are likely to be outgrown before they are worn out. Some camps, as well as outfitters, have found a solution by keeping an assortment of hiking footwear on hand to rent or make available.

A good pair of boots represents a sizeable investment, but if properly cared for, they will serve you well for many years. The manufacturer of boots will generally tell you the best way to care for them, or you can find that information on the Internet.

In addition to boots, a hiker should also consider the socks that will be worn. Socks absorb perspiration as well

as moisture from the outside, cushion the feet, and minimize the blister-causing friction between boot and foot. A "wick dry" sock that wicks perspiration from the feet is recommended. Cotton socks are not recommended since they absorb and hold moisture. On a trip, carry several pairs of socks and change to fresh ones at rest stops or at noon, fastening the soiled pair to the outside of your pack to dry.

Loading and Carrying a Pack

Day packs and backpacks allow hikers the freedom and independence to carry gear needed for a trip, whether it lasts a day or more than a week. The pack should be loaded with concern for the weight to carry as well as how to carry it properly. No one has yet been able to accurately measure the maximum amount of weight an individual should carry for efficiency and enjoyment. However, a common rule of thumb is to carry no more than one-third of your body weight if you are in good physical condition, and no more than one-fourth if you are not. A more realistic weight range is for the pack to weigh no more than one-fifth of a person's body weight.

An additional consideration pertains to how the pack is actually loaded. To align the heavy items more closely with your center of gravity and to keep the pack from pulling back on your shoulders, it is generally best to place the heavy objects near the top of the pack and close to your back. You will also want to keep items that are frequently needed, such as maps, rain gear, and snacks, where you can get to them. If you are packing for an extended trip, many good suggestions on the gear to carry and the best way to pack can be found on the Internet.

A realistic weight range for a backpack is between one-fifth and one-fourth of your body weight.

Hiking Techniques

Before starting out on a hike, make any last-minute clothing adjustments. You can expect your body temperature to rise as you exert yourself. Start a little on the cool side since within a few minutes of going along the trail you will feel warmer. This practice eliminates the need for frequent group stops, especially after only a short time.

Remember that perspiration-soaked clothing is just as dangerous as rain-soaked clothing insofar as hypothermia is concerned. This is an important reason for removing outer garments before overheating occurs. When on a trip of any length, always carry a change of clothing with you and slip into it immediately if you get wet.

When hiking, relax your whole body and swing the arms and legs along rhythmically as you walk. Keep your body erect or, if carrying a pack, lean forward slightly from the hips to counterbalance it. The length of stride and walking tempo should be fairly consistent on flat ground. That same tempo should be maintained when going up or down hills, although the stride must be adjusted with a shorter stride when going uphill and a longer one when going down.

Do not make a hike a speed or endurance contest—what you do and see along the way is as important as how far you go. Like a machine, your body works most efficiently at a moderate rate of speed, so establish a steady pace that can be maintained indefinitely by everyone in the group. Three miles an hour is a good speed to maintain for most people and this pace eats up miles steadily without causing undue fatigue. Whatever the pace, it should allow you to have a controlled, rhythmic movement that keeps the heartbeat and breathing rate even.

You should rest a few minutes every hour or so on a long hike, but avoid staying immobile too long or you risk having your leg and back muscles stiffen. Your first stop should actually be within the first half hour so hikers can make adjustments without feeling they are holding up the group.

Group Considerations

When hiking with campers, one counselor should be near the front of the line to act as a pacesetter, striking a moderate pace that all can maintain comfortably. A second counselor should bring up the rear. Everyone else should stay within viewing distance of the person in front of and behind them. This allows each person to set his or her own rhythm and length of stride.

The most successful hiking groups are composed of individuals of approximately the same age and physical stamina so that the strong do not have to wait for the slow, and the slow are not overworked in an effort to keep up. Even when the group is moderately well matched, some may tend to fall behind. This problem often can be remedied by putting slower walkers near or at the front of the line.

Thirst often results from a drying out of the tissues lining the mouth rather than from general dehydration. Consequently, this kind of thirst can be relieved by rinsing the mouth instead of gulping down large quantities of liquid. Keep in mind however that hiking, like any other form of vigorous exercise, demands constant replenishment of liquid to the body. Thus, you should make a practice of encouraging your campers to consume sufficient quantities of water or other liquids at regular intervals along the way, even if they do not feel thirsty.

Each person in the group will usually want to carry a full canteen or water bottle unless there are safe water sources on the way, or unless you plan to purify your water in some way. You can refill it at a suitable stream, if needed, and purify the water in whatever way you can.

Vigorous hiking soon uses up the fuel readily available in the blood stream, so it is a good idea to take along a snack such as a plastic bag of the appropriately named *trail mix* to eat along the way. Although the variation and recipes for this are endless, a popular blend consists of salted peanuts and mixed nuts, raisins, and small candies such as M&Ms. Any other mixture of nuts, seeds, dried

Don't make a hike a speed or endurance contest, since what you do and see along the way is as important as how far you go.

fruits, and granola cereal is a good choice. Such a mixture will furnish a good balance of protein, carbohydrates, and fats that will keep a hiker going throughout the day.

Finding your way on a designated trail is usually not a problem. However, there are times when even well-marked paths may tend to disappear, especially when they lead into meadows, marshy areas, snowy areas, downed timber, or rock slabs. If you have difficulty locating where the trail resumes, the best procedure is to establish a search pattern and then have your group fan out to look for signs of the trail. Keep everyone within hearing distance during the search and also establish a time limit for everyone to return in case the trail is not located. Chances are you will soon find the lost route and be on your way again.

If your party is traveling cross-country or off the trails, additional knowledge is needed beyond simple map and compass techniques. To determine the best route to take, you must study the terrain and elevation changes and then travel in areas that have gradual slopes. This prevents unnecessary gain or loss in elevation and expenditure of valuable energy. Also keep in mind that traveling on ridge tops is usually easier than valley floors, which may be thick with vegetation, downed timber, and other hazards.

Each situation is different and consideration must be given to such factors as the type of ground cover and your distance from drinking water. Sometimes choosing a longer route with easy going is better than a shorter route with potential problems. Whatever you do, keep as many route options open for as long as possible before committing yourself to any of them. You can always alter your plans if the going gets too rough.

Time/distance estimating may be a useful tool on long hikes. Experienced backpackers come to know their hiking speed. Most allow about one hour for every 3 miles traveled on flat terrain and they add an additional hour for every 1,000 feet of steep ascent or descent. To apply this technique to a hypothetical example, assume your map shows that there are 5 miles of trail to the next campsite. The contour lines on the map also show that the trail to the camp climbs 2,000 feet and then descends 1,000 feet. The formula reveals that it will take your group 4 hours and 40 minutes to reach the camp (5 miles = 1 hour and 40 minutes + 3,000 feet of ascent and descent = 3 more hours). Depending on the physical condition and age of your party, however, you may need to adjust these figures slightly. Be sure to allow time for rest stops and lunch breaks.

Hiking Etiquette

When hiking, some common courtesies should be extended to other people and to the property of others. For example, respect "no trespassing" signs. Close gates behind you if they were found that way and avoid climbing fences, since the wear and tear may inflict permanent damage. Do not walk across cultivated fields—stay close to the edges where no crops have been planted. Pick fruit or flowers only when given express permission to do so.

As a common courtesy to resource managers and property owners, always respect their rules and regulations. For example, avoid cutting corners on the trail. Similarly, picking up and carrying out others' litter will help to maintain a clean landscape and will set a good example for others to follow.

When meeting other parties on a trail, those coming downhill should have the right of way and your group should step aside and let them pass. If going the same way as a faster group, you should always let the faster hikers go by.

Groups on horseback or with pack animals should be given plenty of room. To avoid exciting the animals, your party should move to the downhill side of the trail, stand still, and minimize loud noises or voices.

Horses, mules, llamas, and alpacas have individual temperaments and moods. They can be unpredictable. Consequently, your unexpected appearance, sudden movement, or loud voice can put these animals on alert and perhaps cause them to panic and bolt. The problem can be intensified when encountering a string of pack animals or a group of inexperienced horseback riders. The effect could be serious as each animal successively reacts to the fear of the adjacent one. In the worst case, the animals could dump their riders or gear, break tack, hurt people or themselves, and run away.

Additional guidelines concerning trails that might be used by both people and animals are presented in exhibit 25.1.

Exhibit 25.1

Guidelines for Hikers Encountering Trail Animals

- Stop immediately upon seeing the animals and be sure the riders are aware of your presence. If necessary, advise the lead rider of your presence in a quiet voice.

- Ask and wait for instructions from the packer or leader. While waiting, remain still. Don't kick at the ground impatiently or make sudden movements. Horses can sense your energy and respond best to calmness.

- Respond as requested. The leader is in a better position than you to judge what will be safest considering the situation and animals at hand. Often you will be asked to move 10 to 15 feet off the trail, usually to the downhill side, as the animals would be easier to control if they were to spook uphill and away from you.

- Watch for signs that the animals are nervous and be prepared to move if necessary. Warning signs that a horse or mule exhibits when anxious or excited can be any of the following: ears lying back, tail swishing hard or held tightly to buttocks, body tense, dancing around or rearing, feet rapidly pawing the ground, teeth chomping the bit, head thrown around, eyes rolling, or loud snorting.

- Move slowly back on the trail only after the string has completely passed you and is down the trail.

Low and Minimum Impact Hiking and Camping Techniques

Those who hike or backpack generally want to find solitude and be in close contact with the natural environ-

ment. As a result, the less other groups and their impact on the land are seen, the better the experience will be for everyone. Unfortunately, inexperienced young people and many adults have little awareness of the adverse impact they may have on such vulnerable ecological systems as those found in the backwoods or wildlands. Consequently, as is mentioned throughout this text, camp counselors and trip leaders must adopt and then demonstrate a low-impact camping ethic that is based on proper ecological attitudes toward the natural environment. Everyone should respect the fragility of wild areas and must make a personal commitment to treat these areas with care.

The goal of every hiker or backpacker should be to practice minimum-impact camping by leaving the fewest traces of his or her presence as possible, no matter how far or where the hiker travels. Those individuals who are truly skilled in the ways of the outdoors never leave signs such as aluminum foil, cut branches, scarred trees, fire rings, or anything else other than a few blades of bent grass to show where they have been. Everything they carry into the wilderness they also carry out. The following are additional environmental practices that should be considered if the purpose of your hike is to set up a campsite:

1. To protect the scenic view and to prevent pollution, camps should be at least 250 feet from water and 100 feet from a trail, unless an established campsite is available.

2. No permanent structures should be built in the campsite and trenching of tents should not be done.

3. Using green boughs for a bed is obsolete. Keep the campsite as primitive and natural as possible.

4. Use established camps whenever possible rather than destroy the ground cover in a new area. If you come across an undesignated campsite that shows scars from overuse, find an alternative site to bed down.

5. When selecting a campsite, look for a sturdy or rocky spot rather than camp on lush but delicate soils of meadows or streamsides. Use areas that are covered with sand, fallen tree needles or leaves, and be sure the area is on high elevation and dry.

6. Cook with a stove if at all possible and avoid having a campfire unless absolutely necessary. If a fire is used, build it in a shallow pit dug in the earth in an appropriate, safe place. Set the turf aside and keep it moist so that it can be replaced prior to breaking camp. Scatter any fireplace stones and spread the extra wood around the area so no signs of a fire remain.

7. Do not build big or unnecessary fires. Use only fallen timber since even the standing dead trees are part of the natural scene. If there is no wood on the ground, then the area cannot produce enough wood for people to burn, so use a stove. Do not chop down trees or remove dead branches unless absolutely necessary. You do not need to carry an axe.

8. Garbage should be packed out. Do not throw wastes such as aluminum foil into a fire since the aluminum will remain behind for many years without decomposing.

9. Picking flowers causes unnecessary damage in timberline and alpine tundra regions since these areas are delicate and the ecological systems are easily upset.

10. Stay on existing trails and hike in single file to avoid creating multiple lanes. Always avoid cutting across switchbacks even though it may save time and energy. Switchbacks are graded to prevent erosion and cutting across them only increases the problem.

11. Pick up any litter along the route. Have one pocket of your pack available for trash, or carry a plastic bag for this purpose.

12. When traveling cross-country or off the trail, the group should spread out rather than follow one another. A group of people tramping in a row can crush fragile plant tissues beyond recovery and create channels for erosion.

13. Limit your group size to ten or less to minimize your impact. Also be cognizant of the noise your group generates in order to avoid disturbing other campers or wildlife.

These are just a few strategies that can be done to reduce our impact on the land. Many more ideas could be added to the list but, in the final analysis, what is really necessary is the use of common sense.

Hiking Variations for Additional Fun

Even old familiar trails can take on renewed interest when there is a definite purpose for following them. Usually leaders have a certain objective or destination in mind, but hikers should not be in such a hurry that there is not time to stop for the unusual. Exhibit 25.2 lists several possible hiking variations that can add interest to

---

Exhibit 25.2

Hiking Variations

1. **Heads and tails hike.** Flip a coin at each fork in the road to determine whether to turn right or left.

2. **Carefree hike.** Hike to some interesting or beautiful spot to cook an outdoor meal, hold a program, sing, or play nature games.

3. **Breakfast hike.** Go to a good vantage point to watch the sun rise and cook breakfast. Start at daybreak if you want to see and hear the birds at their best.

4. **Star hike.** Go to a hill on a clear evening to study the stars and their legends. Take sleeping gear and stay overnight.

5. **Fishing trip.** Hike out to fish in a nearby stream or lake to fish. Take a lunch to supplement the fresh fish you hope to catch.

6. **Historical hike.** Brief yourself by reading and consulting others about nearby historical spots, then hike out to visit them.

7. **Moonlight hike.** Walk an established trail to note nature's completely different night life.

8. **Camera hike.** See who captures the most interesting photographs along the way.

9. **Nature hike.** Give each hiker a list of nature specimens (flowers, leaves, animals, or insects) to collect or identify, or see who can collect the most interesting pieces of driftwood, sea shells, or other items to use in the craft shop or add to the nature display. Make sure you consider the ecology of your area before coming up with your list.

10. **Rain hike.** Waterproof yourselves completely and splash along, watching how animals and plants behave in the rain.

11. **Creek or rivers hike.** Follow a creek or river to its origin or mouth.

12. **Overnight hike.** Find a good place to spend the night; cook breakfast and return to camp.

13. **Sealed orders hike.** Give the group a set of sealed directions with a new envelope to open at each landmark along the way, or distribute them along the route so the group will find a new set of directions as soon as they have successfully followed the old. Give instructions in compass points and distances such as "Go 50 paces at 75° and look under the three rocks piled below the big pin oak tree; then go straight E and look inside the big hollow oak tree off at the left." For variety, give clues in rhymes, riddles, or codes. Make the clues challenging but not so difficult as to discourage the campers. A group is best limited to five or six.

14. **Hold the front.** The participants draw for positions in line and arrange themselves in single file. The object is to get and maintain the head position. As they hike along, the counselor picks out some nature specimen and asks the lead hiker to identify it. If the person cannot do so, each person behind is in turn given a chance to try. The first to succeed advances to the head of the line. The counselor then asks a question of the person behind the one who has just advanced and the question is repeated down the line as before until someone answers it correctly and advances up ahead of the one who first missed it. The winner is the person at the head of the line when the game ends.

15. **Bus hike.** Ride out by bus or camp vehicle and hike back or let the vehicle meet you at the halfway point on your return. This gives you a chance to venture farther from camp.

16. **"What is it?" hike.** Give each member a list of objects that might be seen along the way such as a particular kind of bird, tree, moss, or flower. Assign points to each object according to its rarity. The hiker who first sees and correctly identifies an item on the list scores the specified number of points.

normal outings. No matter what kind of hike you take, do not let it become merely a "walk," or you will end up with a group of bored, restless campers on your hands. Some of the activities in exhibit 25.2 add additional interest to a regular hike. You must, of course, adapt your methods to the age of the group. *Plan* your hike, no matter how short it is. You can also meet as a group to decide where to go, what to do, what to wear and what equipment to take, how to pack it, and how to divide up the jobs on the way. Returning by a different route is always more interesting.

WEB RESOURCES

Hiking

American Hiking Association (www.americanhiking.org) includes safety tips; advice on preparation, gear, and clothing; and discusses outdoor skills.

Day hiking (www.dayhiker.com) provides tips, general information.

Hiking basics (www.abc-of-hiking.com) includes basic techniques, skills, equipment, trails, safety and first aid.

Hiking boots (http://www.abc-of-hiking.com/hiking-boots/hiking-boot-features.asp)

Backpacking

(http://backpacking-gear.suite101.com/article.cfm/gear_care_hiking_boots)

(http://www.thebackpacker.com/)

(www.hikingandbackpacking.com)

(http://www.rei.com/expertadvice)

Leave No Trace (http://www.lnt.org/)

PRINT RESOURCES

ACA. (2000, May/June). Take a hike. *Camping Magazine, 73*(3). Includes activity ideas for meaningful hikes.

Burek, T. (2005, July/Aug). The nature of trailside discovery. *Camping Magazine, 78*(4). Includes a description of the Trailside Discovery Program and stewardship.

O'Bannon, A. (2001). *Backpackin' book: Traveling and camping skills for a wilderness environment!* Helena, MT: Falcon Publishing.

26

Using a Knife, Axe, and Other Tools

Before discussing knives, axes, and other tools, good camping ethics must be acknowledged. Out of necessity, the old frontier ethic of the pioneers and early campers in North America was to subdue nature and civilize the wilderness. In earlier times natural resources seemed unlimited and their consumption was not a concern. Camping in those days was a matter of survival rather than recreation. This same attitude should NOT exist today. Teaching campers to be aware of and sensitive to the environment is paramount. This awareness will lead to responsible behavior. The minimum impact philosophy must be emphasized when teaching about using knives, axes, and other camp tools. The days when trees could be carved up or chopped down are long past. Campers should be aware of environmental impact before they are allowed to handle camp tools.

As a counselor, you should also be aware of when tools can be appropriately used and when they may not be necessary in a camp program. Some day camps, for example, may not allow knives on the property.

The Camp Knife

Knives were an important tool of the pioneers, and campers engaged in outdoor living will find them equally important. The tool is useful for performing many camp chores and for making utilitarian items such as fuzz sticks to start a stubborn fire, handy gadgets to use around the campsite, and decorative articles such as lapel pins. Young children may lack the hand-eye coordination necessary to use a knife skillfully and safely, but older girls and boys (age 11 years and up) can become quite adept when properly taught.

A pocketknife with multipurpose blades such as a Boy or Girl Scout knife or Swiss Army knife is usually best for general camp use. It probably will have a cutting blade, a combination screwdriver and bottle opener, an awl or reamer for making holes in leather and other materials, and a can opener. Whatever model is chosen, it should be sturdy and fit well in the user's hand. A knife with a bright-colored handle is easier to find if mislaid or dropped on the ground.

Caring for a Knife

A knife should be treated like the valuable tool it is. Wipe the blade off after each use and never put it away wet. Remove any rust or stains with fine steel wool,

A pocketknife with multipurpose blades is usually best for general camp use.

scouring powder, or dampened ashes from your campfire, and occasionally put a drop of oil on the spring and blade joints. Never carelessly leave a knife lying out. Stow it away in a safe place or keep it in a pocket or anchored to the belt or pants by a chain or strong cord long enough to permit it to be used without detaching.

To open the blade on a pocketknife, hold the knife in one hand, insert your other thumbnail in the notch in the blade, and pull it open. Never allow the fingers on your hand to rest across the blade slot at any time in case the strong spring snaps the blade shut on them with disastrous results. To close the blade, again hold the knife in your hand and push the back of the blade with your other hand, being careful not to place your fingers across the blade slot.

When a knife loses its sharpness, use a file to rough-shape it. An *oilstone* or *Carborundum stone* (*whetstone*) is used for the fine edge. The latter is more convenient since water is applied instead of oil to lubricate it to reduce friction and avoid overheating the blade. These stones usually have a coarse side for preliminary fast grinding and a fine one for putting on the finishing touches (*honing* the blade). Remember that a sharp knife is safer to use because it is more likely to do what the user wants it to do. Test the sharpness of the blade by trying to cut a sheet of paper held between your thumb and forefinger. If the blade is really sharp, it will sever the paper cleanly and easily. If not, repeat the whole sharpening process. Campers should take pride in always keeping their knives sharp and should observe the unwritten law of never lending or borrowing a knife.

Using a Knife

Campers can practice whittling on a bar of soap (save the shavings to use later) or a piece of soft wood such as basswood or white pine. Remember that a knife is potentially dangerous and should never be used carelessly. Always have the campers direct their strokes so they cannot cut themselves or anyone else if the knife should slip. Keep the thumb and fingers around the handle and never on the back of the blade where the blade could close on fingers.

Cut with a sliding stroke *straight* down the wood and away from you. Never use diagonal strokes that may carry the blade off the wood. Take your time, and work slowly and deliberately. Haste, carelessness, and overconfidence result in accidents.

A knife should be closed whenever moving about, even for a few steps. Serious accidents have occurred from tripping while carrying an open knife. When passing a knife to someone else, close it or hand it to them handle first.

Axes

The need for axes in a camp has often been overplayed. They do serve their purpose when actually needed, but many times they should be left at home. If a fire needs to be built, it can usually be made using small dead branches on the ground or fallen trees that can be broken and used for firewood. However, since the axe does serve a purpose in some cases, campers should learn how to use it properly.

There are two basic types of axes. The *double-bitted axe* is usually full size and has a bite or blade (cutting edge) on each side of the head. One edge is usually ground thin and sharp for felling trees while the other is left thicker and stronger for splitting wood. This type of axe is attributed to that legendary hero of the North woods, Paul Bunyan. The champions of the double-bitted axe claim that it is better-balanced and easier to handle than the single-bladed axe, called a *pole axe*. However, it has little if any place in the usual organized camp since it is too dangerous for anyone but a mature and experienced person to use.

The double-bitted axe has a bite or blade (cutting edge) on each side of the head.

The head of a pole axe has an edge on one side and a flattened area called the *pole* or *poll* on the other (see figure 26.1). The flattened area can be used as a hammer for such tasks as pounding in tent pegs. The pole axe comes in a variety of styles and weights. The two types most commonly used in organized camps are discussed below.

The *scout axe, hatchet, hand axe,* or *belt axe* is a short 10- to 13½-inch axe that weighs from ½ to 1¼ pounds and is recommended for general light camp use. It is sturdy and rugged, inexpensive, light, easy to handle, and

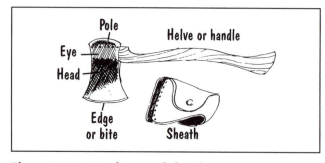

Figure 26.1   Hand axe and sheath.

will meet ordinary needs. It can usually be held in one hand and has a protective sheath that can sometimes be worn on a belt.

A *camp* or *three-quarter axe* is smaller and lighter than a full-sized axe, but is sturdy enough to turn out large amounts of work and so is a favorite with counselors and experienced older campers. It has an 18- to 22-inch handle and a slightly larger and heavier head than that of a scout axe, which gives it more power.

Caring for an Axe

An axe should be treated like any other fine tool and kept in good condition, sharp and ready to go. Inspect the handle of an axe frequently to make sure that it is tight. The danger of a loose head on a swinging axe is easy to see. No matter how tightly a head held in by screws or wedges fits at first, it will probably eventually work loose as the wood dries out. Never leave an axe lying around where it might cut or trip someone. Drive it firmly into a chopping block, a dead log, or a stump, or replace it in its sheath and put it away.

When carrying an unsheathed axe for even a short distance, turn the blade down and grasp the handle close to the head to keep it from cutting you if you should trip or catch it on underbrush. When handing it to another, hold it by the handle and extend it head first and do not let go until the other person has a firm grip on it.

When an axe is sharp, it does a much faster job, biting in to remove sizeable chips of wood instead of chewing it out in small bits. It is also less likely to glance off the wood and injure you or a bystander. Take the time to hone an axe and keep it sharp.

Using an Axe

Get a solid, broad chopping block, 1 to 2 feet high, and level off the top, making a small depression in the middle to hold the wood. If the block tends to roll, drive stakes in solidly against it on both sides. Before beginning, advise campers to look carefully about to make sure there is no one near and no brush or overhanging branches to deflect the axe on the backswing. Wipe the perspiration from your hands frequently. Wet hands are

slippery. Keep your hands and legs well out of the way in case the axe should miss or slide off the wood. Chop at a 45-degree angle (figure 26.2), never directly across the grain of the wood since this makes little progress and quickly dulls the axe. Aim so that the axe will enter the chopping block after you have severed the stick instead of striking you or the ground.

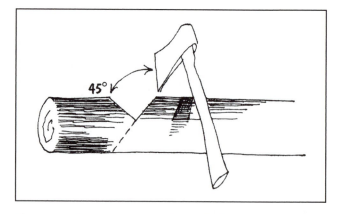

Figure 26.2   Cut at an angle of 45 degrees.

When using a scout axe, grasp it close to the end of the handle and kneel on one knee. With a camp axe, stand with your feet comfortably spread and solidly planted on cleared ground. Grasp the axe with your left hand up near the end of the handle and your right fairly well down toward the head. Take a good backswing to get momentum and slide your right hand down to join the left as the axe bites into the wood. Slide your right hand back up the handle again to help lift and control the axe on the backswing, then repeat. Learn to coordinate your whole body in a rhythmic swing, using the powerful muscles in your back, shoulders, and hips. Skilled and powerful chopping, however, depends more on skill and timing than on muscle power. A long backswing creates good momentum that, when combined with the pull of gravity and the weight of your axe head, produces power. Keep eyes focused constantly on the spot you want to hit and try to score a bull's-eye every time. Rest when you get tired since fatigue lessens coordination and leads to bad accidents. With an axe, a slight miscalculation or a moment of carelessness can result in a serious disabling injury. Always err on the side of being overly cautious.

Never cut a standing tree if you can avoid it. Even dead standing trees have their purpose in providing habitat for nesting birds and other animals, and helping to maintain a sense of beauty in the natural environment. If you destroy something it will take nature many years to replace.

When cutting small sticks in two, avoid the dangerous practice of simply laying the stick loose on the block and hitting it. This leaves both ends free to fly through the air. The *contact method* is one of the safest. Use your left hand to hold the stick crosswise on the block (figure 26.3), and bring the axe down on the stick on the outside edge of the block. If necessary, continue to bring the axe down against the block until the stick is severed. Be sure to direct your strokes so that the axe will enter the block after the stick is severed. With a larger stick, use several strokes, giving the stick a quarter or half turn between each.

Figure 26.3   Chopping small sticks in two.

Figure 26.4   Contact method of splitting kindling.

Since split wood burns much better than whole sticks with the bark on, it is wise to keep some fine kindling and larger split wood on hand. To use the *contact method*, stand at one side of the chopping block, grasp the piece of wood in your left hand, place your axe on top of it, and bring both wood and axe down simultaneously against the edge of the chopping block (figure 26.4). Repeat as many times as necessary to complete a split across the top. Then, turning your axe to face downward in the split, stand the stick upright on the block, remove your left hand, and bring both axe and wood down against the chopping block. Repeat as many times as necessary to complete the split. To get still finer kindling, split the segments. You should never use your foot to hold the stick against the chopping block as it is extremely dangerous.

To sharpen a stake, hold it upright on the chopping block and sharpen it on four sides (figure 26.5). A four-sided point can be made more quickly and will drive into the ground more easily.

Figure 26.5   Sharpening a stake.

Saws

Campers often prefer to use a saw to cut large pieces of wood. In comparison with using an axe, a saw is safer—especially for the inexperienced, wastes less wood, and does the job more quickly and easily. It also leaves the pieces with flat ends, which can be a decided advantage when using them for camp construction or arts and crafts.

A *crosscut saw* or *bucksaw* (figure 26.6A) is an old favorite for use in camp. Some folding types are so light and compact that they are suitable to take on trips. Two

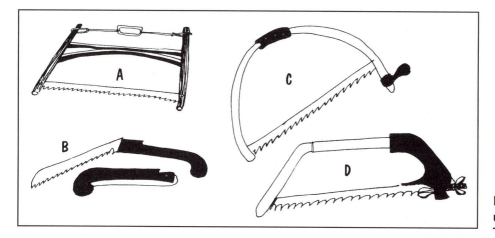

Figure 26.6   Types of saws used in camp.

people can use it, one at each side, with each taking turns pulling. No one ever pushes. Keep the frame perpendicular to the wood and do not bear down on it but let the weight of the saw do the biting.

Figure 26.6B is a *jackknife saw* featuring a blade that folds and is held in place by a wing-nut when in use. It folds to a length of about 12 inches and weighs about 11 ounces.

Figure 26.6C is a one-handed *Swede* or *bow saw* with a tubular metal frame curved over the blade like an archer's bow. Several sizes are available, and some weigh as little as two pounds and can be dismantled and fitted into a case 12 to 18 inches long. Figure 26.6D shows another popular model that works well for most purposes.

The *cable saw* is the lightest and smallest of all. It consists of a thin, wire-like flexible blade with a handle at each end that can be rolled up into a small coil for carrying. One person can use it for light cutting by holding onto both handles, or two can use it with each holding a handle and standing on opposite sides of the piece to be cut. Unfortunately, this saw is simply too inefficient for cutting a considerable amount of wood.

Other Tools

When simple tools are readily available, most campers enjoy using them. It is an imposition to ask the caretaker of the camp to lend tools. Therefore, each living unit could have its own basic set, each painted with a distinguishing color or design so that straying tools can be

instantly recognized. Other special or more expensive tools should be kept available at some central place where they can be checked out when needed.

When many people use the same tools, some will invariably be lost or misplaced. A tool board allows you to arrange tools in an orderly fashion so they can be quickly located. Use a peg board and pegs or make a tool board from any suitable piece of lumber. Lay it flat and place your tools on it in desired locations, then trace the outline of each tool on the board and paint it in solid. Insert nails, hooks, or other suitable holders to suspend each tool and stand or hang the board upright and put the tools in place. Make a card for each tool, with its name and a rough drawing of the tool on it. Punch a hole in the card for hanging it on the board, and file the cards in a box near the board. When borrowing a tool, the user removes its card from the box, signs his or her name on it, enters the date and time, and hangs it on the board in place of the tool. When replacing the tool, the person enters the time and date on the card and re-files it in the box. The outlines of the tools on the board show each person where to replace them and also reveal at a glance which tools are missing. Since people are not always familiar with the correct name of a tool, you may find it advantageous to number as well as name them and file the cards by number.

Hold each user responsible for returning a tool in good condition. Remember a worthwhile rainy day activity for campers is to recondition the tools and other equipment. It is valuable for young people to learn to respect good tools and to understand the need to keep them in top condition.

WEB RESOURCES

Camping, Hiking Tools
(www.theepicenter.com/camping_hiking_and_backpacking_
    accessories.html)
(www.vtarmynavy.com/camp-tools.htm)
(www.campmor.com/.../SubCategory___40000000226_
    200368381)
(www.camptools.com/)

(www.gr8gear.com/)
(www.rei.com/category/40006351)
(www.camping-gear-outlet.com/camping-equipment-175.html)
(www.basecamphq.com)

Outdoor Gear
(www.LLBean.com)

27

Tents and Shelters

Campers sometimes go on overnight or even longer trips and at night simply curl up in their sleeping bags or blankets. Some people prefer to lie out in the open under a star-spangled sky to enjoy the sounds, sights, and smells of nature. This desire is fine in good weather or when there is shelter nearby if a storm threatens. However, on extended trips or when the forecast calls for possible thunderstorms, some sort of shelter is needed. It is wishful thinking to believe that in bad weather you can remain snug and dry for long with only a sleeping bag and ground cloth for protection. In addition, many campers find the idea of living in a tent exciting, the true essence of camping.

An ideal tent would be quick and easy to set up and take down, lightweight and compact to carry, offer protection against rain as well as insects and forest creatures, provide privacy, and be cool and well-ventilated in summer yet warm on cool nights. Unfortunately, such a combination of virtues may not be possible. Several hundred varieties of tents are now on the market with each manufacturer attempting to produce one that is superior to those of the competition.

Types of Tents

Some available tents are variations on old ideas, while others employ new approaches. Most tent makers now take advantage of new materials and technologies to produce tents that are lighter, roomier, and sturdier than ever before. Many tents now feature light, flexible tubular poles made of carbon fiber, fiberglass, and aluminum alloys. Some tents have folding aluminum or plastic frameworks that you can erect in as little as 90 seconds. Others, such as free-standing tents, are suspended from a framework that eliminates the need for pegs and guy lines, and are stable enough to pick up and move about. *Pop-up tents* usually have a light, collapsible, compact framework of aluminum that springs into an igloo-shaped structure almost as quickly as you can open an umbrella. *Wing tents* give added room through flies that extend like wings from two or more of the corners.

In addition to the large tents most suitable for a permanent resident camp, newer *alpine tents* (also called *timberline, mountaineering,* or *backpacking* tents) are more suitable for trip camping with backpacks or canoes. These newer tents are made of lightweight material but are strong enough to hold up in severe weather conditions

Alpine or backpacking tents are more suitable for trip camping with backpacks or canoes.

such as extreme cold, snow, blizzards, and winds up to 100 miles an hour. They are rugged and constructed to conserve heat while providing adequate ventilation for living and even cooking. They have enough room to shelter the people and their gear, yet are compact and light enough to carry in a backpack.

In general, tents can be classified into several basic types according to shape, but many hybrids combine characteristics of the various types. *Conical and pyramidal tents* are usually tall and erected with a center pole or other means of support. Their steeply sloped sides shed rain quickly, which makes them especially well suited to open-plains country where there are often sudden and severe storms. They are sturdy and serve in a permanent or semipermanent camp. In the large sizes, several campers can bed down, lying with their feet toward the center and their bodies arranged like the spokes of a wheel. However, the bulk and weight of these tents usually make them impractical for light-trip camping.

A conical or pyramidal tent. (Photo by Joel Meier)

The *tepee* designed originally by the Plains Indians has no pole in the center and features smoke flaps that adjust to let smoke escape when a small fire is built inside for warmth or cooking. Generally, however, fires should not be built in tents. Not too much waterproofing is required, since the steep walls quickly shed water. When tepees are used in the camp setting, they are generally erected at the beginning of the summer in a remote area of the camp, and seldom moved or taken down until the end of the summer.

Umbrella tents are rather heavy and bulky and sometimes used for family camping or for long trips where transportation is not a problem and the occupants expect to stay put for some time. They are easy to erect, have ample headroom, and have a front porch for additional

shelter. The usual sizes accommodate four or more campers and flaps can be added at the sides of the canopy to house two or three more. Early models were supported by a center pole with side supports that spread out like the ribs of an umbrella, but some of the newer models are suspended from a frame or have side poles that leave the center unobstructed.

Wedge or A-frame tents are favorites for light-trip camping. They are relatively light, easy to pitch, and furnish adequate shelter for the average summer backpacker. The steep roof sheds rain well and some models are tall enough to permit standing. These tents usually accommodate two people.

The familiar *pup tent* design has long been a standby for short-term camping. It is just large enough to provide a crawl-in type shelter for two people and their duffel. Many modern backpacker tents are variations of the pup tent and, when made of light materials, may weigh as little as 2 or 3 pounds. When poles are required, collapsible ones made of lightweight aluminum can be used. In wooded country the smaller models need no poles, since they can be supported on a rope strung between two trees or bushes.

The tepee is a popular choice for a permanent or semi-permanent campsite.

The *explorer tent* is roomy and has enough headroom to permit standing. You can pitch it by stringing ropes from loops on top of the tent and throwing them across the limb of a tree or by using an inside "T" pole. This tent is easy to pitch and strike and sometimes has a screened window in the rear to improve ventilation. It is well adapted to winter camping since you can build a fire in front of the open door. The tent is often used for canoe, pack animal, or automobile camping, since it is not light enough for backpacking. Some types reduce weight and bulk by sloping and narrowing toward the rear.

The *wall tent* is most commonly used for permanent sleeping quarters at the main camp or when a party expects to remain in the same place for several weeks. It provides ample headroom and the sides can usually be rolled up for ventilation. It comes in a variety of sizes, but it is usually too bulky and heavy for light-trip use.

Lean-to tents, which can be used in summer, are also suitable for cold-weather camping because the canopy over the open front will catch the heat from a reflector fire and reflect it inside onto the sleepers. A small fire for cooking can also be built in front of the opening. The walls slope toward the rear to reduce weight and they shed rain well. These shelters are often constructed by using a tarp, cordage/rope, and the assistance of two accurately placed trees. Ground stakes or rocks can be used to secure one end low to the ground.

The *camper tent or canvas tent* has a short ridge and a front porch, and requires two poles for pitching. These tents come in a variety of sizes and are often erected on more permanent platforms.

The *baker tent* is a great favorite for a permanent or semipermanent camp. It is adaptable to both summer and cold-weather use but cannot withstand the high winds characteristic of some areas. It is especially suit- able for automobile or station wagon camping, because the canopy can be suspended from the vehicle to provide added privacy and space. It is really like half a wall tent, with a versatile flap that can be used as an awning in sunny weather or lowered over the front to shut out rain.

Increasing interest is now focused on the new light- weight *dome, box,* and *tunnel tent* designs that are espe- cially popular for backpacking. Most of these tents are free standing with a canopy hung from a self-supporting frame so they can be set up anywhere with a minimum of stakes and guy lines. Recent advances in flexible pole ma- terials have revolutionized the market. Their primary ad- vantage is that there is nearly 50% more volume than in an A-frame tent with the same floor space because the sidewalls are more vertical. This tent is more comfortable to live in when the occupants become stormbound.

Tent Features

Tents vary in size from the huge summer-cottage va- rieties intended to be transported by automobile or truck to the small crawl-in types suited primarily for overnight sleeping or protection during a downpour. Both weight and money can be saved by buying tents that are only large enough for specific needs. A floor size of at least 5 × 7 feet is needed for two or more adults.

Since one of the most important functions of a tent is to protect its occupants and their equipment from rain and heavy dew, the difference between a waterproofed and a water repellent material is important to under- stand. A **waterproofed** material is impervious to rain be- cause the individual fibers have been treated with a wa- terproofing substance or because the material has been coated with one.

Wall tents are commonly used for permanent sleeping quarters.

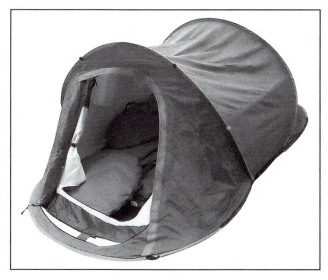

Low profile tunnel tent with flexible poles.

Although a waterpr oofed material may sound ideal, it has disadvantages. Waterproofing makes the material heavier and stiffer, and in time the treatment may crack and lose its effectiveness, necessitating retreatment. In addition, a surface that will not let moisture in will not let it out either. Therefore, in a tightly closed tent, the pint or more of moisture that each occupant gives off during the night through breathing and perspiration remains in the tent. As the evening progresses and the air cools off, this moisture condenses upon contact with the cooler tent walls and ceiling and can eventually drop down on the sleepers below, making them and gear almost as wet as if they had been out in a rain.

Water repellent materials, on the other hand, are made of coated fibers or of fibers that are very closely woven. A tent made of water repellent material may prove satisfactory during a light rain, especially if it has a steep roof to drain the water off rapidly and is pitched tautly leaving no wrinkles or folds to collect and hold moisture. However, in areas that frequently have heavy or steady rains, water repellent materials alone will not be sufficient. The answer to this problem is to use a separate waterproofed tent fly in combination with the tent as described a bit later.

Another problem with a tightly closed waterproof tent is that it will not freely admit oxygen. As the night wears on, a sleeper uses up much of the available oxygen and replaces it with carbon dioxide. The result could be a severe headache, nausea, and lethargy. Inadequate ventilation can have much more serious consequences when a camper succumbs to the temptation to avoid bad weather and cooks inside the tent with a portable stove. Cooking in a tent should NEVER be attempted, although noted previously can be done just outside the tent. Cooking is dangerous in an enclosed space because the burning process creates carbon monoxide, which can make the camper feel drowsy and, in extreme cases, may eventually cause unconsciousness and death. Records show that this fatal result has occurred in several cases.

Fabrics that do allow the passage of air are said to be breathable. A tent obviously has breathability in inverse proportion to how waterproof and airtight it is. Even a tent that is water repellent will need some means of ventilation, which can be provided in various ways. At one extreme are the tarpaulin shelter and the pup tent, which are open at both ends and admit plenty of air as well as unwanted flying and crawling creatures. Do not consider going on a trip without adequate protection from insect pests. Better tents have screened doors, which usually open with one or more zippers, as well as vents or windows.

A **tent fly** consists of a separate piece of waterproofed material that is suspended over the tent itself and solves the problem of protecting a tent that is only water repellent. The fly keeps out the rain, but condensation of body moisture and carbon dioxide is allowed to escape through the breathable inner walls of the tent and dissipate in the space between the roof and the fly. Should any moisture condense on the inside of the fly, it will run down the sides to the ground outside the tent. Another advantage of the fly is that it keeps a tent warmer in the winter by helping to hold heat in, protects against wind, and it also keeps the tent cooler in summer if it is pitched in the sun. The fly should be constructed so that it never touches the tent walls or ceiling, and it should extend well beyond the tent eaves and walls so that slanting rains will not blow in and the dripping from the rain will be well outside the tent walls.

Some tents are equipped with a *vestibule*, which is usually in the form of an extension of the tent's entryway. Its advantage is added space for storing clothing and equipment that otherwise would either have to be left outside or stored directly inside the tent. The vestibule is usually designed as part of the tent fly, and takes the form of a tunnel entrance leading to the front door. Some manufacturers have also designed vestibules that can be zipped on separately.

Shelter Characteristics

Prior to World War II, *cotton* was used in nearly all tents and shelters in such forms as canvas, drill, duck, twill, or poplin. Now, however, it is rarely used except in heavy tents for family or long-term camping or in tents for those who value economy above lightness and compactness. In addition to its heaviness, cotton has other disadvantages. It has low tear strength and it tends to mildew when exposed to moisture and not promptly dried. On the positive side, however, cotton is cheaper than most synthetics and can be tightly woven into a water repellent fabric whose fibers swell when wet to further close up the air spaces between them. Its fibers also readily accept and retain waterproofing.

Breathable dome tent without fly.

Breathable dome tent and waterproof fly with vestibule.

Tent and tent fly with vestibule sealed up for bad weather.

It is desirable to use a separate waterproof tent fly in combination with a breathable tent. The fly keeps out the rain, while the breathable inner walls of the tent allow condensation of body moisture and carbon dioxide to escape and to dissipate in the space between the tent roof and the fly. (Photos by Joel Meier)

Shelters made of some form of *nylon* are now chosen by most light-trip campers. Although more expensive than cotton, it is ultra-light and can be compressed into a small bundle for packing. *Ripstop nylon* has heavier fibers interspersed at quarter-inch intervals to give it added strength and to prevent tears from spreading farther down the fabric. Nylon has good tear strength, will not rot or mildew, and dries out quickly when wet. Tightly woven nylon is water repellent and will prove satisfactory in a light rain, but in a heavy or continuous downpour, the rain will shift through the material as a fine mist. Therefore, a waterproof fly should be used over the roof of the tent. Manufacturers usually treat the flooring of the tent and the fly cover with polymer, polyurethane, or vinyl to keep the rain out. Unfortunately, the coating may eventually crack and disintegrate, necessitating a retreatment.

New materials for tents are introduced all the time. Most tents today are constructed from some type of nylon or polyester taffeta. Materials appear under trade names such as Gore-Tex, Golite, or Klimate as manufacturers compete to find the perfect material that is breathable but will not let in water. Such products work well but are usually expensive.

Tent color is largely a matter of personal preference. White and light colors reflect rather than absorb the sun's rays and are cooler in summer. However, they also soil easily, attract insects, and tend to silhouette the occupants at night to provide an impromptu movie for the neighbors. Although some people prefer the cheerful blues, yellows, oranges, and reds now available, minimum impact advocates are likely to choose somber hues such as khaki, olive-drab, soft brown, or green, which blend in better with woodland surroundings.

For backpacking, tent supports must be light and simple and quick to erect in case of sudden rain. Some poles telescope. Others come apart and nest together for easy packing. Many come in sections that are held together by *shock cords* (i.e., bands of rubber sheathed in nylon running up through the hollow centers), which make the poles easy to assemble and help to prevent loss. Light poles are made of carbon fiber, tubular aluminum, duraluminum, fiberglass, or a still lighter material, magnesium, and each weighs 2 ounces or less.

Because of the need for forest conservation and minimum impact, campers do not need to use a knife and axe to cut and shape their own tent pegs. If your tent needs stakes, take them with you. Figure 27.1A shows a variety of tent pegs that can be purchased or made. Some manufactured ones are of the twisted skewer type and are available in aluminum or chrome alloy steel. They are strong and drive easily, and are especially suited for use in pebbly ground. Others nest together for compactness and can be held together with a rubber band. Lightweight plastic T-pegs are inexpensive but durable and will not bend as aluminum sometimes does. Stakes are usually inexpensive and extremely light, but travelers in woodland

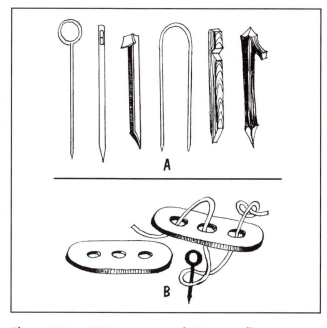

Figure 27.1   (A) Tent pegs and (B) tent adjusters.

Figure 27.2   Ways to use trees in tent or tarp pitching.

areas usually take as few as possible and anchor their tarp or tent lines to rocks, trees, or even bushes (figure 27.2). By using a *guy line hitch,* the rope may be adjusted by sliding the lower knot up and down. The hitch also can be used when tying guy ropes to tent pegs.

Figure 27.1B shows some tent adjusters. These are available in plastic or aluminum and are used to adjust tent lines to the proper degree of tension. Each adjuster has three holes in it and the line is threaded up through one end hole, down through the center hole, around the tent peg, up through the other end hole, and then tied or knotted. To adjust it, pull the guy line slack and slide the adjuster to a new position. The adjuster takes the place of the time-honored taut line hitch that is used for this purpose. Each adjuster weighs only one ounce and costs very little.

A roll of 100-pound test nylon cord provides the best tent lines. It is strong, does not shrink when wet, and resists mildew and rotting. Parachute chord, number 5 manila rope, and window sash cord are also acceptable. Be sure your rope is strong enough to withstand high winds and storms.

Selecting a Tent

When choosing a tent, consider such factors as means of transportation, the duration of your camping trips, how often and how long you expect to use it, what seasons you will be using it in, climatic conditions like rainfall as well as winds and temperatures, the need for protection from insects, and cost. Buy the best tent you can afford. When properly cared for, a quality tent will give many years of solid service.

An inexpensive tent is likely to become an expensive headache in the long run, since it will probably wear out quickly and perform poorly. Although occasionally possible to get an inexpensive tent that will fulfill ordinary camp needs, seek the advice of experienced campers. Usually tents made by a reputable tent maker who takes pride in the product and is willing to stand behind it are best.

Use and Care of Tents

Air out the tent thoroughly on sunny days and roll up the flaps with the edges inside where they won't catch and hold dew. Keep your tent floor clean. Dirt, leaves, and other debris are messy and can damage the fabric and promote mildew. During wet weather place a doormat of old burlap outside to use as a "shoe scraper." Keep an extra pair of soft shoes just inside the door to slip into as you enter the tent. A little warm water on a cloth or sponge will remove mud, pitch or sap, or other dirt from inside the tent.

Your tent will repay you with a longer life and better service if you care for it properly. To pack your tent, fold it neatly or stuff it into the stuff sack (depending upon the manufacturer's suggestion), but avoid creasing it repeatedly in the same places or the fabric will eventually break down. Roll the folded tent into a narrow compact bundle and shape it to fit into your tent stuff bag. This bag simplifies carrying the tent and also protects it from dirt and wear.

Tarp and Poncho Shelters

A *tarp* (*tarpaulin*) is a versatile piece of equipment. You can cover your duffel with it, use it as a ground cloth for your tent or bedroll, convert it into almost any type of shelter desired, erect it as a dining porch or cooking area, use it as a fly over your tent, or string it between two trees to serve as a windbreak. You can use it as an emergency stretcher by pinning it or lashing it through its grommets to two long poles. You can even use a light tarp as a sail.

For summer camping in mild climates, some backpackers prefer a tarp or poncho shelter to a tent. A tarp usually has grommets or tie tapes along all four sides for attaching it to guy lines and tent pegs. Some tarps have snaps along the sides, allowing you to snap two of them together to form one large surface. Several possible ways to construct a tarp or poncho shelter are shown in figure 27.3. You can use one end as a ground cloth, stretching the other above you as a shelter. You will not actually need tent pegs since you can weight the edges with rocks.

Figure 27.3   Tarp and lean-to shelters.

Since tarp shelters are particularly vulnerable in high winds, keep them low to minimize wind ballooning.

Tarps are available in most tent materials and come in a variety of sizes, weights, and colors. A popular choice is 9 × 12 feet made of waterproofed ripstop nylon. This type will shelter two adults, weighs only about a pound, and folds into a small, compact package that can be carried in an outside pocket of your backpack. Since a tarp shelter is open at both ends, you will have no trouble with condensation or lack of ventilation, but you will need some form of protection from insects.

A *plastic tube tent* (figure 27.4) is a popular variation of the plastic sheet shelter and is commonly used by backpackers. You can buy such tents or make your own from rolls of tubing available from outfitters in 3-foot diameters and 3 or 4 millimeter thicknesses. Tube tents can be erected in just a few minutes, weigh only about a pound per person, and cost very little. Tube tents are also available in coated nylon, which lasts much longer but weighs and costs more. Beckets or rope handles can be added by

Figure 27.4   Plastic tube shelter.

doubling over cloth or duct tape, then inserting them under the plastic or nylon and tying cord around them.

WEB RESOURCES

Tents
(http://www.abc-of-hiking.com/hiking-tents/tent-materials.asp)
(http://www.go-camping.org/tents-types.html)

Backpacking Tents (http://www.backpacking.net/)
Tent Guide (http://camping-tent-guide.com/)
Shelters (http://www.natureskills.com/primitive_shelter.html)

28

Sleeping Outdoors

Since a third or more of the day is spent sleeping, the camper's bed deserves thought and attention. A good night's rest means at least eight hours of sleep for adults and even more for younger people—especially when undergoing all the activities of camp.

If campers are traveling by horseback or have other means of transporting heavy baggage, the bulk and weight of bedding are not significant. When they are traveling on foot with all equipment on their backs, it becomes a challenge to provide a comfortable bed that is lightweight and not too bulky. When traveling via canoe, it is possible to take a little more than when backpacking, although materials should be light and compact.

Requirements for Sleeping Comfort

A good outdoor bed should provide warmth. Summer nights can be cool and the ground is always more or less cold and damp. The bed should be light and compact for carrying, provide a reasonable amount of comfort with freedom from bumps, and provide protection from the ground.

Most people who expect to do much outdoor sleeping will invest in a sleeping bag. A good-quality bag, properly cared for, will last for years and will provide convenience, comfort, warmth, and maximum lightness and compactness. Sleeping bags come in four basic shapes, and the shape you choose will have a definite effect on your warmth.

Rectangular or square-cut bags have plenty of room for restless sleepers. However, their ample proportions add bulk and weight, making them more suitable for car camping than backpacking. They are also not as warm as the other types since the excess space inside does not absorb body heat. *Mummy bags* represent the opposite extreme in shape. They follow the shape of the body, and this reduces bulk and weight and increases warmth. Although some find a mummy bag too confining, its advantages are so great that most backpackers prefer it. The *barrel bag* is a variation on the mummy bag and has, as the name suggests, a rounded portion in the middle to permit bending the knees and maneuvering about a bit more freely. The *semi-mummy bag* is a cross between the mummy and the rectangular bag. For comfort, all bags should have an oval enlargement or "box" at the foot to permit room for the sleeper's feet.

A sleeping bag consists of an *inner* and an *outer shell* with a filler (a thick layer of insulating material) in between. Neither shell should be waterproof or even ex-

Rectangular sleeping bag.

The semi-mummy bag is a cross between the mummy and rectangular bag.

tremely water repellent, since it is essential that the bag "breathe" to allow a person's body moisture to evaporate. Various materials are used for the shells, the most common being nylon. All nylon should be the ripstop kind to keep little rips and holes from becoming big ones.

When sleeping, people's muscles relax and metabolism slows down markedly, causing a corresponding drop in the production of body heat. When cold, muscles automatically contract (perhaps even to the point of causing shivering) to step up heat production. This situation causes fitful sleep and people often arise stiff, tired, and decidedly unenthusiastic about starting out for another day on the trail.

Bedding cannot supply any heat in itself, but serves as insulation to keep out cold air and prevent the loss of body heat by conduction and convection. In a sleeping bag, insulation is provided by the thick filler between the shells, which is usually a loose, fluffy material containing countless minute air pockets that trap and render motionless large amounts of warm air generated by the body. This still or "dead" air provides insulation. Two types of insulation used primarily in sleeping bags are the down of waterfowl and polyester fiberfill. However, new materials continue to appear as manufacturers attempt to find a more nearly perfect filler.

The thickness, or *loft*, of the insulation is all important in determining how well it will insulate. Loft is customarily measured by zipping up the bag, fluffing it up as full of air as possible, and measuring the height from the floor to the top of the bag.

Some bags, particularly the warmer mummy types, have an opening at the top and a zippered opening extending most of the way down one side. Another arrangement is a zipper that runs all the way down the side and across the bottom. This structure allows the bag to be completely opened for ventilation. Some bags are designed so that two different bags can be zipped together for double sleeping.

Metal zippers are seldom found in bags since they transmit cold and are more likely to jam. They have been largely supplanted by those made of nylon or plastic, which are lighter, work more smoothly, and have less tendency to jam. If a zipper does become balky, apply a little wax or Zip-Eaze and work it up and down several times.

Rectangular bags are usually left open at the top or have a drawstring to draw them close about the neck. This makes it necessary to carry some sort of supplementary protection for the head and neck in cold weather. Separate hoods are available for this purpose, and some bags have detachable hoods that can be left at home during warm weather. Mummy bags and their variations usually have an extension at the top that can be pulled tight about the face and neck in cold weather, leaving only the nose and eyes exposed, and some have an extra drawstring around the shoulders to make them fit even more snugly.

Some bags come with removable liners to protect the inside of the bag from dirt and abrasion. These liners can be taken out for laundering. They come in a variety of materials such as cotton shirting, outing flannel, ripstop nylon, or silk and sometimes are anchored in place with tapes or snaps to keep them from twisting or rolling up as the occupant turns. If a bag has no such liner, you can easily make one from material of your choice. A twin-bed size sheet or cotton "bed blanket" works well in summer and is about the right size for an adult bag. You may want a warmer material for cold weather. The problem of fitting the liner to the bag is simplified if your bag is the type that opens down one side and across the bottom.

The Use and Care of a Sleeping Bag

A sleeping bag usually comes with its own *stuff sack* into which you literally stuff it, handful by handful, being sure to work at least half of the bag down into the bottom half of the sack. As soon as you arrive at your campsite,

Mummy bags and their variations usually have an extension at the top that can be pulled tight about the face and neck in cold weather, leaving only the nose and eyes exposed.

remove the sleeping bag from the stuff sack. With the zipper closed, pick up the bag by the edges and shake it with a sort of whip-like motion to get as much air as possible into the insulation. Shake at least an hour before retiring to give the insulating material time to attain its full loft. Leave the zipper closed until you are ready to crawl into the bag to prevent the bag from collecting moisture. Always keep the bag well away from any open flame, since a stray spark can burn a hole in it.

Air out your bag every day if possible, turning it inside out and placing it outside on sunny days. This practice will prevent mildew and odors. Before storing it, fasten a plastic bag such as dry cleaners use around it and suspend it in a dry, clean room or otherwise store it loosely so the down can maintain its loft.

Make every effort to keep a sleeping bag clean, since it is difficult to wash satisfactorily without damage occurring. Some people advise against doing anything other than simply using a damp cloth to wipe the surface of the bag. Others claim to have good results by hand washing the bag with mild soap, but natural oils and loft can be reduced by soap and water. Care must also be taken not to cause interior structural damage while washing, since the baffles between the inner and outer shells can be torn easily from the pressure caused by lifting a water-soaked bag.

Selecting a Sleeping Bag

A sleeping bag is a highly personal item and there is no one bag that will suit everyone's tastes and needs. In selecting the particular one for you or your campers, consider such factors as the season of the year, the altitude and probable minimum and maximum temperatures to be encountered, the prevalence of winds, the likelihood of rain or other precipitation, your own personal characteristics (i.e., some people sleep "warmer" than others), how extensively it will be used, how much bulk and weight you are willing to carry, and how much you are willing to spend.

Three-season bags are satisfactory in all but the coldest weather. Some of them come with an extra-warm inner bag that zips inside, and this can sometimes be used separately to provide an extra bag. A camper who sleeps outdoors in all types of weather may want to invest in two bags, a light one for summer and a heavy one for winter.

Since there are now so many bags on the market, you should delay making a final choice until you have looked at several different types. Study the websites and catalogs of outfitters, visit stores, and talk to experienced campers. If possible, borrow several bags from friends or rent them from outfitters so that you can test them in actual use. A "bargain" bag made by a relatively unknown manufacturer is rarely a good choice. Stick to reputable companies who are willing to stand behind their products.

Read all the labels on the bag—the government requires that the manufacturer disclose such information as (1) the amount and type of filling used, (2) the type of outer covering, and (3) the cut and size of the bag (these dimensions usually are given in terms of the uncut material with no allowance for hems and seams).

Buying quality bags for children may be difficult since many manufacturers do not make them and others use inferior materials. Fortunately, there is now a greater selection of bags made from synthetic materials that are generally inexpensive and serve quite well for summer camping.

Blanket Beds

In this day of ultra-lightweight camping gear, most people prefer a sleeping bag. However, since it is one of the more costly camping items, blankets can still provide reasonable warmth for those with limited resources or those who sleep outdoors so rarely that they cannot justify buying a bag. Blankets have some advantages because they can be easily altered to suit weather conditions and are easy to wash. Dark strong blankets that won't show soil are preferable.

Cold weather calls for blankets of wool or fleece. Two relatively thin blankets are better than one thick one, since they are easier to manipulate and trap a layer of dead air between them to provide extra insulation.

To make a bedroll, some people simply roll up in their blankets and claim to sleep in perfect comfort throughout the night. This approach may not work for everyone since the average person changes position many times during the night. If you want to try it, wrap yourself in an *envelope bed;* spread a blanket on the ground, bring the two sides up over you, tucking one edge of the blanket under you, then lift your feet and tuck the blanket under them. To use two blankets, place the edge of one blanket at the center of the other, lie down and proceed as before.

When using two blankets, it is usually best to pin them together in some way. A *Klondike bedroll* (figure 28.1) is easy to make. The one illustrated is made from two blankets and four 3-inch horse blanket pins. First place a tarp or ground cloth on the ground and spread one blanket over about half of it. Add as many blankets as you want, placing the edge of each at the center of the one below. Finish with a folded sheet or light cotton blanket that will be next to you. Now begin folding the blankets over, starting with the top one and working your way down to the bottom blanket. If needed, insert two blanket pins along the outside edge and two along the bottom (make sure that the pins go through all thicknesses). For carrying, fold or snap your poncho or ground cloth around the outside and roll and tie it for carrying as shown in figure 28.1. Be sure to make the bedroll wide enough to allow some movement, since most people do not want to feel confined and find that it interferes with their rest.

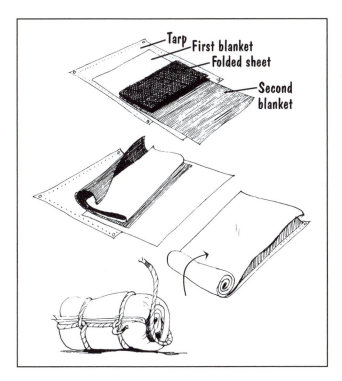

Figure 28.1   Klondike bedroll.

Mattresses

Some hikers sleep with only a sleeping bag and ground tarp for a mattress. Most people, however, prefer more cushioning between themselves and the ground. The weight of your body will compress the bottom of your sleeping bag until very little thickness or loft remains, thus reducing softness and insulation. There was a time when campers would cut branches or gather leaves, grass, or hay to supply a comfortable "mattress," but such practices are not consistent with the minimal impact ethic. Therefore, most people decide to carry some sort of ground pad or mattress. The lightest and most compact option is a "shorty" pad that is just long enough to support the body from shoulders to hips or mid thighs. For a pillow, simply stuff soft clothing into a stuff sack or other bag.

Three types of outdoor mattresses are in current use: (1) air mattresses, (2) open cell foam pads, and (3) closed cell foam pads.

Air mattresses have been favorites for many years. Although they provide softness when properly used, they take some time to get used to and have other drawbacks. They make for cold sleeping since they confine quantities of air in relatively large air spaces; this air moves about with every movement of the sleeper and carries away body heat. This characteristic, of course, might be welcome in hot weather. The main advantage of air mattresses is that they can be deflated and compressed into a small package for transporting. To carry one, roll it up

and place it vertically in your pack. Do not fold it because repeated folding in the same place will cause the material to deteriorate, resulting in leaks. The secret of sleeping comfortably on an air mattress is to underinflate it so that you sleep *in* and not *on* it. Inflate the mattress fully, then lie down on your side on it and slowly let out air until your hip almost touches the ground.

An *open cell foam pad*, as the name suggests, has cells that open into each other like cells of a sponge. The pad is soft to sleep on if it is at least 1½ inches thick. Like a sponge, it absorbs dampness. Therefore, it must be enclosed in a waterproof nylon covering. If the covering has cotton on the upper surface it will be less slick, reducing the tendency for the sleeper to slide off in the night. In addition, the cotton reduces the build-up of body heat and moisture.

A *closed cell foam pad* is much warmer to sleep on since the cells are completely separate and so confine the air in small spaces. Since it does not absorb moisture, it needs no covering, although you may want to use a ground sheet or a washable cover to protect it from soil and abrasion. Although the closed cell pad may not be as soft as other types of mattresses, it is quite washable, smoothes out ground bumps nicely, and provides good insulation. As a result, it is used by many backpackers. A pad can be purchased ready to use or can be cut from a sheet of the material. This type of pad is less bulky and expensive than the open cell pad and can be rolled up into a compact package to attach to your pack.

A closed cell foam sleeping pad may not be as soft as other types of mattresses, but it smoothes out ground bumps nicely and provides good insulation.

Ground Sheet or Tarp

The ground is always more or less cold and damp, and since neither a blanket roll nor a sleeping bag is (or should be) completely waterproof, you will need a waterproof tent floor, a sleeping pad, and a good tarp or ground sheet to protect your bedroll from dampness, dirt, and abrasion. Even if you do use a tent, it is still a good idea to place a ground sheet under it for additional protection. Since any material used for this purpose will eventually develop tiny tears and even larger holes from contact with the rough ground, many people use only an inexpensive, lightweight sheet of plastic (polyethylene) because it is expendable and easily replaceable. Although coated nylon costs more, it will last longer than polyethylene.

WEB RESOURCES

(http://www.backcountry.com/hiking-camping-gear)
(http://www.thebackpacker.com/gear/)

(http://www.backpacking.net/gearbags-tips.html)

PRINT RESOURCES

O'Bannon, A. (2001). *Backpackin' book: Traveling and camping skills for a wilderness environment!* Helena, MT: Falcon Publishing.

29

Camp Stoves and Wood Fires

If early settlers could return today, they would likely be astounded at the concern for conserving wilderness areas and other places imbued with outstanding natural beauty. To them, the supply of natural resources seemed inexhaustible. The dense forests provided wood for their needs as well as fruit, herbs, and wild game for their tables. *Chop and burn* was a way of life for them to make room for growing crops. Timber was also a major industry.

Managing natural resources is the way of life today as people seek to use land in ways most beneficial to both present and future generations. These well-managed natural areas now serve several purposes. Of special interest to campers is that they provide the environment for organized camping, where people can live surrounded by plants and animals in their natural habitats. These same benefits also are available to the people who enjoy going to the woods for such pastimes as backpacking, hiking, swimming, boating, fishing, hunting, and family or group camping. However, large numbers of people are placing increased pressure on the capability of the environment to withstand the demands placed upon it. To preserve the naturalness of the outdoors as well as the accompanying values and benefits derived from it, people must act responsibly and do everything possible to reduce impact on these lands.

Campfires are a big problem facing resource managers. Too many campers and backpackers leave behind an assortment of ugly pock-marked fire sites. In many backcountry campsites, wood is not available. Therefore, campers are now either discouraged or prohibited from building wood fires in backcountry areas. Some areas that still permit controlled wood fires have compromised by establishing fire sites and requiring that all fires be built in them using only dead wood provided or available nearby.

An understanding of ecology shows that burning wood can disrupt nature's balance by permanently destroying a natural resource instead of leaving it to decay and return its nutrients to the soil as nature intended. Another obvious concern is forest fires, usually caused by carelessness, that annually burn thousands of acres of woodlands. They destroy timber and undergrowth and ruin the habitat of countless wild creatures.

Although wood fires can no longer be widely encouraged for general camp use, they are still permissible in some situations. For example, some resident camps have extensive woodlands that they have maintained and replaced. Such management of land can provide valuable conservation lessons as campers observe what is being done and learn to be selective in choosing what wood to use and how to use it. For this reason and for the benefit of those who feel that all campers should attain some proficiency in building wood fires, this chapter describes some of the principles of fire building.

Alternatives to Wood Fires

The sight of a camper using a camp stove was rare 35 years ago. Today it is commonplace. In addition to reducing the impact of wood fires, stoves are useful for several reasons. A stove is more convenient in that it can be unpacked, assembled, and put into operation in a matter of minutes. There is no need to search for suitable dry wood, arrange it carefully, and wait for it to burn down to a good bed of coals for successful cooking. Stoves produce an even heat with an intensity that varies according to need. Moreover, cookware is not coated with smoke or soot as with a campfire. When handled properly, a stove offers little chance of starting a destructive forest fire.

When finished, you simply turn it off. You do not have to wait for it to burn down and then carefully extinguish each ember and partially burned stick. A stove is generally light, compact, and easy to use.

Several alternative sources of fuel have enjoyed various degrees of popularity. *Canned heat* or jellied fuel such as that found in Sterno brand fuel is relatively safe for use by even young campers. These fuels, however, give off so little heat that they are not useful for anything beyond heating a bowl of soup or stew or cooking an egg. To use jellied fuel, place the can of fuel between two rocks to support the pan or use the portable folding wind screen and kettle support that are available.

Cooking with *charcoal* remains a backyard activity familiar to some children and is a fairly safe and satisfactory method to use in the main campsite or on short jaunts. Charcoal briquettes are relatively light and easy to carry and you can extinguish them when through and save them for future use. Charcoal starter is often used. You will need a grill to contain the fire and support cooking utensils.

Several grill types are available commercially that fold up to fit in a carrying case. Grills can also be handmade with a 5-gallon tin can in which ventilator holes are punched in the sides with a juice can opener. If needed, a metal grate can be placed on top to support the pan, and the charcoal can be supported on a metal disc or screen inserted about half way up the side of the can. One of the most serious drawbacks of most homemade grills is that they cannot be folded up and are somewhat cumbersome to take on a trip.

Gasoline, better known as *white gas*, is a convenient and efficient fuel for stoves because of the ease of operating the stove as well as the efficiency of the fuel itself. Although slightly more dangerous than other types of fuels, gas stoves are preferred by many experienced campers. White, unleaded appliance gas is relatively inexpensive and available at most outfitters. Ordinary automobile gasoline is NOT suitable. Gas stoves are efficient and maintain a steady heat as long as any fuel remains in the tank. Gas's volatility, however, makes careful handling mandatory. Any spilled gas or even vapors can ignite when exposed to a spark, flame, or hot surface.

A gas stove should NEVER be used in a small enclosed area such as a tent. A cabin or any other area used for cooking should be well ventilated. All fuel-burning stoves produce carbon monoxide, which if inhaled, can cause serious illness or even death from asphyxiation or carbon monoxide poisoning. They also give off vapors from unburned and partially burned fuels that are highly flammable and can easily build up to dangerous proportions. Using a stove in cramped quarters also increases the danger of tipping it over or having something flammable come in contact with it.

Carry extra fuel in a conspicuously marked, leak-proof round or flat container preferably of aluminum and with a tightly fitting rubber gasket and screw-on lid. These canisters are available at outdoor equipment stores. Gasoline weighs about 1.5 pounds per quart and two people on a 7-day trip should need no more than 2 quarts. However, consideration must be given to what kinds of foods are prepared as well as your altitude—the

There are several popular types of backpacking stoves on the market that are light, compact, and easy to use. (Photo on right by Joel Meier)

higher you are, the longer the cooking time. Stoves weigh from 1 to 3 pounds with a variety of choices available.

Propane and butane stoves are quite popular. Propane and butane are gases compressed under low pressure (LP) and contained in a thin metal cylinder or cartridge that attaches directly to the stove. The danger and messiness of having to pour a flammable liquid is eliminated. They are clean burning, soot free, and as easy to light and regulate as a kitchen stove. They require no priming or preheating. A new cylinder of fuel is easy to attach. Propane-powered stoves compare favorably to butane-burners except that propane has been recommended for use in cold weather. Fortunately, however, fuel cartridges containing a small amount of propane mixed with butane are now available on the market.

When propane and/or butane are used with caution, there is little danger of starting a forest fire or causing an explosion. However, you should never crush or puncture a used cartridge. Instead, place the used cartridge in your pack to carry out and dispose of properly. Propane and butane stoves, however, have several disadvantages. These fuels are less efficient than gasoline. Cooking, therefore, may take more time. They weigh more per unit of heat, largely because of the weight of the non-refillable cartridge. Another disadvantage is that both pressure and heat decrease during the last 10 minutes of burning a cartridge. You cannot accurately determine the amount of fuel remaining in a partly used cartridge so you may run out in the middle of cooking and have to wait until the stove gets cold before adding a new cartridge.

Use a windscreen to concentrate the heat under the cooking vessel, and turn off the fuel supply before you extinguish the stove. As with all fuel-burning stoves, avoid using a propane or butane stove in a small poorly ventilated area such as a tent or cabin.

Wood Fires

Among the fondest memories of resident campers is sitting with good friends around a blazing campfire. Although wood fires can no longer be widely encouraged for general camp use, they are permissible in some situations.

When selecting a fire site, you must always choose one that will offer little chance for a fire to spread. No matter how pleasant and romantic a fire in a deeply wooded area sounds, it is always dangerous. Choose one spot and confine all fires to it to avoid destroying any more of the natural environment than necessary. If you are in an area where no previous fire rings or scars exist, do everything possible to build your fire in such a way that no signs of it will remain once you leave.

The least impactful method for building a campfire would be to use an existing fire pit. If there are none, use a small shovel or hand spade to remove the top layer of sod, set it aside carefully, and keep it moist for replace-

ment after your fire is out and the ground has cooled. Secondly, find inorganic matter to build up the fire pit. This material is often exposed in the root ball of a fallen tree or beneath the organic humus layer of the soil. By building up the fire pit with inorganic soil, the organic soil will be protected from the heat and sterilization. Prior to replacing the sod, however, be sure to douse the ashes and scatter them so they will not be noticed by others.

The floor of the forest is usually covered with a litter of dead leaves, broken branches, and other debris called *duff,* with some underlying organic matter such as leaf mold and decomposing branches, which is called *humus.* These are combustible, and a fire may smolder in them and break out in an open blaze several hours after you have left the vicinity and forgotten about it. To be safe, clear away all this material from an area of at least 6 to 10 feet in diameter. Find a sandy area if possible, since there is no worry about spreading the fire and less likelihood of showing a fire scar. A ring of rocks placed around the fire site is traditional, but avoid it if you can since they blacken from the smoke and leave signs of your presence. If rocks are already blackened from previous campfires, use them instead of new ones. Never build a fire against a tree. If it is dead, it might catch on fire. If it is green, you will injure or even kill it.

Choose a fire site that offers little chance for the fire to spread, and confine all fires to that location to avoid destroying any more of the natural environment than necessary.

Never leave a campfire unattended. Be prepared to react quickly if it spreads. Likewise, put the fire completely out when done with it. A small, compact shovel or hand spade comes in handy for removing sod and clearing off combustible debris before building your fire. It is also useful for smothering a spreading fire with dirt. Always keep water nearby for this purpose as well. If the fire starts to run wild, quick action is imperative. Get help immediately unless you are *absolutely certain* you can handle it yourself.

To extinguish a fire, cut off the supply of oxygen or combustible material by dousing it with water, beating it with a wet burlap bag or other heavy material saturated with water, or covering it with sand, dirt, or gravel. Watch over the area long enough to make sure it does not blaze up again.

Expertise at building the right fire in the right place at the right time tells a great deal about a camper's skills. Three components are necessary for successful fire building:

- Good tinder
- Kindling
- Firewood

You must select, prepare, and arrange each of these to get a fire going. A balky fire that burns sluggishly or sputters and finally dies results from choosing the wrong kind of wood or from arranging it incorrectly.

Many things will serve satisfactorily as *tinder*, highly flammable material that ignites at the touch of a match. Curls of white birch bark or the twigs from a sassafras tree are excellent. They burn well even when wet or rotten. Look for them on a dead or fallen tree or where quantities of them are hanging loose off a live tree and fallen to the ground. Dry pine needles, dry evergreen cones, last year's dry weed stalks, dried goldenrod, grape, and honeysuckle vines, Queen Anne's lace, old birds' or squirrels' nests, milkweed silk, sagebrush, dried cactus, corn stalks, and dry corncobs are also excellent. Three fuzz clumps or fuzz sticks, pyramided together at the base of a fire (figure 29.1), make good tinder. Thin curly shavings or a handful of twigs each hardly bigger than a match, split and broken in the middle, also serve adequately.

You will need *kindling* that will catch readily from the tinder and burn strongly enough to ignite the firewood. Split it for best results and keep it small in size, ranging from the size of a matchstick to about the length of your little finger or longer. Fat pine, cedar, or paper birch are best, but all the birches are satisfactory as are evergreen, basswood, tulip, sumac, white pine and nearly all other kinds of pine, spruce, balsam, or box elder. Frayed bark of cedar or hemlock also works well.

Firewood is divided roughly into hard woods and soft woods, each with special uses for camping. The timber industry regards as soft woods only the *evergreens* or *conifers,* while the broad-leaved trees (*deciduous,* or those that shed their leaves annually) are considered hard woods.

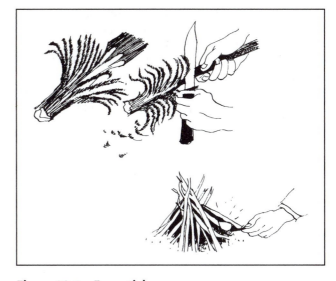

Figure 29.1   Fuzz sticks.

To distinguish between soft woods and hard woods, pick them up and weigh them in your hand. Hard woods are more compact and weigh more. Soft woods burn quickly and briskly, making them good for kindling. They provide quick flames for rapid boiling or baking, and blaze brightly for a campfire gathering. Hard woods are preferable for extended cooking and a long-lasting fire. They kindle slowly, so soft wood must be mixed with them to get them started. Once ablaze, they last a long time and provide a good bed of glowing coals that remains hot indefinitely. Hickory, oak, and maple are usually considered best.

Making a Selection

You must use discrimination when selecting firewood. Green wood, because of its moisture content, seldom burns well. On the other hand, wood that is extremely old has lost much of its valuable heat-producing qualities. A little intelligent experimentation will help you select wisely.

The forest floor tends to hold moisture, so even in comparatively dry weather, branches lying on it may be somewhat damp and questionable as firewood. As each tree in a crowded forest grows, it constantly struggles with its neighbors to reach up and absorb as much sunlight as possible. As the tree grows, its bottom limbs get so little sunlight that they often die. Their position under the tree keeps them quite dry except during a severe storm.

Break wood to test it for dryness. Small dry sticks snap and break cleanly. Wet or green ones bend and finally break with jagged edges. Large dry sticks feel firm and heavy in the hand and will usually snap if you hit them sharply against the edge of a rock. If you tap two of them together, they emit a clear sharp sound instead of the dull muffled sound of wet or green sticks. Sticks that crumble or break up too easily when you give them a sharp blow are rotten and would only smolder and smoke if put on a fire. Wood picked up from the ground should be used rather than dead wood still on a standing tree.

Practices differ regarding the extent to which a hatchet should be used for preparing firewood. It is only common sense to break sticks by hand or under your foot if you can do it easily. You can also avoid chopping by laying long pieces of wood across the fire to burn apart. On the other hand, skill in using a hatchet is a big asset for splitting large pieces of wood. However, *a general rule of thumb is to not burn anything that you cannot break without mechanical or tool assistance.*

If you are going to stay at a campsite for any length of time, arrange your wood in piles, ranging in size from large sticks for extensive cooking and council fires down to kindling and tinder. Place the wood conveniently near but not in the way of activity around the fire site. Throw a tarpaulin or poncho over the woodpile to keep it dry.

Building and Starting the Fire

Collect a big handful of tinder, about twice as much kindling, and a substantial supply of firewood before you start. Place these materials within easy reach. Make a fire foundation by crossing three small sticks with an end of each resting on one of the others to provide good air circulation. Pile the tinder loosely within this framework,

Tinder and kindling must be arranged just right to get a fire going.

leaving a little tunnel at the bottom on the *windward side* (i.e., side from which the wind is blowing). Pile on sufficient kindling in a loose pyramid. This procedure completes what is known as a *basic fire lay* and forms the basis of any kind of fire you want to build.

Add some larger pieces of wood in a pyramid or tepee fashion. Burning consists of *combustion,* or the uniting of fuel with oxygen. When you apply a match through the tunnel to the bottom of the tinder, this loose structure permits the flame to travel upward and soon sets all ablaze. Most fire failures result from piling the fuel on too compactly so that it smothers itself resulting in a dead fire or at best one that is smoky and balky. Remember that fire burns upward and only materials directly in its path will ignite. Keep cautiously adding still larger pieces of wood until your fire is as big as you need.

Using *kitchen* or *torch matches* to start your fire is best since safety or book matches can be worthless for camp use when they become wet from rain or moisture. Matches are so essential to comfortable camping that you should pack them in several different waterproof containers and keep them in a well-protected spot in your pack. Also, carrying a small emergency supply in your pocket is useful. Several kinds of containers will do a good job of protecting the matches, such as a plastic pill bottle. A common and inexpensive metal case, available at most supply houses and equipment stores, is watertight and its screw-on top is attached.

Individual matches can be waterproofed with paraffin. Simply place the paraffin in an old tin can, immerse the can in a pan of water, and heat the water until the paraffin melts. Do not cover the paraffin or place it directly over the fire since it is quite flammable and can ignite into a ball of fire in a matter of seconds. Use tongs or pliers to remove the can of hot paraffin from the water. Tie your matches in bundles of six to eight, leaving a piece of string attached to *each* bundle with which to manipulate it. Dip each bundle of matches into the melted paraffin to coat them. When you are ready to use a match, pick it out of its paraffin cover and scrape off any excess paraffin. What little paraffin remains will make the match burn better. Only counselors or older, responsible campers should handle paraffin because of the fire danger and because hot paraffin causes nasty burns. Never pour paraffin down a sink since it will clog it as it hardens. You can also waterproof matches by dipping them in a thin solution of shellac, varnish, or fingernail polish, or by dripping wax on them from a candle.

Your goal should be to lay your fire so well that you will need only one match to start it. Strike the match and hold it downward so the flame burns up the shaft. Cup your hands to shield the match from the wind. As soon as the match is burning well, cautiously insert it through the tunnel to the *bottom* of the tinder. If your fire lay is good, it will blaze up immediately. Add more fuel as needed, placing it on loosely to avoid smothering the fire.

If your fire does not catch after two or three matches, the fault probably lies in your fire lay and you will save time in the long run by tearing it down and starting over.

One of the most common errors in building fires is to build one much bigger than you need. A small fire will cook a simple meal. Big fires take more work, are hot, waste fuel, burn the food or cook it too rapidly, create greater fire hazards, and are more likely to scar the landscape. In addition, let your fire burn down to coals before you start to cook. Coals cook the food slowly and thoroughly instead of leaving it charcoaled on the outside and raw on the inside. Coals are also more comfortable to cook over and do not leave cookware with a black, sooty mask. To get good coals, light a good hardwood fire well in advance and keep it going until there is a thick bed of glowing embers.

Kinds of Fires

Several kinds of fires are possible. An 18-inch *wigwam* or *tepee fire* (figure 29.2) burns quickly with enough heat to boil water or cook a quick one-pot meal or provide light and warmth for a small group meeting. Its rapid flame renders it a good foundation for getting more long-lasting fires going.

The *hunter-trapper fire* is a good cooking fire. Lay rocks in the form of an open V with the wide end toward the wind and about 15 to 16 inches wide, tapering to the small end, which is just wide enough to support your smallest kettle. Build a tepee fire inside and keep it going until you have a good bed of coals to distribute along under your kettles. Keep a brisk fire going at one end to produce coals to replenish those under your kettles. This fire is cooler to cook by and conserves fuel because the rocks reflect all the heat up onto your kettles.

Figure 29.2   Tepee fire in hunter-trapper design.

The *keyhole fire* (figure 29.3) is somewhat similar in technique to the hunter-trapper fire. The difference is that rocks are laid in a keyhole pattern that provides a corridor in which the burning wood and hot coals can be separated at one end for warmth and for cooking at the other. Two green logs can be used in place of the rocks.

Figure 29.3   The keyhole fire provides warmth on one end and cooking on the other.

The *log cabin* or *crisscross fire* (figure 29.4) also is a good cooking fire, especially when you need a good bed of coals for continued heat. It also makes a good council ring fire. Use sticks an inch or less in diameter if you want it to burn briskly. Build the structure loosely and light a small tepee fire underneath to set the whole thing going quickly.

Reflector fires give steady heat for baking in a reflector oven or for throwing heat into an open tent. Place the reflector on the leeward side of the fire so that it will draw the smoke and flames and reflect back only the heat. You can make a *fire bank* by piling up stones or stacking green logs (figure 29.5) against uprights driven into the ground at a 75° angle. Dirt also can be piled in front to keep it from catching on fire. Figure 29.6 shows an aluminum foil reflector oven made by wrapping the foil around two forked sticks that are separated by another stick placed behind the "V" of the forked ones.

Altar fires are labor-saving devices for permanent campsites since you do not have to stoop either to tend the fire or to stir your food. They also minimize the dan-

Figure 29.4   Log cabin fire.

Figure 29.5   Reflector fireplaces.

ger of having the fire spread through the duff. Cement rocks together or notch logs and fit them together to form a hollow base and fill it with some nonflammable material such as flattened tin cans, sand, or rocks. Build it to a convenient height for those using it—1½ to 2 feet high for children, 2½ to 3 feet high for adults. If you extend one side of the base up a foot or two, it will make an excellent reflector fire.

When a group meets for a summer campfire program, they use a *council fire*. They want a maximum of light and ambiance with a minimum of heat. Adapt the size of your fire to the size of your group and avoid using varieties of wood that crackle and pop. They are dangerous and distract attention from the program. Use a plentiful supply of tinder and kindling as a base and intersperse larger split kindling among your logs so that the fire will get underway quickly. A mixture of soft and hard woods usually gives best results. Since the average campfire program seldom lasts more than an hour or so, you should be able to lay a fire that will last that long without having to replenish it. However, have fuel available in case needed.

Extinguishing Your Campfire

Water is the best thing to use for extinguishing a campfire. Scatter all the embers that remain and douse them thoroughly. Make sure that every bit of fire is thoroughly drenched. Carefully pull aside all blazing pieces for a special dousing, saturating them or immersing them

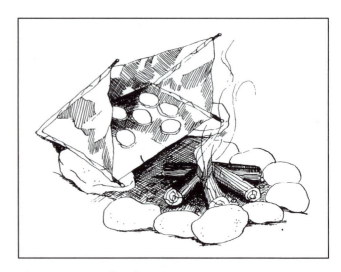

Figure 29.6   Foil reflector oven.

in a nearby stream or lake. Stir the fire bed repeatedly and keep sprinkling it with water. Place your hand at various spots over the fire bed to search for any remaining heat. Make sure it is *dead out*. Leaving it with even a trace of heat, flame, smoke, or steam is NOT safe.

If water is unavailable, smother the fire with sand, gravel, or dirt. Choose the soil carefully, however, for some types contain enough vegetable matter to smolder for days before breaking out into a full-fledged flame. If you have to move hot ashes, wet them down thoroughly and deposit them at a fireproof spot.

Wet Weather Fires

An amateur has enough trouble producing a bright steady flame in clear dry weather, but nothing compares to the difficulty of building a fire when it is damp or raining. A fire may be even more important to campers during foul weather than at any other time. Sending everyone to bed with dry clothing, hot food in their stomachs, and memories of fellowship around a cheerful blaze is quite important psychologically as well as physically.

Whenever you are in camp, always keep a supply of dry tinder, kindling, and firewood under a tent or tarpaulin. If caught without it, search under overhanging rocks or fallen trees or on the dead bottom limbs of standing trees. Even wet wood is usually damp only on the top layers and dry wood can be found by stripping off the bark or shaving off a few layers. Splitting large sticks also will reveal an inner core of dry wood to use as kindling or to make fuzz clumps or fuzz sticks.

Trench candles carried in a plastic bag or waterproof tin box are excellent for starting a fire anytime, but especially on a rainy day. To make them, lay a strip of cloth, twine, or thick cord in the center of six to ten sheets of newspaper and roll and twist them into a tight cylinder. Tie pieces of string snugly about the roll at intervals of 2 to 4 inches, leaving an end of the string on each section long enough to handle it by. Sever the roll midway between the strings and pull out the center cloth or cord of each segment far enough to serve as a wick. Dip each piece several times in melted paraffin or old candle wax, letting it harden a few minutes in between so that the paper becomes thoroughly saturated with the wax. Trench candles are almost impervious to rain and wind and will burn long enough to start a fire under almost any condition. By themselves, they will provide enough heat to cook on a tin can stove or give a fairly adequate light when burned flat in a dish or other container. A plain candle stub or, even better, a plumber's candle will serve the same purpose, although not nearly so well.

A fire built on sopping-wet ground can produce enough steam to smother itself. To avoid the smothering, build a little platform of aluminum foil, stones, or sticks as a base. A tepee fire works best on wet ground. Lay it with more care than usual using fuzz sticks or trench candles and good tinder and kindling at first. Add other fuel gradually as the fire gains momentum. Damp fuel dries out surprising quickly when leaned against already flaming sticks. You can place an additional supply close to the fire to gradually dry out.

If rain is falling, suspend a piece of tarpaulin or a poncho on a framework of sticks at least 5 feet above the fire to shield it until you have it going well. If it is windy, anchor the corners with guy ropes. If the wind is especially strong, erect a tarpaulin windbreak on the windward side.

WEB RESOURCES

Fires and Stoves (http://outside.away.com/outside/gear/index.html)

Stoves (http://www.consumersearch.com/www/sports_and_leisure/camping-stoves/reviews.html)

PRINT RESOURCES

Curtis, R. (2005). *The backpacker's field manual: A comprehensive guide to mastering backcountry skills.* New York: Three Rivers Press.

Getchell, A., & Getchell, D. (2000). *The essential outdoor gear manual: Equipment care, repair, and selection* (2nd ed.). Camden, ME: Ragged Mountain Press.

Townsend, C. (2005). *The backpacker's handbook.* Camden, ME: Ragged Mountain Press.

30

Food and Outdoor Cooking

No matter how much other fun in camp, nothing can take the place of a delicious meal prepared outdoors. With the variety of options on the market, there's no reason for meals to be dull and monotonous. All that is required is a little imagination, some forethought and planning, and a good outdoor recipe book.

Some of the more elaborate dishes and methods of cooking may be good choices when you are near the main camp and have ample time and supplies. However, longer trips will require you to stick to simple meals that can be prepared quickly with a minimum of utensils. Stews and other one-pot meals are popular.

Young campers could start out by planning simple lunches such as sandwiches, fruit, and a cold drink to be packed at the main camp and taken out and eaten. The next step might be cooking a one-pot meal for a supper cookout and then an aluminum-foil menu with meat and vegetables all cooked together in a package. Cooking in hot coals represents the whole category of cooking methods available in primitive surroundings. Adding only one new item at a time is usually best so that the whole meal will not be ruined if the new technique does not turn out as anticipated. These ventures give experience in gauging appetites and preparing food before longer trips are taken.

Avoid the uncreative picnic menu of hot dogs, buns, potato chips, pickles, and marshmallows. These items can be easily prepared at home and there are many more interesting options. It is important from a psychological as well as a health standpoint to have meals that are just as nutritious, well cooked, and attractively served as those indoors. Let campers share in planning and cooking their own meals so they learn the principles of proper nutrition and food selection as they do so. Toward this end, many camps make it possible for campers and counselors to work closely with the food service manager or a well-trained trip counselor. To make it more interesting, you can include a consideration of costs, giving campers a budget and letting them figure costs per meal, per day, and per week. Many excellent outdoor recipe books exist and countless recipes are available on the Internet.

Planning Meals

On the trail, breakfast is usually simple but must be substantial enough to keep campers going during a morning of activity. Lunch is also hearty and likewise simple, often consisting of sandwiches and other cold foods possibly supplemented by hot soup or a hot drink if the weather is rainy or chilly. A cold lunch enables you to get back on the trail quickly without having to take the time to build and put out a fire or unpack your stove. Dinner can be a more leisurely hot meal. If time allows, perhaps a hot bread, side dish, and dessert can supplement the meal.

Vitamins and minerals consumed through normal meals are usually sufficient to meet daily needs, but when hiking or backpacking, it is important to provide plenty of proteins, carbohydrates and fats—the essentials for energy. Proteins maintain muscle mass and keep the body in good working order. Carbohydrates and fats allow quick replenishment of lost energy to meet the increased demands on the body. Fats provide a long-term reserve, while carbohydrates give quick energy for work beyond the normal level.

Carbohydrates are the body's most efficient source of energy. Active campers should eat plenty of carbohydrates. Fruits, vegetables, whole grains, cereals, legumes, and milk products are sources of carbohydrates. The carbohydrates are converted to glycogen, which is stored in the muscles and liver. During exercise, your body calls on these glycogen reserves to give energy. Unlike fats or protein, carbohydrates can be used by the body during any phase of exercise.

In addition to glycogen, the body also gets energy from fats, which supply the body with a concentrated source of energy. After continually exercising for a long period of time, the body begins to burn its fat reserves. However, to stay healthy, you must eat fats in moderation—limiting saturated fats and altogether avoiding trans fat. Sources of fat include oils, cheese, nuts, and chocolate.

Protein is needed to make your body grow. Protein builds, maintains, and replaces body tissue. Although protein can also be used as an energy source, it is a last resort when no carbohydrates or fats are available. When the body burns protein, muscles and other body components suffer. Four to six ounces of rich protein from sources such as meat, poultry, and beans will usually provide all the protein you need each day.

Because of the body's continual need to replenish itself with calories, most campers should carry some sort of snack food to munch along the trail or at brief rest stops. These may consist of a combination of such items as dried fruits, unsalted peanuts or other nuts, and cereal or trail mix. Each camper should carry his or her own supply in a plastic bag. Sweets can be mixed with the trail mix, but they are not necessary. Eating sugary snacks can give a quick rush of energy, but usually is followed by hunger, irritability, and sleepiness a little farther down the trail. Sugar is absorbed quickly into the bloodstream, sending blood sugar soaring. The pancreas produces a hormone called insulin that transports blood sugar into the body's cells where it is used for energy. However, because sugar and refined grains are so quickly converted to blood sugar, the resulting insulin surge causes too much blood sugar to be transported out of the blood, which leaves a person feeling tired and hungry. Fruits, vegetables, popcorn, nuts, and cheeses make for better energy snacks. Thanks to the fiber in plant foods and the protein in dairy, your body takes longer to break down and absorb these substances. The blood sugar then rises slowly and sustains energy.

Including enough roughage in the diet to prevent constipation is often a problem, but it can be remedied by including dried fruit (e.g., prunes, figs, dates). If you want the fruits soft for breakfast, soak them the night before.

Plan each meal in detail, following recipes exactly by putting down the amount of each ingredient needed. In selecting recipes consider such aspects as:

- ease of preparation
- time required for cooking
- number and type of utensils needed (these add bulk and weight to the pack)
- amount of fuel required
- amount and type of weight to be disposed of or carried back with you
- age and personal preferences of those going on the trip
- religious and cultural characteristics of the group

If possible, try out each recipe before using it on a trip.

Most camps furnish blank trip forms to be filled out before the trip. These forms ask for such information as the names of those going, the date and time of departure, destination, date and time of return, number of days and meals planned for, the actual menus planned for each meal, the exact quantities of foodstuff needed, and a summary of the total number of utensils needed for the trip. After the plans have been approved, copy the menu for each meal on a 3 × 5 inch card stating the exact quantities of food required, cooking utensils needed, type of fire required, and complete directions for preparing everything. Representative campers with one or more counselors can work with the food service manager or trip counselor to assemble and pack the supplies requisitioned.

Coping with food preparation for large numbers sometimes proves overwhelming to inexperienced campers. Therefore, you might consider dividing a large group into small groups of six to eight, with each smaller group cooking and perhaps even planning its own meals.

Lightweight Foods

Fresh foods are generally not taken on a trip of any duration. In addition to the danger of eating certain foods that have been kept for even a few hours without refrigeration, they are too bulky and heavy for comfortable carrying. Since most of this weight is simply water, it makes sense to utilize methods of food preparation that

Nothing can take the place of a delicious meal cooked outdoors.

remove much of this water—leaving foods that are dry, light, and compact. When properly packed, they will keep a year or more without refrigeration. Such foods can usually be reconstituted in 10 to 30 minutes by adding water and cooking quickly. They produce a finished product that closely resembles the original food in taste, visual appearance, and nutritional value.

Various methods are used to make these lightweight, dehydrated foods. Freeze-drying is superior for many foods since it removes as much as 97% of the water content, but it is the most expensive method because of the large investment in plant and equipment that is required. After being freeze-dried, a pound of meat weighs only 2 ounces, 10 pounds of potatoes only 1.7 pounds, and a pound of peaches that will serve four, only 3 ounces. A whole cooked meal can be freeze-dried and then reconstituted merely by adding boiling water. Many foods referred to as freeze-dried are actually dehydrated. Although not as much of the water is removed through dehydration, this is a less expensive process and often works quite well.

A number of specialized firms produce such freeze-dried foods as fruits, puddings, stews, breads, eggs and egg products, applesauce, milk shakes, fruit juices, hamburger, casseroles, beefsteak, chicken, pork chops, pizza, chow mien, and even ice cream. In addition to individual foodstuffs, whole meals are available in 1-person, 2-person, 4-person, and 8-person packets. However, some users find the portions in some brands too skimpy to satisfy appetites. An active teenager or adult will burn up 3,000 to 6,000 calories a day. Daily rations per person usually weigh from 1¾ to 2 pounds.

Lightweight freeze-dried foods can be somewhat expensive, but there is little waste and their convenience may make them a good investment. On the other hand, the disadvantage of using such foods exclusively is that campers miss out on the valuable experience of planning well-balanced meals. Using preplanned meals also fails to give campers experience in using various outdoor cooking methods.

Fortunately, there are less expensive alternatives to freeze-dried food available in your local grocery store. For a negligible amount of extra weight to your pack and about half the price of conventional prepackaged trail meals, you can find simple grocery-store provisions that work well for backcountry cooking. The average grocery store contains a surprising variety of dry or dehydrated foods with weight and longevity to suit your trip, as seen in exhibit 30.1.

Packing Food

Any kind of trip, particularly one on foot, challenges counselors and campers to plan menus using foods that require no refrigeration and are not too bulky. Many items purchased at the grocery store come in packages that will not withstand the wear and tear of a trip or have sharp corners. They also may not contain the exact amounts you need. To eliminate excess bulk and weight, measure out and package exactly what you need for each meal. Be careful to detach any essential directions for preparation.

Exhibit 30.1

Lightweight Foods Available at Your Grocery Store

Beef jerky

Bouillon cubes, dried mushrooms, and gravy mixes (excellent for adding flavor to soups and casseroles)

Bread sticks or hard crackers

Bread, biscuit, muffin, corn bread, and pancake mixes

Cake, cookie, brownie, and gingerbread mixes

Dried beef, codfish flakes and cakes

Dried fruits (apricots, raisins, apples, prunes, dates, figs, fruit cocktail)

Dried milk (a pound makes a gallon of milk)—this is usually skim milk, but dried whole milk is available

Dried peas, lentils, and beans of all types

Dried soups

Hard cheese

Hard cookies, such as ginger snaps

Herbs and spices—choose a few favorites such as ground cumin, oregano, thyme, herb mixtures, cinnamon, cloves, bay leaves, dried dill, rosemary, and sage

Instant cocoa, coffee and tea, Ovaltine

Instant potatoes

Instant pudding, Jell-O (cool in a stream)

Instant rice

Macaroni, spaghetti, noodles, pizza

Oatmeal, grits, cornmeal, farina, Granola, Grape nuts, and other cold cereals

Parsley, onion, and carrot flakes

Peanuts and other nuts, hard candy, and non-melting chocolate

Pemmican (dried meat pounded to a pulp and then mashed with fat and sometimes raisins and sugar and formed into cakes or bars)

Pie and cobbler mixes

Popcorn (excellent for campfire nibbling)

Powdered fruit juices

Skillet dinners

Pack semiliquids such as syrup, peanut butter, jams, jellies, or honey in refillable wide-mouthed squeeze tubes or in plastic (poly) bottles that are available at outfitting shops. Lightweight aluminum cans such as those that contain baking powder also may be used. Other packing possibilities are old plastic prescription bottles and plastic containers intended for home freezing.

Place dry materials in strong plastic bags, squeeze out excess air, and fasten them at the top. By double bagging any fine-particle foods such as flour and sugar, you will be sure the bags are strong enough to hold up under trail use. Label each bag with a felt tip pen, indicating the contents, the amount, and the meal for which they are to be used. Printed directions for preparation should be placed inside so they can be read through the clear plastic. When planning flapjacks, biscuits, soups, and cakes, mix all the dry ingredients before leaving and pack them in a labeled plastic bag. This procedure cuts down on the number of bags necessary and saves measuring and mixing ingredients on the trail.

Glass bottles are heavy and breakable, so place the contents in wide-mouthed plastic bottles or lightweight aluminum cans with screw-on or press-in tops saved from commercial products or purchased from outfitters.

Hard cheese (not processed) in chunk form will keep well without refrigeration if properly packed. Package in meal-size quantities and wrap each portion in two or three layers of cheesecloth, pressed lightly against the cheese. Dip each package quickly into melted paraffin so that it acquires a good coating, then place the packages in a rigid container to prevent other objects from breaking the paraffin shield. A little mold may form around the edges of the cheese, but is merely a harmless form of penicillin, which can be scraped off if you find it objectionable. Refrain from touching the unused cheese with your bare hands. Handle the cheese with a plastic bag to keep the bacteria on your skin from taking residence on the cheese.

Spices and other flavorings do wonders in perking up foods. Include a few well-chosen favorites. Since salt draws moisture, it will eventually rust out tin containers. Carry it in a plastic bottle or bag in one of the poly shakers for both salt and pepper that are available from suppliers.

For trips, assemble all the bags for a single meal into a larger bag, carefully labeled as to the meal for which it is intended. Place all bags for a day (breakfast, lunch, and supper) into a larger bag labeled with the day for which it is intended. Place these bags in your food duffel bag or plastic bear canister with food to be used first on top.

When going on an extended trip, investigate the possibility of lightening your load and adding fresh supplies by purchasing groceries along the way. You may also be able to arrange a rendezvous at some point en route to get fresh food or arrange with some supplier to make a drop shipment at a post office along the way. It may also be possible to add variety to your diet by picking fruit or catching fish along the way, but do not count on it.

Outdoor Cooking

Since camps often have cookout sites near their cabins or the main camp or offer short trips involving only one or two meals, we have included some recipes and cooking methods that are especially suitable for use with wood fires in such situations. For additional recipes and cooking methods, consult the references at the end of the chapter.

General Notes about Outdoor Cooking

1. Canvas or other work gloves and a large bandanna are useful for handling hot objects around the fire and for keeping your hands clean for cooking. When cooking over a wood fire, a green forked-stick fire poker and a shovel are indispensable for moving hot rocks, burning embers, and glowing coals into more advantageous positions for cooking.

2. For general cooking over wood fires, ordinary kettles with wire handles that can be hung over lug poles or on pot hooks (see figure 30.1) are recommended. When cooking over a wood fire, coat the outside surfaces of your kettles with a thick paste of detergent and water or rub a moistened bar of laundry soap over them. When the kettle is washed, the soap comes off easily taking the smoke and soot with it. Not all campers agree, however, with this process. Some people feel that kettles heat better and more

Figure 30.1   Ways of suspending pots.

Ordinary kettles with wire handles that can be hung over lug poles work well for general cooking over wood fires.

evenly if you leave the coating of smoke and soot on them. In that case, carry each kettle in its own carrying bag so the soot will not rub off on other things in your pack.

3. Use a tin can or round water bottle for a rolling pin.

4. Grease the vessel in which you melt chocolate or measure molasses or honey to keep it from adhering to the sides.

5. Put a container of water over the fire when you first light it. You will have hot water ready for cooking by the time the fire burns down to coals.

6. You can improvise double boilers for cooking rice and other cereals by supporting the food vessel on three or four small stones inside a larger vessel partly filled with water.

7. Boil a little vinegar and water in the pans in which fish has been cooked to remove the fishy odor.

8. When cooking meat, use low or moderate heat. This procedure requires more time, but the meat will not shrink so much and will be more tender. When you want to draw the juices and flavor out of meat, like when making soup or stew, start it in cold water and cook it with low heat. To seal the juices and flavor in, drop it into boiling water or sear it on all sides over a hot fire, then cook it over low or moderate heat. Do not season meat until it is nearly done. Seasonings draw out juices.

9. Dried milk will taste better if mixed and allowed to stand for some time before drinking it. Place it in a plastic bottle and weight at the bottom of a stream, pond, or lake to chill.

10. To test breads and cakes for doneness, stick a straw or sliver of wood into them. If it comes out clean, they are done. If doughy or sticky, they need to bake longer.

11. Long, slow cooking usually improves the flavor of food. When using a wood fire, start the fire early and let it burn down to a glowing bed of coals. You can regulate the heat by changing the distance of the food from the fire or by drawing more coals under the pot, keeping a brisk fire going over at one side to produce more coals if they are needed.

12. Allow more time for cooking at high altitudes.

13. In general, keep a cover on your cook pot to conserve heat and help preserve moisture.

14. When preparing to cook, spread a plastic sheet on the ground and place all your food and cooking utensils on it. This step will keep them readily visible and prevent misplacing some essential item.

Frying is frequently overused in camp cookery and, when incorrectly done, results in a soggy, unappetizing dish. The chief problem comes from letting fried foods absorb too much fat as they cook. To avoid this problem, have the food as dry as possible and heat the cooking oil to just under the smoking stage before you put the food in. The hot oil sears the food, sealing the juices in and the oil out. Drain fried foods on a paper napkin or paper towel to remove excess oil. When frying in a skillet over an open fire, avoid high flames since they can set fire to the oil in the pan.

Pan broiling is a healthier form of frying that uses low heat. Start with a little cooking oil in the pan and pour off the excess as it forms leaving barely enough in the pan to keep the food from sticking. Turn the meat several times.

Broiling is cooking by direct exposure to the heat from glowing coals. Build a fire of hard wood well in advance of cooking time and keep it going until it burns down to a bed of coals. Place the meat over the flame to sear it quickly on both sides and then place it over the coals. Watch it carefully. Beware of letting fat drip into the flame, since it may catch fire and burn the meat. Avoid using resinous or strong-tasting woods as they may impart an unpleasant flavor to the food.

Wilderness cookery is done without cookware or utensils and includes cooking in ashes or coals, in an imu or beanhole, or on a stick or spit. Planning a whole meal using only wilderness cookery is fun, and there is a surprising variety of foods you can serve.

Cooking Techniques and Outdoor Recipes

One-pot meals include stews or mixtures that are cooked in one kettle and furnish a whole meal in themselves. They are usually built upon a base of macaroni, spaghetti, dumplings, rice, potatoes, or noodles with various dehydrated vegetables, broth cubes, and your favorite seasonings. They may be served hot on rice, toast, or crackers. Here are two examples:

1. *Irish Stew* (serves 5)
   5 onions, sliced
   1 lb. meat cut in 1-inch cubes
   5 potatoes
   Other vegetables such as carrots, as desired
   Salt and pepper

   Heat a little oil in a kettle and fry the onions and meat until brown. Cover with cold water and bring to a boil. Cook slowly for 1½ hours. Add the potatoes and continue to cook slowly until they are tender. Season to taste.

A one-pot meal cooked on a backpacking stove. (Photo by Joel Meier)

2. *Ring Tum Diddy* (serves 5)
   6 slices bacon, diced
   2 onions, sliced
   ¼ lb. cheese, diced
   2½ cups (20 ounces) canned tomatoes
   2½ cups (20 ounces) canned corn
   Salt and pepper

   Fry the bacon and onions until brown, and pour off part of the fat. Add the tomatoes and corn and bring to a boil. Add the cheese and cook slowly until it is melted. Season to taste.

For *stick cookery*, use a metal skewer or peel and sharpen a green stick about 2 feet long. Resinous woods and willow impart an unpleasant taste. If in doubt about the suitability of the wood, peel the end and bite it. Cook over coals, not flames. You can support the stick above the fire by laying it across a rock or forked stick and weighting the handle end down with a rock or other heavy object. Here are several favorites:

1. *Bread Twister or Doughboy*
   Use a regular biscuit mix, adding just enough water to make it sticky. Roll out flat about ¼ to ½ inch thick and cut into long strips about 2 inches wide. Remove the bark from the end of a stick about twice the size of your thumb, heat the end, flour it, and wind a strip of dough spirally around it, leaving a slight gap between the spirals. Bake for 10 to 15 minutes over coals, turning it so that all sides bake evenly. It will come off the stick in the form of a cylinder closed at one end. When filled with jam, jelly, or cheese, it is known as a *cave woman cream puff.*

2. *Pigs-in-a-Blanket*
   Cook a wiener or long sausage on a stick, and then cover it with biscuit dough and bake.

3. *Pioneer Drumsticks* (serves 5)
   1¼ lbs. beef, chopped fine
   ¾ cup cornflakes, crumbled fine
   1 egg
   Onion (if desired)
   Salt and pepper

   Thoroughly mix the ingredients and wrap a thin portion tightly around the peeled end of the stick and squeeze firmly into place. Toast it slowly over coals, turning frequently, and serve in a roll. Some prefer to put the cornflakes on after the meat has been placed on the stick, so that they form a sort of crust over the outside.

4. *Shish Kebabs*
   Lace a slice of bacon in and out among alternate 1-inch squares of steak, pork, or chicken; slices of onion, small tomatoes, green peppers, and so forth, as desired, impaled on a stick. Place the pieces close together if you want the meat rare, farther apart if well done. The bacon will serve to baste them. Broil over

gradual heat from coals. Shish kebab got its name from two Turkish words, *shish* meaning skewer, and *kebab* meaning broiled meat.

5. *Date Dreams*
Make these by alternating pitted dates with halved marshmallows on a stick and toasting slowly over the fire.

The secret of cooking in *ashes or coals* is to build a hardwood fire early and let it burn to coals. To keep a new supply of hot coals coming, keep a fire going at one side and draw coals over as you need them. Parsnips, fish (wrapped in clay), oysters (in the shell), squash, hamburger (wrapped in aluminum foil), and lasagna in a Dutch oven may be cooked in this way.

1. *Potatoes*
Scrub potatoes, sweet potatoes, or yams of medium size and without blemishes, and place them on hot coals in a single layer so that they do not touch each other; cover with coals to a depth of about 1 inch, replenishing them frequently. They are done when a sharp stick will penetrate them easily (45 to 60 minutes, depending on their size). Jab a small hole in each to let the steam escape. Some campers like to coat potatoes with skins on with a thick layer of wet mud or clay before roasting; both skins and mud come off cleanly when they are done. Alternatively, the potatoes can be wrapped in foil. Cook fish in the same way.

2. *Little Pig Potatoes*
Slice the end off a potato and hollow out enough of the center to insert a small, thin sausage (cheese, bacon, or raw egg may be used instead). Replace the end of the potato and fasten it with slivers of wood and bake it as previously described.

3. *Roasting Ears*
Turn back the husks from young, tender roasting ears and remove the silks. Sprinkle lightly with salt, replace the husks, soak the whole thing in water a few moments, and bake in the same way as potatoes.

4. *Roasted Apples*
Core the apple and fill the cavity with raisins, brown sugar, nuts, and the like. Bake them as you bake a potato.

Reflector ovens are useful cooking devices and may be a part of every outdoor cooking kit, although you might hesitate to carry their two or three pounds of weight on a trip. They are available from commercial manufacturers or you can fashion an oven on the spot using heavy duty aluminum foil (see figure 29.6). Some examples of food to cook in a reflector oven include:

1. *General Baking*
Rolls, biscuits, pies, gingerbread, corn bread, cakes, cookies, meat, and small cut up birds such as chickens can be baked in a reflector oven.

2. *Eggs Baked in Orange Shells*
Hollow an orange (making sure to remove the bitter lining) and break an egg into it; season, and set in the reflector oven to bake.

3. *S'mores*
Make a sandwich of a marshmallow and a piece of a chocolate candy bar between two graham crackers. Press gently together and place in a reflector oven to bake.

4. *Banana Boats*
Peel back a narrow strip of peeling from the inside curve of a banana, scoop out part of the banana and fill with marshmallow, chocolate, nuts, or raisins. Replace the strip of peeling and bake in a reflector oven.

Baking can also be done in a *skillet*. Support the skillet at a 45° angle against rocks on the windward side of the fire and over coals (figure 30.2).

Figure 30.2   Baking in a skillet.

1. *Bannock*
This is traditional outdoor bread made by baking biscuit dough in a floured skillet. Shape the dough about one inch thick and of a form just big enough to fit the skillet. Flour it on both sides. Turn the loaf over when done on one side; both sides will be ready in about 15 minutes. Coals shoveled out and put behind the pan hasten the baking of the underside.

2. *Pancakes (Flapjacks)*
Oil the skillet lightly and brace as described. Use only moderate heat from a small fire or from coals and heat the skillet to just under the smoking point. Drop the batter from a spoon and turn the flapjacks as soon as bubbles appear on top. Avoid too much heat for it is easy to burn them. Add blueberries or other fruit for variety. You can make your own syrup by mixing a cup of white or brown sugar with ½ cup of water, then bringing it to a boil as you stir it. Add a small amount of vanilla for a different flavor.

The heavy black cast iron *Dutch oven* (figure 30.3) is a favorite for many people. You can bake, broil, fry, roast,

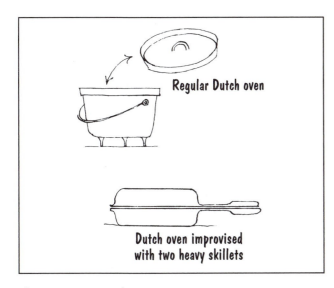

Figure 30.3   Dutch ovens.

or stew in it. You can do anything you could in your oven at home. Unlike the reflector oven, which reflects heat, the Dutch oven absorbs heat slowly and steadily and stays hot for a long time. An outdoor Dutch oven has three stubby legs that leave enough room to rake coals under it to heat it from below, and its flat, tight-fitting lid with a turned-up edge lets you put coals on top to heat from above. Its tight-fitting lid and heavy construction retain the heat and steam so it cooks the food thoroughly without letting moisture and any of the flavors escape. Be careful not to let the hot coals under the oven actually touch the bottom or it may burn the food. The oven has a strong wire handle with which to manipulate it. Ovens come in diameters of 10, 12, and 14 inches. You will not want to carry an oven on a long trip but you will enjoy using it near camp or while on a canoe trip.

The first step in Dutch oven cooking is the preparation of coals. Heat distribution is critical in Dutch oven cooking. Place the coals on top of the oven, arranging them on the edge of the lid, nearly touching each other. Underneath the oven, position them close but not touching the bottom, and about an inch in from the outside edge. Avoid lifting the lid to look at the food. Every peek can cost five to ten minutes cooking time. Here are three examples of Dutch oven cooking:

1. *Pot Roast*
   Put oil in the bottom of the kettle. Sear all sides of the roast over an open fire and put it in the kettle, adding such vegetables as onions, parsnips, carrots, turnips, potatoes, or sweet potatoes about a half hour before it is ready to serve. This provides a delicious meal in itself, and you can use the stock left in the bottom to make gravy if desired. A five-pound piece of meat requires about three hours to cook. The long exposure to even, moderate temperature tenderizes almost any cut.

2. *Baking*
   Baking is the specialty of Dutch oven cooking. First, prepare the batter from scratch or Bisquick. Before pouring the batter into the Dutch oven, grease the oven well with shortening or cooking oil. If preparing a cobbler, put the fruit on the bottom of the oven and pour the batter on top. Place about three-fourths of the coals on the lid and use the remainder underneath (but not touching) the oven. To check whether the baking is done, quickly lift the lid of the oven and stick a fork or twig through the middle of the pastry. If the fork or twig comes out clean, the cooking is done.

3. *Lasagna* (serves 5)
   1 box of lasagna noodles
   1 pint of marinara sauce
   2 lbs. of ground beef
   1½ lbs. of mozzarella cheese
   Spices to taste (garlic, oregano, salt, pepper)

   Layer the ingredients beginning with a thin layer of ground beef. Continue with a layer of sauce, noodles, cheese, spices. Repeat the layering until you reach the

Dutch oven cooking is very versatile and is a favorite method for many people.

top of the kettle. Place lid on the kettle and bury it in the hot coals, with about half the coals on the lid and the remainder underneath the oven. Let the dish cook for 30–45 minutes, depending upon the size of the oven. The juices from the meat and sauce will boil the noodles and cook the meat.

The *imu* or *pit barbecue* (figure 30.4) is another method to cook by steam with moderate even heat. It is really a variety of fireless cookery, and the excellent results obtained justify the long cooking time required. About 3 hours are necessary to cook a chicken and about a half-day for a ten-pound roast. To begin the *imu*, dig a hole about two to three times as large as the food to be cooked and line the sides and bottom with non-popping rocks. Build a good hardwood fire and keep it going for an hour or two until the rocks are sizzling hot with a good bed of coals. Get all the food ready and place it in the pit as rapidly as possible so that no more heat than necessary escapes. Remove part of the coals and hot rocks, place the food in the pit, and pack the hot rocks and coals back in around and over it. Shovel about 6 inches of dirt to make a steam-proof covering. If you see smoke or steam escaping, shovel more dirt over the leak. You can now forget the food until you dig it up ready to eat. You can cook green corn, parsnips, carrots, onions, ham, clams, potatoes with meat, and many other foods in this way.

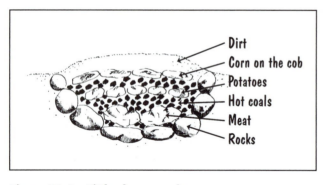

Figure 30.4   Pit barbeque or imu.

A preheated Dutch oven makes the best container for food, but if none is available you may wrap the meat and vegetables in damp butcher paper, damp paper towels, damp grass or seaweed, or damp non-tasting leaves such as lettuce, cabbage, sassafras, or sycamore.

Meat can be *barbecued* in several ways. You can place it directly over coals (but never in the flames) or a short distance away at the side of the fire. Barbecuing is a satisfactory method for cooking anything from a small chicken to large cuts of meat.

To barbecue on a spit over the fire, first dig a pit, build a good hardwood fire in it, and let it burn down to

coals (see figure 30.5). Place the meat on the spit and fasten it firmly in place so that it will turn as the stick does and so cook evenly on all sides. The coals will cool off and must be replaced frequently. Keep a separate fire at one side of the pit to provide a constantly fresh supply. Make the handle of the spit long enough to let you stay well back from the fire and place nails at varying heights on the uprights for adjusting the spit to the proper height above the heat. You can use a peeled green stick for a spit, but a metal rod with a non-heating handle does a better job, since it conveys the heat into the meat and cooks it from the inside as well as the outside. When barbecuing a chicken, select a young, tender bird commonly known as a broiler. One bird weighing two pounds serves two people and you can cook several side by side on the same spit. Clean the chicken well and insert the spit firmly from tail to neck. Protect the wings and legs from burning by pinning them close to the body with wooden slivers. Rotate the spit slowly over the coals, and baste the bird every 10 minutes with melted butter, bacon fat, or other shortening applied with a swab made by tying a cloth to the end of a stick.

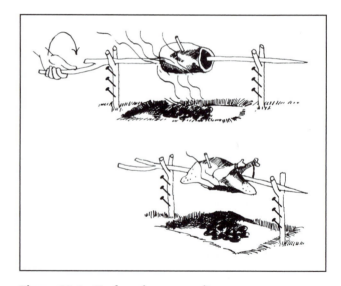

Figure 30.5   Barbequing on a spit.

To barbecue on a wire grill, fit a wire grill or piece of gravel screen on a framework of rocks, two logs, or metal poles over a pit. Build a fire of charcoal or hard wood and let it burn down to coals. Place the food to be cooked (e.g., hot dogs, chickens, spareribs, chops, steaks) on the grill over at one side of the pit. Two people using garden forks or similar tools can fasten them in the food-laden grill to draw it into position over the coals. Use a long-handled spatula, further lengthened by tying a long stick to the end of it, to turn the meat. Do not prick the meat with a fork, since holes allow juices to escape. Baste the meat occasionally with a cloth swab to keep it from drying out.

Barbequing is a satisfactory method for cooking anything from a small chicken to a large cut of meat.

Heavy duty *aluminum foil* is best for outdoor cooking, since it is about twice as thick as the ordinary variety. To prepare a meal in it, tear off a piece large enough to surround the food, allowing 2 to 3 inches of excess on the three open sides. Lay the food on one half of the piece, bring the other half over, and fold the two edges up into at least ½-inch folds and crimp them to make an airtight envelope; the all-important thing is to make it absolutely airtight so that no steam can escape, carrying with it the juices and wonderful flavor. If you have ordinary rather than heavy-duty foil, use two layers, wrapping them around in opposite directions and crimping each separately. Cook in a good bed of coals from a hardwood fire, made well ahead of time. Round out a depression in the coals big enough for the food, place the package in it, and pull the coals back over and around it. Turn the food over halfway through the cooking process. When it is done, let it sit a minute to cool, and then make a slit down the center or open the ends and eat right from the foil. Vegetables should be washed just before they are wrapped in the foil; the moisture will provide the necessary steam to cook them.

1. To cook a hamburger meal, place a patty in the foil along with strips of potato, green pepper, onions, carrots, and tomato. Flavor with a pinch of salt and cook 15 minutes.

2. Lamb or pork chops, steaks, fish, and chicken can be cooked in this way, surrounding them with such vegetables as sliced carrots, turnips, potatoes, onions, or green beans.

3. Wet an ear of corn thoroughly, leaving it in its husks; wrap a hot dog in biscuit dough; core an apple and fill the hole with brown or white sugar, cinnamon, and raisins, and cook similarly.

You can wrap the ingredients for several meals before you start out, labeling them so that you can select the right one and toss it into the coals when ready to eat. If you want to take extra foil with you, tear off a strip and roll it around a small stick. Folding it might cause holes at the creases.

Cooking time will depend on such factors as the size of the package and the heat of the coals. If necessary, look into the package to see if it is done but be sure to seal it up airtight again before replacing it in the coals. When cooking several things together, allow enough time for the slowest one to cook. Suggested cooking times are listed in exhibit 30.2.

Exhibit 30.2	
Cooking Times for Foods in Aluminum Foil Packets	
Meats	
Chicken (cut up)	20–30 minutes
Fish (whole)	15–20 minutes
Fish (fillets)	10–15 minutes
Shish kebab	14 minutes
Beef cubes (1 inch)	20–30 minutes
Frankfurters	10–15 minutes
Pigs-in-blanket	15–17 minutes
Lamb chops	20–30 minutes
Pork chops	30–40 minutes
Vegetables	
Corn (silks and husks removed)	6–10 minutes
Potatoes	60–70 minutes
Potatoes (sweet)	45–50 minutes
Carrots (sticks)	15–20 minutes
Squash (acorn)	30 minutes
Miscellaneous	
Apple (whole)	20–30 minutes
Banana (whole)	8–10 minutes
Biscuits (wrap loosely in foil to allow for rising)	6–10 minutes
Stew (1-inch meat chunks, potato cubes, onions, carrots, salt, etc.)	20 minutes

Campers should be adaptable enough to use whatever resources they can find or can convert into cooking devices for use around the campsite. Ingenuity and skill will aid in improvising cooking devices, and your satisfaction will be greatly enhanced by building your creation from scratch.

Keeping Food Safe

Cooking outdoors can be a fun, satisfying experience. However, you also must consider problems that might be encountered. For example, many curious creatures may want to investigate the people who have established themselves in their forest home. These creatures will nibble on anything and everything they can find after you've finished the meal and gone to bed.

There are no guaranteed methods of storing food. If camping in true wilderness country, you may experience wolves, foxes, or bears. In or near most resident camps, you are far more likely to see chipmunks, squirrels, mice, raccoon, opossum, pack rats, and even roving dogs or cats. In some regions, porcupines are numerous and may prove troublesome. Note that anything with a salty taste has an irresistible attraction for porcupines, and perspiration-soaked paddles, axes, shoes, belts, bridles, and saddles must be kept well beyond their reach. Any food with an odor is particularly likely to draw uninvited guests.

You also must anticipate the ever-present flies, ants, and other tiny crawling and flying insects that love to sample your food. To protect food from ants and other crawling insects, you can erect a water barrier by placing the food on a table with each leg resting in a small container of water. Also effective is a sprinkling of common moth flakes or moth balls around the legs of a table or on the path ants would have to take to reach the food. To keep out flying insects, place the food in jars or cans with tight-fitting lids. Food can also be wrapped in cloth, mosquito netting, and cheesecloth, or sealed in plastic bags.

The type of animals you expect to encounter will determine the kind of cache or protection you must provide. Even tin cans are not safe. Some animals, including dogs, can pierce them with their teeth and suck out the contents. The traditional method of caching food is to suspend it on a tree limb about 8–15 feet above the ground, far enough away from the tree trunk and overhanging branches that neither jumping nor climbing animals can get to it. Another method would be to safely secure a rope between two trees, with an additional pulley placed in the middle with a second rope through the pulley. Pull the first rope taut between the two trees, tying it off at the base of the trunks. When ready, put all food, cooking gear, and toiletries in a sturdy bag and hoist it up using the rope that runs through the pulley. Tie this rope to the base of a nearby tree.

The recommended method of preventing animals from getting into food, and the requirement for camping on many federal lands today, is to have a food or bear canister where all food and any other odiferous items (e.g., chewing gum, snacks, toothpaste) are stored. These heavy duty plastic canisters have a lid that is lockable to prevent any animal from penetrating it. The canister should be placed a distance away from the tents. These canisters can be rented or purchased from an outfitting store.

WEB RESOURCES

Camp Cooking (www.free-camping-recipes.com) offers a database of recipes sorted by category, as well as cooking tips.

Camp Recipes (www.camprecipes.com) includes a database of recipes sorted by category.

Campfire Safety Guidelines (www.windsorfire.com/divisions-prevention-campfire-safety-guidelines) discusses general fire safety, specific information on good campfire skills.

Dutch Ovens (http://www.ceedubs.com) and (http://www.idos.com).

Earth Easy (http://www.eartheasy.com/play_campfire_cooking.htm) offers tips on building campfires, recipes, general information, safety, and other cooking techniques.

Proper Campfire Ring/Enclosure Design Guidelines (http://dnr.wa.gov/Publications/rp_fire_campfirebrochure.pdf) provides a brochure on campfire facts and safety tips and design.

Menu Planning and Suggestions

(http://www.netwoods.com/d-cooking.html)

(http://www.pathfindersrus.com/camp-cooking.html)

(http://www.wilderness-backpacking.com/backpacking-cooking.html)

PRINT RESOURCES

Jacobson, C. (1999). *Cooking in the outdoors.* Guilford, CT: Globe Pequot Press.

Jacobson, J. (2005). *The one pan gourmet: Fresh food on the trail* (2nd ed.). Camden, ME: Ragged Mountain Press.

Pearson, C. (Ed.). (2004). *NOLS cookery* (5th ed.). Mechanicsburg, PA: Stackpole Books.

31

Gear for Camping and Trips

Newcomers to camp usually bring along *duffel* or *gear* (camp jargon for your possessions). The secret of camp living is to have everything that is needed for health, safety, and happiness without being surrounded by a collection of unnecessary accoutrements. Camp living is about simplicity. Your camp quarters probably will be clean, comfortable, and adequate for your needs but without extra embellishments or an unlimited amount of storage space. Therefore, you need to help campers plan for what they need to make the camp experience most beneficial both while at camp and when away on trips.

When packing for camp, particularly a residential or trip camp, choosing what to take and how to pack it is important, especially if you have to transport the gear. Transportation by watercraft or animal allows a bit more latitude, but space is still at a premium and every unnecessary item will need to be picked up and handled many times as you search for needed items.

Long expeditions into the backcountry should not be undertaken unless you have the minimum of equipment for doing it comfortably and safely. However, elaborate outlays are usually not necessary. Campers can initially get along with little more than the gear they or the camp already has. Camps sometimes rent or lend pieces of personal equipment to campers and customarily furnish group equipment such as tents, tools, and group cooking and eating utensils. Campers also can make some items. Whatever the case, a brief description of the various kinds of gear needed for camping and trips follows.

Ditty Bags and Stuff Sacks

A camper's pack is a series of bags within bags with similar things such as toiletries or underwear collected in small *ditty bags* or *stuff sacks*. This procedure allows an individual to locate items quickly without having to turn everything inside-out. Articles packed singly or randomly have a way of dropping to the bottom of your pack or being lost or forgotten.

The number of sacks or bags needed depends upon the length of the trip and your personal preferences. A minimum is one bag for toiletries, one for clothing, one for eating utensils, and one for miscellaneous items. You may want to add others for tools and food.

Many experienced campers like stuff sacks made of clear plastic since they are waterproof, tough, and readily reveal what's inside. Collect your own assortment by saving home freezer bags and bags in which food and other items are sold. Outfitters offer zippered pouches and bags that close with drawstrings, which are usually water-

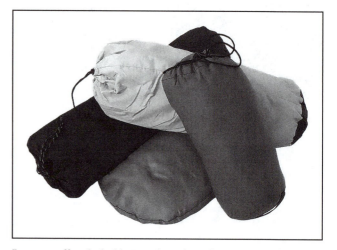

Larger stuff sacks hold a number of smaller sacks or ditty bags in which campers can organize their gear.

proofed and made from lightweight materials. New materials like Cuben fiber offer high performance, lightweight fabrics that resist tearing and are waterproof.

Clothing

Clothing and outfitting stores display attractive camping outfits of almost every type and description. You would be wise, however, to go slowly and choose carefully before making a large investment. Although everyone wants to look well dressed, it is far more important to choose clothing based on comfort, suitability, and durability. Choice of clothing should be influenced by factors such as the season and weather expected, the length of the trip, and the type of terrain in which you will travel. Garments should be comfortable and fit snugly, yet be cut full enough to permit freedom of movement for hiking, climbing, canoeing, working around camp, or whatever else. Clothes need to be serviceable, snag resistant, and washable.

Layering

The human body has a built-in thermostat with its own heating and cooling devices. Choosing clothing that will help the body perform efficiently is important. The principle of *layering* works well. To fully understand the importance of layering as well as proper clothing selection, the basics of thermodynamics and heat transmission are at work. The body loses heat in four ways:

1. *Convection* is the transfer of heat by currents of air, and it occurs when cool air carries your body's heat out and away from you.

2. *Radiation* occurs continually as a body's natural inner heat dissipates out just like a stove. Much of this loss takes place through the head and neck.

3. *Evaporation* and cooling comes about from air moving over the moisture on skin. The body's sweat is a natural evaporative cooling system.

4. *Conduction* is the conveying of heat from the body when it comes into contact with something cold or wet (i.e., your back against a wet T-shirt, your hand in an icy stream, your nose against a cold pane of glass). A danger in low temperatures is sweaty, wet clothes against the skin. The moisture is warmed by body heat, and the heat flows to the cold outdoors.

Heat loss through convection and radiation are readily managed through simple covering and layering to create thermal traps to hold warmth close to the body. On the other hand, the best defense against evaporation and conduction is getting the moisture away from the skin as quickly as possible without interfering with the warmed air layer that exists between the skin and the closest garment.

An example is that on a cool summer morning, you start out wearing underwear, pants, a shirt or two, and even a sweater and lightweight windbreaker. As the day warms up, simply remove the garments as needed. In reverse order, clothing is added to meet the cool of the evening. The advantage to this system is that several layers of clothing provide more warmth than does a single thick garment because immobile air is trapped between the various layers. A person is also better able to make clothing adjustments to adapt readily to changing weather conditions. Another important consideration is a person's ability to control perspiration caused by overheating. The collection of moisture on clothing, whether from perspiration or any other source, can lead to a dangerous condition called hypothermia, which can sometimes be fatal.

Regardless of how many piles of clothing used for layering, the system has three primary components.

Vapor Transmission Layer

This layer consists of *breathable* garments next to the skin that allow body moisture to pass quickly and efficiently through them. To wick away moisture in cold weather, wear underwear made of wool, silk, or synthetics such as olefin, polypropylene, Capilene, Thermax, and Dryline. Although wool has long been the traditional standby and still works well, more people are now choosing undergarments made of lightweight nonabsorbent synthetic fibers that keep skin dry by transferring moisture out to the next layer of clothing. Above all, in cold climates be sure to avoid garments made of cotton since they provide no insulation when wet. Collected moisture in cotton fabrics actually can draw heat away from the body faster than it can be generated.

Insulating Layer

Shirts, sweaters, vests, jackets, or parkas commonly are used to hold the warm air around the body. A variety of garment materials works well for the insulating layer including wool, down, or any of the newer synthetics such as pile, Polarguard, Hollofil II, or Thinsulate. Wool has a disadvantage of being heavy when wet, and down is worthless if wet. On the other hand, pile—a thermal fleece made of polyester, nylon, or acrylic—is now widely recognized as excellent insulation from the cold as well as from the wet. The advantage that pile has over many other insulators is that it is durable, relatively inexpensive, insulates well even when damp, and it continues the wicking process that proper undergarments start.

Protective Layer

The outermost layer protects the inner layers from abrasion and also shelters the wearer from water and wind. As with the insulating layer, a variety of suitable garments are available including jackets, anoraks, wind shirts, cagoules (pullover parka), and other variations. Since the moisture protecting element of the outer layer must protect against rain or even snow, a dilemma arises in selecting proper materials. Waterproof shells (usually made of coated nylon or plastic) are impervious to moisture and consequently, they do not breathe. Thus, a person can become soaked from body moisture that collects inside, especially when involved in hard physical activity. Waterproof ponchos are popular since air can circulate under them. The other choice is to wear a breathable garment made of water repellent material that allows body moisture to escape to the outside. Materials such as 60/40 cloth (40 percent cotton, 60 percent nylon) work well, but they can only resist rain for a short duration before becoming saturated. The market also offers PTFE (polytetrafluoroethylene) laminates under such registered trademarks as Gore-Tex and Klimate. Under most conditions these materials actually do keep out the rain. Yet because of microscopic pores in the laminate, body moisture is allowed to pass through in the form of water vapor molecules. The major disadvantage of clothing made of PTFE laminates is the cost. Although these garments are expensive, they do work in most circumstances, so they may well be worth the money for those who spend a great deal of time outdoors. Keep in mind, however, that the only rain gear that is really *waterproof* is made with either plastic or rubber coating. Therefore, for maximum rain protection, many experienced outdoor persons rely only on garments that have a layer of PVC or rubber.

Specific Garments

Not all of the items mentioned earlier can be or necessarily should be part of every camper's attire. Expense as well as the different settings and climates in which camps operate throughout the country are factors to consider. Nonetheless, a helpful checklist of equipment and clothing that might be desired appears later in this chapter. A more specific discussion of some garments that can be considered for summer use is described below.

Although well-fitting, comfortable cotton *underwear* is suitable for summer wear, many experienced backpackers prefer polyester or nylon underwear because it washes easily and dries quickly. Another underwear option is made with open-weave materials. The mesh feels quite comfortable as it soaks up perspiration and allows it to evaporate. When cool, the weave also provides warmth if covered with outer garments, since the open spaces between the netting trap dead air. At least one extra pair of underwear is needed so that you can wash out the ones you've worn at night to always have a pair in reserve for an emergency.

Pants should be of sturdy, closely woven material that will resist snagging and picking up trailside nuisances like burrs and nettles. Although wool is preferable for cold weather, cotton or cotton blend is better for summer as long as it stays dry. When wet, however, cotton provides little insulation and becomes quite heavy and difficult to dry. Various synthetic fabrics work best. In addition, good rain protection gear is needed. Blue jeans,

once a camping favorite except during cold or rainy weather, are not the best choice. A large selection of clothing is available from outfitters. Look for designs that have large pockets, and for those with pocket closures.

Shorts are comfortable for walking along country roads or on open woodland trails. They should be ruggedly constructed and comfortably cut. On most occasions, however, long pants are recommended for general hiking through the woods since they offer protection from scratches, poison ivy or oak, insect bites, chiggers, and too much sun. If the legs are cut wide enough, you can pull them up or roll them up for coolness when such protection is not needed. Many outdoor designers now make *zip-off* pants that can be easily converted to shorts as needed. While walking through sand or an infestation of insects, pant legs can be taped or tied snugly about your ankles.

Cotton or cotton blend *shirts* may become uncomfortably soggy and chilly when wet. For this reason, many prefer the new fibers as well as lightweight fleece. A synthetic fiber blend is an excellent choice for a torso garment. Synthetics wick moisture away from the body, while keeping one warm when it is wet. A mixture of polypropylene and other synthetic material can be quite comfortable. Long sleeves discourage mosquitoes and other biting insects and protect against sunburn, scratches, and poison ivy and oak. A long shirt tail keeps the shirt tucked inside your pants, or can be worn outside for better ventilation when hot. One or two breast pockets with button down flaps are a convenience. Take at least one extra shirt to wear for extra warmth and to allow you to wash one out at night.

Your summer outfit should include a lightweight *windbreaker jacket*. One with a hood is called a *parka*. It should be of closely woven, water repellent (not waterproof) material so that it breathes to keep perspiration from being trapped inside where it will condense. Nylon is a satisfactory material. The garment should be long enough to cover the hips and should be roomy enough to permit free arm movement even when worn over several layers of clothing. Most jackets have elasticized wrists or Velcro closures with several large pockets. Windbreakers come in two styles—a pullover jacket or opening down the front. Although a pullover is simpler and lighter, it cannot be worn open to adjust to temperature changes.

A *hat* with a fairly wide brim will be needed to protect from sun glare and to keep rain water from running down the neck. It should fasten under your chin with a strap or ties so it cannot blow away. A roller-crusher type hat of soft material, which can be rolled up and stored in your pack, is good. Some people prefer to wear a hat of terry cloth that can be kept wet to cool your head. Other campers like a duckbill, visored tennis, hunting, or baseball cap. For cooling your head, try knotting a bandanna into the semblance of a hat and wear it damp. It also can be used as a headband to keep perspiration from running down into your eyes.

For *sleepwear,* never sleep in the clothes you have worn all day. They are likely to be perspiration-soaked and clammy. While on the trail, most campers prefer to change into a fresh T-shirt and shorts rather than carry along pajamas.

Keep *raingear* near the top of your pack where you can find it in a hurry. As already mentioned, there is little agreement as to the best material, but no one disputes the importance of good protection. Snug-fitting waterproof garments trap perspiration and make a person wet. Therefore, you should have rainwear that fits loosely to admit some ventilation and make sure that wrists, collars, and fronts can be opened during breaks in the weather.

A frequently used garment for general rainwear around camp is a poncho. This waterproof sheet has a center hole and hood for the head. Some types have a long flap in the back that can be draped over your pack to protect it. This loose construction provides ample ventilation. The hood can be held close about your face with a drawstring. A poncho is especially useful in a canoe, where the loose flap can be draped over your gear on the bottom of the canoe. A poncho, however, is not well-suited when trying to walk in a strong wind, which sets it flapping, or when trying to walk through heavy brush or weeds. A poncho is particularly valuable because of its versatility. It can be converted into a flat waterproof sheet to cover gear, used as a ground cloth under your sleeping bag, or used as an improvised shelter. Some ponchos can be snapped together to form a larger sheet.

A *rain suit* consists of a hip length jacket with a hood and full cut pants that slip on or off easily over shoes and are roomy enough to wear over several other garments. The suit should be well constructed and of a strong, lightweight, and durable material. *Rain chaps* slip onto each leg individually and tie at the waist. Since they have no front, back, or crotch, they weigh very little. They protect your legs well and should be worn with a fairly long rain jacket to protect the rest of the body. Many items of rainwear come with built-in or detachable head protectors. If you need a separate *hat,* you can either carry a rainproof cover for your regular hat or get one of the various light waterproof hats with medium brim and strings to tie under your chin.

Although your *boots* may be made water resistant, it is practically impossible to waterproof them completely. Treating them with liquid silicone or silicone wax will help, however. Light rubber overshoes are handy if you expect to do extensive walking in wet conditions.

A pair of lightweight leather *gloves* or washable canvas work gloves can be an important part of your equipment. They are indispensable for handling hot cooking utensils and for protecting hands from blisters, abrasions, and splinters when doing heavy work or building fires.

A large *bandanna* is another piece of equipment that adapts itself to many purposes. It can be used to handle hot pans, to double as a triangular bandage or tourniquet, shield your neck and face from sunburn and insects, to wear around your forehead to keep perspiration out of your eyes, or to dampen and make into a turban to wear wet around your head for cooling.

Miscellaneous Articles and Equipment

Carry a few well-chosen toiletries in a ditty bag or in a lightweight, protective case. For a trip, only small quantities are needed such as a small bar or tube of biodegradable soap, a toothbrush and small quantity of paste, dental floss, comb, toilet paper, a small mirror, and a washcloth. Pack all liquids in unbreakable containers. Such planning is the secret of successful *go-light* trips.

A few tools may be needed for your trip, but there is no need to burden each member of the party with duplicates. If one axe or bow saw will serve the whole party, then take turns carrying it. Depending on the nature of your outing, such tools as a small screwdriver and pliers with wire cutter can be useful. Each party should carry at least one trowel or small shovel, preferably with detachable handle, for digging sanitary facilities, cooking pits, and possibly manipulating and putting out fires.

Some lengths of strong nylon cord, thin copper or picture wire, canoe and tent repair kits, and a small assortment of cotter pins (for pack frame problems) may prove helpful. You also may find many uses for 1/2-inch strips of older inner tube (tying packages, fastening items to your pack, and so on). A mending kit should include such items as needles (laced through a small piece of cardboard), both straight and safety pins, a few yards of thread wound on a piece of cardboard, small pointed scissors, buttons, patches of cloth and leather, assorted rubber bands, adhesive tape, and strong waxed linen thread.

No expedition, even a brief one, should leave camp without the necessary supplies for emergencies, which should be available in a first aid kit (see exhibit 31.1). You may not actually need a map to find your way, but a topographical map of the region is advisable. A compass is also a standard piece of equipment for any trip.

Exhibit 31.1

Minimum Contents of an Expedition First Aid Kit

• Acetaminophen	• Gauze pads (3" × 3")
• Adhesive bandages (4" × 3")	• Ibuprofen
• Alcohol pads	• Latex gloves
• Antihistamine	• Moleskin
• Antiseptic ointment	• Nonstick dressing (2" × 3")
• Athletic tape	• Sting-relief pads
• Burn cream	• Tweezers
• Cotton-tipped applicators	

In addition to a broad-brimmed hat or visored cap, long sleeves, full-length pants, and a bandanna, you also need a good pair of sunglasses and some sunscreen. Sunglasses not only protect your eyes from bright sunlight, but also help to keep out dust and wind. Take a good insect repellent and, if needed, a head net to cover the face and neck. If there is no built-in insect protection for your tent, you may want to add some netting or screening for the tent door.

Sleeping equipment should consist of a ground cloth to place under your tent and sleeping bag, and a sleeping pad for additional insulation from the ground. A stuff sack filled with clothing can serve as a pillow. A lightweight alpine tent or tarpaulin is necessary for protection against the elements.

Each person should have a small pocket-sized flashlight with extra bulbs and batteries. Long-lasting LED flashlights are especially useful. When not using your flashlight, reverse the top battery so that the two negative poles meet. This trick will prevent any possibility of the light being turned on in your pack accidentally. When on an outing you should take advantage of daylight hours by stopping early to make camp, eat supper, and clean up before dark. By doing so you will use the flashlight sparingly.

Short, fat plumbers' or miners' candles provide good light and are also handy for starting a wet-weather fire. Some prefer to use a candle in a lantern (figure 31.1) that has a shatterproof plastic chimney to shield the flame and a chain at the top by which to hang it. The lantern folds down compactly for carrying. Remember to never use open or closed flames inside a structure such as a tent.

Carry a water bottle, canteen, or camelback and a supply of water with you. The amount depends upon known safe water sources along the way. Several types of water containers are available. Popular models are made from plastics like copolyester and polyethylene, stainless steel, and aluminum, all of which are now manufactured without BPA (a chemical that has raised health safety concerns). A wide-mouth bottle is easier to clean and more convenient for mixing powdered drinks.

A lighter is handy for starting fires. Also, an ample supply of matches should be waterproofed and carried in a waterproof container. Trench candles or plumbers' candles, and bits of dry tinder help to start a fire in wet weather.

Several whistles on lanyards should be available so that any person or group going even a short distance away from the main group can carry one. When traveling in thick woods it is easy to become confused or lost when going even a short distance, which can be a serious matter. A whistle blast carries much farther than the voice. The universal signal for help is three blasts on the whistle.

Popular water bottles are made from hard plastic and feature a wide-mouth opening that makes them easy to clean and more convenient for mixing powdered drinks.

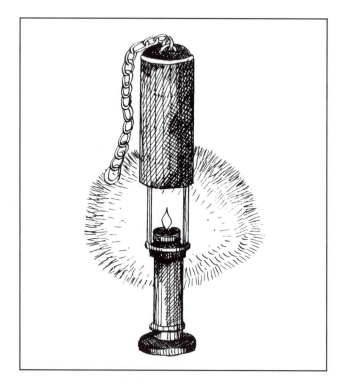

Figure 31.1   Candle lantern.

A lightweight backpacking stove is necessary equipment for a trip. No matter what your heating source may be, cooking utensils are a must. Nested cooking kits are available to serve from 1 to 12 people. These cooking utensils usually have no handles, but instead are manipulated by a detachable handle that fits any of them. This arrangement has an added advantage in that the handle stays comfortably cool to the touch, since it is never left over the fire. You can assemble your own mess kit with a minimum of eating utensils such as a cup and a spoon. Non-breakable plastic is considered by many to be superior for cups, plates, and other dishes, and sectioned plates are available. Others prefer pie tins or aluminum plates. Each person will need a spoon and possibly a fork, but the pocket knife substitutes well for a table knife.

Most of the items already mentioned in this chapter should be considered as necessities for safe camping. A few additional things can be taken along to enhance the pleasure of a trip. Carrying such items as a camera, fishing gear, pencil and notebook, playing cards, and binoculars may be considered a sacrifice in weight, but may be worth the effort for the satisfaction and enjoyment gained.

Checklists for Packing Equipment

To best meet particular needs for camping and tripping, go over the items listed then make out a checklist. Recheck the list and eliminate everything not really essential. After returning from a trip, revise the list on the basis of your experience and keep it handy for use the next time. Exhibits 31.2 and 31.3 (on pp. 318–319) suggest checklists for personal and group equipment.

Traveling on foot with your bedding, food, and clothing on your back offers freedom. All equipment for such a trip must obviously be stored in some form of pack, even when you are only going on a day hike. Packs of almost any size and description are available to suit your needs.

Packs

Packs come in all sizes and designs. The pack known as a *belt, waist,* or *fanny pack* is the smallest of all, consisting simply of a small container attached to a nylon or web belt that is worn around the waist. It will hold from 3 to 5 pounds of supplies including your lunch, a camera, and a water bottle. These packs are made of the same materials as larger packs and they usually open by means of a zipper on top that is covered by a protective rain flap. Some packs also have zippered pockets on the side and a place for a water bottle. The belt is worn with enough slack so that you can turn it around to extract the contents without having to remove the belt.

Rucksack is a term of German origin and literally means "back sack." Rucksacks or backpacks come in many sizes and designs, varying from those just large enough to carry a lunch to others more suitable for extended overnight excursions of several days or more. To avoid confusion in discussing packs, they are usually classified by their size or intended use. They may be classified into three types: (1) day packs, (2) overnight packs, and (3) expedition packs.

Day packs are the smallest of the choices and are generally limited to day trips or brief excursions away from the central camp area. One kind of day pack is the *knapsack,* which is just large enough to carry a lunch and possibly a garment or two. Another, the *haversack,* is slightly larger and more suitable for daylight jaunts and cookouts.

A midsize pack is the *overnight pack*, which is big enough for limited food and clothing as well as a sleeping bag. The user must plan carefully if this pack is to serve satisfactorily for anything more than a night or two in the woods.

Expedition packs are the largest packs of all and are intended primarily for carrying loads on extended trips of up to a week or longer. Many are designed to carry 40 pounds or more, but such quantities of camping gear are usually more than is desired or necessary.

The first thing to consider when selecting a pack is its intended use. What kinds of trips will you be taking? Will you be doing day trips, staying overnight, or traveling for several days? Will you travel mostly on trails? Do you intend to do some technical climbing or backcountry traveling off the trail? What kinds of equipment will you need to carry and how much?

In addition to size or intended use, packs can also be grouped by the types of suspension systems used to sup-

Day packs (*left*) work well for brief excursions away from camp where overnight gear is not needed. Expedition packs (*right*) are the largest packs and are designed for trips of a week or more. This pack has an internal frame.

Exhibit 31.2

Personal Gear for a Camping Trip

Personal Equipment (depending on the season)

Essential	Optional
Wearing Apparel	**Wearing Apparel**
Long pants	Insect head-net or mosquito netting
Walking shorts	Swim suit
Shirts	
Sunglasses	
Boots	
Extra shoes for around camp	
Socks (several pairs)	
Wide-brimmed hat or duckbill visor cap	
Sleeping clothes or pajamas	
Rainwear (poncho, parka, chaps, etc.)	
Gloves	
Bandanna	
Underclothes (including long underwear, if needed)	
Windbreaker, wool shirt, jacket, or sweater	
Sleeping Gear	**Sleeping Gear**
Ground sheet or poncho	Sleeping bag liner or sheet
Pad or mattress	
Tent or tarp	
Sleeping bag or bedroll	
Toiletries	**Toiletries**
Biodegradable soap in plastic box or tube	Lotions for skin
Towel and washcloth	ChapStick
Pocket mirror (metal preferred)	
Toothbrush and paste	
Dental floss	
Comb	
Sunscreen	
Insect repellent	
Toilet paper	
For Food	
Canteen or water bottle	
Mess kit, including cup, fork, and spoon	
Tools and Other Items	**Tools and Other Items**
Pocketknife	Hatchets or saws
Waterproofed matches or matches in waterproof matchbox	Fishing equipment and license
Flashlight, extra bulb and batteries	Whistle
Packsack	Pedometer
Rope or nylon cord	Day pack
Stuff sacks or ditty bags	Money (especially a few coins)
Maps	Binoculars
Compass	Camera (in waterproof bag)
Mending kit	Nature books, poetry books, games
Pocket notebook	Stationery (already stamped)
Pencil	Musical instrument
	Songbooks
	Extra eyeglasses in case
	Watch
	Hammock (can be rolled up to size of a fist)

Exhibit 31.3

Group Gear for a Camping Trip

Group Equipment

Essential	Optional
For Food	**For Food**
Menus and recipes	Reflector oven, Dutch oven
Water purification equipment	Paper towels
Cooking forks, spatula, spoons	Grates
Cooking utensils	Aluminum foil
Plastic food bags	Water container (plastic or canvas folding)
Salt and pepper, as well as other spices	
Food (carefully checked against checklist)	
Stoves and fuel containers	
Can opener (on multi knife utensil)	
Tools	**Tools**
Repair kit for mending tents, air mattresses, etc.	Extra paddles for canoe or kayak trip
Tarpaulins or tents for sheltering equipment	No. 10 tin can buckets, etc.
Spade or shovel	Candles
Nylon cord, wire, etc.	25 or 50 feet of strong cord
	Camp lantern
	Axes or saws
	File and sharpening stone
Fires and Sanitation	**Fires and Sanitation**
Extra supply of waterproofed matches	Inspirator, trench candles, etc.
Toilet paper	
Insect repellent	
Wash pan or canvas wash basin	
Dishcloths, towels	
Biodegradable soap or detergent	
Metal or plastic sponge for cleaning pans	
Steel wool	
Miscellaneous	**Miscellaneous**
Checklist of equipment	Extra shoelaces (twine or nylon cord will do)
Mending kit (buttons, thread, shoelaces, etc.)	
First aid kit and instruction book	
Tents or tarps and accessories	
Maps of area	

port them. Most can be classified as either a *frameless pack* or one with a frame. Frame packs are further divided into those with *external frames* and those with built-in frames (referred to as *internal frame packs*) (see figure 31.2). Both have advantages and disadvantages that should be discussed when they are purchased or when a counselor is determining what is best for his or her campers. A great deal of information about various expedition packs is available on the Internet and from various outdoor stores that sell them.

You can choose from many models of packs, and new ones are constantly appearing on the market. In general, select the smallest pack that will carry what you need. If you will be taking trips of various lengths, especially in different seasons or by various means, you may want to invest in several models and sizes. The advantage

of an external frame pack is that it achieves excellent weight distribution. The frame gives the load a higher center of gravity which puts more weight over the hips, and as long as you travel mostly on trails, this will be the most comfortable method of carrying your gear. Another plus is that the frame and back band create airspace for ventilation between you and your load, which is much appreciated on hot days.

On the other hand, if you try to do some climbing or travel on rough terrain with an external frame pack, you will discover why internal frame packs were invented. When you try to look up, your head hits the back of your pack. Likewise, when you try to maneuver a tricky foothold or walk through heavy underbrush, your pack will tend to throw you off balance. Internal frame packs and soft packs were made to alleviate such problems. These

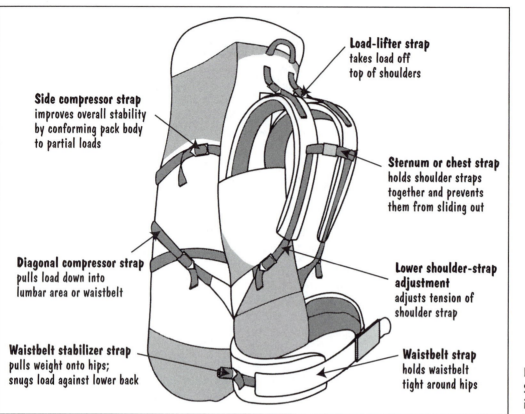

Load-lifter strap
takes load off
top of shoulders

Side compressor strap
improves overall stability
by conforming pack body
to partial loads

Sternum or chest strap
holds shoulder straps
together and prevents
them from sliding out

Diagonal compressor strap
pulls load down into
lumbar area or waistbelt

**Lower shoulder-strap
adjustment**
adjusts tension of
shoulder strap

Waistbelt stabilizer strap
pulls weight onto hips;
snugs load against lower back

Waistbelt strap
holds waistbelt
tight around hips

Figure 31.2
Schematic of an
internal frame pack.

packs are designed to hug your body and have a much lower center of gravity, providing optimum balance and allowing you more upper body mobility and flexibility. Although not as comfortable for carrying heavy loads on a trail as an external frame pack, this type of design gives a load that is stabilized on your back. It allows the freedom of movement and the balance needed for scrambling, climbing, or even activities such as cross-country skiing.

Improvised Packs

The following information is intended for camps that cannot afford to purchase backpacks or for those individuals who do not have their own. A lack of resources to obtain manufactured equipment does not necessarily mean tripping cannot be a part of the camp program. Some of the improvised packsacks discussed may not always work or look like manufactured models, but at times they will do fine.

A child may enjoy rolling gear in a *blanket*, securing it with 3-inch horse blanket pins and a short strap or rope, and wearing it in a U that is draped around one shoulder after buckling or tying it together near the opposite hip. This technique works well enough for a short trip, but the roll will make the hiker hot and sweaty and can catch on every tree and branch along the way making

it ill-adapted for any but short excursions. A poncho or ground cloth should be used as the outside layer to offer protection from rain.

Another novel way to make a pack is to use *blue jeans or long pants*. You can slip gear into the body and legs of the slacks and secure it by cinching a strap through the belt loops and running it around your waistline. The legs are converted into pack straps by bringing them up across your shoulders and under your arms. Fasten them to the waistline strap about 2 inches apart near the center so the legs hug your shoulders snugly in order to center the weight of the pack well down on your back.

A *large burlap bag* or something similar can be converted into a pack. Four pebbles and two lengths of nylon webbing or strong rope about 3 feet long will also be needed. To make shoulder straps, place one pebble in a lower corner of the sack and tightly fasten one rope around it with a clove hitch. Place another pebble in the upper corner on the same side and fasten the long end of the rope around it. Repeat on the other side of the bag using the other rope. Since these ropes serve as carrying straps, be sure to leave enough slack to slip your arms through them. Foam rubber, old socks, or other improvised materials can be used to pad the ropes where they cross the shoulders.

WEB RESOURCES

Camping Gear
- (www.thecampingguy.com) has suggestions for purchasing gear and for making campfires and cooking.
- (www.camping-tips.com)
- (http://sierrabackpacker.com/)
- (http://www.backpacking.net/)
- (http://www.hikingandbackpacking.com/gear_buying_advice.html)
- (http://www.gorp.com)

Camping Earth (www.campingearth.com) has suggestions for building a fire, equipment, tips, and stewardship.

Checklists (www.howtocampingtips.com) provides several types of checklists and gives tips for both experienced backpackers and beginners.

Love the Outdoors (www.lovetheoutdoors.com) has advice for planning trips, safety and cooking suggestions, and much more.

PRINT RESOURCES

Curtis, R. (2005). *The backpacker's field manual: A comprehensive guide to mastering backcountry skills.* New York: Three Rivers Press.

Townsend, C. (2005). *The backpacker's handbook* (3rd ed.). Camden, ME: Ragged Mountain Press.

Appendix A

Suggestions for Conducting Courses in Camp Counseling

This book has been designed as a text for college courses in camp counseling. It will be equally useful for participants in CIT (counselor-in-training), precamp, and in-service training as well as for individuals already employed in a camp situation. The purposes of the four sections of this book have been discussed in the Preface. Successful camp counselors must be well rounded, understand human nature, maintain proper attitudes, and possess specialized skills. To do their job well, prospective counselors must be well trained and adequately prepared. Like the campers with whom they expect to work, counselors will profit most from a lively and varied course that is relevant and meaningful to them.

The theoretical aspects of the course can be covered with the usual lectures, discussions, and testing, but more is needed. Experiential opportunities are needed to provide practice in camping skills, including the use of equipment and tools and working effectively with groups. Outdoor excursions to practice camping and trail skills would be useful. Moreover, actual work with children, like leading them in games, would be desirable.

Some people learn best by *seeing*, others by *hearing*, and still others by *doing*. Incorporating all these methods of instruction is the best way to engage students. This approach also is a good model for counselors who will be using a variety of teaching and leadership techniques on the job. Here are some suggestions that may prove helpful:

1. Use supplementary reading from journals, books, and the World Wide Web. Every student should be exposed to different opinions and methods, as well as to some of the resources available in the field. In addition to requiring certain readings, it is also wise to allow students to choose from diverse fields such as ecology, aquatics, and group dynamics to allow for personal interests and to help counselors prepare for specific jobs.

2. Hold discussions—round table, panel, or led by a group member—about topics of general interest, perhaps chosen by the class. Have class members make oral presentations and/or write special reports concerning some phase of camping. Encourage students to seek out innovative ways to present material in a dynamic manner. The class can evaluate the methods used.

3. Individuals should take turns instructing classmates on chosen topics, like how to lead a discussion, talk to a camper about a possible problem, plan a campfire program, lay a fire, pitch a tent, or use and care for a knife. Discuss methods of presenting such material to campers.

4. Assign special projects such as collecting songs suitable for camp use or making articles for camp or personal use.

5. Schedule visiting speakers or consultants such as a camp director, first aid instructor, conservation agent, or forest ranger. Also invite speakers from related teaching fields such as psychology, sociology, child development, or food science.

6. Compile a list of resources like camp websites, resources available from the American Camp Association and other organizations, and other available resources.

7. Schedule experiential opportunities for practicing camp craft skills. You might invite a group of children to receive instruction from members of the class.

8. Have students prepare their own resource list of information on camping, which will enable them to quickly locate needed information.

9. Have class members plan and participate in cookouts, overnights, and longer trips. This opportunity provides a chance to use the committee system, delegate

responsibility, and work democratically with others to put into practice some of the theories discussed.

10. Individual class members can make lesson plans to use when explaining techniques to others.

11. Videotape students as they lead sessions or discussions, and let them evaluate the playback.

12. Use various group methods such as role playing, circular discussion, and others described in the text.

13. Study various types of camping equipment available (use catalogs of various outfitters or visit local supply stores).

14. Encourage attendance at meetings and workshops sponsored by the ACA or related organizations and encourage student memberships.

15. Sponsor a camp staff job fair or placement day, and invite various camps to send representatives. Provide areas for displays and private interviews.

Although camp leadership training courses are available, the supply of those completing such courses still lags behind the potential demand. Anyone who contemplates offering such training is urged to contact the American Camp Association about their leadership courses, which are conducted by approved instructors. Appropriate professional development certificates are available for those who satisfactorily complete these programs.

An outstanding example of a pre-camp training program is presented in appendix B.

Appendix B

The Best, Most Incredible Staff Training Ever Known to a Summer Camp in the History of Summer Camps, Even Better than Last Summer

Key Elements Needed

☑ Staff Bonding
— From Individuals to a Team to a Family

☑ Relationship Building
— Getting campers to move through the ranks

☑ Being an Intentional Camp
— A clear vision of what we want to happen this summer and how we get there from here
— One Mission, One Vision, One Camp

☑ Creating Magic Moments
— The Wow factor for our campers

☑ Character Development
— Move from a head knowledge to a heart knowledge

☑ Building Skills
— Creating lifelong activities in the lives of campers

☑ Creativity
— Everything can be done with a twist

☑ Communication
— Increased in all facets of camp

☑ Safety
— Proactive

☑ Fun
— Says it all

Courtesy of the YMCA Camp of Greater Des Moines.

Day 1

10:00 All Staff Check In
  • Begin the greatest staff check-in of all time

12:00–12:45 Lunch
  • Welcome Speeches

1:30–2:15 Games
  • Begin with introduction games
  • Introduce the first part of Initiatives in a Backpack
    ▪ Should play at least 8–10 games
    ▪ Games of all types (running, sit down, quiet, loud, etc. . . .)

2:30–3:15 Song Practice for the Bonfire
  • Have leadership staff, and program staff leading groups
  • Split into Peer Groups

3:30–4:00 Who am I, and where do I want to go?
  • Read Dr. Seuss "Green Eggs and Ham"
    ▪ Relate this to trying new things
    ▪ Stepping outside of the comfort zone
  • Quiet reflection of who they are
  • 5–7 questions about what they want to be, where they want to go, fears, excitements etc. . . .

4:00–5:00 Mission Statement

5:00–5:45 Swim Tests
- Go through pool rules by the pool Circle Leader
- Tests
  - Done exactly how they are done in the summer with the kids
- Pool expectations
- Play pool games

6–6:45 Dinner

7:00 Go over summer schedule
- What does the summer look like
- What does a day look like
- Explain the parking lot (questions)
- Share a game/song list
- Introduce Cimbers

8:00 Get Ready for Bonfire

8:30 Bonfire at BJ's
- Songs
- Devotions

12:00 Lights Out (Mandatory)

Day 2

7:30 Clean Cabin
- Have them meet outside the cabin at 7:30
- Go over the list with them of what he is looking for
- Can you do it as a competition between bunk mates

7:50 Chapel
- Box of ideas and possibilities needs to be created with all kinds of stories
  - Creation of a binder that staff can use and pull from
- Done really well so they start off with how it should look every time
- Explain how important this is and that it sets the tone for the rest of the day

8:00 Breakfast

9:00 Y Camp Purpose Statement

10:00 Y Camp Statement of Excellence
- Begin with a song
- Broken down into specific parts

11:00 The five most important things at Y Camp
- The kids, the kids, the kids, the kids, the kids

12:00 Lunch

12:45 Great Staff Skit

1:00 Creating Magic—Staff are the magic
- Magic does not just happen, it takes work, dedication, and practice
- Magic is a matter of the details

- Doing all of the little things right that make a camper's experience amazing
- Little things that can happen
- Initiatives in a backpack

1:45 What makes a GREAT Y Camp Leader
- Who were your heroes
  - What did they do to make them your hero–not who they were, but what specific actions
  - Being a great leader means taking action—doing stuff—refer to SSE
  - Think of the best customer service you have ever had

1:45 List of what great staff DO
- Draw out what a great staff looks like

2:30 Great Programs
- Start with the Envelope
  - Giving them the secret to great programs
- What each means to program areas

3:15 Archery
- How to string the bow, parts of the bow, commands, how to shoot
- How do we teach character
- What are Rainy Day Alternatives

4:15 Processing activities—done at Archery Range
- The Magnificent Mortar—do the demonstration
  - Why it is so important
- How do you do it
- Initiatives in a backpack

5:00 Dinner

5:30 Dave's Creative Speech
- Taking it to the next level

6:30 Group Camping Discussion
- Tanya and Abby Lead
- What it is they have coming in
- Expectations
- The groups are kids

7:00 Leader Show and the Art of the Camp Skit
- How to effectively use skits
- What is the purpose
- What is the Leader Show
- The importance of the Leader Show
- History
- Ideas
- Skits to work on

8:00 Watch Movie at Dave's
- Begin with why we are watching it
- What to look for
- The power of relationships
  - How they are built
- The power of creativity

10:00 Leading Great Evening Devotions
- Done in small groups led by leadership staff
  - What is the purpose
  - What can they look like
  - What they should include
  - How they can be used
  - What are the expectations
  - What to avoid with them
  - Give out sheet with all the different ideas to be used

12:00 Lights Out (Mandatory)

Day 3

7:50 Chapel
- Staff begin to lead

8:00 Breakfast

8:30 Kids—Child Development
- Why we do what we do
- What kids are going through

9:00 Building relationships means listening to campers
- "Balloon Exercise"
- Time to practice

11:30 The Pathway Process
- Where staff go
- What the limits of "Free Travel" and Perceived Freedom may be

12:00 Lunch

1:00 Get into Suits

1:30 Canoes

3:00 Free Swim and Showers

3:30 Trading Post Procedures

4:15 Riflery

5:00 Arts and Crafts

5:30 Dinner

Night Off
Staff must be at breakfast by 8:00 AM
Optional Chapel and Time of Prayer for the summer
If staying on camp Quiet Hours start at 11 PM

Day 4

8:00 Breakfast

8:30 Fire Building

9:30 ½ Horses, ½ Climbing Tower
(Great Programming and Character Development)
- Horses
  - Everyone learns how to put kids on horses and get them into line
  - What to do while your kids are on a trail ride and you are not
  - How to put helmets on
  - Go for a ride
  - What to do with the kid that does not go
  - The importance of speed
- Climbing Tower
  - Knot tying
  - What the kids that are not climbing can be doing
  - How to put harnesses on kids (everyone learns)
  - Encouragement Training
  - What we want the kids to realize

12:00 Lunch

12:45 Day Camp Magic / Day Campers are still campers
- Why Day Camp is so important\ one of our largest priorities
- What to expect
- What our expectations are
- The day camp overnight
- Bus Transportation

2:00 OLS
- 3–5 activities
  - some for Pathways only
  - some for Rotations only

3:30 Risk Management

4:30 5 Minute Rule and why it works / more child development
- Re-hit what it is about
- Why is it so important
- Practice, Practice, Practice

5:30 Dinner (Go through Heart Connection and Day camp assignments)

6:30 The "coolest" cabin and the check-in
- The importance of a cool cabin
- Check-in happenings
- Greeting parents practice (handshake, smile, name tag, and introductions)
- How kids are feeling
- What should the other kids be doing (i.e., making name tags, get to know you games, etc. . . .)

7:30 Chapel

8:30 Embers

9:30 Making Friends practice

10:15 Leadershow practice

10:45 Devos

12:00 Lights Out (Mandatory)

Day 5

7:50 Chapel

8:00 Catch up and open-ended question time

8:30 Breakfast

9:00 Leave to set-up program areas
  - Staff are working program areas
    - 4–5 staff stay back to go through in-service training

12:30 Lunch

1:15 Emergency Procedures

Afternoon works like the morning with program areas and in-service training—Staff getting CPR are assigned

5:30 Dinner

6:15 Character Development
  - What this means for camp
  - The guarantee
  - How do we develop the character of every camper in camp and why it is important
  - Making a world of difference

7:30 Trail of Five Fires

9:30 Behavior Management and Zero Tolerance
  - Justin Campbell Story
  - What is proper discipline
  - When to discipline
  - Why the zero tolerance policy
    - What it means
  - When to involve leadership staff
  - How to avoid having discipline problems
  - Role Play situations

10:30 Devos

12:00 Lights

Day 6

7:50 Chapel

8:00 Open-ended questions

8:30 Breakfast

9:00 Staff to areas

12:00 Lunch

12:45 Policy Manual

Afternoon Schedule of Groups and In-Service Training—CPR Training

5:30 N.U.T.S.
  - What meals to cook
  - What makes this time so special
  - Night programming and what can be done
  - How it all works

Day 7

8:30 Breakfast

9:00 Program Areas

12:30 Lunch

1:00 Finish Policy Manual

5:30 Dinner and a Break

7:00 Sensitive Issues and Homesickness
  - The dangers of it
  - Protecting yourself
  - Why it happens
  - What can be done to prevent it
  - What can be done to treat it
  - When enough is enough
  - Role playing

8:30 Inspiration Point

10:00 Staying motivated throughout the entire summer
  - Effectively using your break
  - Write letters to yourself to get mid-summer
  - What are things that we as a leadership staff can do to help

12:00 Lights Out (Mandatory)

Day 8

7:50 Chapel

8:00 Family Camp and Hertko Hollow

8:30 Breakfast

9:00 Work Projects

12:00 Lunch

Afternoon Program Areas and In-service Training

5:30 Dinner

6:00 Dave Keck to Visit Camp
  - Ice Cream Social

7:15 The Arty Show
  - What to expect
  - What to do, how you can prepare your kids
  - Keeping it appropriate

8:15 Leadershow Practice

9:00 Aunt FiFi—Talk through it

9:30 Role Playing

10:30 Nap Room
  - Purpose
  - What it is, and what it is not
  - Why it is there
  - Expectations of what happens

12:30 Lights Out (Mandatory)

Day 9

7:50 Chapel

8:00 Perceptions rule the world
  - How you are perceived in the world and what it means for camp

8:30 Breakfast

9:00 Leave to set-up program areas
- Staff are working program areas
  - 4–5 staff stay back to go through in-service training

12:30 Lunch

Afternoon works like the morning, with program areas and in-service training

5:30 Dinner

6:15 Parent Closing program
- why we are doing it
- checklists to get the cleaning done
- what the program will look like

7:15 Awards and why they are so important
- Read "Oh the Places You'll Go"
- What each area is going to do
- Begin making them for the next week

8:15 Honor Point
- Shirt Ceremony is done then
- Give them their awards
- Opportunity for final questions

9:30 Released until Sunday at 11:00

Appendix C

Suggestions for Conducting Camp CIT (Counselor-in-Training) Courses

Introduction

Many camps conduct their own Counselor-in-Training (CIT) or Leader-in-Training (LIT) programs. These in-camp leadership training courses have a strong emphasis on in-service experiences designed to prepare older youth for their future role as camp counselors. The participants in such a program are referred to as CITs or whatever name the individual camp may give them. Although CITs are still campers, they are in a specific category. Therefore, in addition to their own specific training program, they usually have their own separate living quarters apart from the younger campers.

Basic guidelines that should apply to any CIT program include the development of specific learning activities for the individuals who participate. On a regularly scheduled basis, CITs should be assigned outside readings as well as responsibility for leading discussions and giving reports. These experiences should be mixed with chances for observation and opportunities to acquire basic skills. In addition, follow-up and evaluation must be a continuous part of the program so that CITs can recognize their growth and judge the progress of their own performance.

For the first year of a two-year course, CITs are usually more involved in observation and skill development rather than actual leadership. After they have been exposed to skills and principles of leadership, they should be given more opportunities to practice and demonstrate their knowledge during the second year. This second year is also the time for more in-depth exploration of the total workings of the camp.

The nature of the CIT course and its implementation will depend upon such factors as the philosophy of the camp, the number of CIT personnel involved, and the facilities available. The following two-year course outline is intended to serve as a possible guideline for those who are responsible for organizing and leading the CIT program. This text should serve as a resource for trainees as well as for leaders of CIT courses.

Suggested CIT Program for a Two-Year Course

I. First Summer
   A. *Philosophy and objectives.* What are the objectives of camp generally, and specifically of your own camp? Develop a program of learning that includes information and understanding to be gained about these objectives, including:
      1. Skills and habits to be developed.
      2. Attitudes and interests to be encouraged.
   B. *History and current trends in camping.* Examine the following:
      1. The background of the camping field.
      2. Types of camps and their sponsors.
      3. Issues and problems, campers' needs, and various camp programs.
   C. *Leadership skills in program areas.* Emphasis should be on observation and discussion for the first year to help CITs develop knowledge and leadership abilities in camp activities. Discuss and demonstrate the logic model, teaching-learning process and teaching methods including proper activity

progression, and ways to evaluate outcomes. Opportunities should be available for CITs to gain experience by functioning as aids and assistants to counselors and other staff. Opportunities should be provided in some of the following areas:

1. Land sports—tennis, archery, riding, etc.

2. Music—songs and song leading.

3. Creative activities—arts and crafts, dramatics, storytelling, dance, etc.

4. Special activities—campfire and evening programs, rainy day activities, and other special programs.

5. Campcraft, trip camping, and outdoor living skills.

   (a) Basic skills—hiking, backpacking, canoeing, kayaking, toolcraft, ropecraft, firecraft, map and compass skills, food and menu planning, outdoor cooking.

   (b) Conservation, nature, and ecology.

   (c) Waterfront activities—swimming, life saving, sailing, canoeing, kayaking, waterskiing, etc.

   (d) Health, safety, and first aid.

D. *Leadership skills in social aspects of camp life.* Provide opportunities for observation of groups in camp including factors leading to their success or failure.

1. Methods and techniques of leadership.

   (a) Leadership and guidance of both individuals and groups.

   (b) Analysis of skills.

2. Serve as aids to counselors while working with youngsters of various ages in activities and settings.

   (a) Observe campers during activities in living quarters and on trips.

   (b) Develop an understanding of camper behavior and age group characteristics.

3. Assist in organizing specific camp activities and special events.

E. *CIT evaluation.*

1. Several times throughout the CIT session (beginning, middle, end), review and discuss with each trainee such matters as background, attitude, experience, strengths and weaknesses, leadership potential.

2. Counselor evaluations.

3. Self-evaluation.

4. Recommendations concerning each CIT's continuation in the course the following summer.

II. Second Summer

A. *Continue the development of skills, techniques, and knowledge of camping activities.*

B. *Further experience in assisting and serving as an aide to counselors and other staff.*

1. Live in different age group units to acquire experiences and assume camp roles.

2. Practice teaching and leading camp activities under the direction of counselors.

3. Assist on trips and other camp activities.

C. *Group interaction and discussion concerning campers.*

1. Backgrounds and needs.

2. Means of assessing individual abilities and problems.

3. Discussions of specific situations.

D. *Observe and learn about other camp functions and responsibilities* such as maintenance, business procedures, records and reports, supplies and inventory, administration, food service, and ACA camp standards.

E. *CIT evaluation* (as in I-E). The trainee program should end with each person receiving a recommendation concerning future employment as a member of the camp staff.

Appendix D

21st Century Camp Bibliography

American Camp Association. (2002). *Camp health record log.* Monterey, CA: Healthy Learning.

American Camp Association. (2002). *Designing quality youth programs: Strategic changes across structures, policies, and activities.* Monterey, CA: Healthy Learning.

American Camp Association. (2007). *American Camp Association's accreditation process guide.* Monterey, CA: Healthy Learning.

American Camp Association. (2007). *Creating positive youth outcomes: A staff-training resource for camps and other youth development programs.* Martinsville, IN: American Camp Association.

Ball, A., & Ball, B. (2004). *Basic camp management: An introduction to camp administration.* Martinsville, IN: American Camp Association.

Bany-Winters, L. (2000). *Show time: Music, dance, and drama activities for kids.* Chicago: Chicago Review Press.

Barrows, R. E. (2001). *Recreation handbook for camp, conference and community.* Jefferson, NC: McFarland & Company.

Beard, D. C. (2006). *Camp-lore and woodcraft.* Mineola, NY: Dover Publications.

Becker-Doyle, E. (2010). *Leadership isn't rocket science: 6 ways to boost your leadership IQ.* Monterey, CA: Healthy Learning.

Benson, R., & Benson, T. (2009). *Survival guide for coaching youth softball: Only the essential drills, practice plans, plays, and coaching tips.* Champaign, IL: Human Kinetics.

Bentinck-Smith, M. (2010). *It wood be fun: Woodworking with children.* Groton, MA: Martin and Lawrence Press.

Bordessa, K. (2005). *Team challenges: 170+ group activities to build cooperation, communication, and creativity.* Chicago: Zephyr Press.

Brummer, M. (2010). *Contemporary dyecraft: Over 50 tie-dye projects for scarves, dresses, t-shirts and more.* Tonawanda, NY: Firefly Books.

Calhoun, Y., & Calhoun, M. R. (2006). *Create a yoga practice for kids.* Santa Fe, NM: Sunstone Press.

Campbell, D. (2010). *Beginners guide to fishing: And survival guide for supervising adults.* Scotts Valley, CA: CreateSpace.

Campbell, M., & Long, D. (2006). *Digital photography for teens.* Florence, KY: Course Technology PTR.

Carter Beard, D. (2008). *The American boy's handy book: Build a fort, sail a boat, shoot an arrow, throw a boomerang, catch spiders, fish in the ice, camp without a tent and 150 other activities.* Berkeley, CA: Ulysses Press.

Cohen, C. (2007). *Stepping stones to building friendships: A guide for camp counselors.* Washington, DC: Advantage Books.

Coleman, M., & Coleman, J. (2009). *Crisis communications weathering the storm: A handbook for camps and other youth programs.* Monterey, CA: Healthy Learning.

Coutellier, C. (2004). *Day camps from day one: A hands-on guide for day camp administration.* Martinsville, IN: American Camp Association.

Coutellier, C. (2007). *Camp is for the camper: A counselor's guide to youth development.* Marina, CA: Coaches Choice Books.

Coutts, J. (2002). *Start windsurfing right.* Portsmouth, RI: U.S. Sailing Association.

Dawson, C. D. (2008). *Sailing is fun!: A beginner's manual for young sailors.* Scotts Valley, CA: CreateSpace.

Decker, M. (2001). *Rainy day games.* Martinsville, IN: American Camp Association.

Delano, M. (2003). *Summer jobs and opportunities for teenagers: A planning guide.* Jackson, TN: Da Capo Press.

Dinoffer, J. (2001). *101 hoop games for kids.* Monterey, CA: Healthy Learning.

Donovan, R. (2006). *Campfire cuisine: Gourmet recipes for the great outdoors.* Philadelphia: Quirk Books.

Ellis, M. (2004). *Ceramics for kids: Creative projects to pinch, roll, coil, slam and twist.* Asheville, NC: Lark Books.

Elpel, T. J. (2009). *Participating in nature: Wilderness survival and primitive living skills.* Silver Star, MT: HOPS Press.

Erceg, L. E., Pravada, M., & American Camping Association. (2001). *The basics of camp nursing.* Martinsville, IN: American Camp Association.

Fanjoy, J. (2008). *Teaching archery to kids.* Scotts Valley, CA: CreateSpace.

Ferguson, N. (2002). *Training staff to be spiritual leaders: Activities and resources for Christian camps.* Monterey, CA: Healthy Learning.

Ferguson, N. (2009). *Grab-and-go activities: Teaching older children (ages 9 to 11) about God's creation.* Monterey, CA: Healthy Learning.

Ferguson, N. (2009). *Grab-and-go activities: Teaching younger children (ages 6 to 8) about God's creation.* Monterey, CA: Healthy Learning.

Fraser, K., Fraser, L., & Fraser, M. (2009). *The 175 best camp games: A handbook for leaders.* Tonawanda, NY: Boston Mills Press.

Friedman, D. (2003). *Picture this: Fun photography and crafts.* Tonawanda, NY: Kids Can Press.

Garst, B. A. (2009). *Volunteer development 101: Empowering organizations to work with volunteers.* Monterey, CA: Healthy Learning.

Gerling, I. E. (2009). *Teaching children's gymnastics: Spotting and securing.* Germany: Meyer & Meyer Fachverlad und Buchhandel GmbH.

Gilbertson, K., Bates, T., McLaughlin, T., & Ewert, A. (2005). *Outdoor education: Methods and strategies.* Champaign, IL: Human Kinetics.

Gordon, I. H. (2001). *The complete book of canoeing.* Guilford, CT: Falcon.

Hamlett, C. (2006). *Screenwriting for teens: The 100 principles of screenwriting every budding writer must know.* Studio City, CA: Michael Wiese Productions.

Hammett, C. T., & Atkins, Z. (2010). *Campcraft ABC's for camp counselors.* Whitefish, MT: Kessinger Publishing.

Hart, P. (2005). *Windsurfing.* Wiltshire, UK: Crowood Press.

Hauserman, T. (2007). *Monsters in the woods: Backpacking with children.* Reno: University of Nevada Press.

Hickey, J. J., Fleischner, D., & Silver, Y. (2010). *How long to visiting day? Creative role-playing for training camp counselors.* Scotts Valley, CA: CreateSpace.

Hiebert, H. (2000). *The papermaker's companion: The ultimate guide to making and using handmade paper.* North Adams, MA: Storey Publishing.

Hudson, J. (2005). *Cabins, canoes and campfires: Guidelines for establishing a summer camp for children with Autism spectrum disorders.* Overland Park, KS: Autism Asperger Publishing.

Hufford, D. (2005). *Candle making: Work with wicks and wax.* Mankato, MN: Capstone Press.

Hurni, M. (2002). *Coaching climbing: A complete program for coaching youth climbing for high performance and safety.* Guilford, CT: Falcon.

Katz, A. (2011). *Mosquitoes are ruining my summer!: And other silly dilly camp songs.* New York: Margaret K. McElderry.

Kelly, N. (2004). *Orienteering made simple: An instructional handbook.* Fairfield, CA: 1st Books Library.

Kibble, G. (2006). *Sailing for kids.* Hoboken, NJ: Wiley.

Kjellstrom, B., & Kjellstrom Elgin, C. (2009). *Be expert with map and compass: The complete orienteering handbook.* Hoboken, NJ: Wiley.

Knight, J. R. (2002). *101 age-appropriate camp activities.* Monterey, CA: Healthy Learning.

Knight, J. R. (2007). *101 creative programs for children.* Monterey, CA: Healthy Learning.

Koger, R. (2005). *101 great youth soccer drills: Skills and drills for better fundamental play.* New York: McGraw-Hill.

Kohl, H. R. (2007). *Making theater: Developing plays with young people.* New York: Teachers & Writers Collaborative.

Krause Publications (Eds.). (2002). *Kids 1st summer crafts: 20 projects and activities for camp, the car, and beyond.* Iola, WI: Krause Publications.

Lanier, T., & Nichols, C. (2010). *Filmmaking for teens: Pulling off your shorts.* Studio City, CA: Michael Wiese Productions.

Latshaw, G. (2000). *The complete book of puppetry.* Mineola, NY: Dover Publications.

Lessels, B. (2002). *Paddling with kids: AMC essential handbook for fun and safe paddling.* Boston: Appalachian Mountain Club Books.

Lightfoot, A., & Ewald, W. (2002). *I wanna take me a picture: Teaching photography and writing to children.* Boston: Beacon Press.

Lowe, H. (2007). *Child and youth development: By the experts.* Marina, CA: Coaches Choice Books.

Malmberg, E. (2003). *Kidnastics: A child-centered approach to teaching gymnastics.* Champaign, IL: Human Kinetics.

McKee, J. (2005). *Woodshop for kids.* Bellingham, WA: Hands On Books.

McWhirter, J. J., McShirter, B. T., McWhirter, E. H., & McWhirter, R. J. (2006). *At risk youth: A comprehensive response for counselors, teachers, psychologists, and human services professionals.* Florence, KY: Brooks Cole.

Meachen Rau, D. (2008). *Candle making for fun!* Mankato, MN: Compass Point Books.

Miniscalo, K., & Kot, G. (2008). *Survival guide for coaching youth basketball: Only the essential drills, practice plans, plays, and coaching tips.* Champaign, IL: Human Kinetics.

Mitchell, D., Davis, B., & Lopez, R. (2002). *Teaching fundamental gymnastics skills.* Champaign, IL: Human Kinetics.

Montgomery, D. (2008). *Native American crafts and skills: A fully illustrated guide to wilderness living and survival.* Guilford, CT: Lyons Press.

National Museum of Forest Service History. (2004). *Camp cooking: 100 years.* Layton, UT: Gibbs Smith.

Nierman, K., & Arima, E. (2000). *The kids 'n' clay ceramics book: Handbuilding and wheel-throwing projects from the kids 'n' clay pottery studio.* New York: Tricycle Press.

Noble, J., & Cregeen, A. (2004). *Swimming games and activities: For individuals, partners and groups of children.* London, UK: A & C Black.

Paris, L. (2010). *Children's nature: The rise of the American summer camp.* New York: NYU Press.

Peck, S. (2007). *101 fun, creative, and interactive games for kids.* Monterey, CA: Healthy Learning.

Peterson, L., & O'Connor, D. (2006). *Kids take the stage: Helping young people discover the creative outlet of theater.* Washington, DC: Back Stage Books.

Prouty, D., Panicucci, J., & Collinson, R. (Eds.). (2007). *Adventure education: Theory and applications.* Project Adventure. Champaign, IL: Human Kinetics.

Prusak, K. (2005). *Basketball fun and games: 50 skill-building activities for children.* Champaign, IL: Human Kinetics.

Purcell Cone, T., & Cone, S. (2004). *Teaching children dance* (2nd ed.). Champaign, IL: Human Kinetics.

Redmond, K., Foran, A., & Dwyer, S. (2009). *Quality lesson plans for outdoor education.* Champaign, IL: Human Kinetics.

Richman, M. S. (2006). *The ultimate camp counselor manual: How to survive and succeed magnificently at summer camp.* Bloomington, IN: iUniverse, Inc.

Rodomista, K. (2006). *101 cool pool games for children: Fun and fitness for swimmers of all levels.* Alameda, CA: Hunter House.

Rohnke, K. E., & Tait, C. M. (2007). *The complete ropes course manual.* Dubuque, IA: Kendall Hunt Publishing.

Rooyackers, P. (2002). *101 more drama games for children: New fun and learning with acting and make-believe.* Alameda, CA: Hunter House.

Rooyackers, P. (2003). *101 more dance games for children: New fun and creativity with movement.* Alameda, CA: Hunter House.

Rudick, J. (2007). *101 marketing essentials every camp needs to know.* Monterey, CA: Healthy Learning.

Ruis, S. (2009). *Coaching archery.* Chicago: Watching Arrows Fly, LLC.

Sales, A. L., & Saxe, L. (2003). *"How goodly are thy tents": Summer camps as Jewish socializing experiences.* Waltham, MA: Brandeis.

Scheder, C. M. (2002). *Outdoor living skills program manual: An environmentally friendly guide.* Martinsville, IN: American Camp Association.

Schinas, J. (2005). *Kids in the cockpit: A pilot book to safe and happy sailing with children.* London, UK: Adlard Coles.

Schnell, J. (2009). *The camp counselor's guide to interpersonal communication.* Monterey, CA: Healthy Learning.

Shelton, M. (2003). *Secret encounters: Addressing sexual behaviors in group settings.* Martinsville, IN: American Camp Association.

Sherman, E. (2004). *Geocaching: Hike and seek with your GPS.* New York: Apress.

Spainhour, D. (2007). *How to run a basketball camp: A guide to directing a successful basketball camp.* Winston-Salem, NC: Educational Coaching & Business Communications.

Sparrow, A. (2010). *Complete caving manual.* Wiltshire, UK: Crowood Press.

Stuhaug, D. (2006). *Kayaking made easy: A manual for beginners with tips for the experienced.* Guilford, CT: Falcon.

Stull, K., & McGuffee, J. (2001). *Hands on crafts for kids: Camp hands on.* Austin, TX: Greenleaf Book Group.

Tawney Nichols, R. (2006). *Hiking with kids: Taking those first steps with young hikers.* Guilford, CT: Falcon.

Thomas, B. (2009). *Creative coping skills for children: Emotional support through arts and crafts activities.* Philadelphia: Jessica Kingsley.

Thompson, L. (2000). *Essential waterskiing for teens.* Danbury, CT: Children's Press.

Thurber, C. A., & Malinowski, J. C. (2000). *The summer camp handbook: Everything you need to find, choose and get ready for overnight camp—and skip the homesickness.* Glendale, CA: Perspective Publishing.

Tilton, B. (2005). *The complete book of fire: Building campfires for warmth, light, cooking, and survival.* Birmingham, AL: Menasha Ridge Press.

Tilton, B. (2006). *Outdoor safety handbook.* Mechanicsburg, PA: Stackpole Books.

Utley, C., & Magson, M. (2007). *Exploring clay with children: 20 simple projects.* London, UK: A & C Black.

Van der Smissen, B., Goering, O. H., & Brookhiser, J. K. (2005). *Nature-oriented activities: A leader's guide.* Martinsville, IN: American Camp Association.

Van Slyck, A. A. (2010). *A manufactured wilderness: Summer camps and the shaping of American youth 1890–1960.* Minneapolis: University of Minnesota Press.

Vasquez Jr., R. (2001). *Tennis for kids: Over 150 games to teach children the sport of a lifetime.* Yucca Valley, CA: Citadel.

Voelke Studelska, J. (2008). *Archery for fun.* Mankato, MN: Compass Point Books.

Warner, P. (2002). *Parent's and kid's complete guide to summer camp fun: Everything you need to prepare for an incredible camp adventure.* Roseville, CA: Prima Lifestyles.

Wenig, M. (2003). *Yoga kids: Educating the whole child through yoga.* New York: Stewart, Tabori and Chang.

Werner, P. (2003). *Teaching children gymnastics* (2nd ed.). Champaign, IL: Human Kinetics.

Index

337